MARY C. McCALL JR.

MARY C. McCALL JR.

The Rise and Fall of Hollywood's Most Powerful Screenwriter

J. E. SMYTH

Columbia University Press

New York

Columbia University Press
Publishers Since 1893
New York Chichester, West Sussex
cup.columbia.edu
Copyright © 2024 Columbia University Press
All rights reserved

Library of Congress Cataloging-in-Publication Data
Names: Smyth, J. E., 1977- author.
Title: Mary C. McCall Jr. : the rise and fall of Hollywood's most powerful
    screenwriter / J. E. Smyth.
Description: New York, NY : Columbia University Press, 2024. | Includes
    bibliographical references and index.
Identifiers: LCCN 2024000105 (print) | LCCN 2024000106 (ebook) |
    ISBN 9780231215275 (hardback) | ISBN 9780231215282 (trade paperback) |
    ISBN 9780231560719 (ebook)
Subjects: LCSH: McCall, Mary C., Jr., 1904–1986 | Women screenwriters—United
    States—Biography. | Women labor leaders—United States—Biography. | Hollywood
    (Los Angeles, Calif.)—Biography. Screen Writers' Guild. | Women in the motion
    picture industry—United States—History—20th century. | Motion picture industry—
    California—Los Angeles—History—20th century.
Classification: LCC PS3525.A1265 Z86 2024 (print) | LCC PS3525.A1265 (ebook) | DDC
    813/.54 [B]—dc23/eng/20240418
LC record available at https://lccn.loc.gov/2024000105
LC ebook record available at https://lccn.loc.gov/2024000106

Printed in the United States of America

Cover design: Elliott S. Cairns
Cover image: Writers Guild Foundation Library

For Mary-David, Ned, and Zoe

When Heaven forgets to protect the working girl, she has to do the best she can on her own.

—Mary C. McCall Jr.

Contents

Introduction: 1943—the Turning Point   1

1. Mary Jr.   13

2. The Pirate   26

3. It's Tough Being Famous   40

4. A Second Chance   52

5. Bending the Codes   64

6. Breaking the Rules   76

7. Independence   94

8. The Invention of Maisie   110

9. Golden Girls and Brass Rings   123

10. A President at War   135

11. A Woman in the Establishment   150

12. The Party Is Over   161

13. Scarlet Woman   178

14. Smaller Screens   194

15. The Stuff That Dreams Are Made Of   211

x   Contents

Acknowledgments   227

Notes   231

Bibliography   263

Index   271

Introduction

1943—the Turning Point

On the afternoon of Thursday, March 4, 1943, a crowd had gathered outside Los Angeles's Ambassador Hotel. By 7:30 p.m., the police had herded a throng of journalists, photographers, and film fans on the pavement as Hollywood's elite arrived for the fifteenth annual Academy Awards. With well over a thousand guests expected that night, it was the largest Oscars event since the ceremonies began back in 1929. Celebrity spotters cheered when Hedy Lamarr, Gary Cooper, Rosalind Russell, Walt Disney, and Joan Fontaine appeared. But when a petite brunette stepped out of her limousine and maneuvered her way toward the lobby, the autograph collectors were puzzled. Who was she? But while they had no idea who the woman was, the journalists, Academy members, and others invited to that star-studded Oscars event knew her. She was Mary C. McCall Jr., president of the Screen Writers Guild.

Her trademark frizzy bob tended to become more disordered when she was attending labor meetings between the Screen Writers Guild and the studio producers. But not a lock was out of place that night. A small pillbox hat and veil held her hair in check, and her plain black dress swept to her feet in a ripple of velvet. There was a wartime ban on formal wear at the ceremony that, as a member of the Board of Governors of the Academy of Motion Picture Arts and Sciences, McCall had voted to uphold since the previous year. She was happy to play by the rules when she was involved in writing them.

Hundreds of people packed the lobby, and even more had moved into the Cocoanut Grove nightclub inside the hotel. After ten years as a Hollywood screenwriter and prominent labor organizer for her guild, McCall knew just about everyone attending the awards dinner that night. Her pale blue eyes could sparkle and snap as she traded wisecracks with writing colleagues Dorothy Parker and

Charles Brackett, or they could glow as bright and cold as an x-ray when she was in a committee meeting surrounded by executives and yes-men. That night, she was looking for her old friend Bette Davis.

The two-time Best Actress winner for *Dangerous* (1935) and *Jezebel* (1938) was nominated again that year for *Now, Voyager* (1942). Davis had been president of the Academy when war was first declared in December 1941 and had urged the organization to scale back its lavish ceremonies "for the duration." The plain-spoken New Englander believed that even Hollywood should make sacrifices and tone down the displays of glamor and money while American men and women were fighting and dying in Europe and in the Pacific. But some of her male colleagues, unaccustomed to being told they were overdressed and out of touch by a woman, had demanded her resignation. In a public spat over the Christmas holidays, Davis turned to columnists Louella Parsons and Hedda Hopper, who were also friendly with McCall, asking "that they explain her position to the fans."[1] Thanks to the power of Hollywood's female press corps and Davis's widespread popularity, the Academy soon faced a public relations backlash. Fourteen months later, with McCall's urging as a governor, the Academy adopted Davis's Spartan war spirit.

But it was a Pyrrhic victory for Davis. She had burned her bridges with the Academy's male elite and would never regain her footing as a behind-the-scenes powerbroker. Most awards insiders agreed she was not a popular favorite to win a third Oscar that year—the producers would see to that. But, according to Davis's boss Jack Warner, "the meanest bitch in town" was not Davis but another one-time Warner Bros. employee: McCall.[2] The two women had met years ago, and their friendship had deepened as they learned to survive in the male-dominated studio environment. But while both were fighters, McCall knew how to outlast her enemies by negotiating, pivoting, and in some cases, ducking. That night she steered clear of both Warner and his Paramount colleague, executive Y. Frank Freeman.

Freeman, the current head of the Association of Motion Picture Producers, had first met McCall several years before at one of the many polarized labor meetings between the Screen Writers Guild and the producers. He was deeply opposed to Hollywood producers signing any contract with screenwriters and formally legitimizing the guild's power to arbitrate disputes between screenwriters and their employers. At one of these meetings, as he paused for breath in the middle of another tirade, McCall blew smoke from her cigarette into his face and asked, "Is Y. Frank Freeman a rhetorical question?"[3] The quip spread like fire and became the stuff of Screen Writers Guild legend.

It was thanks in no small part to McCall's efforts with the National Labor Relations Board in Washington, D.C., that Hollywood screenwriters won the right to unionize and forced the producers to sign the contract granting screen credit protection and arbitration, a minimum wage, and the right to strike. The contract had been in full force since the summer of 1942, and after several months as acting president, at the annual meeting in November, McCall was officially elected president of the Screen Writers Guild—the first woman ever to hold such an office.

The fifteenth Oscars ceremony was the first one that McCall attended as Screen Writers Guild president, and it was also her first as an Academy governor. This had special significance, since the conservative Academy had for years been a producer-controlled stronghold and enemy of the guild. Now that they were backed by Washington and legally recognized by the studios, screenwriters at the awards dinner in 1943 were the first to experience Hollywood's pomp and ceremony on an equal footing with their employers. McCall was there as a presenter, not as a nominated "guest." Her election signaled a new era for Hollywood writers and was a benchmark for gender equality.

California's Republican governor, Earl Warren, was in attendance that night, and McCall stopped to talk with him. Although she was a diehard Roosevelt Democrat, she still shook hands with some Republicans. Warren was friendly with her current studio boss, MGM's Louis B. Mayer, who had been chairman of the California Republican Party before Warren took over.

Lowell Mellett, a former journalist and current head of the Bureau of Motion Pictures attached to the Office of War Information (OWI), was also there. Despite their shared allegiance to Roosevelt and the New Deal, McCall was wary of Mellett. Although he was in town that night to give an award to the motion picture industry, according to the trade papers, he was also there to reassure Hollywood that the U.S. government was not interested in "dictating film content" or "competing with the entertainment film" in wartime.[4]

Many of McCall's colleagues, remembering the government propaganda and excesses of the First World War era, were concerned that government censorship and restrictions on film stock, staff, and other resources would end up hurting the industry. In addition to her other jobs, earlier that week McCall had been elected chairwoman of the Hollywood branch of the War Activities Committee, replacing Freeman. Back in November, Hollywood insiders had hoped she would head the film industry's branch of the OWI in Washington. But Mellett had objected, stating that "the job shouldn't go to anyone associated with the film industry," and many guests at the awards ceremony were understandably still anxious about the government's future wartime role in motion pictures.[5]

As a high-ranking member of the Hollywood establishment, but also as a friend of First Lady Eleanor Roosevelt and other members of the Roosevelt administration, McCall was instrumental in smoothing relations between the two camps. Though anti-Hollywood government politics had nixed her OWI job, she and Mellett were polite. With the support of the current head of the Academy, producer Walter Wanger, McCall had arranged the attendance of a number of political and military guests at the ceremony. Wanger was expected to read the Academy members a letter of commendation from President Roosevelt, assuring them of his gratitude and a continued hands-off approach to relations with Hollywood. McCall also held a telegram from the secretary of war, which, as chair of the War Activities Committee, she was expected to read to the assembly that night.[6]

Unlike the other women at the event, McCall wasn't leaning on any man's arm. Normally, women at the Academy Awards were expected to bring a male date, either a husband or a studio-appointed escort. Sometimes they brought relatives. Greer Garson, the current Oscar favorite for her work in *Mrs. Miniver* (1942), had brought her mother more than once, and that night Bette Davis was accompanied by her sister Bobby. In the many years that she had been a fixture of the Hollywood social scene, McCall had appeared at big events with her husband, costume designer and artist Dwight Franklin. Though often mentioned in the columns as "Miss Mary McCall" and "Dwight Franklin," they were still a well-known Hollywood couple and parents of three children. People who knew her casually or at the studio, from her bosses Mayer and Eddie Mannix to ex-employers Warner and David Selznick, all at the Grove, would until recently have expected her to be on the arm of the tall, dapper Franklin. Bette Davis was one of the few people in Hollywood who knew the whole story behind McCall's solo appearance. In fact, she was to a certain extent indirectly responsible for it.

For the past few months, Davis had been serving as president of the Hollywood Canteen, a converted club on Cahuenga Boulevard where U.S. servicemen about to embark on overseas combat tours could relax, drink, and dance with Hollywood stars. When the canteen opened in October 1942, Davis asked McCall to help out as a hostess to take her mind off things. One of McCall's closest friends,

Jack Ruben, had died of a heart attack that September. For the past five years McCall and Ruben had been a writing and producing team and were riding the crest of the wave at MGM as helmers of the *Maisie* franchise, starring blonde comedian Ann Sothern. McCall was hit hard, personally and creatively, by Ruben's death. It was at the canteen a few weeks later that McCall first met Lieutenant David Bramson, stationed at nearby Fort MacArthur. And it was because of Bramson that the first time McCall walked into that Oscars banquet room, she was alone.

More than a few heads turned that night. There was an awkward moment when she locked eyes with star James Cagney on her way into the banquet hall. Cagney was the favorite to win Best Actor in Warner Bros.' biopic of legendary Broadway entertainer George M. Cohan, *Yankee Doodle Dandy* (1942). McCall had known Cagney since the 1920s when they were both building their careers in Manhattan. She was the pretty rich girl breaking away from her family; he was the alluring bad boy from the wrong side of the tracks. Although they were both married to others, the sparks used to fly when they were out on the town together, and she had based the eponymous hero of her popular short story "The Hoofer" (1934) on "Jimmy." After moving to Hollywood in the early 1930s, they had grown closer in their efforts to secure actors and writers a union. While McCall headed the Screen Writers Guild, Cagney had been elected president of the Screen Actors Guild in September. It should have been a night to remember the good and bad times together and to celebrate a future with more job protections for their colleagues.

But Cagney was also an old friend of Dwight Franklin, and, like the rest of Hollywood, he had read about the end of his friends' marriage in Hedda Hopper's *Los Angeles Times* column exactly one month earlier. Franklin had driven to Reno for a divorce in late January, citing "extreme mental cruelty," since McCall couldn't afford to take time off work for the required divorce residency. In early February, the day after her divorce came through, McCall married Bramson in, as Hopper put it, "a marriage which will surprise many of their friends."[7] It was the understatement of the year, as far as Cagney was concerned.

Bramson was not only Jewish but also almost seven years younger than McCall. Years before, McCall had seen her own wealthy Irish Catholic family cold-shoulder her uncle Tod's Jewish wife, Rose Traube. The couple had fled Manhattan in the 1920s for a life as innkeepers in Massachusetts.[8] Even in 1940s Hollywood, Irish Catholic anti-Semitism died hard. But though mixed second marriages such as the Goldwyns or the Cohns could just about survive public censure, Sam Goldwyn and Harry Cohn were older, powerful Jewish men who had married younger, less wealthy women.[9] In marrying a younger Jewish man of modest circumstances, McCall was flagrantly violating the social hypocrisies of the era that governed wealth, sex, and power. She was acting as if men and women were completely equal.

McCall had never lost sleep over what other people thought about her before. But she was devastated to discover that in divorcing Franklin, Cagney had divorced her from his life. From that night on, when they saw each other at War Activities Committee meetings (Cagney was also a member of the executive board) or at cross-guild benefits and fundraisers, their friendship was over.

But apart from Hopper's coverage and something similar in Parsons's rival *Los Angeles Examiner*, the press had kept things low-key; only a handful of Eastern papers mentioned the McCall-Franklin divorce. This was fortunate. With all eyes on the newly accredited union and its attractive woman president, McCall didn't need adverse publicity about her private life. She recognized that maintaining a good relationship with the Hollywood and national press corps was essential for the survival of the guild and her own career. She was friendly with all the columnists, from Sheilah Graham to Sidney Skolsky, and felt she could expect some slack from the press. But even her close friends had observed a worrying change in her.

Over the last ten years, McCall's blazing talent and energy, which she channeled into her writing and Screen Writers Guild work, propelled her into the top ranks of Hollywood screenwriters. Once the guild had its contract, McCall became one of the industry's accepted powerbrokers. But the delicate key to her influence was her carefully curated public image, on the one hand as a sexually attractive woman who could get away with saying outrageous things precisely because she was desirable to men and on the other as a married mother of three young children whose "solid" home life made Hollywood look good to the public. She was steel-nerved Miss Mary C. McCall Jr., feminist, labor leader, and writer, but she was also Mrs. Franklin of Bainbridge Avenue. Furthermore, her marriage with Franklin had tied her to Hollywood's large New York communities which included powerful Irish American connections from Cagney to MGM fixer Eddie Mannix. With her divorce and remarriage to Bramson, McCall burned the networks that had sustained her rise to power in a cutthroat industry. McCall had never been afraid of courting controversy, but her personal life was in danger of damaging her career.

One of the few safe havens in the packed room that night was next to her colleague Charles Brackett. A fellow New Yorker who dressed more like a rich banker than a scruffy screenwriter, Brackett was a staunch Republican who nonetheless had fought alongside McCall for the writers' contract over many years. While producers knew that McCall dined with Mrs. Roosevelt and was one of the guild's "very militant" advocates, a Twentieth Century-Fox attorney attending one of the joint labor meetings hilariously misread Brackett, telling writer Philip Dunne, "You ought to get rid of that damn communist!"[10]

For the past seven years, McCall and Brackett had been planning a politically moderate takeover of the Screen Writers Guild in the shrewd belief it would ultimately get them union recognition and power. Though years later, journalists and film critics claimed that Brackett and writer-director Billy Wilder formed "Hollywood's happiest couple," offscreen McCall and Brackett's relationship was not only as influential on Hollywood's history, but closer.[11]

In 1941 Budd Schulberg had immortalized the pair in his debut Hollywood novel, *What Makes Sammy Run?* Although Schulberg's antihero, Sammy Glick, was a composite of writers Jerry Wald, Norman Krasna, and the anti-guild John Lee Mahin, Schulberg's heroine, screenwriter and guild leader Kit Sargent, was, like McCall, a Vassar graduate from a powerful East Coast family.[12] Everyone in the guild recognized Schulberg's portrait of McCall, but it was somewhat embarrassing for McCall, since Kit Sargent sleeps with Glick and graphically discusses the affair with the novel's Brackettesque narrator, ex-drama critic-turned-screenwriter Al Manheim, whom Kit/McCall eventually decides to marry. As Brackett noted soon after the novel's publication, "Frank Partos, Sam Lauren, and I took Mary McCall to the bar and we all viewed with alarm and I laughed with Mary about the portrait of her Budd Schulberg did in the heroine of *What Makes Sammy Run?*. 'I want it distinctly understood,' she said, 'that I did *not* sleep with Norman Krasna.'"[13]

More recently, when McCall and Brackett weren't dining together at Lucey's or Perino's or in McCall's dining room talking shop, they met at meetings of the Academy of Motion Picture Arts and Sciences as fellow "Academy governors." That Oscars night, Brackett's curly hair (also inclined to disarray) was slicked back and McCall's was more or less in control under her hat as they slowly emptied a bottle of her favorite Irish single malt, Tullamore Dew. Nearby, Louis B. Mayer held court, confident that his studio's top film, *Mrs. Miniver*, would sweep the awards. He had block-booked the Grove's tables closest to the awards platform and microphone, wired for coast-to-coast radio coverage, and the rival studio heads were fuming.

Jeannette MacDonald set the longwinded tone of the evening by singing the national anthem, but Oscars host Bob Hope's jokes revived the crowd. Early on in the ceremony, after Freeman finished giving out the first awards for editing, sound, and special effects, Hope used McCall's now-iconic quip on stage: "Why [Y.] Frank Freeman?"[14] One by one, McCall's male colleagues stood up to give awards: director of photography James Wong Howe, Hope, songwriting legend Irving Berlin, director Frank Capra, and Mervyn Leroy all bestowed the awards for cinematography, shorts, music, direction, and special awards.

Then Hope introduced McCall, who would give the numerous writing awards. It was another first: the first time a woman writer stood up to give the awards for screenwriting. In the past it had always been men who gave out the writing Oscars, whether it was writers, actors, or producers. She walked up to the microphone, looked over the crowd with a triumphant gleam in her eyes, and quoted the famous line from the Bible: "In the beginning was the Word."[15] All the writers in the room cheered loudly. McCall's longtime champion, syndicated columnist Sidney Skolsky, remembered it as the best line of the best speech of the evening. McCall wasn't afraid of reminding her colleagues that their industry would always stand or fall by its story material, and that writers, the last major filmmaking cohort to secure a union contract, were no longer powerless.

She was proud that the Academy had moved outside its insular comfort zone and had given awards to British films. Earlier, Noël Coward's and David Lean's *In Which We Serve* (1942) won best foreign film. She read telegrams from Washington bigwigs about "our allies, the British," displaying to her producer colleagues just how well connected she was—and possibly taking another dig at Freeman, who had been an outspoken opponent of hiring "foreign talent" in the early days of the war. Another British film, *The Invaders*, written by Emeric Pressburger and Rodney Ackland, won best original story, beating Warner Bros.' *Yankee Doodle Dandy* and the personal favorite of many in the room, the Lou Gehrig biopic starring Gary Cooper, *Pride of the Yankees*. McCall's other statuettes went to friends and fellow guild members Ring Lardner Jr. and Michael Kanin (*Woman of the Year*) and Claudine West, Arthur Wimperis, George Froeschel, and James Hilton (*Mrs. Miniver*) for films produced by her own studio, MGM.

McCall couldn't have been happier for her colleague, the English-born West, who was nominated for two films (*Random Harvest* was the other) and won for her shared work on *Mrs. Miniver*. She was the only writer nominated twice and the only woman nominated in any of the writing categories. But West was dying of cancer and unable to attend the ceremony. She would pass away on April 11, with her devoted friend, producer Sidney Franklin, at her bedside.[16]

MGM's reputation for employing women writers was matched by its films about women and aimed at women audiences, and its top 1942 releases were no exception. Jan Struther's episodic novel focused on the everyday life of Mrs. Kay Miniver and her family, before and after war was declared in England. In the film adaptation, Greer Garson played a housewife and mother of three who supports her family through the Blitz and even captures a German Luftwaffe pilot in her kitchen. After years at RKO, Katharine Hepburn had moved to MGM and had overseen the development of Lardner and Kanin's original script about journalist and public figure Tess Harding, *Woman of the Year*. Tess's story was a barely disguised biopic of journalist Dorothy Thompson and her difficult marriage with novelist Sinclair Lewis.[17]

McCall understood these women. Like comfortable, middle-class Kay Miniver, she was also a mother of three who liked fancy hats and roses and was rich enough to hire other women to cook and clean for her and her family. Like Tess Harding, she was also a writer who knew everyone, went everywhere, was quoted everywhere, and yet had a problematic private life. But in *Woman of the Year*'s much-debated ending, when Tess tries to be a good housewife and completely screws up making breakfast for her husband (Spencer Tracy), he tells her that she doesn't have to choose a life of the housewife over a career. McCall had been doing both since she earned her first paycheck in the 1920s, but it was nice to have one of the top films that year validate her and her female colleagues' complicated lives.

Although over the years, Hollywood has acquired a reputation as a man's business, the golden age of the studio system (roughly spanning the 1920s and 1940s) was also a golden age for women's employment. Despite the impact of the Great Depression, more and more American women entered the workforce in the 1930s and by 1940 experienced a net gain in jobs since 1929, in stark contrast to American men.[18] Some statistics estimate Hollywood's workforce was 40 percent female, between 10 percent and 15 percent higher than the total national percentage of women in work at that time.[19] And while women worked in dozens of film industry occupations, they were perhaps best represented in the Screen Writers Guild, where they made up over 25 percent of the industry's unionized screenwriters.[20] Screenwriting was one of a handful of key professions in Hollywood where women built upon their successes from the silent era, when June Mathis and Frances Marion took home some of the highest paychecks in the business.

McCall always contended that writing was "a wonderful field for women" and that she had never found it "sex-conditioned." "You can earn equally with men. It is one of the few careers that combines pretty well with marriage and a family. There must be adjustments made, certainly, but to be a writer," she argued, was "easier than having to go to a factory or a department store. And it's also more satisfying."[21] While she had survived many frustrating encounters with male producers, actors, and writers, McCall recognized that the industry's range of career opportunities for women had to be championed and supported in order for true equality to thrive. Hollywood's men weren't perfect, but McCall was a negotiator. She also believed that in order to be successful, women of her generation had to embrace the freedom and fear of being totally responsible for their own income as artists: "Van Gogh never sold a picture during his lifetime except to his brother, yet he kept on painting," she reminded her colleagues. "I had no Dear Theo. If I'd been unable to support myself by writing, I would have had to stop and to search for some other way of earning my living."[22] While Hollywood's women may not have had the nepotistic perks of being studio men, they had McCall, the most prominent female labor leader in Hollywood.

But McCall's faith in Hollywood as a community where equality and better working conditions could thrive in peace and war was about to change. In one sense it all began to unravel the day after that Oscars night. Although the awards had always been a banquet, where the various members of the film community all sat down and broke bread together, March 4, 1943 would be the last time the Oscars ceremony was held in a glorified dining room. All the extra guests and telegram reading had made the event much longer, and Greer Garson's six-minute acceptance speech pushed many over the edge. The press complained volubly about the 1,200-plus people packed into the Grove, and so in late November, McCall and her other governors voted to move the event to a theater and dispense with the dinner, a blueprint for the next eighty years of Oscars.[23] It became an awards show where stars picked up their statuettes rather than a dinner for the film community.

Late that night, actress and producer Mary Pickford slammed the lengthy ceremony and her industry, telling the press, "No one person could arrange anything so boring."[24] Twenty years before Pickford had been the queen of Hollywood and "America's sweetheart," a cofounder of the legendary United Artists film company, and easily the most highly paid and powerful star in movies. She had presided over a period in Hollywood's history when she and other women exerted considerable influence over the industry. Although Pickford knew McCall through her ex-husband Douglas Fairbanks, as well as through their shared involvement in a Hollywood charity, the Motion Picture Relief Fund, the women were on distant rather than cordial terms. Pickford's seat at the banquet was so far away from the action it might have been "in Arizona," she quipped to the press.[25] She was one of many formerly prominent Hollywood women who had been pushed to the margins.

McCall, then at the height of her power and influence, didn't give much thought to her senior colleague. Perhaps she believed that as a prominent writer and labor leader she was more protected than Pickford, whose acting career had waned with her advancing age. One of McCall's screenplays, *Desirable* (1934), had been on this very subject. But the writer also knew that surviving in Hollywood for any length of time was a struggle. Things had looked bleak for her back in 1936 when Jack Warner fired her for union activities; if Harry Cohn hadn't picked up her contract and given her work at Columbia, McCall might have quit and returned to New York and her old life as a successful freelance short fiction writer. Some skilled negotiations by her agent at the Jaffe Agency, Mary Baker, had landed her a lucrative contract with MGM in 1938, and after she and producer Jack Ruben created Maisie Ravier in 1939, her reputation at the studio was made. By 1943, *Maisie* and the sequels had turned the series' star, Ann Sothern, into a household name, and McCall's colleagues addressed her as "Madam President" or, when she was in a grim mood on the phone, "Sir."[26] Though she gave Warner a wide berth and chuckled at Hope's remarks about Freeman, McCall was loyal to the town she had called home for ten years. Long before December 1941 she had been working overtime to support her industry and country in the fight against fascism.

The next morning McCall was up early and out the door of her fancy Bainbridge Avenue house before the nanny Miss Chapman got twelve-year-old Sheila and McCall's eight-year-old twin boys up for school. Her ex had moved out months ago and left her the family home. Franklin was a gentleman to the end, and McCall missed him. Despite Bramson's complaint that his wife was still living at her old address, McCall refused to sell the house. It was a magazine showplace, and she and the kids loved the location, close to UCLA.

That spring, she was working on the latest *Maisie* script, which had her eponymous heroine working in a California aircraft factory. Then the writer had hours of guild meetings for the war effort long after her colleagues' normal workdays ended. She was never home to eat with her children; even when she did have the odd meal at the weekend with them, she hired another woman to prepare it. McCall wryly admitted that she "was not skilled in the domestic arts." If she had a dinner in town, she'd breeze in and out, "a whirl of taffeta, silver fox, and perfume."[27] McCall didn't have time to be exhausted or lonely, and she didn't have time for regret.

It is rare to look back at any person's life and find one moment when the drama, the years of hard work, the tragedy, and the power are in play. If there were ever such a pivotal moment in McCall's life, it was at that Oscars ceremony in 1943. That said, it was the culmination of years spent at the heart of Hollywood's longest, bitterest battle over money, influence, and creative control.

McCall was no stranger to leadership or feminism or the desire for money, fame, and power that drove the core of Hollywood's immigrant elites. All those elements flowed in her blood and determined even the different parts of her name. When she was seven years old, her mother set up a bank account for her in the name of "Mary C. McCall Jr."[28] Like her grandfather John A. McCall, the legendary former president of New York Life, the little girl was determined to make the balance grow with hard work. When the boys at school had laughed at her, saying "a girl couldn't be a junior" and "a girl couldn't be her own boss," she faced them down. No one told her what a girl could or could not do. She knew from an early age that she would be a writer. Her most enduring literary creation, Maisie Ravier, was a survivor, facing life with humor and courage. McCall revealed in one interview: "I know her as well as I know myself."[29] Both women were stubborn and generous and unafraid of speaking out, even if it lost them a man—or, more important, a job.

In 1943 McCall had her share of problems, but unemployment wasn't one of them. Whether she did it in the pages of a script or on a speaker's platform, on the radio or in a journalist's column, Mary C. McCall Jr.'s name was all over Hollywood. She was the studio system's most powerful woman and was respected and resented across the political spectrum. She used to joke about her far left- and right-wing film colleagues: "When the revolution comes, they can put me up against a cellophane wall and shoot at me from both sides."[30] There was a revolution on its way, and it would end up being more devastating for Hollywood than any world war. But for the time being, McCall still had the luck of the Irish.

CHAPTER 1

Mary Jr.

Mary C. McCall Jr. made her first public appearance one balmy July afternoon in 1904 at her grandparents' Jersey Shore estate—at a party to celebrate their thirty-fourth wedding anniversary.[1] Like all the other women present, she wore a variation of the season's diaphanous white gown and was escorted on the arm of a gentleman. But she was only a few weeks old and sat magisterially against her grandfather's shoulder, surveying New York's elite assembled on the lawn.

She was a chip off the old block. Grandfather and granddaughter had the same frosty blue eyes and dark hair, and John A. McCall couldn't have been prouder of the latest addition to his family. She had been born April 4, 1904, at 49 West 72nd Street, the upscale address where McCall housed all his children and their families. His son Leo's wife, the former society debutante Mary "Mazie" Caldwell Burke, thought her father-in-law could be a bit domineering at times, and she named her daughter "Mary Jr." as a way of preserving women's inherited power in a world of men.

Despite Mazie's reservations, it was a good time to be a McCall. Since 1892, John A. McCall had been president of the country's largest insurance company, New York Life, having beaten future president Grover Cleveland for the job.[2] As a young man he had wanted to play professional baseball—he went as far as playing first base for the semipro Live Oaks—but his middle-class Irish American parents had insisted on business school.[3] Within two decades he had risen to the top of his profession and was one of the most influential men in the state, earning $100,000 a year, over $2.6 million in today's currency. In addition to his Jersey Shore estate, designed by Henry Edward Creiger and nicknamed Sliwoccam (the Gaelic of McCall spelled backward), he owned 52–56 West 72nd Street, where he lived with his cold-blooded, red-headed wife, Mary Smyth Horan. When he wasn't at home or at the office he could be found hobnobbing with President Theodore Roosevelt at the White House, dispensing insurance and investment advice.[4] As New York Life's president, McCall had been making campaign contributions to the Republicans for some years (with the knowledge and consent of the board), since it was believed that Democratic candidates were not pursuing economic policies favorable to big business.

John A. McCall may not have been a Gilded Age "robber baron," but he worked with them and underwrote their investments. In an era when wealth inequality and exploitation of workers were at their most extreme, John A. McCall was neither a social reformer nor concerned with the lives of ethnic minorities who had a tenuous connection to his family origins. He worked hard, made his money, and protected his family's interests.

But even as he presided over his elaborate anniversary bash in the summer of 1904, progressive reformers were coming for him. Journalist Ida Tarbell's exposure of the Standard Oil Company from 1902 to 1904 would break Rockefeller's monopoly and create significant antitrust legislation from 1906 to 1914. After months of research into the meatpacking monopoly of the "Big Five" in Chicago, journalist Upton Sinclair published his serialized exposé, *The Jungle*, in 1905. That same year New York's governor, Frank Higgins, opened a state investigation into tax evasion and appointed Charles Evans Hughes as counsel for the new Armstrong Insurance Commission, which would put an end to companies' widely practiced (though illegal) campaign contribution policies.

McCall was the most prominent businessman to testify that autumn before the New York committee. Most of his colleagues fled to Europe in disgrace, including Andrew Hamilton, who had headed New York Life's "legislation" branch. When Hamilton, hiding in Paris, refused to account for $235,000 of missing funds, the committee ordered McCall to pay. He complied, cashing in his $400,000 life insurance policy and selling the $500,000 Jersey Shore estate for a fraction of its value.[5] Then he resigned from the company. By February 1906 he was dead, worn out by the shame of the investigation and a lifetime of hard work and hard drinking.[6]

Mary Jr. began life as a privileged member of an elite New York family, and her parents struggled to keep it that way. Her father, Leo, like all of the McCall men, continued to work for New York Life, and gradually the family fortunes revived under the leadership of her uncle, Darwin P. Kingsley. But her mother,

Mazie, whose father Francis Burke had also been in the insurance business, was less focused on the past glories of her husband's family and more concerned with her daughter's future. In 1906 the trio traded the glamor of Midtown Manhattan for a modest white Victorian on Lydecker Street in the sleepy middleclass suburb of Englewood, New Jersey. Leo played golf on his one day off, and Mazie took her daughter to the occasional society wedding of her wealthy Manhattan friends.[7] At one such event in June 1910, the New York press took note of six-year-old Mary Jr., "the granddaughter of the late John A. McCall," who wore a frock of "white muslin with sashes of pink ribbon" and carried a basket of sweet peas for Gladys Torrance Benjamin.[8]

That fall she matriculated at the Franklin Elementary School and made a few good friends in the neighborhood, including the lively Elisabeth Morrow and her younger, quieter sister Anne. Mary Jr. excelled at school, especially English and history. Usually little girls of her social class had to spend hours at singing or piano lessons, but Mary Jr. was born tone-deaf, and her spare time was freed up for reading and writing. As she recalled, "From the time a composition of mine written in first grade was well received by the teacher and even most of the kids, I had only one ambition—to be a professional writer."[9] She did so well that the teachers at Franklin let her skip the fourth grade.

Their neighbor Mrs. Morrow looked on Mary Jr. with approval and recommended to Mazie that the youngster be sent to a women's college in a few years. The McCalls' normal college of choice, Yale, wasn't an option; the university wouldn't admit women until 1969. Mrs. Morrow had graduated from Smith, one of the prestigious "Seven Sisters," a group of Northeastern women's colleges offering a rigorous academic program without the constant sexism of coed institutions such as Oberlin, the University of Chicago, and Berkeley. There were opportunities for smart girls with supportive parents, but gender, class, and race barriers were everywhere in the 1910s. Women of any background still couldn't vote in every state, though suffrage rallies were making headlines. But it was Mary Jr.'s Uncle Arthur who encouraged the girl to see women's fight for equal opportunity as part of a wider struggle for progressive reform. Years later his niece would remember him talking to her about "syndicalism" and the history of the American labor movement.[10]

She was pushed outside the comfortable borders of Englewood when Mazie took her to Washington during the war years to be nearer to Leo, who had enlisted in the National Guard. Mary Jr. was sent to the elite Miss Madeira's School, but even in that high-society atmosphere, she experienced the culture shock of a completely segregated South, where white women were treated as if they were mindless dolls and Black women as if the slave-owning Confederacy had never lost the Civil War. By the time they all returned to Englewood in 1919 (with a baby brother Leo Jr. in tow), Mary Jr. knew she was going to be one of society's critics and commentators, not one of its ornaments. She led her class at the Dwight School for Girls and, as she recalled, after "surviving entrance exams" in everything from algebra and geometry to Latin and history, she entered Vassar College in Poughkeepsie, New York, in the fall of 1921.[11] With the passage of the Nineteenth Amendment, giving women the right to vote, she was part of the first college class selected when women were legally men's political equals. It would be up to her and her peers to pursue the goal of complete equality.

McCall loved Vassar and its history of supporting women's higher education. As she recalled, "The corridors in Main Hall . . . were very wide, so that the young ladies, who wore hoop skirts, could take their exercise indoors in bad weather without bumping into one another."[12] The founder, a local beer baron named Matthew Vassar, believed that since God made woman "with the same natural faculties as man," women were "entitled to the benefits of an equal education." For Vassar, an equal education meant spacious grounds, a well-stocked library, comfortable living quarters, and a range of disciplines to study from science to the arts.

In his will Vassar wanted his tombstone to be in the simple shape of an acorn, since he hoped that his ideas for women's education might grow into "an oak of true equality." In her senior year, as chairwoman of Founder's Day, she was proud to "put a wreath on Matthew's grave with its acorn headstone down by the Hudson."[13] But her years at Vassar taught her more than gratitude for the few rich men who cared enough to support women's higher education. It was there that she discovered the importance of a community of women in changing the future.

The boom in American higher education began in the 1860s, helped along by westward expansion and the passage of the Land-Grant College Act (1862). When the federal Office of Education first began surveying statistics in 1870, about 1 percent of the country's population was attending college; women made up 21 percent of that student body. By 1900, 36 percent of all American college students were women.[14] In 1920, after women had won the right to vote in all U.S. elections, many reformers predicted a new era in women's and America's history. By 1921, there were as many women as men attending college, and Vassar, with the rest of the prestigious Seven Sisters, seemed poised at the vanguard of feminist empowerment.

Vassar earned its reputation for scholarly excellence thanks to its female faculty members. But while three-quarters of the faculty were women, men were usually department heads and key administrators. Senior women did not take kindly to being "managed" by younger and less qualified men. In 1915 Professor Lucy Salmon of the history department led a faculty revolt, forcing the male president of the college, Baptist minister James Monroe Taylor, to resign. When Henry Noble MacCracken took over the job later that year his predecessor allegedly bequeathed him a loaded pistol to defend himself from his Amazonian colleagues. The battles over faculty appointments and women's representation continued through the 1920s. Yet the women who fought for equal political rights and taught McCall and her peers were very different feminists from the young women arriving on campus in the fall of 1921. Educators such as Vassar's Elizabeth Hazelton Haight were concerned that unlike the "stern pioneers," the new generation of women "wear all their learning . . . lightly like a flower."[15]

Certainly, for some, a women's college was no more than an expensive finishing school or just a gap between adolescence and marriage. Other women, imbued with the ethos of the suffragettes, continued to believe in the need for a women's community, founded on trust and intellectual respect, without the incursions of male students. And there were those who carried the tenets of Alice Paul's Equal Rights Amendment to its logical conclusion in American society. Vassar's "Adamless Eden" had to prepare its women for a world where they worked alongside men, earning the same financial and spiritual rewards from their work.

Admittedly, McCall's parents had selected Vassar for their daughter not because they were suffragists who admired Vassar's "dangerous women," but because they had a smart girl they wanted educated in a safe, upper middle-class environment not too far away from home. But Mary Jr. was not the sort to wear her intellectual armor lightly in order to be a dutiful daughter or fiancée or wife. She was not interested in boys but in learning how to build a career as a writer. The moment she arrived on campus, she declared her English major and minored in political science.

Thanks to the efforts of Uncle Arthur, labor history still fascinated her, and she was sharply articulate in seminars and, as she discovered, a gifted public speaker. In the spring of her junior year, she was invited to address members of the Women's Guild of Poughkeepsie's First Congregationalist Church on "Child

Labor."[16] She learned about women's dominance in New York labor organizing and discovered that freelance writers had their own union, the Authors Guild. She vowed to join as soon as she was a paid writer.

In the meantime she took literature and composition classes, continued with her work in history and languages, and pursued political science so seriously that one professor offered to put her up for a year's fellowship abroad in Belgium to study international law. But there was a catch. She would have had to accept a two-year teaching contract upon her return to the United States, and McCall knew that the only thing she really wanted was "to write fiction." The thought of teaching—the lot of generations of impoverished, genteel women—nauseated her. Instead, influenced by Professor Gertrude Buck, she took up dramatic writing. In her junior year, she won the Philaletheis Prize Play competition with a work called *The Beaten Path*.[17] In her senior year, Hallie Flanagan (future head of the New Deal's Federal Theatre Project) joined the faculty, and McCall and fellow student Elizabeth Hawes (the future feminist designer) took the play production seminar and had leading roles in organizing the school play. McCall also edited the college newspaper.

She relished being a "big wheel" on campus.[18] In her senior year, the fourteen women on the staff of Vassar's newspaper had their photo taken. Squarely in the middle of the frame, her black Underwood typewriter in front of her, Mary Jr. lowers her chin like a prizefighter and stares directly into the camera. That fearless, confident look would become her trademark.

Slightly taller than the average woman of the era at five feet six inches, her legs advantageously displayed in the new short-skirted fashions, Mary Jr. turned heads in any room. She had piercing blue eyes under dark brows and a mass of curly black hair that fell down to her waist. She usually gathered it up into a chignon, but it was so thick and heavy that it would escape any bobby pins, slipping down over her shoulders in wild disarray in the middle of a seminar. In her senior year, she considered shingling it, like some of the girls she worked with on the paper. Before the war, fashion icon and star Irene Castle had her hair clipped as short as a man, and after the war the style went mainstream chic. Hollywood star Colleen Moore's famous cut in *Flaming Youth* (1923) and Brooklyn girl Clara Bow's style (*Down to the Sea in Ships* and *The Daring Years*, both 1923) persuaded many American women to visit the hairdresser.

She was captivated by the movie industry and wondered whether she could combine her writing interests with Hollywood. Many women had their start as screenwriters, such as Anita Loos, who had begun as a teenaged scenario writer for D. W. Griffith and Douglas Fairbanks, and by 1925 was at the top of the best-seller list with her comic novel *Gentlemen Prefer Blondes*. Other women worked as prominent story editors and film critics. On one of her trips to New York, Mary Jr. walked into the offices of the film magazine *Cinema Art* and got a job as a film critic.[19] It earned her extra pocket money, but it didn't lead to anything more substantial in the motion picture business. As far as her father was concerned, this was just fine. As he said of her new job, "If your work brings you in contact with producers of, or actors in film, I must ask you not to accept it."[20] At first McCall didn't challenge her father. Instead, she concentrated on reworking and editing her portfolio of short stories. She even wrote humorous poetry and considered submitting something to a new literary magazine that had just appeared in the winter of her senior year, *The New Yorker*.

But McCall's college years were not perfect. As she acknowledged, she was not a complete liberal arts scholar: "Chemistry and higher mathematics, both required, which turned many hours of my freshman year into a nightmare, are the only subjects I felt were a complete waste of my time—and the instructors'." Since Vassar required all of its young women to be well rounded scholastically, McCall acknowledged that her two Ds in these subjects "pretty well wrecked my chances of election to Phi Beta Kappa." It also meant that she was unlikely to get a scholarship or fellowship from the college to study after graduation, something that would have eased her parents' financial burden considerably. But as far as her father was concerned, a deal was a deal; since she had skipped a grade in elementary school, she would graduate at twenty-one. He had promised to educate her until age twenty-two, and so, she wrote, "he told me I had a year coming to me."[21]

McCall wanted to get a fellowship but, as she recalled years later, one of her professors, Winifred Smith, told her "quite bluntly . . . she did not consider me a scholar."[22] When McCall admitted that she wanted to write fiction rather than scholarly articles, Smith told her that fellowships weren't available for students who wanted to write fiction, since "you have a sporting chance to earn your living. You take the scholar's way and you will never yield enough to feed you."

McCall wanted to see a little of the world, in her words, "before I settled down to earning my living by writing," and so it made sense to go overseas for a year.[23] She could get ideas for more stories that way. After all, the young writers Ernest Hemingway (*In Our Time*, 1925) and F. Scott Fitzgerald (*The Great Gatsby*, 1925) seemed to do all right in an expatriate environment. With graduation approaching, she asked President MacCracken where she should go in her last year of family-financed higher education. She knew MacCracken well from her weekly college newspaper board meetings and shared his love of shaking up stale traditions (it was he who had ditched Founder's Day lectures in favor of faculty-student baseball games and plays). McCall had set the college on its ear when she endorsed *Treasure Island* as the final offering of the class of 1925, with a cast made up almost entirely of men from the faculty.[24] It amused her to have Vassar's male professors told what to do by the female students in charge of the production.

Vassar's women had done postgraduate fellowship years in Europe, with Great Britain especially popular, given that Oxford and Cambridge now had female colleges, and University College London had also offered her a place. But MacCracken said that thanks to the postwar vogue for the Oxbridge atmosphere among wealthy Americans and ex-soldiers, the English were getting "very fed up" with "foreign" college students. She was ambivalent about London and inquired about Ireland. "You are the most Irish looking girl in the College, and it seems appropriate that you should go to Trinity College," he told her.[25]

MacCracken was right: England was too stuffy for McCall. Ireland, though another patriarchal island, was in her blood. Her grandmother Katie Green Burke was pleased that her granddaughter was going back to the country of her birth as an elegant college graduate. But the summer after her graduation was a bittersweet one for the family. Though Mazie and Leo were thrilled with their daughter's performance at Vassar, they learned in July that John A. McCall's former penthouse, now owned by Leroy Coventry, had been sold to developers Louis Gold and Co.[26] It was scheduled to be razed to the ground to make way for a fifteen-story building with 225 rooms. With her family's history disappearing before her eyes, McCall concentrated on making her own tracks.

She sailed that fall. The American men in the Irish consulate saw the pretty, well-connected American student "as a novelty" and flocked to take her to the Abbey Theater and on excursions to family landmarks in western Ireland. While in Dublin she also met celebrity writer Liam O'Flaherty at the Radical Club. O'Flaherty had just published *The Informer*, the story of a friend's betrayal during the Irish Civil War. But while she enjoyed being in the company of actors and writers, she hated the dreary weather, saying she "could understand why the Irish drank, as the washcloth one wrung out after the morning wash-up remained as cold and wet as ever at the end of the day's occupations."[27]

University life was an even bigger disappointment. Trinity refused to recognize her undergraduate degree from an American women's college. She was "allowed" to go to all lectures, but only with the status of a new undergraduate. Women never spoke in class and even had to sit on opposite sides of the lecture hall, well away from the men. Even though Trinity had been one of the first colleges in Europe to admit women, they were there, she recalled, "very much on sufferance."[28] She remembered her first attempt to speak out in class "prompted the male members . . . to pound on the floor with their feet." She was puzzled, since she knew her comment "couldn't have been that far off the mark." She found out afterward it was the first time *any* woman had ever spoken in class.

The stifling misogyny infuriated her, but McCall's privileged background and education had given her already robust ego additional protection. Although money wasn't that plentiful at home, McCall was still part of one of New York's premier business families. Her uncle Darwin P. Kingsley was rich, and the cultural residue of John A. McCall's wealth lingered in the lives of his children and grandchildren. Coming as she did from a lineage of wealth and privilege, Mary Jr. possessed two assets that lasted longer than any permanent income: social confidence and the time to develop her own ideas without caring too much what other people thought.

Her year in Dublin paid long-term dividends. The time away from her family, from the supervision and the middle-class mundaneness of her life, gave her the necessary distance to discover how to turn life experience into fiction. If she couldn't do more at the university than attend lectures and annoy male scholars by speaking in class, then she would spend her time in coffeehouses and theaters, watching, thinking, learning—being a detached observer, an outsider, free to develop her own loyalties.

But her time as an expatriate made her realize the core of her literary imagination was in her everyday American experience: "I think one of the soundest ways to approach a writing career is to 'mine your own front yard.' Certainly at the start," she stated. "To write out of your own experience and your own background: to write what you know about. Surely you know more about a certain block in Englewood, New Jersey . . . better than some other place . . . there are plenty of stories on every block." So in those early days she chose to write about being at a woman's college or going to Ireland or being a New Yorker. And, even as a novice, she found she had a process. She'd spend about a month on each story.

First, she'd write in long hand and then type it up, revising as she went: "I write fast once I know what I want to do," she confessed. "I used to spend about three weeks sitting around looking stupid or riding on busses, but when I was ready to go, it only took it a day-and-a-half to put it on paper."[29] She followed the technique all her working life.

McCall returned home in the spring of 1926 and continued writing, sending the stories she had begun in Dublin out to some of New York's "slick paper magazines." Americans' addiction to weekly or monthly magazines and periodicals had started in the late nineteenth century, and the appetite for short fiction, current affairs, Progressive era exposés, and serialized fiction helped many young women writers intent on a career to support themselves financially through their writing. In the 1920s a family's ability to subscribe to several magazines at home was a marker of middle-class success.[30] *Collier's, The Saturday Evening Post, The Pictorial Review,* and *Redbook* were what McCall was really aiming for, and given high circulation, editors could pay hundreds if not thousands for a story. These "top-drawer" magazines had an unrivaled national readership, and Hemingway, Fitzgerald, Edna Ferber, and Dorothy Parker routinely contributed their material. Mary C. McCall Jr.'s work did not make an immediate hit, but she kept trying.

She had her first real heartbreak when her seventy-seven-year-old grandmother died after suffering a stroke. Katie Green was born during the Irish potato famine, and as a baby she miraculously survived the crossing to America on one of the "coffin ships."[31] Katie had been Mary Jr.'s childhood companion and, unlike the wealthy McCalls, could tell her granddaughter stories about poverty and living as an Irish immigrant in the Lower East Side of Manhattan. It was she who had always encouraged Mary Jr.'s writing.

In a brief period of loneliness, Mary Jr. allowed herself to get engaged to Julian Harrington, a young foreign service officer from Natick, Massachusetts, whom she had met in Dublin. But she didn't let it interfere with her writing. That summer, *The New Yorker* accepted her poem "Aquarium Reverie" for publication in the October 2, 1926 issue.[32] McCall's humorous piece was told from the perspective of a careworn young woman watching a fish that "swishes his bright tail about," free from "the vicious business of our world." In a life of "pleasant ease, with all care without," he can be as ambitious as he likes. But, as McCall wrote, she "could never change my lot with him . . . Because I simply cannot learn to swim." The life of a beautiful goldfish was not for her.

Encouraged, McCall followed up with *The New Yorker*, sending them a short sketch, "Peek A Boo," about a young woman worried that her taxi driver does not match the photograph on the displayed rate card.[33] As the cab speeds through the streets, her imagination jumps from one terrifying conclusion to another (the man in the driver's seat could not only be a potential rapist but may also have murdered the real owner of the taxi . . .). But when she finally arrives at her destination and pays her fare, she meets the driver's eye and realizes the photo was taken years ago when he was younger and had all his teeth. *The New Yorker* appreciated the humor and let her know it would welcome more submissions.

Her parents, focused on bringing up Leo Jr., left McCall to her own devices. Young Leo was a round-faced charmer with a droll sense of humor, but his chronic love of a good time would later get him kicked out of Hotchkiss and Stanford. McCall, less coddled by her parents, turned out to be more resilient. Beginning in 1927, she realized that without an agent or any high-powered contacts in the writing business she needed some other means of making money. She didn't like living at home, still dependent on her parents, without contributing to the household budget. Because her modest sales to *The New Yorker* were too sporadic to count as regular income, she decided to join her father on the daily commute to the city.

At first she tried breaking into journalism. "I hoped maybe I could get a job as a second-string motion picture critic on a paper or a very junior editorial job on a magazine."[34] Although she applied everywhere, as she put it, "from the *Police Gazette* to *Vanity Fair*," she "struck out." Finally, armed with a letter of introduction from one of her "august uncles," she landed a job at Barton, Durstine and Osborne, one of Manhattan's most innovative advertising agencies, as an "assistant account executive." In 1923, the agency moved from 25 West 45th Street to the more upscale Knapp Building at 383 Madison Avenue. It had established a radio department in 1925 and had its own hour-long radio show and exclusive rights to broadcast Metropolitan Opera performances. She worked five and a half days a week.

As McCall admitted, "I was very much interested in the business until I learned how to do it pretty well."[35] There were few businesses that had the glamor and pace of Manhattan advertising in the 1920s. She was initially flattered when the office had her voicing her own copy over the radio. Her low-pitched, "profundo" mid-Atlantic voice had a persuasive elegance. She also liked the fact that as an assistant executive she got to wear a fashionable hat in the office, unlike the lowly secretaries. In later years she laughed at this pathetic little bit of snobbery.

But even as a young woman she realized that she was hired to handle a cosmetics account only because she was a woman and management assumed she could offer "the consumer's perspective." (She rarely used cosmetics.) McCall explained: "We were selling things to people which they really didn't need for more money than they could afford to pay."[36] Although ad agencies seemed to offer modern women the prospect of self-empowerment in the creation of their own public image, McCall knew that the Madison Avenue game was based on the manipulation of women.[37] Women were encouraged to purchase cosmetics to attract male marital partners, eventually removing them from the workforce to marital drudgery.

It wasn't just the gender politics of her advertising account that bothered her. The year McCall joined as an assistant account manager, the agency hired copy guru John Caples. A few years later, Caples declared in his book *Tested Advertising Methods* (1932) that the average American has the intelligence of a thirteen-year-old.[38] Caples told copyists to lay off humor and keep words simple because American consumers were stupid. Style was wasted on them.

If McCall found it a challenge to accept the bland, one-size-fits-all masculine ethos at the office, then it was even tougher commuting in her smart suits and hats, doing the 9:00 to 6:00 days, trying to save something—anything—of her pay in an industry where the men were routinely paid more than women for the same work. She made only $25 a week. A good stenographer in Hollywood earned twice that amount. By 1927, when audiences heard vaudeville star Al Jolson talk and sing in *The Jazz Singer*, the movies had revolutionized entertainment and had become an even more intriguing market for writers. In the new sound era, screenwriters had more than filler title cards to write, and good screenwriters with an ear for snappy dialog were in demand. But without any major writing credits under her belt or inside connections, McCall, as a new studio employee, would have been put in the story or reading department looking at other writers' work and forgotten.

At least in New York, despite the poor pay, McCall was writing, rubbing shoulders with other writers, and picking up tips to become a self-supporting freelancer. But among the ranks of young women swarming the offices and streets of New York in their short gossamer dresses, clacking heels, and shorn hair, she didn't feel like the modern pro she aspired to be. She didn't want to be the wife of a diplomat, and Julian no longer fit in the life she visualized for herself. As she recalled with a sigh of relief, "fortunately for me this romance broke up in '27."[39]

McCall's proper aunts and great-aunts were appalled by the news, but Mazie, who had once dreamed of a creative career, sympathized. Like countless modern daughters before her, McCall explained to her mother that she needed a fresh start. Her sensible Irish name, her plain impeccably made clothes, her well-scrubbed young face, and above all her Victorian hair dated her like a George M. Cohan ingénue.

One day that fall she came home from the hairdressers several pounds lighter, her sleek bob tucked under a cloche. According to McCall family legend, Leo Sr., much like the father from Frank Bunker Gilbreth Jr. and Ernestine Gilbreth Carey's classic memoir *Cheaper by the Dozen*, was outraged at his daughter's act of tonsorial rebellion. As McCall's own daughter later recalled, when her mother was chatting in a room with Mazie, "he supposedly walked out the French doors and around rather than be in the same room with my mother once she cut her hair."[40] He wouldn't speak with McCall for months. But she wasn't fazed. And that spring, the twenty-three-year-old flapper had finally dated a man who impressed her—and who liked her hair. His name was Dwight Franklin, and in his spare time he was a pirate.

CHAPTER 2

The Pirate

Dwight Franklin was unlike any man McCall had ever met. He wasn't an insurance executive or stockbroker or bootlegger or advertising man. But he was an artist, design historian, explorer, denizen of every New York gin house from the Players to the Hotsy Totsy—and a pirate. His credentials had been on movie screens all over America in 1926, when he appeared with Douglas Fairbanks in *The Black Pirate*. Like most American women of her generation, McCall found Douglas Fairbanks irresistible. She soon felt that way about Franklin.

But there was a sixteen-year age difference between them. Born on January 28, 1888, to Jean Whittemore Dwight and Joseph Frederick Franklin, he was only eight years younger than Mazie and nine years younger than her own father. But any reservations her parents may have had about his age were assuaged by his connections, for he was distantly related to former Yale president Timothy Dwight IV as well as Mazie's former Veltin School headmistress. His mother had raised him alone. Two months after Franklin's birth, the notorious blizzard of 1888 struck the Northeast on Sunday, March 11. There were gale force winds in Manhattan, and the streetcars weren't running in the snow. His father, who worked downtown, caught pneumonia after having "walked through the blinding snow" to his job.[1] The pneumonia became tuberculosis, and he died in 1890.

Jean Dwight Franklin had too much gumption to become a poor widow. She invested the inheritance from her husband's estate wisely and supplemented her comfortable income by opening and closing rich people's town houses for the summer and winter social seasons, teaching, and boarding students from Columbia University. She also designed book covers and wrote poetry for the local New York papers.[2] Dwight Franklin went to private schools in New York thanks to family connections and the money that his mother saved, but unlike the boys in the McCall family, he was not destined for a normal office job. Stylish and extravagant, with a mischievous sense of humor, he was hardly the type to put on a sober suit six days a week. When he wasn't off carousing with friends, he was in the New York Public Library hunched over piles of art books. He was fascinated with the history of design and studied European and early American costume exhaustively. He told his mother he wanted to be an artist but "didn't know exactly what he wanted to do in the arts." Rather than tell him to get a safe office job, Jean Franklin "stood up to the members of her family" and supported her son's career aspirations.[3]

In 1906, at age eighteen, he got a job as an artist with the American Museum of Natural History. He joined the museum under the controversial presidency of Henry Fairfield Osborn, working as a researcher, taxidermist, and display artist and designer. Osborn's chief impact on the museum was in investment in displays and exhibitions for the public. Franklin was a perfect collaborator in this vision, and the two revolutionized the museum's popular reputation and visual appeal. The younger man believed in the use of theatrical lighting, painted backgrounds, and realistic staging of animals, birds, and fish in exhibits. Although many senior curators felt alienated by the popularizing trends at the museum that kept them from scientific work, Franklin was a favorite of Osborn and had lots of opportunities for offsite research. In 1912, when he and A. E. Butler traveled to the Wisconsin lakes and "camped out on lake and river" to collect fish specimens for the museum's new displays, their glorified fishing trip was widely covered in the New York press.[4] Franklin, who always liked to shake things up, discovered that the male dogfish, "an eccentric aristocrat of the fish family . . . does the female's domestic work."

But Franklin's greatest contribution to the art world was his work as a miniature artist, or, as he described himself to McCall, "a three-dimensional illustrator."[5] During the 1910s, he developed miniature display group types in pliable wax—eight inches tall, painted, and complete with landscape art and lighting. By 1914 Franklin's reputation had grown to such an extent that he left the museum to freelance for the competition. A punctured eardrum kept him from active war service between 1917 and 1918, but Franklin worked as a propaganda artist designing posters, also creating patriotic miniature displays for public viewing and reproduction. After the war his career took off, with his miniatures appearing in the Wanamaker Galleries, the Cleveland Museum, the Metropolitan Museum, the Brooklyn Children's Museum, and the Museum of the City of New York.[6] His numerous private clients included Franklin D. Roosevelt. Years later, Franklin's miniature display of naval hero John Paul Jones ("I have not yet begun to fight!") was in the president's study at the White House.[7]

But pirates were Franklin's true passion, and his figurines of Robert Louis Stevenson's pirates were huge favorites with audiences of all ages. Journalists often referred to him as a "disciple of Howard Pyle," but Franklin's approach was distinctive.[8] Commissions rolled in for models of the American pioneers in James Fenimore Cooper's novels and Teddy Roosevelt on horseback. Soon Franklin was at the forefront of a postwar cultural movement that made history fun. Collectors, whether they were young children or wealthy business executives, could hold their favorite action heroes and heroines, and a sense of history, in their hands.

In addition to being a gifted artist and researcher, Franklin was a savvy businessman. He had many contacts in the theater and film worlds that were closely entwined in 1920s New York.[9] When actress Pola Negri arrived from Europe to start her Hollywood career in September 1922, he was among the members of the Coffee House Club at the luncheon reception in her honor.[10] The guests included actresses Ethel Barrymore, Tallulah Bankhead, and Blanche Bates; theater director Theresa Helburn; the new chairman of the Motion Picture Producers and Distributors of America, Will Hays; and critics Alexander Woollcott and George Jean Nathan. Franklin was friendly with all of them. While chatting with Negri and other stars about their upcoming pictures, he took note of Hollywood's investment in historical epics. Later that fall, *Film Daily* announced that Franklin had abandoned his work for the Metropolitan Museum of Art to open "a research bureau for Eastern motion picture production."[11] One of his early films was the Film Guild witch drama, *The Scarecrow* (1923), starring Glenn Hunter. Franklin worked as the production's researcher, art director, and costume designer, and his drawings and miniatures were photographed and reproduced as publicity for the film.[12]

Though Franklin's knowledge of history and design was broad, "pirates . . . are Mr. Franklin's chief interest," journalist Barbara Little revealed in *Picture Play*.[13] In early 1923, Hollywood's golden couple, Mary Pickford and Douglas Fairbanks, visited Franklin's studio in Greenwich Village. "It was shortly after that that [Fairbanks] announced his plans to play a pirate," Little claimed. Since making *The Mark of Zorro* in 1920 and *Robin Hood* in 1922, the swashbuckling star had spent the past few years trying to put another outlaw project together using the new color technologies. In 1923, the French period drama *Monsieur Beaucaire*, an adaptation of Booth Tarkington's novel, was touted to be Fairbanks's next film, but after visiting Franklin's studio "the sight of his fascinating pirate figures ... inspired Douglas Fairbanks to postpone *Monsieur Beaucaire* in favor of a pirate romance." As Little predicted, "The coming of pirates to the screen means the coming into motion picture production of the man who knows most about pirates, Dwight Franklin." Just as Hollywood's historical productions were attempting to bridge the divide between history and the public, so Franklin's wax miniature models "have invaded even the sacred precincts of staid art museums and universities."

Fairbanks realized that in Franklin he had found an expert whose research could give his new film a plot and some prestige. But the star still had to arrange financing and work with the Technicolor company on the possibility of shooting in color. He returned to Hollywood, and Franklin continued his freelance research and commissions. He went on to work with Gloria Swanson in *The Hummingbird* (1924), making a famous miniature of the actress in her role (which the director, Sidney Olcott, then gave to her). At one of the sessions the impish Swanson turned the tables on Franklin and sketched him.[14]

Tired of waiting for Fairbanks, Franklin took off to the Pacific with naturalist, explorer, and friend Charles William Beebe, whom he knew through Osborn. Beebe needed a staff artist aboard his steam yacht Arcturus for his second expedition to the Galapagos Islands in 1925.[15] Though largely forgotten today, Beebe was a towering figure in the world of zoology and oceanography and a firm believer in making science accessible to the public. He was also a charismatic popular figure in New York society who, like Franklin, enjoyed a good party. They were away several months, and Beebe would eventually publish an illustrated book covering their findings. One of the photographs shows Beebe and Franklin posing with a twenty-foot manta ray the team caught on the voyage. Then in his late thirties, Franklin was tall and slim, with blue eyes, cut-glass cheekbones, and thinning brown hair.

Upon his return to New York, Franklin read in the trade papers that Fairbanks was going ahead with *The Black Pirate* and had assigned his old friend Albert Parker (*Knickerbocker Buckaroo*, 1919) to direct. He sent Fairbanks a wire that morning ("How dare you make *The Black Pirate* without me?"). A few days later, Franklin was headed to Los Angeles as technical advisor, design consultant, costume designer, and extra. He helped Fairbanks on details of the treatment and even drew storyboards to help the director visualize individual shots. As journalists covering the lavish production explained, "Every night during six weeks filming, the assistant director handed him a layout of the scenes to be shot the following day."[16] Franklin would then "sketch in the figures, number them, and then have the cast fit into the figure position, with the result that the pirate crew had no haphazard grouping of themselves but were placed in accordance with definite laws of composition where they were most eye-compelling." The action of every scene was timed in accordance with Franklin's view of the material, and sometimes more than a hundred pirates were involved in a sequence.

But most of all Franklin enjoyed dressing himself and his friends as pirates. *New York World* critic Heywood Broun wrote about Franklin dressing him for the famed Beaux Arts Ball in 1926, a month before the premiere of *The Black Pirate*. It "took me out of the narrow confines of my own life," Broun remembered, and he confessed that later in the evening he fought off half a dozen bouncers who objected to his entering and exiting without a party stamp on his hand.[17] Franklin's costume "induced a recklessness" that the critic found exhilarating. Broun was neither the first nor the last to find Franklin's company addictive.

Fairbanks wanted Franklin to remain in Hollywood and collaborate on future projects with him. But Franklin also possessed something of the pirate in his nature, at least in terms of his independence and fear of settling down to work at one job. He enjoyed California and the film crowd, but he was a New Yorker and a scholar at heart who was happiest working in his own studio. Though he was a member of the Players Club and was considered one of the best-dressed men in New York, Franklin preferred historical costume research and design (he was also a founding member of the Armor and Arms Club, created by the Met's curator, Bashford Dean, in 1921). He knew little bits of everything on every possible topic, from botany to Renaissance dress to military history to how to get into the most exclusive clubs in the city. He knew everyone, from Hollywood stars to unknowns Jimmy Cagney and Humphrey Bogart. The life of an elegant New York bachelor, a first-nighter and fixture in the city's artistic scene, suited him just fine. With the successful publicity campaign and opening of *The Black Pirate*, Franklin found there were plenty of pretty women in New York ready to take him out of the library on weekends.

Then, through the efforts of some family friends in the fall of 1927, he met McCall, who was charting her own independent career path. Though she had steered clear of romance to focus on her writing, Dwight Franklin's elegance and experience were attractive. Unlike so many men she had met through her family or in the office, he was not condescending or unpleasantly aggressive or threatened by women with careers—even if the woman should become his wife. Jean Dwight Franklin had raised him alone, after all, and he respected women's strength and intelligence as well as their looks. Franklin made up his mind quickly about McCall; he asked her to marry him a few weeks after their first meeting. Despite her initial worries that marriage and women's careers couldn't mix, she accepted. They planned the wedding for early in the new year, and he gave her an engagement ring of a diamond flanked by pink and blue tourmalines.

McCall's present was a sonnet, but it was no tribute to wild passion or doomed longing.

> Let us keep something secret and unknown
> Always. Possessed, you would be dead, clay-cold
> And pitiful. It is the free, alone
> And living you I love. Dear, let us hold
> Inviolate the spirit's solitude.
> Adventuring together, we shall be
> Gay fellow-players in the salty, rude
> Boisterous comedy of life, yet we
> Will never lose our joy in quiet things.
> Sharers in laughter and in ecstasy,
> Loving each other while the young blood sings
> Thru all our veins, such friends shall we two be
> There will enfold us when our youth is spent
> The lovely mantle of a deep content.[18]

McCall cast herself and her future husband as pirates on an adventure, and as lovers who would never smother each other with affection. Her view that even when a man and woman were in love they had to preserve their individuality was unique and a fine tribute to her and Franklin as emancipated equals in 1920s America. Franklin also proposed an open marriage, something radical even in the Roaring Twenties. She was young, he acknowledged, and "could have her fun" as long as she didn't try to hide anything from him and was "discreet in public." Flings were "no reason to cause fights or a vulgar divorce."[19] It worked both ways; he was entitled to his discreet fun, too. It appeared to be the ideal marriage.

They wed January 16, 1928, and Mazie and Jean saw to it that the New York society papers covered the wedding.[20] But rather than marry in Englewood, the couple decided to do things a bit more stylishly. They were married at Franklin's mother's Manhattan home by a handsome Presbyterian pastor from Englewood whom Mazie had taken a fancy to, and McCall's little brother Leo was Franklin's best man. One wonders what all McCall's Catholic family members thought of this unusual ceremony. But Franklin was not about to convert, and McCall was no longer a churchgoer. Mazie was happy enough to have her daughter marry into one of the oldest families in New York and to have the papers mention her daughter as "a popular member of the younger set." Franklin had the best wedding present of all for his bride. Beebe had recommended that the couple escape the arctic New York weather for Bermuda, where he had done a lot of his scientific research. Franklin took McCall on a two-month pirate-themed honeymoon.[21]

Upon their return, she settled into a slightly more prosaic existence at 247 Lexington Avenue before moving into a larger apartment at 215 East 73rd Street. McCall wrote in any nook she could find. Things were slightly easier for her husband. Through his wife's family connections, Franklin had snagged a top-floor studio in the brand-new New York Life Building, at 51 Madison Avenue, set to open that December.[22] This glamorous real estate was a wedding present from McCall's uncle, the president of "The Company," Darwin P. Kingsley. By day it gave Franklin the artist some of the best light in the city. At night it would become a favorite setting for the couple's parties for their many friends in the theater.

Two of them, James and Lucile Gleason, the stars of *The Shannons of Broadway*, held a coming-home dinner for the newlyweds at Don Dickerman's pirate-themed restaurant at 133 Washington Place on March 27.[23] In the Twenties it was one of the hottest nightspots in the Village, and it was perfect for Franklin since the waiters were all dressed as pirates and staged hourly duels. In addition to the cast of the play, Norman Rockwell, artist Ruth Eastman, and publisher George Palmer Putnam were among the guests. On her husband's arm, McCall had entrées into the city's most elite cultural gatherings, from the Village to Park Avenue. If she felt a little miffed about their different working arrangements, his palatial studio versus her cramped little desk, she kept it to herself. Franklin brought other things to the marriage.

Wherever the couple went, he saw to it that they turned heads and enjoyed making elaborate gowns for his wife's appearances at the costume balls at the Astor Hotel. Once she appeared as an eighteenth-century French aristocrat, and at another party he dressed her as Shakespeare, complete with skullcap, whiskers, and colored hose. But on January 24, 1930, they made their most stunning joint appearance to date, attending the Beaux Arts Ball at the Astor Hotel as "Le Connetable de Bourbon and Anne de Montmorency." Even among the three thousand guests who could afford the most outrageous couture, they stood out in their faultless French Renaissance brocade. Franklin was on the ball's planning committee and would continue to be an advisor on the décor throughout the 1930s, working alongside *Vanity Fair* editor Frank Crowninshield and architect William Adams Delano.[24] For a while, McCall enjoyed being dressed up like a doll by an adoring husband.

McCall had left her job at the advertising agency when she married, ostensibly to transition fulltime to freelance writing, but it was hard to get back into a daily writing routine, particularly when she didn't have her own "studio." After a yearlong grind writing trite copy, she had let her discipline slip. She did a bit of freelance advertising work after her honeymoon, including a return to radio voiceover work impersonating "an internationally famous beauty expert," Madame Jeannette de Cordet.[25] Franklin, who had a thriving national clientele for his wax figures, dioramas, and museum exhibitions, became worried when he found her bored and out of sorts. He reminded her that she was "always talking about stories" but never writing them down. If she was going to earn her living doing what she loved, now was the time to do it because they had bills to pay. Given that her husband's commissions were sporadic, she *had* to start writing. And as she put it once, she had a "terrible feeling about using money that my husband had worked hard for for frivolity. . . . If I wanted a pair of red shoes," then, as she put it, "it's got to be my money that I spend on red shoes."[26]

Two New Yorkers she met through her husband shared her cash-strapped restlessness and became her good friends. James Cagney, then a struggling actor, was six years older than McCall and had the kind of education a person didn't get at college. His working-class Irish upbringing on the Lower East Side was worlds away from McCall's safe suburban existence, and she learned a lot from his stories about hunting for work, taking chances, and stretching a dime. Soon she started writing about him.

While in hindsight they seemed like a well-matched pair, Cagney was more traditional in his attitudes than Franklin. When the Cagneys had briefly traveled to California in the mid-1920s hoping to break into the movies, *his* career was more important than his wife Billie's. The couple returned East, still broke, but Cagney soon won good stage parts in *Outside Looking In* (1925), *Broadway* (1926–27), and the hit *Grand Street Follies of 1928* while Billie's career stalled.

McCall and Franklin were always there for Jimmy's first nights and the epic parties afterward that lasted till dawn. But at the close of the 1920s those happy days were numbered. Luckily, with the help of Al Jolson, Cagney would head west to Hollywood again, attached to a play that Warner Bros. optioned with him and a vivacious blonde actress named Joan Blondell. This time he became a star.

On the surface, Mary Caldwell McCall Jr. and Humphrey DeForest Bogart were more alike. He was born on the Upper West Side at 245 West 103rd Street, and the Bogarts had a summer estate while his parents' work flourished. Belmont DeForest Bogart, a prominent surgeon, was the son of heiress Julia Stiles, but even so, his wife, the successful commercial artist Maud Humphrey, earned more than twice as much as her husband did in a good year. A former student of James Whistler, she frequently used little Bogie as her model, and a portrait of him served in the advertising campaign for Mellin's Baby Food. Bogart's parents had intended that their son to go to Yale, like the rest of the Bogart men, but he was expelled from Phillips Academy prep school in 1918, putting an end to his academic career and mortifying his father.

After Bogart served in the U.S. Navy for a brief stint in World War I, childhood connections with the famous Brady theatrical family led to his theater career, and by the end of the decade, he was commuting from the East Coast to California, playing an assortment of handsome juvenile "Tennis, anyone?" leads. In 1928, when he grew close to McCall, Bogart was also newly divorced from Helen Mencken and about to remarry the popular stage actress Mary Philips. But even as an up-and-coming theater actor, he still had time for old-fashioned social engagements with the family. McCall and Franklin would join him and Philips at an enormous "debutante's tea" given in honor of his cousin, Beatrice Bogart, in September 1929, one of the last of such lavish events before the Wall Street crash and the onset of the Great Depression.[27]

These were the sort of stuck-up dos McCall occasionally went to that made Cagney tease her. Though McCall and Cagney maintained a fun-loving relationship seasoned with plenty of humor, her friendship with Bogart was sometimes more difficult to manage. Although they came from the same background and social class, McCall liked about Bogart what Franklin so conspicuously lacked. Bogart was dangerous. When he was around, the atmosphere and the repartee had a charge. If McCall began to contemplate the flexible borders of her marriage to Franklin, then it was Bogart's looks in her direction that got her thinking about it. But it wasn't just a sexual attraction that brought them closer in those early years. Behind his blasé, well-bred exterior, Bogart was a fiercely gifted actor and as ambitious as she was. Frustrated with his limited roles and slightly contemptuous of the profession, he was already a heavy drinker.

McCall shared his sense of purposeless frustration at the end of the Twenties but didn't turn to alcohol as a cure. She pulled herself together and wrote, returning to *The New Yorker* in July for a burlesque of the popular British detective fiction genre, "The Persian Rug Mystery."[28] Her pompous drone of a detective, Mordaunt Rice, refers to other glorious cases he's solved, patronizes the police, and describes a preposterously intricate hypothesis for the crime (only to have a policeman interrupt him mid-speech to witness the butler's confession). It was a hilarious takedown of the kind of Bulldog Drummond fare Hollywood obsessed over.

McCall then turned her satirical eye on the modern smart set with "Defeat" in March 1929.[29] Told from the perspective of the female half of a "bright young" couple from the Village ("We wrote our own ceremony. He had his basement and I had my attic. We breakfasted together on alternate Tuesdays"), McCall nailed the smug cultural influencers of the 1920s and their artistic pretensions ("We read Ambrose Bierce, and Samuel Butler meant a lot to us even before Gene Tunney took him up"). But after twelve years at the top, these self-consciously brilliant people have run out of original things to do. As McCall puts it, their Sutton Place "nest" once had "black linoleum and one early Matisse. Then we made the room Victorian."

Her follow-up, "Sesame Lollard," published in April, pursued the theme of modern celebrity culture, profiling a beautiful young woman who "had no aloneness" because all her opinions and tastes were trumpeted in the popular press.[30] She was one of the new beauties who had no mystery simply because she "would endorse anything for five thousand dollars." McCall had more sympathy for the protagonist of "Butterfly" (out in *The New Yorker*'s May issue), a chorus girl with an obsession for cultural self-improvement.[31] But however much fun she had taking down pretension and poking fun at so-called highbrow culture, McCall needed to make more money. It wasn't enough to appear in the same issue as James Thurber, Alexander Woollcott, and Robert Benchley. *The New Yorker*, although prestigious, didn't pay well.

"So I took myself by the back of the neck," as she put it, and wrote a "shamelessly autobiographical" story and sent to the editor Percy Waxman of *The*

Pictorial Review, whom she "had met once at a cocktail party." He offered her an astonishing $300 for it. This was a big deal. Edith Wharton's *The Children* was serialized there in 1928. But soon after publication she had an irritating encounter with Edwin Balmer, the editor of *Redbook*, who "went off into guffaws of laughter" when he identified her as the "girl" who called herself "Jr." "All right chum," she thought. "But you remember, and any way I can make you remember is all to the good."[32]

She had no agent at the time, but then Sydney A. Sanders approached her, saying he could do "what you cannot do gracefully yourself"—namely, sell the material to editors and the public. McCall at first wasn't so sure she needed an agent (a man) to sell her work, which could stand up on its own merits, and then take 10 percent of her earnings. He informed her that men ran the publishing world, but "I know every editor in New York. I lunch with them every day. I ride on the train with them from Westport every day. . . . I think I can talk up your work and create a demand for it, and so raise your price and raise my commission."[33] She hired him, and Sanders remained her literary agent until his death. When she later moved to Hollywood, she insisted that Sanders be cut in on any deals her motion picture agents secured for her.

Then, in the late spring of 1930, just as she seemed to hit her career stride, she discovered to her dismay that she was pregnant. All her past worries about getting married resurfaced, and she remembered with horror the time she was at Dublin's Abbey Theatre and saw a crowd of young children sitting together in the stalls. "A school party?" she had innocently asked her male escort. "No," he replied, "a family."[34] As her stomach grew bigger each month, McCall was in a race with the clock to put as many stories on paper as she could before motherhood took all her writing time away. She wrote about ordinary people struggling to make a living in the city; working women coping with romantic disappointment; married women looking back on betrayal and shattered dreams; lonely people haunted by the past. She wrote about college girls and artists' models and cops and secretaries and little girls. Mostly they were from the working class. Sometimes they were Irish. Always they tried to define themselves against the forces that were crushing them through telling stories. Nothing was ever easy. In the early years of the Great Depression, when so many were blindsided by fate, these were the tales that people wanted to read.

In many of her stories the heroes were inspired by what she knew of Jimmy Cagney. He was the poor but talented Irish American hoofer Joey in "Wooden

Shoes," the romantic tale of two broke young dancers.[35] The story appeared in *Redbook*'s July 1930 issue and got a "Magna Cum Laude" from playwright Russel Crouse in the *New York Post*.[36] It remained one of her favorite pieces of fiction to the end of her life. "Subway Diamonds" and "Mr. Nolan's World" appeared in *Redbook* that fall.[37] With Sanders negotiating on her behalf with editors, she was soon making thousands of dollars per story rather than hundreds.

All the extra money came in handy. On December 4, 1930, her daughter was born. They called her Sheila. The name was newly popular, and she and Franklin liked the modern spelling of the old Irish name, which was also slang for "girl." "Granmazie" was there to help, and now that McCall's short story writing was on a roll, she realized with relief that she could afford a nanny to give her some time to write. She hired a formidable lady named Justine Prickell.

By 1931 McCall's work was always in one New York magazine or another. *The Pictorial Review* published most of her stories, but "Crazy—Or Something" came out in *Redbook* in July and "Let's Not Pretend" appeared in the November issue.[38] *Redbook* favored lighter romantic fare, but McCall's favorite piece of work, the Irish immigrant tale "The Horse with the Flaming Mane," appeared in the October issue of *Collier's*.[39] Hollywood headhunters often turned to *Collier's* for grist for the motion picture mills.

McCall had finally broken into the career she wanted since she was a little girl. All the fashionable and smart people in New York were reading her stories. She and cultural critic Gilbert Seldes, author of the acclaimed *Seven Lively Arts* (1924), were praised in the same sentence. And she sold everything that she wrote—"always to the slick paper magazines," she said, "never to the pulps." Though she relished success and admired other writers whose work appeared in the more high-toned *Harper's* and *Scribner's*, she wanted to remain true to the kind of stories she wanted to tell. As she explained, "I am a storyteller. I write a good deal better than I think. . . . I am not a profound thinker. I always wrote just as well as I know how to, because I had a story in mind which seemed to me to be an awfully good story and I wanted to tell it as good as I was able. Then, when I got it all done and a clean typescript, I would read it over and say, 'Dear God! I have written a good buckeye story for *The Redbook*.'"[40] But it wasn't enough. Remembering one of her childhood literary idols, Charlotte Brontë, "Onward and upward" became her motto.

She realized that if she wanted to climb to the top she had to write a novel, and one that would appeal to Hollywood. Mary Pickford had sponsored many female writers over the years, including Frances Marion, whose recent script for *The Big House* (1930) won an Academy Award. But McCall disliked the idea of getting a film job because she was "a friend of a friend." Though many other female screenwriters during the silent era had earned their credits through the word of a friend or climbing the career ladder from story editor or cutter to title writer and screenwriter or through some one-off story in a monthly magazine, jobs were getting competitive. "Talkies" appealed to East Coast actors and writers. As new arrival Herman Mankiewicz wired Ben Hecht in 1927, "Millions are to be grabbed out here and your only competition is idiots."[41] Hecht went west with his wife, Rose Caylor, who would collaborate on many of his screenplays but receive no credit. This was not a fate McCall wanted; she wanted credit for a career she created herself.

The Wall Street crash in the fall of 1929 and the onset of the Great Depression exacerbated the situation. Despite McCall's prolific story hawking, her income depended on the continued solvency of glossy magazines, which depended on the existence of middle-class patrons. She and Franklin spent lavishly on parties and clothes and vacations. If any of her regular clients folded, they would be in a precarious financial situation. Franklin's work as an artist and design consultant was even less secure, and she realized that she was the chief breadwinner in the family.

Friends were out of work, but a few were lucky. Bogart signed a contract with Fox in 1930, and Cagney left Broadway permanently for Warner Bros. soon after. Even her own family members were fleeing to the West. Her father had developed asthma, and when it grew worse, her parents and brother Leo left Englewood for Westport, Connecticut, and began taking long winter vacations in Arizona, avoiding the pollution of New York City.

Cagney's new boss at Warner Bros., twenty-eight-year-old Darryl F. Zanuck, was making a name for his studio producing contemporary stories that were "ripped from the headlines." Rather than cut back on production, Zanuck's response to the economic depression in the early 1930s was to invest in new story material to lure audiences into the theaters. He was employing a range of new screenwriters who, even if they weren't Hollywood insiders, understood the dynamics of this fast-paced, modern era.

McCall needed a great story to crack this Hollywood market. The advice always given to young writers was "write what you know." Although she lived in the most exciting and modern city in the world, the hub of so-called great writers, at first the twenty-six-year-old struggled to define what distinguished her experience from the hundreds of other young freelancers trying to make more than a ripple in New York's literary scene. What could a girl who grew up in Englewood bring to a world of stars, publicity, glamor, and money? True, she had come a long way since that little *New Yorker* poem about a posh fish swimming in its little aquarium, flashing its fins at drab tourists. Then, as she remembered years later, she reflected on her suburban childhood in Englewood—sleepy, middle-class, average old Englewood—and woke up. One of her girlfriends from grade school had just married Charles A. Lindbergh. And just like that, her plot fell into place.

CHAPTER 3

It's Tough Being Famous

When McCall began writing her first novel, Charles Lindbergh was a national hero. Three years before, in May 1927, he had become the first man to fly solo across the Atlantic Ocean from New York to Paris. Tall, blond, smiling, and untouched by the tragedy and death of the First World War, his "Lone Eagle" image modernized traditional ideals of American "frontier" individualism with a film star's good looks.[1] Lindbergh's brand of glamor also fed the American public's class snobbery and racism. He was from a rich, well-connected political family. According to the media, he was a catch for any young woman.

McCall's close friend Elisabeth Morrow was teaching at the Dwight School in Englewood in 1927, but her parents were in Mexico City, where Mr. Morrow was ambassador to Mexico. Elisabeth and her sister Anne, who was then a senior at Smith College, visited their parents for Christmas, where they met Lindbergh. As McCall remembered, when Elisabeth returned, "she was wearing Lindbergh's wings, which sent the school into a tailspin."[2] Elisabeth was beautiful and spirited, but McCall believed that Lindbergh was put off by Elisabeth's independence. Elisabeth, she recalled, "was very much an individual." He shifted his affections to the shy, more compliant Anne, and they married in May 1929 in Englewood. Their first child, Charles Lindbergh Jr., was born in June 1930. The press never left them alone.

McCall observed all this with amused interest and decided to base her novel on the media's construction of the Lindbergh image and modern America's insatiable appetite for news—but with a twist. She changed a few things to avoid a potential libel suit. Her hero was Irish rather than Swedish American like Lindbergh; he was a submariner rather than an aviator; he was from an average family of nobodies rather than wealthy; and in order to thwart any comparisons with the famous aviator, she made her protagonist prone to airsickness![3]

McCall's premise was simple. After a freak, daring rescue of his crew, a young submarine officer becomes a hero overnight, and it nearly ruins his life and that of the woman he loves. Scotty McClenahan just wants to get out of the navy and marry his girlfriend Janet and settle down to a boring domestic existence. Just before he is due to return home from sea duty, a ship accidentally rams their sub. They can't surface, and the only way Scotty can save his crewmembers is by ejecting them through the torpedo tubes one at a time. He elects to stay behind and expects to suffocate, alone, and go down with his ship. But he is rescued at the last minute, and from that moment, "Scotty belongs to the nation. His life is lived in a goldfish bowl, with ten million newspaper readers peering in through the glass slides."[4] He has to negotiate agents, tabloids, radio shows, public appearances, being stared at, managed, misquoted, and manipulated. He can't get drunk, swear, or have a fight with his girlfriend without its becoming national news.

McCall's title, *The Goldfish Bowl*, was inspired by famed *New York World* journalist and "Judge Priest" creator Irvin Cobb's line, "No more privacy than a gold fish" and was also the subject of her poem "Aquarium Reverie." But while the gaping hordes ogle Scotty for nearly three hundred pages, the hero isn't any more unique than a goldfish you could buy at your local pet store. He's no steely-eyed hero like Lindbergh, and he's not particularly interested in becoming a role model, either. When he won't invite one of his wife Janet's young cousins over to stay with them (he's tired of being gaped at), she replies: "Suppose you'd been invited to spend a week with Douglas Fairbanks when you were twelve?" When he grunts, "I'm not Douglas Fairbanks," she pointedly agrees with him, precipitating another fight.[5]

Janet recognizes that the whole press circus has to be played as "a kind of game," and that if they let the media "get under our skin, then they've won."[6] Scotty may be the hero to the public, but Janet is more resilient and determined to find humor even in "the triumph of vulgarity" that they are living through. Newly married and, they hope, alone at long last in their hotel room, she is only half-joking when she asks Scotty to "look under the bed for reporters."[7] But she has even less respect for an American public that sees her as "Scotty's sweetheart" rather than as an "independent" woman. "People," she reminds him, are "just a lot of driveling idiots" because they want to see her as a young housewife in a house managed by a troop of servants. Janet tells Scotty firmly, "I don't think I want to be taken care of. I don't like asking you for clothes, money, and taxis—things like that. I'd like to have something of my own." When Scotty responds, uncomfortably, that they "are equal partners," Janet agrees, but tells him, "I've got to have a job."

Unfortunately, Scotty's success increasingly restricts what Janet can do. She can't get a job using her old name; potential bosses only want to hire her as Scotty's wife. They separate, plan to divorce, and then tentatively reconcile. Everything will be all right, they reason, once they leave the great American success story and drive across the border to Canada. Like modern outlaws escaping over a frontier, they set off in their car. But at a railway crossing, the car ahead of them stalls on the tracks. In a last-minute save worthy of serial stunt actress Pearl White, Scotty nudges the vehicle off the tracks to safety. As stunned witnesses approach them, they realize they are again in danger of becoming page-one news. They drive away in the nick of time.

McCall's novel satirized the American public's mania for news and heroes, while casting a sympathetic look at a young, somewhat dull-witted Irish American guy and his skeptical mate. McCall knew what the average reader wanted, just as librettist and fellow Irish American George M. Cohan knew at the turn of the century: a spirited American boy who works hard and gets the girl in the end. It was the formula for Cohan's musicals *Little Johnny Jones* (1904), *Forty-Five Minutes from Broadway* (1905), and *George Washington, Jr.* (1906). But, unlike Cohan, who on stage and off worshipped the mantra of male success, McCall took aim at the national obsession with celebrity and revealed how those loved "individuals" were merely average people constructed by a network of crass promoters and freeloading journalists. Janet, objectified by the press as Scotty's girlfriend and wife, ultimately rejects the "Best Supporting Actress" role in Scotty's big story. She articulates why women need to work and achieve things on their own terms, regardless of whether they are married. Janet's average, girl-next-door persona makes her beliefs even more revolutionary.

Sanders sold the magazine serial rights to the *Pictorial Review* on April 18, 1931, for $7,500 and negotiated a book contract with Little, Brown.[8] As McCall remembered, Sanders told her that he chose Little, Brown because "I'm trying to pick a publisher for the rest of your literary life and I think Little and Brown, which has a small light-fiction list, would be very willing if, later, you wanted to do another book of quite a different nature."[9] Simon & Schuster, in contrast, "would want you to keep on doing the same thing."

Just as things were falling into place that spring, a potential disaster appeared. McCall and Franklin, like many in their social circle, had started vacationing in Skowhegan, Maine, where new plays were tried out for Broadway's fall and winter seasons. One night, they had tickets to a play called *Zoom* by William E. Barry and John B. Hymer. The play, to McCall's horror, had "the same story" as her *Goldfish Bowl*. She saw months of hard work and career strategies vanish. But, being McCall, after the curtain went down, she went backstage and confronted William Barry. She told him straight out: "I want you to know that I have the galley proofs of a novel which has been sold to Little and Brown and is to be serialized, and it is on exactly the same theme. I don't want you to think I rushed up here, saw your play, and quickly wrote something."[10] Barry replied that the theme would appeal to a lot of writers and not to worry. But, she confessed, she put a call through to Sydney Sanders in New York that night letting him know that they "should move forward on a motion picture sale because if this play opens in New York, we're dead." The play, starring Russell Hardie and Joyce Arling, was produced by the Shuberts, and went to Philadelphia's Chestnut Street Opera House for a few weeks in January for an out-of-town tryout before closing on the road.[11] McCall was in luck.

The Goldfish Bowl was ideal content for Hollywood, and someone with a quick eye at Warner Bros. brought it to Darryl F. Zanuck's attention. The book targeted the newspaper business, the tabloids, public relations, advertising, and radio, had a good conventional love story, and focused on a handsome male protagonist putting up with fame. It fit in with the studio's 1931 hits *Five Star Final*, *Little Caesar*, and *The Public Enemy* (the latter starring Cagney in a breakout role). Zanuck offered McCall $8,750 for the rights in early November 1931.[12] Since no other offers were forthcoming, on November 5, 1931, she signed the contract at Morris Ebenstein's studio offices at 321 West 44th Street.[13] It was just over a thousand dollars more than *The Pictorial Review* had paid. Perhaps a more experienced Hollywood agent might have worked up the price or brought in other studios. But national unemployment stood at 15 percent, and who knew whether anyone would have a job by the spring, when the novel was slated for publication.

Ironically, Warner Bros.' hottest young star was Douglas Fairbanks Jr., the son of her husband's old pirate buddy. The actor was even more handsome than his legendary father. While they were on the phone discussing the deal, McCall told Zanuck that she wrote the role of Scotty with Doug Jr. in mind and casually dropped that she knew Doug Sr. rather well through her husband.[14] Zanuck was intrigued but explained that Fairbanks's contract specified story approval. But that wouldn't take long: by a strange coincidence, having just finished work on his latest picture, *Union Depot*, Doug Jr. was planning to visit New York that November with his new wife, Joan Crawford.[15] Zanuck suggested that Mary Jr. and Doug Jr. could meet and discuss the story then. But, Zanuck said, the studio had to change the title. *The Goldfish Bowl* was too arty; audiences would think it was a movie about fish. *It's Tough to Be Famous* wouldn't confuse them. McCall agreed. Warner Bros. had a quick production turnaround. As long as Doug Jr. concurred, they would start shooting in January 1932 and release the film in early May.[16]

Then, as she recalled, she "timorously" suggested that she "would like to work on the screenplay." Zanuck stalled. "The answer was that they *never* employed writers on their own work," McCall remembered. "They didn't think the writer had the proper perspective."[17] Robert Lord, who had worked on the exposé of modern journalism *Five Star Final*, would get the assignment. But Zanuck wanted her to be on hand to read the script and advise on dialogue. He promised to get back in touch when they had a draft ready.

Fairbanks Jr. and Crawford had first met in 1927 and married in 1929. His stepmother Mary Pickford and Doug Sr. did not attend the ceremony. They allegedly didn't like Crawford, thinking the young woman was too "common" for the more sensitive and cultured Doug Jr. A year later, Crawford was already having affairs, and her relationship with Clark Gable, her costar in *Possessed* (1931), nearly wrecked the marriage. By the time he met McCall in the winter of 1931, Doug Jr. was ready to even the score with his wife. McCall was pretty enough to qualify as a starlet, but she had several advantages over the typical Hollywood glamor girl. She was educated, with a wide range of interests, an amusing raconteur, and had a droll, stylish sense of humor. She was developing material for *his* career as much as her own. Finally—and perhaps most appealingly—McCall was a married woman, so not as likely to hire a publicist to follow them to hotel rooms and create an expensive divorce.

It was a recipe for an affair, and that November in Manhattan, she and Doug Jr. fell for each other.[18] There's no evidence that the actor told Zanuck to get McCall out to Los Angeles, but a week or so later, Zanuck called her again, asking if she'd like to work "on another property."[19] He'd taken a look at her other material and noted how prolific she had been over the past couple of years. They were having trouble with the adaptation of a new picture for Kay Francis, an acquisition from Paramount they were trying to build up with her own vehicles. They offered to pay all her expenses and a few hundred dollars a week.[20]

Since, as McCall later joked, she'd "never been west of Newark" and the studio was offering to cover all her travel expenses, she agreed.[21] Her parents were spending the winter in Scottsdale with twelve-year-old Leo Jr. and offered to host little Sheila and the nanny. Franklin was delighted to have a breathing space from the wife and new baby. Zanuck offered McCall $300 a week "to write dialogue" for a period of six weeks, with the option of an extension if she was developing a script they both agreed on.[22] He also told her he would buy any new stories she wrote during that time. He asked her to report at the studio on December 21, 1931.

On December 15 McCall signed the contract, packed her bags, had a goodbye drink with Sydney, and went to Grand Central Station to catch the Century Limited. She saw the Midwest through a train window but didn't have time to indulge her curiosity about American life between the two coasts. Like so many before her, she was headed for California and could see only Hollywood on the horizon. Anything else was peripheral. She dropped Sheila and Justine Prickell off in Scottsdale and continued to Los Angeles. She and Zanuck connected instantly, and Fairbanks kept her company over the Christmas holidays. Presumably they looked over Robert Lord's script together at some point.

If Zanuck was aware of what was going on with his star and new writer, he didn't say, but concentrated on laying the groundwork for a smash hit. The most powerful columnist in Hollywood, Louella Parsons, reported "I haven't seen Jack Warner and Darryl Zanuck as excited over a play in months as they are over *The Goldfish Bowl*. . . . Jack told me he considered it the greatest thing he had bought in many a day."[23] She even claimed that Zanuck himself would direct McCall's story. Though her novel hadn't been published, already McCall was the latest buzzword in the industry. Parsons then wrote to McCall and teased her about whether she'd abandon writing for an acting career. Perhaps she'd heard the gossip that McCall was keeping company with *a certain actor.* McCall, wanting to keep Parsons as an ally, gently deflected the reference to Doug Jr. and replied, "I promise to keep this Irish face on the lee side of the camera."[24]

Although some papers maintained that McCall had been asked out to Hollywood to write the treatment, Zanuck knew what he was doing in assigning the property to Lord, one of the studio's top writers.[25] Lord had his start in the mid-1920s writing westerns for William Fox. After a few years, he moved to Warner Bros., earning over $1,000 a week writing *Hold Everything* (1930), *Little Caesar*, and *Five Star Final*. Although McCall later admitted she was gutted not to get the chance to adapt her own work and was ready "to burst into tears" when Zanuck asked if she'd like to read the script, to her surprise, it was good— though, in contrast to McCall's *Goldfish Bowl*, Lord's script began with Scotty's actions in the submarine, thereby somewhat justifying the media's decision to hail him as a hero. McCall avoided opening her novel with any typically heroic material.

But Lord exploited McCall's funny one-liners and extended the repartee between Scotty and his media "handlers" in a series of spiraling comedic scenes. When one promoter offers Scotty $3,000 a week in vaudeville for sixteen weeks, his friend says, "For three thousand dollars a week they can exhibit me naked in Times Square." When an admiral congratulates Scotty for his heroic act in saving his men, the newsreel guys flub the sound, and they have to arrange another take. That's show business! And when Scotty point-blank refuses to read a speech with highfalutin' phrases about "the angel of death" brushing his cheek in that submarine, director Al Green (*Disraeli*, 1929) cut to Scotty in a tux later that night uncomfortably trying to remember the notes from his ridiculous script at a fancy dinner. Lord also preserved McCall's connections between her hero and Fairbanks Sr., having one of Scotty's colleagues remark soon after his media stardom, "From now on, you're America's sweetheart" (the media's longstanding nickname for Mary Pickford).[26] But Scotty's ineptness with the media is part of his charm (as he and Janet, played by Mary Brian, find out when they witness a hilariously awkward staging of his first day at work on a newsreel in a New York movie theater). Unfortunately, Lord focused almost entirely on Scotty and turned Janet into a bland supporting character.

If McCall was dismayed by Janet's fate, she held her tongue and focused on expanding her Hollywood network. Lord and Green became her lifelong friends. Green had worked for Pickford throughout the 1920s, and so they had lots to talk about when she wasn't with Fairbanks. Green even invited her on set to discuss shooting with the star. So it caused little stir with the gossip columnists when she was photographed in a sexy new leopard coat, lounging on the set of *It's Tough to Be Famous* with Fairbanks at her side, pretending to be absorbed with the star's new Great Dane. For the first time in McCall's romantic life, she was the older woman (Crawford, ironically, was also McCall's age and five years older than

Fairbanks). The perfect, no-strings-attached affair turned into an enduring friendship.

While they were shooting *It's Tough to Be Famous*, as promised, Zanuck paid her to write for Kay Francis and to come up with any additional ideas which might lead to a longer stint at the studio. She was hired to rework veteran Charles Kenyon's adaptation of Polan Banks's novel *Street of Women*, and associate producer Hal Wallis gave her a crash course in how to stage material to Zanuck's liking.[27] McCall's six weeks would stretch to ten.

Kay Francis, who had started her career on Broadway in the mid-1920s, switched to films and made several hits at Paramount, often paired with William Powell. Taller than almost all her male costars, glamorous, and with a trademark lisp (she had trouble pronouncing the letter "R"), women loved her projection of elegant world-weariness. In 1932, she left Paramount for Warner Bros. after being offered $4,000 a week. This made her one of the highest paid actresses in the business, so Zanuck was paying novice screenwriter McCall a compliment in assigning her to craft Francis's material.[28]

The trouble was, McCall didn't feel that way. She disliked the sex-ridden, victimized woman dramas Francis was known for (*Passion Flower*, 1930; *Scandal Sheet*, 1931; *Ladies' Man*, 1931) and thought Francis was more of a clotheshorse than an actress. Perhaps McCall would have preferred writing something to boost the career of the then-unknown Bette Davis, who had just arrived at the studio following a lackluster stint at Universal, where she'd worked with Bogart in *Bad Sister* (1931). But what McCall didn't realize, since she didn't mix socially with Francis, was that the star had grown tired of the tripe the studios made her work with—endless plots of men betraying women, and women paying endlessly for their transgressions against the patriarchy. Eventually, Francis's complaints about the material assigned to her at Warner Bros. contributed to the studio's decision to terminate her contract in 1939.[29]

McCall picked up the language of scripts quickly, rewriting *Street of Women* in January and handing it to Zanuck on February 2. For someone who didn't warm to the actress's on or offscreen persona, McCall did her best to refashion Francis's role into an independent working woman. As the famous Manhattan designer "Natalie Upton," Francis plays a woman who crafts her own style and shapes the tastes of modern women. McCall staged scenes with Natalie at her office, designing, managing the books and clients, and appearing to be a paragon of the emancipated woman. The costume designer followed the script's lead: Natalie wears a variety of chic sportswear, wide-leg pantsuits, and tuxedo tops, in keeping with her active, modern lifestyle.

But the narrative focused on the long-term adulterous affair between Natalie and architect Larry Gibson (Alan Dinehart), and the fallout when the man's daughter (Gloria Stuart) and Natalie's younger brother (Allen Vincent) find out. His debutante daughter Dodo (not idly named!), who has never had to work a day in her life, doesn't get her father's attraction to independent women. Calling New York a "man's town," she laughs, "Can you imagine mother if I went into trade or on the stage or something?" So much for the liberated younger generation.

Although over the past few decades, popular film critics have celebrated Hollywood films produced from 1930 to 1934 as "Pre-Code"—more sexually explicit, violent, and fun in comparison with what came after the formalized 1934 Production Code—*Street of Women* is a relatively tame adultery drama. Natalie and Larry are in love but riddled with guilt about their affair, and the plot is a mixture of nineteenth-century moral melodrama and stale sex. If modern New York really is a "Street of Women," then its denizens are riven by discord, jealousy, and class divisions (unless they're working-class salesgirls).

With baby daughter Sheila vacationing with her grandparents and Franklin back East, McCall stayed in town through the end of February. She completed the first draft of a novella, *Revolt*, and showed it to Zanuck and Fairbanks. The story of an aristocratic officer and a maid who leave postrevolutionary Russia in hopes of marrying and starting a new life, it was obviously intended to showcase the considerable romantic talents of her new lover. Nikita (Fairbanks) was young, brave, and like any handsome member of the Czar's guards, slept with as many beautiful women as he could manage. Things don't go so well for him after the revolution, of course, but he manages to escape to the West, taking a pretty former servant (Nancy Carroll) along with him.[30] They marry, and he gets his young wife pregnant, but he leaves her after an old flame tempts him with a jewelry scam that will make them both rich. Inevitably he abandons the deal, returning to poverty and love with his honor intact. It was a nice Valentine's Day present for her lover. Fairbanks was one of two actors at Warner Bros. who had story approval at the time (the other was matinee idol Richard Barthelmess), and he told Zanuck he wanted to make *Revolt* that summer. Fairbanks would later write that he "enjoyed the picture as an exercise in narcissism—and escapism."[31]

On February 16, Zanuck directed Roy Obringer "to see her personally" and pay McCall $5,000 for the story: $2,500 up front and "the balance upon delivery of completed treatment."[32] The treatment was due by February 27, and, incredibly, McCall made the tight deadline. She accepted that another writer would later rework her treatment and that in selling it to Zanuck upfront she had lost any opportunity of publishing it as a novel. But she let it go. *Revolt* was fodder for Fairbanks's career, and both she and Joan Crawford would be out of Fairbanks's life soon. What was important was that Zanuck would be impressed enough with her work ethic to extend her contract. But it didn't happen.

A combination of the Great Depression and Kay Francis very likely settled her fate at the studio. Although McCall never confirmed the details, in later years, the writer would dismiss *Street of Women* (1932) as "a dog" of a picture that the studio undoubtedly thought was more suitable material for a new female screenwriter. Twenty years later, she still wasn't above taking cheap shots at Francis: "Had I been told before I started the first screenplay on which I ever worked that the star for whom I was writing couldn't pronounce the letter 'R,' I would never have written the line for her 'Sawah, I want my bwothew's woom wedecowated.'"[33] It was an uncharacteristic bit of spite directed at another woman.

Studio politics aside, *It's Tough to Be Famous* had a good preview, and she looked forward to a sudden burst of publicity in early April with the release of her book. Franklin had arrived in Los Angeles and spent the last two weeks of February with her before they headed back to Arizona to pick up Sheila.

Then, as she recalled, on March 1, "at breakfast . . . I saw a newspaper with banner headlines: 'Lindbergh Baby Kidnapped.' My first thought was of Anne, but my second thought, I admit, was: 'There goes the book!' And how right I was! The big bookstores said they would stock it in case anyone asked for it, but they certainly would not feature or promote it in any way, since, as a satirical comedy, it was in such execrable taste, with the Lindbergh family undergoing such suffering."[34] She, Franklin, Ms. Prickell, and Sheila caught the train back to New York.

But Zanuck saved the situation. First, he called Morris Ebenstein of Warner's legal department and arranged for an addendum to McCall's contract, giving her consent to release *It's Tough to Be Famous* in April rather than May. Though McCall wasn't due back in New York until March 11, they located her and got her signature on March 8.[35] Then the studio negotiated with the exhibitors, changed the release schedule, and told the studio publicists to get to work.

Sadly, the New York literary world lacked Zanuck's energy. Only *The New York Evening Post* promoted the novel with a glamorous picture of McCall, calling it "an amusing account of the experiences of a national hero."[36] Some smaller papers, reviewing the film, credited McCall with collaborating on the script and dialogue and revealed that she "had a prominent national hero in mind" when she wrote the book.[37] But this careful allusion to Lindbergh created little stir in all the publicity about the kidnapping. Warner Bros. film publicists went with the lead: "His private love-life was public property," thereby subtly connecting Fairbanks's own high-profile Hollywood marriage to Scotty's closely monitored private life onscreen.[38] The *New York Times* reviewed *It's Tough to Be Famous* in early April, praising the film's "hilarious situations" and "subtle" critiques of the modern press and publicity industries.[39]

McCall attended the New York premiere with Cagney. Fairbanks wasn't there. The critics commented that throughout the screening, there was "continuous chuckling at the tribulations of the hero who did not aspire to heroics," and at the end, when the lights went up, the audience applauded. Other papers praised the film's "radical" departure from "the ordinary routine story" and claimed that it was Fairbanks's and Green's best work. *The Buffalo Courier* commented: "America's well known hero-worship, and the attendant tendency of smart businessmen and publicity experts to capitalize on that failing, or quality" was a touchy subject for a film, since the public was often the butt of the story's wit.[40]

McCall's name was again in the papers that June, thanks to the release of *Street of Women*. It was only Kay Francis's second starring vehicle for the studio, and whatever the star's feelings about the script, the film did well at the box office. How could it not, with the publicity lead: "She gave her heart to a married man! Learn the secret of a love sacrifice which gave a man a future—and gave a woman a past!"[41] Given its short running time, Warner Bros. paired the film with another adultery drama, starring Ruth Chatterton and Bette Davis, *The Rich Are Always With Us*, but one critic singled out Francis's "captivating" performance in a film that "delicately and magnificently" handles "an age old problem."[42] Francis's legions of fans were content to count the gorgeous gowns she wore (twenty-two).[43]

She may have had two hits on her record, but McCall was out of a job. *Revolt* was handed over to two newly hired men, Niven Busch and Erwin S. Gelsey, and retitled *Scarlet Dawn*. Facing her first major career setback at the age of twenty-eight, McCall was philosophical. It wasn't all bad news: She had made some good friends at Warner Bros., and she and Bette Davis, who had managed to hang onto her job after a successful pairing with George Arliss in *The Man Who Played God* (1932), discovered that their birthdays overlapped (April 4 and April 5). The women made a pact that in the future, whenever they were together, they'd celebrate in one marathon party. But at that point, without a studio contract, it seemed unlikely that McCall would see Davis or Hollywood again.

That summer she returned to her typewriter. Being true to her word in their open marriage, McCall told her husband about her affair with Doug Jr. He didn't mind, though it was a little awkward that her paramour was the son of his old friend. But it wasn't quite over. Later that September, she and Franklin met Doug Jr. and Crawford at the premiere of the actor's latest film, *Life Begins*, at the Hollywood Theater on Broadway.[44] It was all very friendly on the surface, but Fairbanks and Crawford's marriage was over. They would divorce a few months later. If Doug Jr. and Mary Jr. decided to meet for a drink during his latest sojourn to New York, no one commented. Unlike Scotty and Janet, they could still escape the attention of the press. They were colleagues, after all, as well as friends.

CHAPTER 4

A Second Chance

McCall spent the rest of 1932 and 1933 working on short stories and giving dreary talks to local women's clubs about "her stay in Hollywood" in the hopes that it would promote sales of *The Goldfish Bowl*.[1] She had more fun drafting *The Lady Surrenders*, a novella about a young woman who falls in love with her actress-mother's new lover.

Book sales from *The Goldfish Bowl* were disappointing, so out of necessity McCall developed a knack for living well from story to story. Top-paying *Redbook* bought "Unknown Master," "Handed Down," and "As Cheaply As One."[2] A longer piece of fiction, inspired from her days at Vassar, "Lure," was published over two months in early 1933.[3] But she also used her time in Hollywood as copy, creating a fascinating story about a dedicated Hollywood script girl, "She Said What She Meant," which appeared in *The American Magazine* later in July.[4] *McCall's*, *Collier's*, *Cosmopolitan*, and *The Delineator* also printed McCall's work.[5] She continued to write about life in the city, struggles to find and keep a job, failed romances, making do, and fleeting moments of success and excitement.

At heart, she was a creative risk-taker. Yet her monthly freelance scramble for money in the middle of the worst-ever economic depression took its toll. Years later, she would remember, "I wasn't born to a lot of money, and nothing I want tremendously really costs a whale of a lot." But, as she admitted, "I like money, because when I am broke my mind is constantly occupied with small, dirty problems of subtraction. For an intelligent person to spend most of his waking and sleepless hours adding up the bills and subtracting is dreadful."[6]

Franklin wasn't particularly concerned by her struggles with domestic mathematics. Despite "doing the best work of his life" in the early 1930s, the Great Depression had killed off most of his commissions.[7] Working in the apartment on East 73rd Street, McCall managed to produce enough work each month to make ends meet and even arranged for a business manager to put savings aside for her and dole out a monthly allowance for the family's expenses. But it was no substitute for life as a Hollywood contract writer, where management defined the assignments and each week one got a regular paycheck.

Despite her success at keeping her name in print, there were no more calls from Hollywood. The Depression was taking its toll on the film industry, and in January 1933 Paramount and RKO announced that their theater chains were bankrupt. The other major studios, including Warner Bros., felt the bite as ticket sales declined, and two months later, only MGM could afford to meet its staff payrolls. Wage cuts threw workers into a panic and studios took out hefty loans from New York banks. It was no time to ask for a studio job.

Franklin knew his wife longed to return to Hollywood. As McCall remembered, the continued impact of the Depression eventually convinced the couple that "more and better paid employment for both of us lay in Hollywood rather than New York."[8] Even if, as President Roosevelt's National Recovery Administration reported, 50 percent of screenwriters made less than $4,000 a year, Los Angeles was less expensive to live in. She could still send material to Sanders in New York. But without the immediate prospect of a studio job for either of them, a move to the West Coast seemed unlikely.

Then on April 26, 1933, pirates came to their rescue. Headlines in the *Hollywood Reporter* announced that MGM was planning *Treasure Island* with Wallace Beery and Jackie Cooper in the lead roles of Long John Silver and Jim Hawkins.[9] Franklin didn't know the director, W. S. Van Dyke, but he and McCall were acquainted with the studio's top art director, Cedric Gibbons, a New York Irish American who had attended the Art Students League and moved in the same Greenwich Village social circles as Franklin. In a repeat of his telegram to Douglas Fairbanks Sr., Franklin wired Gibbons: "How do you dare to make *Treasure Island* without me?" McCall remembered, "It worked. He was hired."[10]

MGM wasn't offering McCall a job in the writing department, so she and Franklin decided to be practical and at first kept their furniture in their Manhattan apartment on East 73rd Street while the family moved into temporary accommodation at 336 North Croft Avenue. Between Beverly Hills and West Hollywood, it was convenient to the studios. Then, just as everything seemed set, MGM put the picture on hold for several months, later reassigning it to director Victor Fleming in February.[11] McCall continued writing fiction and, at the invitation of her friends James and Lucile Gleason and Robert Montgomery, joined the Riviera Country Club, where she rode and occasionally rubbed shoulders with the polo-playing studio set. Her old boss Darryl Zanuck was a member and played competitively.

As their sixth wedding anniversary approached, Franklin designed a special present with horses in mind—an engraved bookplate. An Irish linen scroll reads "Mary McCall her book," and a traditional harp and Irish clovers adorn the scroll. To the left, sheets of paper fly off a typewriter. To the right, a slim young woman with wild, cropped hair leans out, as if poised to fly away into thin air. At the top, a winged horse sails off with beating wings. One can almost hear Yeats's words,

> I will arise and go now, for always night and day
> I hear lake water lapping with low sounds by the shore;
> While I stand on the roadway, or on the pavements grey,
> I hear it in the deep heart's core.

Of course, he pasted the plate into a volume of Yeats's poetry, "with all my love." Dwight Franklin knew his wife as a person who always carried a love of beauty with her, wherever she went. If other men were part of that fascination, he lived with it. To a certain extent, this was less important than knowing the better part of her, which was her fearless desire to explore, to create, to work. Yeats's own casual remarks in everyday life, as much as his poetry, mattered to her. "Art knows no politics—art knows no morality," she would often quote. If Franklin ever recognized his friend Cagney or anyone else in the pages of her short fiction, he let it be. No one in her life would ever love, encourage, or understand McCall so well as Dwight Franklin. For a time they shared the same dreams and luck.

While he went back to his pirates in March, McCall called Hal Wallis, her associate producer on *Street of Women*, and said she was back in town and looking for work. Wallis was now running day-to-day production following Zanuck's departure, and he liked McCall. He considered adapting one of her favorite short stories, "The Horse with the Flaming Mane," for the screen but asked whether she had "anything in the trunk to suit a blonde girl named Jean Muir."[12]

As it so happened, Muir, a statuesque New Yorker, was a fellow alumna of the Dwight School in Englewood, but was a few years behind McCall. She made her Broadway debut in 1930 and became a Hollywood contract star in 1933. By 1934 she had played a succession of not-so-innocent single women and was cast as second lead to Kay Francis's physician in the racy melodrama, *Dr. Monica* (1934). With the implementation of the newly strengthened Production Code in June, which required that all films have a seal of approval for release from July 1, Wallis wanted Muir's image scrubbed without making her too pure and boring.[13] As it so happened, McCall's *The Lady Surrenders*, as yet unpublished (and, she would later joke, "unpublishable"), would be a perfect antidote to Wallis's censorship woes in the post-Code era. Wallis initially offered her $2,100, but she raised it to $3,000 and had him hire her at $300 a week in April and May.[14] A New York friend, playwright and screenwriter Edward Chodorov, was assigned to associate produce the picture.

At the end of April, Louella Parsons headed her column with Muir, noting that in opting for McCall's original story, Wallis "has done considerable scouting to get Miss Muir the right vehicle."[15] Parsons hinted that "the name Mary McCall brings to mind *It's Tough to Be Famous*, which she wrote for Douglas Fairbanks, Jr.," so the writer was adept at creating star vehicles. During the Great Depression, Hollywood studios would stand or fall on their ability to develop tailored material for their stars and to market them to the public. It was easy for McCall to master the Hollywood star system because thanks in part to her years with Franklin, she simply "loved actors in general" (Kay Francis excepted).[16] There was something exhilarating in her varied relationships with them that inspired her writing. Throughout her Hollywood career, she created dialog attuned to a particular actor's speech patterns and style. Parsons appreciated this quality in McCall's writing and would continue to be her staunch supporter in the years to come.

Desirable explored a famous New York actress's complicated relationship with her daughter. Helen Walbridge (Verree Teasdale), McCall explained, is a Broadway star "in the old-fashioned sense—she had a huge following which is quite unrelated to the play she appears in."[17] For the past two years, a younger man, Stuart McAllister (played by another of McCall's acquaintances, Bette Davis's on-again, off-again boyfriend George Brent), has been in hot pursuit. But the first evening he arrives at Helen's apartment with her latchkey, she's not there. Instead, a young woman is sitting by the fire. He soon discovers that it is Helen's daughter, Lois (Muir), whom the actress has hidden from the public. "There is no criticism of Helen in her conversation," but Lois "makes it clear to Mac that for years she has been shunted from school to summer camp, and never permitted to be with her mother." Mac realizes that Helen's concern is to appear youthful and sexually attractive; her daughter Lois is only a reminder to the "vain, silly woman" that she is no longer twenty.

Lois has been to college and graduate school (Wallis later cut McCall's allusions to women's higher education). But Helen has paid for her daughter's education to keep her out of the way, *not* because she has some deeply cherished belief in equal opportunities for women. Of course, Mac and Lois form an attachment, discouraged by Helen, who tries to destroy the relationship by claiming that she and Mac were lovers. Lois flees from the apartment, determined to get away from everyone who has manipulated her, but Mac corners her in the elevator. McCall planned "the last shot of the picture [to show] people on all the floors of the apartment house furiously ringing the elevator bells"—clever romantic shorthand that circumvented a potentially censorable clinch.[18]

Family melodramas and society romances were (and still are) a dime a dozen on Hollywood screens, but the women in *Desirable* are not totally devoid of interest. She may be manipulative and selfish, but Helen's career success as a Broadway actress is connected to her identity as a single woman. Being married would have killed Helen's career just as surely as public knowledge of her motherhood. The best stage (and screen) parts always go to younger women, so a successful actress must appear as young as possible for as long as possible. Helen occasionally elicits sympathy for being trapped in a business that focuses on displaying and sexualizing the female body, but McCall never shows Helen onstage and objectified for multiple audiences; instead, she is seen in the fullness of her social success as a public woman—at parties, with other men—where she can do her own looking. But career success and independence are stepping-stones to social position, and Helen defends hers brutally against the incursions of her daughter.

Lois, unused to the competitive atmosphere of her mother's parties, has not learned the gendered rules dictating women's conduct and image in New York's social season. She is "unconventional" and "hates flattery, affectation, and ostentation." The only genuine conversation she has with another woman is a brief exchange with a Black maid working in a hotel powder room—possibly McCall was taking a leaf out of Mae West's scripts for *She Done Him Wrong* (1933) and *I'm No Angel* (1934). It was a solid part for an ingénue with nonconformist talents such as Muir (dubbed "the enigma of Hollywood" by publicists), and the actress made the most of it.[19]

Wallis was impressed with McCall's ability to turn out good work in record time and couldn't fail to notice that her stories were regularly appearing in the best popular magazines on the East Coast.[20] So, following the completion of her work on *Desirable*, the producer offered her a permanent studio contract at $300 a week.[21] It was a respectable salary; Dalton Trumbo made only $100 per week at Warner Bros. She joined Lillie Hayward as the only other woman writer at the studio and was put to work on a range of material.

Another business "issue" had arisen in McCall's absence. The Screen Writers Guild, which had formed in the early Twenties as a social club, had morphed into a fledgling union in 1933. There was still no national right to strike, and of all big cities in the United States, Los Angeles was the most notoriously "open shop" and anti-union. But the impact of the Depression and the election of Roosevelt in November 1932 inspired Hollywood writers to revive the power of the unions and reassert the integrity of the screenwriter.

Many contract writers in Hollywood made less money per week than secretaries, and freelancers were treated far worse. Producers often took credit for writers' work or refused to give them credit altogether. There was no respect for intellectual property, and writers were hired and fired like disposable commodities by a new breed of cost-cutting producer.

Most commercial writers belonged to the Authors League of America in New York. On March 29, 1933, the screenwriters belonging to the league held a meeting at the Writers' Club in Hollywood. Jane Murfin, Dudley Nichols, Oliver H. P. Garrett, Tom Geraghty, Ralph Block, Alfred Cohen, Frank Woods, Vernon Smith, and President Howard J. Green voted to engage two attorneys to draft bylaws and a new constitution for the Screen Writers Guild. They drew up codes of conduct and employment, buoyed by the new presidential administration's avowed crusade for a minimum wage and the right to strike. Members were required to pay dues and sign the first contract of April 6, 1933, the "birthday" of the Screen Writers Guild. Original signers included Doris Anderson, John Bright, Boris Ingster, Lenore Coffee, Frances Goodrich, Albert Hackett, Anita Loos, Marguerite Roberts, Nunnally Johnson, and the new guild's first president, John "Jack" Howard Lawson.[22]

Hostility to unions and a wave of violently suppressed strikes dominated the national headlines in the spring of 1934. That June, Roosevelt issued Public Resolution Number 44 to guarantee the right to strike, and that same month he replaced the struggling National Labor Board with the National Labor Relations

Board while Secretary of Labor Frances Perkins hammered out the historic Wagner Act. Soon, individual unions and guilds could go to the National Labor Relations Board with grievances, forcing employers to comply with federal labor standards. It was the high tide of American labor organizing, and screenwriters wanted to be part of the crusade to reform the workplace.[23]

But as far as the studio heads were concerned, the barbarians were inside the gates. They feared that caving into the unions would kill the industry's slim profit margin. Since writers were the most eloquent advocates for unions and encouraging other craft guilds to unionize, management believed it was essential to take a hard line against them. Executives threatened to fire and blacklist anyone for suspected membership. As a result, organizers kept membership lists secret. Looking back on the struggle in 1941, writer Leo Rosten commented, "The obstinacy and indiscretion with which the producers opposed Hollywood writers in their fight for recognition, basic working conditions, and a code of fair practices, is one of the less flattering commentaries on the men who control movie production."[24]

Hiring McCall, a writer with no known guild affiliations and hailing from a family of conservative businessmen, seemed like a good bet to Warner Bros. Plus she made her deadlines. Although McCall stated she didn't want "to settle down to one studio for a long period of time," she conceded, "I needed money. I liked money."[25] Jack Warner and Wallis probably hoped that if they paid her well she wouldn't join the Screen Writers Guild. But one of the founding guild members, Boris Ingster, had already quietly approached McCall about joining the ranks. Wallis hadn't figured on John A. McCall's granddaughter being a liberal advocate for the working class. It was far worse than that. In joining the guild, Mary C. McCall Jr. had found her second calling. Throughout her long career in Hollywood, the tenets of the Screen Writers Guild contract would always be sacrosanct.

Desirable was a hit that fall, with the *New York Times* focusing on Muir's "delightfully fresh and truthful" performance as one of the highlights in "a drama of surprising delicacy and force." The critic André Sennwald, without noting any specific examples, chose to praise director Archie Mayo for putting "the fragile story back on its course" rather than credit McCall's fresh take on a "school of cinema romance."[26] But another New York reviewer led with McCall's contribution, calling her "the famous magazine writer" and commended a film "filled with highly dramatic and intensely emotional situations, with rapier-like dialogue and a climactic clash between a woman of the world and her unsophisticated daughter that fairly takes the breath."[27] Although Lois was nominally an ingénue, McCall and Muir turned her into a young woman whose "unconventionality and utter frankness" headlined a "dynamic and colorful drama." On the West Coast, *Variety* concurred, singling out McCall's "beautifully contrived and balanced" story.[28] He didn't raise her salary, but Wallis handed her a project that would give her the national fame and industry prestige she craved: Sinclair Lewis's best-selling, *Babbitt* (1922).

The studio had purchased the screen rights to Lewis's novel when it was still known as First National. A silent version of the film had appeared in 1924 directed by Harry Beaumont. It didn't make much of an impression on audiences; complex satires of middle-class businessmen weren't exactly in high demand with an American filmgoing public obsessed with Fairbanks, Pickford, and Valentino. But after Lewis became the first American writer to win the Nobel Prize in literature in 1930, the studio took another look at the property.

During the 1930s, all the major studios appealed to middle-class cinemagoers with prestigious literary and historical adaptations.[29] MGM's colorful period adventures such as *Treasure Island* represented one way of approaching the trend; but American dramas did well. In 1932, RKO won an Oscar adapting Edna Ferber's bestseller *Cimarron* and, with the guidance of story editor Kay Brown, continued to experiment with period material for stars Ann Harding, Katharine Hepburn, and Irene Dunne. Under Zanuck, Warner Bros. combined relatable tales from modern history with more old-fashioned biopics such as *Disraeli* (1929), and by the 1930s the studio was spending more money on adaptations of good literature.

Lewis was fashionable in early 1930s Hollywood, and the adaptation of *Arrowsmith*, produced by Samuel Goldwyn, had reaffirmed Ronald Colman's star status in 1931. RKO produced an acclaimed version of *Ann Vickers* in 1933, and Goldwyn was developing Lewis's *Dodsworth* with actor Walter Huston. *Babbitt* was easily Lewis's most famous novel, and Warner Bros. wanted to prove that even during the Depression it could still compete with rival studios for the prestige picture market.

At first Hal Wallis assigned the adaptation to contract writers Tom Reed and Niven Busch. Wallis wasn't an expert in American literature, but he thought that the script they sent him didn't bear much resemblance to what he thought *Babbitt* was about. McCall was one of the few writers on Warner Bros.' roster with a college degree, and that may have been why Wallis sent her the script for her opinion that summer. McCall wrote back that the script wasn't *Babbitt* at all.

On July 25 Wallis wrote to production supervisor Samuel Bischoff, "The attached note from Mary McCall is self-explanatory and confirms my belief that the writers wrote an entirely new story after writing a treatment and getting that okayed." He continued: "Will you contact Miss McCall and let her go ahead on the re-writing of this script, as I am sure she will do a good job on it." He aimed a parting shot at his associate producer: "Incidentally, however, after this treatment was written and approved, I don't see why you let the writers get so far away from the story line that we had all agreed on."[30]

Nevertheless, Reed and Busch still received screen credit for their "adaptation." Reed, who had a string of writing credits at Universal and Warner Bros., was paid $7,167, and Busch, despite his reputation as a former writer for *The New Yorker* and client of agent Myron Selznick, got $3,583. McCall handed in her script a few weeks later in record time and got single credit for the screenplay, even though she was paid only $983 for her efforts.[31] William Keighley directed Guy Kibbee and Warner Bros. regular Aline MacMahon (who got star billing) as Mr. and Mrs. Babbitt in a cast featuring Hattie McDaniel, Alan Hale, and Bert Churchill.

The film begins with a montage of men's club signs outside the mythical Midwestern city of Zenith (the "fastest growing community in America"). No other textual explanation is needed. It is the age of advertising. Kibbee, plump, balding, and bad-tempered, doesn't wear his success too well. In his sleep he dreams he's still driving his car; when the alarm rings to wake him, he reaches for it and accidently smacks a glass of water in his face. He has a fat reduction machine in his bathroom (which isn't helping him) and a fancy egg timer for his chatty, musical cook (McDaniel) that she doesn't use. Telegrams keep coming to him mysteriously, and his middle-class family (pretty daughter, college-age son, and efficient wife) all imagine some business deal that will make them richer than ever before. But, as we learn on the sly, they're all signed "Maureen," threatening him with attorneys if he doesn't pay attention to her. It's a setup for the audience, believing Babbitt is just another dirty old businessman with a woman on the side he's trying to hide from his family. But, as it turns out, it's also a setup for Babbitt. He really *hasn't* heard of Maureen; his fellow Zebra Lodge members have arranged a prank to "celebrate" his elevation at the lodge.

Initially, McCall's George Babbitt appears to be just a brash but harmless citizen, who gets along with his even-tempered wife, barks at his cynical secretary, can't quit smoking (he locks his cigars in the safe), and tries to help out a down-on-his-luck college friend, Paul (Minor Watson). But Babbitt is also a social climber, a cheerful grafter, and a husband who frets on his domestic tether. He only agrees to serve on the board of the library when he hears a well-connected banker is the president and is hosting the first meeting in his home. He casually arranges a land scam and picks up an enterprising mistress when she throws herself his way.

McCall's script, which grew from 58 to 121 pages in August 1934, depicts an overfed, middle-aged white man of privilege surrounded by the props of a comfortable, middle-class existence.[32] It was a life she recognized, since she had grown up with a variety of Babbitts—albeit more cultured ("Mary Had a Little Lamb" is George Babbitt's idea of great literature). Paul's shrewish wife, played to a neurotic extreme by Mina Gombel, would wreck anyone's evening at the country club, but the scene has eerie and unintended extratextual depth: The club orchestra plays "Midnight," the iconic final song of Stanley Kubrick's 1980 horror film *The Shining*, as the couples squabble. McCall spoofed the Prohibition era in a scene where a local oligarch offers Babbitt and his colleagues homemade "root beer." The guests look utterly disgusted—until they taste whiskey and exchange delighted guffaws.

Ironically, McCall's main liberty with Lewis's novel was not in editing his romance with the bohemian Tanis Judique (Maxine Doyle) and her crowd to focus on a shady real estate deal. Babbitt becomes involved with corrupt civic leaders in land speculation over a proposed town airport and is later blackmailed by his ex-mistress and roasted by the local press. Only the last-minute efforts of his wife get him out of hot water. His lodge brothers invite him back into the fold, and he and his family celebrate the importance of another kind of conformism: family loyalty. The abruptly executed "happy ending" isn't convincing—and it wasn't meant to be.

McCall's focus on Babbitt's double-dealing and lack of morality resonated with the cluster of businessmen biopics and melodramas produced in the early 1930s, including *Match King* (1932). But it also must have touched a nerve for her to write the story of a lumpy, mediocre Midwesterner's ability to get off the hook when her own grandfather was unfairly scapegoated for business malpractice in a much more unforgiving era. In McCall's original script, Babbitt's daughter was a socialist and the biggest questioner of his conformist lifestyle. But Warner Bros. wouldn't tolerate this character trait, and so in the final cut, she merely appears in a few scenes as decoration.

In the *New York Times*, Sennwald, who had failed even to mention McCall by name in his review of *Desirable*, now praised her adaptation of *Babbitt*. "Although the cinematized *Babbitt* lacks the remorseless irony of the printed page," he wrote, "it is in its own right a skillfully managed motion picture which regards the immortal George F. with a human and sympathetic eye."[33] Kibbee's delightful impersonation of Babbitt was rendered "in a kaleidoscopic procession of briefly etched scenes," and the filmmakers, "far from desiring to dip this noble and confused gentleman into the acid bath," had his wife and son save his reputation, creating "broad-humored entertainment out of his adventures." *Variety* was even more complimentary, praising "McCall's shrewd screen play" as "an excellent, intelligent, and well-proportioned translation of the book."[34] Released in time for Christmas, *Babbitt* was hardly anyone's idea of a warmhearted family film. The satire may have pulled many of its punches with humor, but the final scenes only half-heartedly propped up the ultimate expression of American Babbittry—the middle-class family.

McCall's efforts saving *Babbitt* did not earn her an immediate pay raise; she had to be content with the honor of adapting a man's prizewinning novel. Even though her successful short fiction career set her a cut above the other contract writers and her sales of original material earned her extra money, Wallis handed her a mixed bag of assignments. While she occasionally was allowed to adapt her own material or that of a "prestige" male author, more often than not she was a "corpse rouger," putting smart dialogue on an already dead-boring script written by male colleagues. She later acknowledged this was part of her Hollywood success: Producers brought her in to doctor weak writing on a range of pictures for which she never received screen credit. As she remembered in a 1970 interview: "I have a good ear. I say that because I think that is one part of a writer's equipment with which you must be born. I think you can sharpen it, but I don't think you can acquire it."[35]

That summer of 1934, while she was working on *Babbitt*, she was assigned to do a rush job on playwright Leonard Ide's (*These Few Ashes*, 1928; *Peacock*, 1932; *Ringside Seat*, 1938) unproduced play *Concealment*. Writers Tom Buckingham and F. Hugh Herbert had drafted the treatment, and it was McCall's job to "brighten the dialog." Although she and Herbert would end up the best of friends, neither liked the script. Even when retitled *The Secret Bride* and starring rising actress Barbara Stanwyck as Ruth Vincent, the daughter of a state governor, it was still a fast-paced disaster in search of a plot. Publicists advertised it as political melodrama: a young couple conceals their marriage from the public after Vincent's father is accused of taking bribes. Things are a bit more complicated, since Stanwyck's bride is married to the district attorney assigned to investigate her father.

Up until that point Stanwyck, who avoided long-term studio contracts, had divided her time between Columbia, where she got raves for her work with Frank Capra (*Ladies of Leisure*, 1930; *The Bitter Tea of General Yen*, 1933), and Warner Bros., where Zanuck had found her an occasional role worthy of her talent (*So Big*, 1932; *Baby Face*, 1933). Her 1932 contract with Warner Bros. included story approval, and her roles often reflected her independent lifestyle and career.[36] But since Zanuck's departure, Stanwyck felt increasingly trapped by indifferent roles and pay. She had turned down several scripts before reaching the end of her rope with *Concealment*. The only things that could be said for it were that the role of a well-connected daddy's girl was a departure from her usual working-class heroines—and she earned $50,000 for the part.[37] André Sennwald was grateful only that the film "kills off its victims at such breakneck speed that it is pretty easy to sit through," and other critics concurred.[38]

But with another two hits and a flop, McCall had definitely arrived as a Hollywood screenwriter. Meanwhile, after *Treasure Island* wrapped, MGM rehired Franklin in October to design the men's costumes and serve as technical advisor on *Naughty Marietta* (released later in 1935), a lavish period musical project starring Jeannette MacDonald and Nelson Eddy in their first screen pairing. Of all the studios, MGM had been the least affected by the crisis of 1933 and had money to spare for Franklin's expertise. The couple, certain they had landed on their feet, sent for their New York furniture. While Franklin traveled to New York several times a year to see his mother and to oversee preparations for the annual Beaux Arts Ball, McCall was more content to settle into the Hollywood scene. However hard she worked at the studio, she made sure she had time to play. Bette Davis, on loan to RKO for *Of Human Bondage* (1934), had introduced McCall to her costar, Leslie Howard.

CHAPTER 5

Bending the Codes

I n later years, McCall's family, friends, and colleagues would remember her dedication to her craft, her indefatigable energy, her sense of humor, her refusal to back down in a labor dispute, her support of all writers, her feminism. But it should also be remembered that for a while, McCall was an astute and even brilliant player in Hollywood's social scene. In 1934 she rode at the Riviera Country Club, one of Hollywood's power hubs, and made sure Zanuck saw her.[1] Her current boss, Jack Warner, also patronized the club, and though she privately loathed him, cultivating a relationship away from the studio made good business sense. If she occasionally contemplated whacking him over the head with one of his polo mallets, no one knew for sure.

But not all of McCall's Riviera relationships were so business casual. Consider her affair with Leslie Howard. Howard bore an uncanny resemblance to Dwight Franklin. He was older, debonair, very experienced with women, and had a spare, athletic build. But he also had the same shade of wavy, coppery blond hair as Cagney. While McCall's daughters were unable to confirm how long their mother's affair with Howard lasted in the mid-1930s, the star began playing polo in mid-1934, learning from the Riviera's famous Snowy Baker.[2] It's possible that meeting at the Riviera was a convenient way for the affair to progress without too much surveillance from gossip columnists.

That spring she was already several months pregnant by Franklin, and as her figure changed over the summer months, with some regrets, she set Howard and horses aside. The actor went back to England to shoot *The Scarlet Pimpernel* (1934) for Alexander Korda but found time to complain about the new Production Code's censorship of sex onscreen.[3] Howard didn't have any complaints about matters off the set in either country: While in England, he replaced McCall with his costar, Merle Oberon. But he wasn't away from Hollywood for that long. Warner Bros. lined up a biopic of British style icon Beau Brummel for him, and Louella Parsons reported that fall that "Warners have already assigned Mary McCall Jr. to the adaptation."[4]

Hal Wallis was in a relatively generous mood. That summer McCall had been given a small raise of $50 to $350 per week.[5] It was an acceptable salary, but still less than most of her seasoned male colleagues' rates. She had been working on an adaptation of Tom Buckingham's original story "The Skipper of the Ispahan" that summer when Wallis sent another memo asking her to work on a horse picture, *North Shore*, for Bette Davis.[6] But when Davis's shooting schedule didn't work out, he tried matching McCall with Stanwyck again. Mercifully, he let her work alone at first. She read Wallace Irwin's risqué popular society novel and drafted the script, though the studio later brought Peter Milne (*Modern Mothers*, 1928) in to write his own version. Milne had worked on the studio's *Registered Nurse* (1934) with Lillie Hayward, and although Hayward did more work on the script, Milne was paid substantially more. The same thing would happen to McCall on *North Shore*, which she and Wallis retitled *The Woman in Red*. Although today Stanwyck's films remain some of the most widely seen studio classics, *The Woman in Red* is rarely screened and unfairly overlooked.

Stanwyck plays Shelby Barret, a professional equestrian from Kentucky. She does equitation, dressage, and show jumping, and at the San Hernando show, where we first see her, she collects all the blue ribbons for her boss, "Nicko" (played by a sleekly poisonous Genevieve Tobin). Shelby rides against women and men and beats them all. Not all the riders are professionals who earn their livelihoods from horses. Many are rich, like Gene (John Eldredge), the millionaire head of a large bank, who loses to Shelby with a smile and prefers the "straight shooter" to his bored girlfriend. Shelby is different from the other women on the circuit, the pros, the owners, and the social crowd. While most of the younger women in the cast sport platinum bleach jobs, Stanwyck's no-nonsense dark bob is her natural color. She wears breeches and seems uncomfortable in dresses. She also lacks her rich blonde boss's high prey drive for men.

Enter Johnny Wyatt (Gene Raymond), the son of an old Long Island family (take note that the clan lives in "Wyattville"). Raymond, never more than pretty scenery in his films, smiles a lot in *The Woman in Red*. At first Stanwyck's Shelby is wary of him. She knows her employer would fire her in a heartbeat should Johnny turn his romantic attentions to her. At the post-show party, Shelby knows her cues and tries to keep her distance, but by the end of the evening Johnny has cost Shelby her job and life as a single woman.

Warner Bros. may have been a macho studio where women had little to do except look pretty, but the studio dared to look at America's class issues—and occasionally, thanks in part to McCall and Stanwyck, they occasionally looked at independent women. Shelby's faux English in-laws, living on income from inherited wealth, despise Shelby and her plans to involve Johnny in a horse-training business. Shelby sees the potential for the new business as a metaphor for her equal partnership with Johnny. Unfortunately, Johnny's unilateral business decisions, made from his sense of male entitlement, nearly wreck them.

Following Warner Bros. tradition, the film builds to a romantic bust-up, death, and a wild courtroom circus before Shelby and her pale but wealthy male are reconciled. But McCall gives Johnny some uncharacteristically forward-thinking lines: "We're partners, a closed corporation." Shelby wanted them to be equals in all aspects of their life together, and at last she has made a professional of him. In its way, *The Woman in Red* is as much a transformative story for Johnny as it is for Shelby. He leaves the curse of idle wealth and family for a true working partnership, and she leaves the life of a single woman dependent on a dishonest employer to be her own boss.

McCall was relieved to work on a story about a heroine who had to earn her living (even if it was in part by pleasing rich people). Despite their starkly different social backgrounds and political outlooks (Stanwyck was a conservative Republican), both she and Stanwyck were New York–born Hollywood immigrants and could relate to Shelby's outsider status, need for independence, and love of horses. But McCall had reservations about most of the scripts at Warner Bros.—and most of the men she had to work with. Although she liked Wallis and respected one of his key associate producers, the German-born Henry Blanke, who had been Ernst Lubitsch's assistant early in his career, she was less impressed with the other associate producer, Samuel Bischoff, particularly after his mismanagement of *Babbitt*.

One incident in the summer of 1934 stood out in her memory. As she recalled, "I was doing my job and not begging off because of my condition, but I was obviously pregnant. I was doing a rewrite. . . . The woman was quite well-drawn in the script . . . but the man was an absolute clod. And I was told that I must write a scene in which this woman said that she worshipped and adored him." McCall then told Bischoff, "I don't know how to write *this* scene, because I do not know what attracts this woman, who is quite intelligent and charming, to this man. He is a nothing. I don't see why she should give *him* the time of day." The producer looked her over and said, "How did you get what you've got inside you?" The casual crassness that was part of her day-to-day life as a woman at Warner Bros. hit her. Then McCall thought, "If I let this vulgar, nasty guy drive me out of the medium I love with all my heart, he has won, and I have lost." She replied drily, "Suppose we leave my quite uninteresting condition out of the discussion and just stick to the script."[7]

McCall discussed her advancing pregnancy with Wallis soon afterward and insisted that she could work right up until the birth. Writers, unlike actresses, didn't need to worry about photographing well below the waist. But she didn't want her pregnancy to get her fired and said she'd need only a week or two off. Wallis was happy to keep getting his money's worth out of McCall and wanted to reward her for her string of hits. He reteamed her with Charles Kenyon to adapt *A Midsummer Night's Dream*, the studio's prestige production for 1935. Hollywood had been cautious about adapting Shakespeare for the screen (Doug Sr. and Mary Pickford's 1929 version of *The Taming of the Shrew* had been a disaster), but Max Reinhardt's theatrical production at the Hollywood Bowl the previous year had been a success, and Wallis didn't anticipate much difficulty in transposing the play to the screen. He wanted lots of stars to soften the dialogue, and assigned two directors for the project, Reinhardt and McCall's *Secret Bride* colleague, William Dieterle. She and Kenyon set to work cutting and shaping the comedy to suit a broad audience.

Once again she wasn't getting paid equally with Kenyon: McCall got $2,275 for her work compared to Kenyon's $3,534.[8] But, possibly even worse, she noticed that she was nearly double the size she had been when she had Sheila. After she had a minor health scare in late October, Franklin suggested that she make an appointment at the hospital and stay at home for a couple of days. Wallis agreed and wrote to Henry Blanke that McCall was more than happy to continue working and to just "send her out" anything she needed at home.[9]

McCall, for her part, tried to ignore her stomach and set to work. She wrote to Blanke on October 24: "Henry, my dear, In order to bring our new time arrangement out right, I have taken liberties with Mr. Shakespeare's text which make me break out into a cold sweat."[10] The tweaks were as minor as she could manage, and she pleaded for him to pay attention to the rhythm of the dialogue in cutting the film: "A lot of this is written not in blank verse, but in rhyming couplets—and it would be barbarous, unethical, and lousy to divorce a rhyming line from its mate. The whole couplet must be preserved or stricken out—but don't leave the rhymes hanging in mid-air, or our audience will go cuckoo waiting for the other shoe to drop."

She enjoyed working with the cultured Blanke, and she loved that Cagney, the adorable Frank McHugh, and pal Hugh Herbert were all involved with the project. However, McCall was allegedly less enthusiastic about her directors. According to her daughter Sheila, McCall said with some menace that "if Max Reinhardt or William Dieterle mentioned to the writers one more time that to truly appreciate Shakespeare, one had to read him in German," they would have her to contend with.[11]

Then, in early November, she went for her scan at St. Vincent's and nearly fainted. She was carrying twins.[12] But she just sucked it up and worked through her due date. Years later she described the situation simply in a collection of reminiscences intended for her children: "Gerald McCall Franklin and Alan McCall Franklin were born on November 16, 1934, just 24 hours after my last conference—at home—on *A Midsummer Night's Dream*."[13] As she told Louella Parsons, one of the boys weighed six pounds and the other six and a half pounds.[14] They weren't identical twins, but at the time no one could really tell. All McCall knew was that even with the efforts of Ms. Prickell and Sheila's new nanny Miss Chapman, she found herself longing for the peace and quiet of her Warner Bros. office. Ten days later, while she was recuperating, Warner Bros. notified her that she was on suspension.[15]

Though she now was the mother of three young children, it never occurred to McCall or to Franklin that she should quit writing to become a full-time hausfrau. Even if the idea of cooking and cleaning didn't already drive her mad, the household would never have been able to afford it. Thanks to the twins, they also needed a bigger house. On December 10, 1934, she was back at work at the usual $350 a week.[16] Wallis tried to make some amends for the mediocre pay, and on February 2, 1935, her salary was bumped up from $350 to $400 a week. He assigned her and Casey Robinson to another Kay Francis vehicle, an adaptation of John Monk Saunders's story *I Found Stella Parish*.[17] The tale of a famous actress with a shady past and the media's efforts to blackmail her, it was the kind of material McCall could write in her sleep. Ironically, according to Louella Parsons, who covered the news in the press, the story represented the studio's efforts "to get better stories for Kay Francis."[18] Allegedly, Warner Bros. actually valued McCall's talents. But behind the scenes, Wallis hired other writers for the project, in addition to Robinson.

Around the same time, Franklin was hired to design the costumes and act as technical advisor on the adaptation of Raphael Sabatini's *Captain Blood* (1935), temporarily bringing him into the Warner Bros. "family."[19] But while Franklin enjoyed the project, a remake of a 1924 film he had much admired starring J. Warren Kerrigan, he soon found a more lasting working relationship at Paramount. That year, producer-director Cecil B. DeMille called Franklin and made him an offer to join his production company as a costume designer and research specialist on a new Calamity Jane–Wild Bill Hickok western called *The Plainsman* (1936). Dwight was in demand, but he was still a freelancer. Even under a long-term studio contract, he never would have made enough to support them in the lifestyle to which they were happily becoming accustomed. McCall brought the regular paychecks home. The trouble was, she was becoming increasingly frustrated at work. Since she'd signed her contract, her name had disappeared from the contents of New York's top magazines.[20] Warner Bros. owned her and anything she wrote.

She did her best to compartmentalize her life, though it meant that she didn't see much of her children or her husband. During the day Sheila and the twins were with the governess and nurse, while McCall wrote at the studio. At night, instead of reading bedtime stories and changing diapers, McCall was dining out with friends, hosting dinner parties, and, as time went on, attending Screen Writers Guild meetings and hosting many of them in the McCall-Franklin home. Sheila, unlike the boys, was self-confident and could be relied upon to greet the guests before retiring for bedtime stories. She looked like her father, with her long, thin face and decided chin. She also preferred her father's company and was always too overawed by her mother to feel comfortable with her. McCall, making amends, got her a dachshund called Michael, in addition to the governess and nurse, and hoped it would turn into a shorter and more efficient version of Nana, the dog from J. M. Barrie's *Peter and Wendy*. Unfortunately, as it turned out later, the boys were allergic to dogs. Sheila allegedly suggested "they rehome the boys and keep the dog." Mother and father were amused, but alas, Michael had to go.[21]

At the studio, McCall had to be careful not to let Wallis suspect anything of her guild activities. She had built a solid working relationship with the producer, and as one of only two full-time contracted female writers at the studio, she knew there were hostile eyes on her job. McCall covered any sense of favoritism or suspicion she was there on romantic sufferance by doing what successful modern women always seem to do: working twice as hard as every other man in the room. Wallis assigned her to a smattering of projects, but increasingly they weren't scripts she had developed, and she wasn't on assignments long enough to invest any personal interest in them. Perhaps Wallis thought that in lightening her workload he would make things easier for her. But McCall wanted another film with sole screenwriting credit. Finally, in the spring of 1935, she was given a project she was ready to care about.

Once again, as with *Babbitt*, Wallis wanted her to rescue another adaptation that had been derailed by two male screenwriters. It was novelist and screenwriter W. R. Burnett's *Dr. Socrates*, a gangster drama. Burnett's story focused on the dilemma of young Dr. Cardwell, who is forced to treat a wounded gangster named Red Bastian (loosely based on the former Public Enemy Number 1, the late John Dillinger, killed outside a Chicago movie theater in 1934). The FBI's pursuit of Bastian leads them to Cardwell, and the young man is faced with betraying either the law or his principles as a doctor. Like all of Burnett's work, it was a spare, exciting, fast-paced story, an astute mixture of contemporary gangster history and Hollywood melodrama. Burnett, creator of *Little Caesar*, was arguably the most important name in gangster literature.

Robert Lord had recently been promoted to associate producer under Wallis and had hired some contract writers to draft a treatment of Burnett's novel, which was first serialized in *Collier's* that March and April. But the first treatment was a mess. Wallis and others were seriously considering pulling it from production, since apart from its lifeless plot and characterization, Joseph Breen had called for a moratorium on gangster films. All the content producers had relied upon in the early 1930s was now against Production Code rules, and that meant studios would not get a seal or state licenses to exhibit.

But the gangster heroes of the early 1930s—Cagney's electric Tom Powers in *The Public Enemy*, Doug Jr.'s and Edward G. Robinson's work in *Little Caesar*, Paul Muni's sexy and dangerous Tony Camonte/Al Capone in *Scarface* (1932), Lew Ayres's sympathetic hero in *Doorway to Hell* (1930)—were replaced by vicious, unattractive thugs. Audience sympathy was refocused on the gangsters' victims. The hero of *Dr. Socrates* is Paul Muni's honest physician, who is blackmailed into helping gangster Bastian (Barton MacLane). Bastian, on the other hand, may have been from a small town, like Dillinger, but had none of Dillinger's good looks and killer charm.

On May 20, Bob Lord threw Wallis a lifeline when he said that McCall was going to write a new script for them "approximately following the Burnett novel."[22] He wrote, "This morning we hit on a device which solves the major difficulty in the Burnett story." Within four weeks, he promised, she would have a script ready and within one week "we will be able to determine whether or not it is advisable to go ahead with the picture." But he hadn't reckoned on McCall, who for the first time since *Babbitt* finally had a project she could shape to her liking. She worked nonstop for the next seven days and finished the script.

On May 28 she handed in her work, which reflected the spirit of Burnett's novel.[23] In what may go down in history as Wallis's only thank-you note to a contract writer, he told McCall on June 8, "I appreciate the effort you have made on *Dr. Socrates*, and the quick job."[24] He reteamed her for the third time with William Dieterle. After looking at excerpts of her work the director suggested only minimal dialogue changes, and McCall was optimistic about the project. Despite the terrible experience of *The Secret Bride* and the occasional rough patch on *Midsummer*, the writer and director got along well, and Dieterle told Wallis that he would prefer to continue working with McCall rather than with a new writer. Wallis complied, and rather than put her on a new project, he told her to take few days off. "If it looks as though you might be needed from time to time during the shooting of the picture, we will keep you available."[25]

But Muni didn't want a woman writing "his" film. The star had been with Warner Bros. for several years and was considered one of the studio's biggest assets. Wallis, wanting to pacify the star, had Lord tinker with the dialog. Then, at Muni's insistence, Lord was told to do a complete rewrite. When McCall found out on June 12 she was furious. What made it worse was that she considered Lord her friend. "I am naturally terribly disappointed that I was given no opportunity to make the dialog changes Muni wanted," she wrote to Wallis.[26] "Considering I am the only person, with the exception of yourself, who saw possibilities in the Burnett story, that I did the script in a very short time in order to get the studio out of a jam . . . I feel I was entitled to a chance to preserve the piece of work as my work."

If Muni was going to stand on his soapbox as a great actor, she had standards as a writer. "I made the changes Mr. Dieterle wanted. I know that I could have done what Muni wanted." She had enough of the studio's latent or obvious sexism and blasted Muni: "To talk about its being impossible for a woman to write the dialog for that character is just so much nonsense." She reminded him that she wasn't any hack writer they'd picked up off a newsroom floor: "I was writing successfully for national magazines—and often writing about men—for several years before I came to the studio." Both her novel and early films focused on the problems of men. "I hoped, as consideration for the very real strain I underwent during those hectic few days, to have the satisfaction of having done a piece of work to which I could put my name, knowing that I had done it—all of it." What made it especially ironic was that the next day, June 13, she was due to give a primetime radio talk on KMTR: "Women Who Want to Write."[27] Her interview about "how the housewife with an urge to write may turn her talents into cash" obviously avoided everything women writers experienced routinely in the film business.

Wallis was not a dishonest man; by Hollywood standards, he was a model of justice and fair play. He was fed up with Muni's star antics too. (Ironically, nearly a decade later, he would quit Warner Bros. after Jack Warner snatched Wallis's producing statuette for *Casablanca* at the Oscars.) Even if Jack Warner didn't value McCall's contributions, he did. He talked to Lord privately, and later that month Lord agreed with him "that the amount of rewriting I have done on the script after the picture went into production is somewhat distressing and a little absurd."[28] Lord blamed Muni's tantrums. "It was the only procedure possible to keep the company shooting, and to keep Mr. Muni sufficiently cheerful to give even a semblance of a good performance." As an example, he admitted that McCall's original writing for a scene between a federal officer and Muni was "5% better" than Muni's version. But if they went back to McCall's original script and ignored his complaints, "Muni would be so resentful that I can almost guarantee his giving a bad, unconvincing performance. . . . Once you start him in a picture, you have to adjust his scenes so that he is approximately pleased with them or he will be so bad that you can't release the picture." Wallis assured McCall that the bulk of rewriting was over. Muni eventually demanded so much rewriting that McCall's credits were adjusted to merely "adaptation by." Lord got credit for the screenplay.

In his classic Hollywood memoir *Bring on the Empty Horses* (1976), actor David Niven claimed that "the greatest convention of writing brilliance ever assembled" was "watered down, wasted, or filtered out by megalomaniacal producers," so that by the time the actors got the scripts nothing but tripe remained.[29] He forgot to mention when megalomaniacal and misogynist actors undermined scripts.

McCall's rage and disappointment over *Dr. Socrates* radicalized her commitment to the Screen Writers Guild. For a year she had been a dutiful studio employee, completing assignments in a variety of genres and working cordially with male cowriters. She put up with the stagnant salary, knowing that occasionally Wallis would give her a chance to develop some worthwhile content. But after *Dr. Socrates*, she was tired of being reasonable. What was normal at the studio was that she was paid far less than the two other men who were assigned to work on *Dr. Socrates* before her, contract writers Abem Finkel, who was the half-brother of Muni's wife, Bella ($2,700), and Carl C. Erickson ($3,850).[30] Even though two months before the film premiered Erickson shot himself, his body discovered at the end of August in a car in the Hollywood hills overlooking the studio, this didn't make McCall feel any less bitter about the money. William Dieterle got $34,193 for his services, and Robert Lord had graduated to producer/supervisor at $15,188. It may have been some consolation that the film was not particularly successful.

McCall tried to move on. It helped that Bogart had joined her in Hollywood, hired, thanks to Leslie Howard's insistence, to reprise his role as Duke Mantee in *The Petrified Forest*, which had finished its Broadway run at the end of June. Bogart signed with McCall's agent at the Jaffe Agency, Mary Baker, got a long-term contract with Warner Bros., and fell into the West Coast, country-club lifestyle with his old friend.

She invited her parents up for a visit that summer; Mazie and Leo Sr. both adored Bogart. Though her father still didn't think much of people who acted for a living, Bogart, a "gentleman" from a good New York family, was the exception. On his visit to see his daughter and grandchildren he accepted Bogart's present of a guest card to his golf club, the Lakeside Country Club. Leo Sr. still played a very good game, and, as McCall remembered, "one day Poppa came home and his eyes were shining and he said, 'Guess who I saw today on the third tee? Oliver Hardy!'" Mary Jr. caught her mother's eye. They concurred: "We have come full circle."[31] After that her father was a little less dismissive of his daughter's Hollywood career.

McCall later speculated about her father's dislike of acting in general and Hollywood in particular. Ingrained homophobia informed his assumptions about male actors: "I think he felt that anyone who put paint on his face was a fairy . . . that was one of his reservations," McCall remembered. "Through me, he did meet James Cagney who was quite obviously not a fairy, even to him." Cagney had his own reservations about Hollywood in general and Warner Bros. in particular. If it wasn't the long-term contract and frequent suspensions when he didn't like bad scripts, it was Jack Warner's telling him how to vote (though Upton Sinclair's "End Poverty in California" gubernatorial campaign had faltered in 1934, Cagney gloated over Roosevelt's reelection in 1936).

In his downtime Cagney channeled his frustration with his boss by collecting guns and swords with Franklin. Both were longtime weapons enthusiasts, and for years the two of them had been hunting down rare guns and sabers at New York auctions to add to their collections.[32] Very often parties would evolve into a shooting competition. As Franklin's friend, journalist Charles Driscoll, wrote, "You have to be an enthusiastic pirate fan to stand up at twenty paces and pretend to be fighting a duel with him. He assures you that some of the pistols are loaded, but he tries to pick unloaded ones for duel practice."[33] Franklin and Cagney would pop the snails crawling on the hearth in the den with some of his collectible firearms. (If they gave the snails names such as Harry, Jack, and Al, nobody cared.) Sheila would inspect the nicks in the brickwork while her mother talked union business with Lucile Gleason and Bob Montgomery over drinks in the next room, ignoring the gunfire as best she could.

Bob, Jimmy, and Lucile had been founding members of the Screen Actors Guild, inspired by the Screen Writers Guild and founded in July 1933, mainly in opposition to the notorious seven-year studio talent contracts that kept stars locked in at low salaries despite being the studios' major assets. McCall's friends Jean Muir, Bette Davis, Gloria Stuart, and George Murphy, as well as Cagney and Bogart, were all active SAG members and helped to establish strong bonds between the two fledgling guilds.

McCall didn't share her husband's and Cagney's enthusiasm for guns. She got some relief from studio politics by resuming her affair with Leslie Howard when he returned to make *The Petrified Forest*.[34] But it was not enough to distract her from her real problem. She was fed up with Wallis and Lord's wan apologies and life as a hack writer for Hollywood's most macho, cut-rate studio. She figured that the best way to kick against the Hollywood pricks was to work not just for herself but for all writers and all industry professionals who believed in the power of the union.

On July 5, 1935, Congress passed the National Labor Relations Act, and, as McCall noted, ten days later the Screen Writers Guild's executive board "sent a letter to the major studios and principle independents, stating that the guild, with 770 members, was the bargaining agent for writers."[35] Any negotiations the producers were currently carrying on with the thirty-eight writer members of the conservative Academy of Motion Picture Arts and Sciences "were illegal," and "the guild stood ready to appoint a committee for collective bargaining for writers under the Wagner Act and invited the producers to do the same." The war was on.

CHAPTER 6

Breaking the Rules

W hen Mary McCall first worked for Warner Bros. in 1931, she was lucky to have Darryl F. Zanuck as her boss. Unlike many of his producing colleagues, Zanuck, like McCall, was a young outsider. Only two years older than she, he understood what it was like to want to break into an industry where everyone else seemed to know each other or be related by blood or marriage. He started out as an overworked and underpaid screenwriter at Warner Bros. in the early 1920s and was responsible for turning German shepherd and World War I survivor Rin Tin Tin into the studio's biggest star. Zanuck was so productive that he allegedly wrote half the studio's pictures for a while. Jack Warner would reminisce, "Zanuck could write ten times faster than any ordinary man. . . . He could leave on Friday and come back on Monday with a script."[1] He had three aliases: Melville Crossman, Mark Canfield, and Gregory Rogers, who all wrote different genres. But even when he became a producer and production manager, Zanuck retained lingering sympathy for his former writing colleagues. As Douglas Fairbanks Jr. would later say, Zanuck "was a rare example of a Hollywood executive behaving with integrity."[2]

In 1932, when Zanuck managed the studio, McCall's name appeared in all press for *It's Tough to Be Famous*, *Revolt*, and *Street of Women*. She was paid well and given screen credit. But things were different after Zanuck left to form Twentieth Century Pictures in 1933 and she was rehired as a studio contract writer the following year. Jack, Harry, and Al Warner didn't care whether McCall got proper credit or a good salary. In the early days of the studio system, screenwriters were often lured by speculative writing deals, assured they would get a contract, salary, and screen credit, and were then shafted. Screenwriters with a contract weren't treated much better. A producer could hire as many as a dozen writers on a project, with each writer thinking he or she was the sole writer assigned, only to be denied screen credit. As writer Lenore Coffee remarked, "They pick your brains, break your heart, ruin your digestion—and what do you get for it? Nothing but a lousy fortune."[3] But the majority of screenwriters never even got close to a living wage, let alone a fortune. At MGM their stories were stolen outright by producers such as Carey Wilson, who even had the nerve to demand a $5,000 bonus for providing the studio with this kind of "original material."[4] Few in Hollywood were willing to admit that "the greatest mental and creative effort in any film is in the writing of the script."[5]

McCall had officially joined the Screen Writers Guild on April 14, 1934, signing up as an associate member as soon as Zanuck's replacement at Warner Bros., Hal Wallis, rehired her.[6] She had been a member in good standing of the guild-affiliated Authors League in New York since the late 1920s, and so, "as soon as I came to Hollywood," she explained, "I went and joined the Screen Writers Guild."[7] McCall always believed "very strongly in the necessity of a strong writers' union, not only for the financial benefits which can be obtained by collective bargaining, but also for the professional advantages." Unlike some of her colleagues who had to be chased for their dues or cudgeled into working on subcommittees, McCall wanted to make the guild viable. That meant not just joining the union but also putting hours of effort in smaller working groups and on the studio shop floor organizing other writers. She was elected to her first term on the executive board in 1935.[8]

Although in recent years it has been argued that Hollywood's emerging labor culture pushed women out of key professions behind the camera in the 1930s, this cannot be said of the Screen Writers Guild.[9] As with the contemporaneous New York garment industry and the Mexican American civil rights organization El Congreso de Pueblos de Habla Española in California, throughout the 1930s and 1940s, the guild was a haven for female political and labor activists. When it was formed at that fateful March 29 meeting, screenwriting legend Jane Murfin (*What Price Hollywood?*, 1932) was there to vote on the creation of a contract. A week later, Academy Award-winning writer Frances Marion was elected as the organization's first vice president (Jack Lawson was the first president), and Gladys Lehman (*Back Street*, 1932) served on the executive board. In future years, Marion and Anita Loos (*Intolerance*, 1916) served in advisory capacities as senior writers. When McCall served on her first executive board, she wasn't the only woman in the room; the formidable New York wit and woman of letters Dorothy Parker was there too. She and McCall clicked the moment they met and would spend some of their funnier guild committee meetings trading one-liners about film executives—and sometimes their colleagues. But while many of Parker's better-known barbs were aimed at other women (Katharine Hepburn "runs the gamut of emotions from A to B"; "you can lead a horticulture, but you can't make her think"), McCall's main target was bad writing. "While speaking of a picture that shall be grossless," she once quipped, "it must have been written on a tripewriter."[10]

Dozens of other women flocked to join the guild in its infancy. There was Doris Malloy, who would become McCall's close friend and senior organizer, and who specialized in material about women (*The Mad Parade*, 1931; *Bondage*, 1933; *Gambling Lady*, 1934). There were writers who had survived the transition from silent films to sound—women such as Murfin, Doris Anderson, Dorothy Cairns, Adele Buffington, Gladys Lehman, Clara Beranger, Josephine Lovett, Alice D. G. Miller, Ethel Hill, and Dorothy Yost. Other female guild members began their Hollywood careers as stenographers or script readers before moving into screenwriting, such as Virginia Van Upp (until she became a producer and executive producer), MGM's Marguerite Roberts, and Helen Logan (who worked for Zanuck at Twentieth Century-Fox). Other women were even better known in theater, such as Gladys Unger, Rachel Crowthers, Rose Franken, and, of course, Lillian Hellman.

Although another strand of film history has alleged that the number of women writing in Hollywood declined after the 1920s, a substantial number of the Screen Writers Guild's early members were young women who entered the business in the 1930s as sound films fueled the need for good writing.[11] Gertrude Purcell, Frances Goodrich, Virginia Kellogg, Maude Howell, Jane Hinton, Claire Church, and Wanda Tuchock (who also directed) all made names for themselves. There were other women who joined the Screen Writers Guild after aging out of glamorous acting jobs; former actresses Salka Viertel, Olive Cooper, Seena Owen (sister of screenwriter Lillie Hayward), and Ruth and Mitzi Cummings all changed careers. Some guild writers even moved from writing to acting, such as Lucille De Nevers and Gladys Hurlbut.

Lots of screenwriting women supplemented their careers as fiction writers with screenwriting gigs, such as Vera Caspary, Tess Slesinger, Jane Shore, Viña Delmar, Vicki Baum, Mercedes de Acosta, and Dorothy Parker. Anne Morrison Chapin, Laura Perelman, and Dorothy Bennett started out as Broadway playwrights but moved to more lucrative careers as screenwriters. There were women who had occasional big pictures such as Helen Bell (*Susannah of the Mounties*, 1939), but more often were squeezed out of the credits. And there was, of course, a large group of guild women who existed on the margins of the Hollywood economy as freelance writers, such as Florabel Muir, Meta Sterne, Ann Lee Cunningham, Virginia Elston, Ella Joyce, Irene Francis, Sally Unterberger, Marcella Gardner, and Judith Kandel.

Nearly a quarter of all Screen Writers Guild members in the 1930s were women. In her early days as a Warner Bros. contract writer, the guild offered McCall the opportunity to work within a strong community of women, something she did not easily find at the studio. During the life of the Screen Writers Guild (1933 to 1954–which mirrored McCall's own studio career), there was usually one woman serving in one of the top four executive positions and two to three women on an eleven-person executive board (20-27 percent representation, a wider reflection of the overall makeup of the electorate).[12] Murfin and Gladys Lehman would support McCall on the executive board in her first term as president in 1942-43 and were later joined by McCall's collaborator on the *Maisie* franchise, Elizabeth "Betty" Reinhardt, in 1943. Between 1933 and 1954, Parker, Malloy, Marion, Tuchock, Loos, Goodrich, Hellman, Roberts, Cooper, Perelman, Purcell, Kellogg, Brenda Weisberg, Erna Lazarus, and Dorothy Hughes were running and getting elected as guild officers. Guild representatives empowered to arbitrate disputes with the studios in the fractious early years included Lehman (Fox), Malloy (Universal), and Mary McCarthy (the independent production companies).

That said, guild statistics were not always reflected in wider studio employment patterns. Although, as McCall would later point out, MGM and Columbia hired over the 25 percent benchmark in the guild, Warner Bros. had the worst reputation in Hollywood for employing women. When Warner Bros. signed McCall in 1934, she was one of only two women writers under contract–or 6 percent of the writers in the building.[13] The other woman was Lillie Hayward, who began her career in the silent era, adapting the successful women's Revolutionary War epic *Janice Meredith* in 1924, and who had stints at MGM and Columbia before coming to Warner Bros. She was also, like McCall, a Zanuck-era hire, writing *Miss Pinkerton* (1932) and *They Call It Sin* (1932) in additional to creating an original historical drama, *Frisco Jenny* (1933), set during the 1906 earthquake, for megastar Ruth Chatterton. Hayward continued to work on the studio's few films set in the modern era about women and work, including Bette Davis's *Housewife*

(1934) and *Front Page Woman* (1935). She joined the guild thanks to McCall. Although she was risking her job in becoming a member, Hayward was fed up with being paid less than her male colleagues for doing more and better work.

Luci Ward would join them as a contract writer of low-budget B pictures and westerns, moving up from her job as a secretary to writer Ben Markson (also a guild member) and script girl. The trouble was, the studio never bothered to increase Ward's $25-a-week salary, as she would later testify to the National Labor Relations Board in 1938.[14] But in 1936, she was listed as one of three women working among thirty-four contracted male writers (Jerry Wald, Delmer Daves, Casey Robinson, Seton I. Miller, and Dalton Trumbo among them).[15] McCall, who had quickly become one of the guild's most effective organizers, also persuaded Ward to become a member. They had to keep this quiet, since studio executives were firing and blacklisting suspected guild writers. Some quit their membership, terrified at the prospect of being out of work.

Some, like Twentieth Century-Fox's top writer, Sonya Levien, paid their dues and attended the odd meeting but kept a very low political profile. Given boss Darryl F. Zanuck's anti-union feelings, she masked her affiliations so well that even her colleague and collaborator William Ludwig said that Levien "was the least political person I ever met."[16] She remained one of Zanuck's favorite writers for years, going on to share an Academy Award for *Interrupted Melody* (1955) with Ludwig.

Levien's avoidance of political engagement in the interests of self-preservation wasn't an option for McCall. As a woman at Warner Bros., she knew that she and her two female colleagues would always be paid less than the men, regardless of the quality of their work. But in order to get a better deal for women, she had to negotiate for the rights of *all* writers. If her better-paid colleagues Levien or Frances Marion wouldn't take the risks involved, she would. The writer, regardless of gender, was the first and most important creative force in the development of any film, yet they were still paid less than secretaries, or, as McCall once sneered, "less than body makeup men."[17] Charles Brackett, who was accepted as an associate member at the same August 30 meeting in which McCall was promoted to full membership, soon became her closest ally.

Following her fight with Wallis over *Dr. Socrates*, McCall was more or less at a loose end at the studio. Then, in July, Wallis gave her novelist Lloyd Douglas's most recent book to adapt. In 1935 Universal had turned the ex-minister's first novel, a male-centered melodrama called *Magnificent Obsession* (1929), into one of the biggest hits of the year, starring newcomer Robert Taylor and Irene Dunne. Douglas's latest effort, *Green Light* (1935), was the story of a surgeon who takes the blame for a colleague's botched operation and then nobly hides himself away in some backwater town. It was just the sort of improbable nonsense McCall loathed. But Louella Parsons reported in her column that Jack Warner "has re-signed Mary McCall Jr. to write the scenario" since the "fascinating story" required "delicate handling."[18] Initially, Leslie Howard was attached to the project and that sweetened things. She got another small raise on August 26, from $400 to $500 a week, and a contract for an additional fifty-two weeks, with twelve idle weeks.[19]

It didn't last. That September, while she was finishing *Green Light*, the studio bought Joseph Santley's story "Ask for Mrs. Foster" for McCall to develop for Aline MacMahon but then dropped the option.[20] Santley had already done *Harmony Lane*, a low budget biopic of Mr. Foster (the composer, Stephen) released from Mascot Pictures that October, and Warner Bros. wasn't interested in a biopic of the wife. The studio's developing interest in historical-themed pictures and biopics was firmly focused on "great men."

Then McCall found out that Warner Bros. had passed around her old project for Kay Francis, *I Found Stella Parish*, to a succession of male writers. The result was an even more outlandish and confusing melodrama. McCall may have joked to Brackett that she "didn't want anyone to know that she'd worked on the script," but after the film was shot that September and she learned that only Casey Robinson had screen credit, McCall hit the roof.[21] It was even worse than what had taken place with *Dr. Socrates*, and she realized that Warner Bros. was getting personal. She was laid off beginning in January 1936 for what would be twelve weeks.[22] Thanks to her budgeting skills, McCall had saved some money, but she started thinking seriously about returning to New York, where she could at least write what she liked under her own byline. Franklin was in favor of moving back to the city as soon as he completed his work with Gary Cooper and DeMille on *The Plainsman*. California was a cultural desert in comparison to New York. But before they could sell the house, Warner Bros. reinstated her on February 13.[23] Evidently good writers (even if they were suspected guild members) were not expendable—yet.

McCall was back at work on *Green Light*, but she now had to share the script with Milton Krims, a new hire who resented working with a woman. She did her revisions, and then that spring Wallis attached her to a remake of *Everybody's Sweetheart*.[24] The project stalled, and she was assigned to friend Pat O'Brien's *The*

Great O'Malley and flailing dance star Ruby Keeler's new musical, *Ready, Willing, and Able*, to improve the dialog (or corpse rouge), but again she received no credit when the pictures were released. Eventually executives replaced Howard with Errol Flynn on *Green Light*. When the film was released in 1937 only Krims got screen credit.[25] Given Flynn's post–*Captain Blood* popularity at the box office, the film made over a million dollars domestically. Warner Bros. had dozens of ways to exploit scriptwriters, and McCall learned them all firsthand.

Her career at Warner Bros. collapsed for one reason: she was too prominent in Hollywood's labor community. After *Dr. Socrates* she no longer concealed her membership in the guild. Back in 1935 she was asked to head the new *Screen Guilds Magazine*, a joint publication between the Screen Actors Guild and the Screen Writers Guild that she and her friends had cooked up. As part of her role on the magazine, she encouraged her more articulate friends in the actors' guild, Jean Muir and Bette Davis, to contribute articles.[26] But it was *her* articles, written in the summer and fall of 1935, that created the biggest stir in the screen community.

The first, published in the middle of the *Dr. Socrates* controversy, was "Let's Have a Motion Picture Kindergarten."[27] In it, she noted that new writers needed a "training period" if they had never written a shooting script before, and that "cutters, cinematographers, and directors, sound men, process experts, might well be glad to talk and answer questions." The resulting scripts would be better and more appropriate for the film medium, she reasoned, and directors would have to shoot only what was on the page. McCall was tired of directors (and stars such as Muni) who changed the script to suit their own egos, and with this system more knowledgeable writers would be more powerful.

The article was passed around. Producers might have worried about all these other screen professionals talking with writers (as their own rumored secret get-togethers revolved around questions of unionization). But McCall argued that even holding the "kindergarten" on company time would eliminate production waste since, as she put it, "In a business where two highly paid writers often spend twelve weeks pumping the arms and depressing the ribs of a story which has been dead so long even the nose knows it, there must be stringent economies somewhere." Readers knew she was describing the soul-destroying production processes at Warner Bros.

In her second article, "Have You Forgotten Your Life Class?," she urged writers to focus more on real events and the lives of ordinary people and not on the fake Hollywood glamor that producers seemed to demand. "A great deal of screen acting, screen writing, and many screen sets are as florid, lifeless, and phony as a meringue glacé," she said flatly.[28] "We're not selecting and editing from reality, emphasizing its important features and discarding its irrelevancies to create drama. Too often are actors parading tricks learned from other actors while they speak 'dialog' written by someone else whose ear has grown deaf from disuse."

Then she took an explicit swipe at her studio's twin production strands: glammed-up romances and high-toned biopics of great men: "The studios are constantly on the lookout for material based on uncommon, unusual incidents. The further removed a story is from everyday life, the better they seem to like it.... How much longer will audiences pay to see our extraordinary characters sit on their extraordinary beam ends in those never-never land sets, speaking dialog?" Hollywood *was* capable of realism; they only had to watch the performances of Broadway actors James Cagney or Spencer Tracy to find it. But glamorous escapism was killing writers' creativity and audience interest. This issue was all too painful for her, since following *Dr. Socrates*, this frothy fare was the only type of material that was being offered to her. Even then the studio was refusing to give her credit.

While this was happening, the current far left–leaning guild leadership rejected overtures from the Academy of Motion Picture Arts and Sciences, which had secured promises from the producers of advance notice of discharge, "fair" credit assessment, and written contracts. These vague measures gave all the power to the producers, so the guild pursued a merger of all fiction writers from the East Coast Authors League of America in 1936 to increase their bargaining power. Things became more tense when Dudley Nichols rejected his Academy Award for best screenplay for *The Informer*, reminding the Academy that three years earlier he had resigned his Academy membership and stood by his guild, since "there is no other representative autonomous organization for writers which aims at justice."[29]

Then, in May 1936, a cabal of conservative members of the Screen Writers Guild, led by top-earning freelancers Rupert Hughes, James McGuinness, Howard Emmett Rogers, John Lee Mahin, and Morrie Ryskind, broke away, forming a rival guild that was more amendable to the producers' exploitative practices: the Screen Playwrights. Herman Mankiewicz claimed that the left-wing Screen Writers Guild could never have the leverage to work with the producers, and the Screen Playwrights obtained a contract with the producers in an effort to stymie the Screen Writers Guild's more ambitious labor reforms for all writers and to avoid amalgamation with other dramatic and professional writers in New York.

Producers upped their intimidation tactics. As Warner said to McCall and her colleagues at a special meeting he convened at the studio on Saturday May 2, "There are a lot of writers in the business who are active in the Screen Writers Guild now who will find themselves out of the business for good."[30] It was a special warning for McCall, but she held her ground. Later that night she was elected to the Screen Writers Guild's executive board alongside Dorothy Parker and Donald Ogden Stewart.[31] They voted to amalgamate with the Authors League of America, but that spring and early summer members left in droves, succumbing to studio intimidation tactics. The old organization dissolved; the *Screen Guilds Magazine* was handed over to the safekeeping of the Screen Actors Guild. The writers lost their offices at North Cherokee (they couldn't pay the rent), so McCall volunteered to hold meetings at her house.

Just as the guild was falling apart, she was offered a lifeline. She and fellow writer and guild member Edward Chodorov (*Madame du Barry*, 1934) had been working on a comedy for Warner Bros. called *Snowed Under* (1936), about a playwright working under a deadline who gets literally and figuratively snowed under, trapped in a remote cabin with two ex-wives and his current girlfriend. They had a lot of fun writing the gags, but in true Warner Bros. style Chodorov was fired. He moved to Columbia as an associate producer. Knowing how miserable McCall was, he asked studio head Harry Cohn to hire her on loan-out to write his next production. The studio was to adapt George Kelly's Pulitzer Prize–winning play *Craig's Wife* (1925) for the screen, and they needed a writer who understood contemporary literature and its themes of social class and conformism. Columbia approached Warner Bros. in late April about McCall, and Wallis was all too happy to let her go for six weeks.[32]

Kelly was one of the most bankable playwrights on Broadway in the 1920s, known for his trio of hits, *The Torch-Bearers* (1922), *The Show-Off* (1924), and *Craig's Wife* (1925), starring Chrystal Herne in the title role. Back in 1929 he had picked Cagney to star in the lighthearted *Maggie the Magnificent*, which teamed him with Joan Blondell for the first time on Broadway. When Cagney had later asked the playwright why he'd picked him out of dozens of other hopefuls, Kelly allegedly replied, "You were *just* what we were looking for—a fresh mutt."[33]

In contrast, *Craig's Wife* pulled the roof off the middle-class American marriage and its images of compliant, clingingly feminine housewives. Harriet Craig viewed her husband and everyone else in her life merely as inconvenient accessories in her palatial home. Her ingenue niece Ethel, contemplating marriage to one of her college professors, is shocked when her aunt tells her she married Mr. Craig "to be independent of everybody"— including her husband—and that since the "snare of romance" keeps women "in a state of almost primitive feminine dependence," she had decided to reverse the gender-power dynamic.[34] American women in the audience knew that Harriet Craig was no monster; many of them had also traded poorly paid jobs and the life of a single woman for tenancy in a comfortable home. Kelly's unusual approach to gender norms and domesticity attracted the attention of noted producer Rosalie Stewart, known for her work on female-themed plays.[35]

Pathé made a silent version of *Craig's Wife* in 1928, written by Clara Beranger and starring Irene Rich and Warner Baxter, but Columbia wanted to pull out all the stops for a prestigious new sound-era adaptation. Cohn was tired of critics saying his studio was only capable of Poverty Row–style pictures, cut-rate versions of the things Samuel Goldwyn and MGM did on a routine basis. Back in the early 1930s he had tried hiring Dorothy Arzner as a director-producer, but she held him off, saying, "I'll work for you, Mr. Cohn—when your pictures start playing the first-run theaters."[36] On February 27, 1935, he finally got even with his detractors when the studio's top grosser, *It Happened One Night* (1934), swept the Academy Awards for Best Director (Frank Capra), Best Adaptation (Robert Riskin), Best Actor (Clark Gable), Best Actress (Claudette Colbert), and Best Picture (Cohn). Arzner quit freelancing to work at Columbia, but she wasn't happy with the first two projects she began developing. Then she heard about *Craig's Wife*, and Cohn introduced her to McCall, perhaps thinking that his new hires might click on a project about the bitter lives of housewives. It was an inspired decision. Though Cohn has gone down in history as a crude, abusive studio boss, the New Yorker had an unrivaled grasp of strong, challenging story material that would appeal to the public.

In 1936 Arzner was Hollywood's last remaining full-time female director and would be the only woman to join the newly formed Screen Directors Guild until Ida Lupino signed up in 1950. Arzner had her start in the silent era as a stenographer before moving into the editing room, where she cut Valentino's *Blood and Sand* (1922) and the iconic western *The Covered Wagon* (1923). She directed her first picture, *Fashions for Women* (1927), for Paramount, and worked with the studio until 1933, when she began her freelance career with RKO's *Christopher Strong* (1933)

and the ill-fated *Nana* (1934) for Goldwyn. Known as a director of women's pictures for the industry's top stars, Arzner worked with glamorous Lilyan Tashman
(*Manhattan Cocktail*, 1928), Clara Bow (*The Wild Party*, 1929), Ruth Chatterton
(*Sarah and Son*, 1930; *Anybody's Woman*, 1931), and Katharine Hepburn (*Christopher
Strong*). Louella Parsons noted, given the female slant of the material, "It's smart . . .
to hand the direction over to Dorothy Arzner, the only woman director in the
business."[37]

McCall remembered seeing the play in New York when it opened, but she worried that it wasn't going to be motion picture material. As she remembered, "It
takes place in 24 hours in time, in *one* room, and people *talk* to each other. There
is no action to speak of!"[38] Chodorov agreed that *Craig's Wife* wasn't "pure film,"
but argued that "there are no longer any travelling companies or resident stock
companies, so many, many cities and small towns of this country have never seen
a first-class play performed by a first-class cast. I think there is room for that."
McCall bought his argument but remained concerned that the material was too
different for film audiences and a studio system focused on young women and
conventional romance. Kelly, in contrast, she wrote, "never was fond of women
of breeding age; his ingénues were always very shallow and colorless, but the mothers and aunts were dandy."[39]

She felt in her bones that she could not only do justice to Kelly's story, but
also that she could explore areas of Harriet Craig's experience that had never
occurred to the male playwright. She had grown up with women like Mrs. Harriet Craig and knew that their surface materialism was often a reaction to being
little more than an object to their wealthy husbands. Harriet wanted some kind
of authority over her own life, but there was none for a housewife, no matter how
wealthy. And her concern that her niece's romance may be ill advised turns out
to be correct: McCall staged new scenes with the young professor, revealing him
and his colleagues as boorish misogynists.[40]

While Kelly put Harriet Craig's chilly marital philosophy up front in the first
scene with little preamble, McCall took more time to reveal it in her script, planning a long full shot of the interior of the house that would bring a "gasp" of admi-
ration and self-recognition from "every woman in the audience." With this long
slow take, McCall said, "They're seeing Mrs. Craig's soul." McCall included additional scenes of Harriet at her sister's sickbed, consulting the nurse as to what
would be best for her recovery, and later, she is genuinely concerned that Ethel
will make the same romantic mistakes as her mother and sister: "It's better that

the destiny of her home should be in her hands, rather than in any man's." She retained Kelly's substantial speech in which Harriet Craig explains her lifelong fear of poverty was a result of her mother's losing her home to her father's financial mismanagement. The working-class presence in the house grew on screen; there were additional lines for the maid Mazie (Nydia Westman).[41]

Arzner approved but wanted it all articulated, with actors' movements and shots rationalized. As McCall remembered, she wrote the first draft alone, and then the two women worked through each line before meeting with stars Rosalind Russell and John Boles and Cohn's top editor, Viola Lawrence (*The Whole Town's Talking*, 1935).[42] "She questioned every move I made," McCall remembered.[43] "In the script, I would write, 'She walks to the window.' Dorothy would say, 'Why?' And I would answer, 'Well, she's getting the worst of the argument, so she is running away. She turns her back and looks out.'" Arzner responded, "All right, all right, but I have to know why she moves. Otherwise I cannot direct it." Unlike most screenwriters of the time, McCall had a unique opportunity to shape the production and the performances, because Arzner "wanted the writer to be on the set" and not just disappear when shooting commenced. Most directors never invited writers on set, let alone involve them in shooting. Directors were better known for ripping out pages of the script (John Ford) or letting the actors ad lib (Howard Hawks).

As McCall remembered decades later, at the end of every rehearsal, Arzner "would turn to me and say, 'How is that for you?' For the first couple of days, I couldn't believe it. I had never been assigned to a set before."[44] Then, as she put it, at the end of the second day on set, "I decided to crowd my luck." John Boles, playing Mr. Craig, hadn't delivered one of his lines the way she had intended. He spoke as if it were "a direct statement," while she thought "it would be better as a semi-question, with a rising inflection." So, when Arzner asked her again how it had been, McCall replied, "I think that is too definite a statement of that line. I think there's some question in his mind." Arzner then had her read the line as she had intended and called Boles over and told him to redo the last line "with a rising inflection . . . you're not quite sure of it." He did, and Arzner informed everyone, "Fine. That's the way it's going to be." They shot the film in four weeks, at a cost of $280,000.[45] Though economical by any other major studio's standards, this was big money for Columbia.

At one point, they had a serious talk about McCall's career. McCall confessed to Arzner how frustrating it was to be an underpaid hack assigned at random to crank out smart dialogue. She admitted she was thinking of returning to New York. "Don't you have any respect for this medium?" Arzner asked.[46] "Any story-teller who didn't respect this medium would be an idiot, because it is the most flexible, most wonderful way to tell a story that has ever been invented," McCall replied. But, she continued, "it seems to me a medium in which my calling, my profession, has no authority, no dignity, no professional standing at all. We are lent and borrowed, bought and sold, like professional ball players."

When Arzner asked her how she had felt working on *Craig's Wife*, McCall confessed, "It's been the finest weeks of my professional life. I have stopped the work reluctantly every night and have gone to it eagerly the next day." Arzner replied, "Well, it can be like that. . . . But if you turn your back on it and run away, then you will never have anything to say about how a motion picture is made." The trouble was, as far as McCall could tell, there was only one Dorothy Arzner. Chances were slim that the two could work together on the director's next project. After shooting wrapped, she would have to go back to Warner Bros. But she remembered years later, "Miss Arzner's belief that a writer should be a part of the making of a picture from start to finish, and that I had the makings of a good writer for the screen, encouraged me to stay."[47] Their friendship lasted until the director's death, and of all McCall's work in Hollywood, she was proudest of *Craig's Wife* and her partnership with Arzner.

Actress Rosalind Russell, on loan-out from MGM, could tell McCall a thing or two about sticking with it despite setbacks. She had played a long, boring series of second-lead ladies, occasionally opposite the more dynamic Jean Harlow (*Reckless*, *China Seas*, both 1935) and seemed destined to remain typecast for the rest of her career. Playing Mrs. Harriet Craig (an unsympathetic character for men in the audience) was a career risk. But, like Bette Davis's decision to play shrewish waitress Mildred in *Of Human Bondage* two years before for RKO, Russell's re-creation of Kelly's complex, remote housewife brought the actress critical recognition. According to critic Mildred Martin, "*Craig's Wife* may give many women the thrill of recognizing themselves, not retouched. . . . Miss Russell has stopped being a carbon copy—however charming—of Myrna Loy and has played Harriet Craig uncompromisingly and sincerely."[48]

While some male critics worried that the "unsympathetic" Harriet Craig would be the prelude to a cinematic "open season" on women, the majority of female journalists understood Harriet and praised the film as a "revolution" in female representation in front of and behind the camera and "a woman's picture from start to finish."[49] The film was a box office success, not only because of its nuanced critique of marriage and persistent sexual inequality but also thanks to the novelty of its principal female creatives. "That anomalous situation in the motion picture industry, whereby a world of entertainment which relies largely upon its appeal to the feminine audience is almost completely under masculine dominance has undergone, so far as one picture at least is concerned, complete revolution," commented the *New York Post* in September.[50] "Women scenarists, women film editors and cutters, as well as women stars, have been for too long taken for granted in the film world," wrote another critic.[51]

Martin, thrilled that women dominated production, took note of the fact that although a man had written the stage play, the film was even better because "Only women could so deeply get beneath the skin of another woman and so devastatingly expose her." Though Kelly's narrative was sound, Martin pointed out that McCall had written several additional scenes and created "a number of her own" biting lines. McCall's work had given the narrative a depth that it had lacked in the original play, and filmgoers found that Harriet Craig was relatable after all. Writing for the *New York Times*, Frank Nugent agreed: "Hollywood appears to have found the magic stone for turning good plays into better pictures."[52]

Eighty-odd years later, it often surprises audiences that "crude and rough, argumentative, brassy" Harry Cohn was responsible for putting *Craig's Wife*'s female crew together to make such an unabashedly feminist film critiquing the impact of society's limited spheres for women. Sam Bischoff once said his boss was "the wandering Jew without a soul."[53] Years later, Mario Puzo's vicious portrait of Cohn in *The Godfather* (1969), set during the production of Cohn's *From Here to Eternity* (1953), did further damage to his reputation. Many Hollywood women did not like him, including Ben Hecht's wife and fellow screenwriter, Rose Caylor. McCall remembered that one day during her early days at Columbia, "Caylor came down from a conference with Harry, crying and falling apart." Cohn had demanded changes that she found "absolutely destructive of what she had written." Caylor asked McCall how she could stand working there, and then said she "didn't have to write for a living and wanted to quit." McCall responded in the same way Arzner had to her complaints. "Rose, I think you have to ask yourself how much it means to you. I want very much to write for the screen, and I make it a point to get along with Harry Cohn and Darryl Zanuck and J. L. Warner and Louis B. Mayer and with lots of people with whom I truly do not have much in common. But I am not going to have them drive me from the business. I'm going to stay."

McCall's reaction wasn't a case of her abandoning Caylor and her feminist principles to further her own career: The truth was, McCall honestly "liked" Harry
Cohn and said she "got on well with him."[54]

She wasn't the only female colleague to feel this way. Cohn hired more women
as producers at his studio in the 1930s and 1940s than all the other studio heads
combined, and he hired screenwriter-producer Virginia Van Upp as Columbia's
executive producer in 1947. When Cohn discovered that the other male producer
candidates didn't congratulate her on the new job, he sacked them all.[55]

Without doubt he was a legendary womanizer and bully, and he made a pass
at everyone from Hepburn to Hayworth. When McCall was asked, late in life,
whether Cohn had made similar overtures to her, McCall was vague but remarked,
with a glimmer of characteristic humor, "Oh, I certainly got my share of being
chased around desks. I would feel sorry if I had to report that no one ever did."
Evidently, Harry Cohn took McCall's "no" with fairly good grace. Blunt, challenging, and aggressive, the producer was also capable of being fair. He had a sense of
humor, too, if one knew how to handle him. As McCall walked across the Columbia lot on her way out one day, Cohn yelled out the window at her, "Where are
you going?" When she yelled back, "I'm going to lunch," he raged, "No one goes
off the lot to lunch here." "Well, I do, and I'm going," she bellowed, and continued on her way. Any woman who screamed right back at him had Cohn's
respect. As for McCall, when given a choice between Jack Warner the cheap
hypocrite and honest rogue Harry Cohn, McCall took the latter. As she later
said of her old boss, "whereas he might break your jaw, he would never stick a
knife in your back."[56]

Jack Warner had no such scruples. He fired McCall on July 14, right in the
middle of *Craig's Wife*, before the annual review of her contract came up.[57] It could
have been a disastrous situation for her, since being sacked in the middle of the
guild struggle could mean she would be subject to a blanket employment blacklist by all the studios. Luckily, Cohn was famous in the industry for not being
like everybody else. He hired McCall through the autumn of 1936.

One of her first jobs was a quick dialogue polish of an original script written
by guild colleagues Mary McCarthy and Sidney Buchman, *Theodora Goes Wild*
(1936).[58] Small-town, proper Theodora seems to be a pillar of her straightlaced
community, but she has a secret life, thanks to a pseudonym, as the best-selling
author of a newly serialized novel. While on a trip to New York to deal with her
publishers she meets and falls in love with the suave artist involved with the

production of her book. He discovers her double life, follows her back to her hometown, and gleefully blows her cover. But it turns out that he has some skeletons in his closet too, and by the end of the script Theodora gets both her revenge and her man.

Theodora bore an unusually strong resemblance to McCall—from her very proper family and scandalous success as a writer to her free-spirited artist husband and their glamorous New York courtship. She had fun sharpening the wisecracks for Columbia's battle-of-the-sexes comedy of errors. Starring Irene Dunne and Melvyn Douglas (whom McCall knew through his work for the Screen Actors Guild), it became one of Columbia's top hits and arguably the best of Hollywood's early screwball comedies. She didn't get screen credit, since McCarthy and Buchman had done most of the work, but her next projects drew upon her New York background and earned her credits.

The best of the bunch was no comedy. *I Promise to Pay* was about gangsters, loan shark racketeering, and the exploitation of the working class. Eddie Lang (Chester Morris), an overworked and underpaid office worker, wants to take his wife (Helen Mack) and two kids on a vacation to escape the punishing heat wave in the city. But, of course, he can't afford it on his office salary—and, of course, his boss won't give him his expected bonus two weeks early. So, Eddie takes out a small loan of $50 to cover expenses and thinks all is well . . . until the payment plus 1,000 percent interest is due, and racketeer Ricky Farra's (Leo Carrillo) thugs come to collect. Lang struggles to make the payments, but when he doesn't, he's beaten up and his family is threatened. He steals money from his workplace to cover expenses, is fired, and tries to escape by taking a WPA job in another city, but Farra's henchmen find him.

McCall first met Chester Morris through their mutual friend, actor Robert Montgomery. Morris was another prominent member of the Screen Actors Guild and all of them worked together on cross-guild meetings and initiatives. He was utterly believable as the nice guy who's duped by trying to do the right thing for his family. As one critic put it, the film showcased "the most acceptable Chester Morris in ever so long."[59] But off set and onscreen, McCall and audiences were even more taken with the film's other star, California grandee and staunch Republican Carrillo. Carrillo had worked with Edward Chodorov at Warner Bros. on *In Caliente* in 1935, and McCall was delighted to write him a substantial part showcasing his menacing charm free of the exaggerated Latino stereotypes characterizing most contemporary Hollywood films. The two were snapped outside the studio, chatting conspiratorially, as part of the preproduction publicity for the film. Carrillo's Farra is comfortable with the finer things in life and is nobody's fool. His contempt for the WASPy businessmen who want in on his flourishing loan shark business is as breathtakingly frank as his opinion of his underlings. After a late-night meeting with his sharks and enforcers, Farra offhandedly tells his butler to open the window in his apartment. "It smells in here."

Critics reviewed *I Promise to Pay* as a "timely drama" and "a smashing story of one man's fearless war against the loan shark racketeers."[60] It received high praise from the *National Board of Review* for its "vigorous" contemporary material and *Motion Picture Herald* praised its timeliness, with a script "ripped out of newspaper headlines." "Grim and brutal and informative," the *Philadelphia Inquirer* concurred. Reviews took note of McCall's story, "a spine-chilling picture of what can happen to the $27.50-a-week wage-earner who falls into the hands of the loan sharks." Payday loans, unemployment, cancelled bonuses, making do with a family, debt, and more debt were not glamorous stories, but they were at the heart of the American experience in the 1930s.

Her next project for Cohn was less well received, a reworking of *Meet the Wife* playwright Lynn Starling's script for Melvyn Douglas, *Women of Glamour*, a Pygmalion tale costarring Virginia Bruce, in which a middle-class artist tries to mold a working-class nightclub singer into his "ideal woman." It was easy enough to model some of her artist husband's quirks on the urbane Douglas, but this wasn't the type of material McCall enjoyed writing; it was more like what she had tried to escape at Warner Bros. The critics agreed, with one dismissing it as "sweet and sentimental and familiar as an old hat."[61] But whatever its shortcomings, *Women of Glamour*'s costars became McCall's friends and helped shape her public image over the next decade. Douglas's wife, former actress Helen Gahagan, was politically active in California's Democratic Party. Bruce was another committed Democrat, and her new husband, MGM writer-director-producer Jack Ruben, also became the writer's friend.

In the final days of her contract, McCall was one of many screenwriters brought in to brainstorm ideas for *The Awful Truth* (1937) and tailored some of her scenes for cast member and friend Ralph Bellamy.[62] But director Leo McCarey disliked all the scripts he'd seen and moved on to Viña Delmar before winding up improvising scenes with his actors.[63] Her last script for Columbia could have been a screwball gem, but onscreen *It's All Yours* fell rather flat, owing in part to the spectacularly miscast Francis Lederer and his schoolgirlish leading lady, Madeleine Carroll.[64]

Most Hollywood writers between contracts in the Great Depression would have rushed into another exclusive deal for financial security. But McCall had saved her pay, and it bought her the time she needed to bring the Screen Writers Guild back to life. Over the fall and winter of 1936, through whiskey-fueled, chain-smoked Camel evenings, she and Charles Brackett developed a master plan to secure union recognition from Washington and teach the Hollywood bosses a lesson in political moderation.

CHAPTER 7

Independence

O f all the major Hollywood guilds and unions, members of the Screen Writers Guild endured the toughest hazing from studio brass. The year 1936 was particularly brutal. Harry Cohn was one of the few producers who would hire guild-affiliated screenwriters like McCall in 1936.[1] As she remembered, "We were the first of the talent groups to form a guild" but the last to be recognized.[2] SAG would negotiate with producers in 1937, and the Screen Directors Guild, formed in 1936, reached an agreement with producers in 1938. She continued: "The actors borrowed the use of our offices to form *their* guild and were recognized and got a contract. The directors weren't even a gleam in Frank Capra's eye until several years later, but the studios would never sit down and bargain with *us*."

Over the years, colored partially by the cultural fallout from the postwar Hollywood blacklist, the Screen Writers Guild and Hollywood writers more broadly have been associated with left-wing radicalism and communism—ideological enemies of both the Hollywood studio system and U.S. capitalism. But as guild president Jack Lawson acknowledged, "The majority of the people who sustained the organization were not communists. They were just individuals who saw the need for an organization, who realized that the struggle for the guild was both economic and creative."[3] McCall, Charles Brackett, Jane Murfin, Allen Rivkin, Laura Kerr, and Doris Malloy were some of the more prominent moderates instrumental in developing the membership base and a sense of collective identity that went beyond getting members to pay their dues. Guild membership had plummeted and only a handful of stalwarts were attending meetings at her home. In February 1937, dismayed that her colleagues had skipped another guild meeting to hear a British war correspondent talk about the Spanish Civil War, McCall published a semihumorous lament in the *Screen Guilds Magazine*: "Nobody goes to anybody's house any more to sit and talk and have fun. There's a master of ceremonies and a collection basket, because there are no gatherings now except for a Good Cause. We have almost no time to be actors and writers these days."[4] She also poked fun at the many writers who were warming chairs in studio offices rather than writing, liberals who despised the studios wholeheartedly but still took their paychecks: "The clock creeps around to 5.30 and then life begins. Then we listen to speeches, and sign pledges, and feel that warming glow which comes from being packed in close with a lot of people who agree with you—a mild hypnotism, an exhilarating pleasurable hysteria." Rather than pass collection plates in the fancy drawing rooms of Hollywood's so-called intellectual elites for other political causes, writers needed to focus on writing— and the future of the guild.

In the next issue Donald Ogden Stewart, a former Broadway actor turned communist screenwriter, replied, accusing her of abandoning liberal causes for the Hollywood "good life." He wrote: "Miss McCall's indignation at the efforts of the organizers of the good causes sounds not so much like the desire of the true artist for the high lonely peak as the reminiscent whine of the well-fed to be let alone in his feather bed. It is a painful surprise to find so courageous a fighter as Miss McCall . . . counseling . . . adherence to the banners of those defenders of the goose that lays the golden eggs."[5]

That was rich, considering that Stewart had been one of the prominent writers to cross picket lines at the 1934 Academy Awards and "thumb [his] nose at the guild" when it faced its first clash with the producers.[6] Later, when the guild was more fashionable, he became more supportive as an openly communist member. McCall was out of work, but Stewart was comfortably ensconced at MGM writing glitzy stories of the rich (*The Barretts of Wimpole Street*, 1934; *The Prisoner of Zenda*, 1937; *Marie Antoinette*, 1938; *Holiday*, 1938).

The dispute eventually made its way to *The Daily Worker*, where journalist Mike Gold condemned McCall for her "sharp blast" at "screen writers being plunged up to their necks in politics."[7] Though most of the male screenwriters on the far left were gleeful that McCall had "been shouted down," historian Ian Hamilton later concluded that her comments "surely touched a nerve."[8] McCall was neither a conservative stooge nor a fellow traveler; she was merely doing her best to secure the contract and protect her fledging union from too many debilitating political links and "a tenuous existence in a hostile industry." There was a well-justified fear that too many political encumbrances would further compromise the guild's efforts to obtain studio recognition as a union.

Despite Stewart's disdain, McCall had a considerable following among moderate Democrats and Republicans, younger members, and women. Writer William Ludwig was eight years McCall's junior and had just come out to Hollywood under contract to MGM. Together with Aurania Rouverol, the mother of screenwriter Jean Rouverol, he wrote *Love Finds Andy Hardy* (1938) for Mickey Rooney, which proved to be one of the studio's smash hits of the year.[9] He would go on to write five more Andy Hardy films. Like McCall, Ludwig had joined the guild the moment he arrived in Hollywood and found that some more senior writers looked down on him and the kind of "juvenile" films he wrote. But McCall wasn't like this.

Ludwig remembered, "I first met Mary in 1937.... She was already established, and I was a very lowly junior writer but she treated me like a colleague, like a *real* writer. To Mary, there were no 'junior writers.' You were either a writer or you weren't and if you were, she was for you." He pointed out that "too few of us recall that era in our history when we were struggling for certification by the National Labor Relations Board so we could compel the producers to negotiate a contract with us.... And we've come a long way, baby, a long road with a lot of blood on it. And no small part of that blood was Mary's."

McCall inspired Ludwig to become an active executive board member, and he would serve as treasurer and secretary for nearly twenty years. Of all her colleagues, Ludwig was the most eloquent in summarizing her philosophy: "Mary wasn't a radical of the Right or of the Left. She was a radical about writers ... about their rights in their material, about their right to earn a decent living from their work, about their right to be treated with dignity and respect. Mary had the courage, the fire and the integrity to live through those days, not just to join the fight, but to lead it ... visible, a target, but unafraid." He concluded, "She was a good friend, a true friend, and your friend forever. If one writer or the entire guild was under attack no one ever had to look around for Mary. She was up front, leading the fight. An iron backbone, a steely will, and the fury of an avenging goddess."[10]

Provided that the Wagner Act survive its trial before the Supreme Court that spring, federal law would protect any future labor organizing in any industry. Were the guild to resurface and lobby for recognition, McCall realized that it would need a serious PR makeover. After obtaining legal advice, she and Brackett contacted as many members as they could—cold-calling at dinnertime, meeting for drinks in town, arranging casual dinners and picnics—and then asked for their voting proxies for when they could not attend meetings. As McCall remembered, "In the Screen Writers Guild was a small communist minority. They were very active, very hard-working, they were frequently elected to the board. I always felt that, in their activities, the guild came second and the Party came first. I fought them. We finally beat them by using proxies, because we got the guild's solid, middle-of-the-road people who were too lazy to work at defeating them to give their proxies to those of us who were willing to work. This way, the communist members of the guild were eventually run out of office."[11]

Finally on April 12, 1937, there was good news. The Supreme Court declared the Wagner Act constitutional. For the first time in American history, the right to form a union and to strike was recognized and protected by all branches of the federal government. Flush with donations from jubilant members, the Screen Writers Guild board returned to its dismal old address on North Cherokee.

No one was more delighted by this turn of events than Dwight Franklin. Having a sizable chunk of Hollywood's screenwriting community using his house for meetings meant that it was usually too noisy for him to concentrate on his work for DeMille and his private commissions. The house was full to bursting with seven-year-old Sheila and the three-year-old twin boys.[12] That spring, Franklin began building an art studio on Highland where he could get some time away from his family and his wife's colleagues. But "McCall-Franklin Inc.," as their close friend writer and humorist Leo Rosten dubbed them, kept their sense of humor. They put a note in the *Los Angeles Times* that May: "Dwight Franklin, designer for C. B. DeMille, and his wife, Mary McCall Jr., scenarist, want all their friends to know they aren't having marital difficulties. The fact that he is building a studio on Highland Avenue is probably responsible for the rumor."[13]

On June 11 the Screen Writers Guild held its first open meeting on North Cherokee in almost a year. Four hundred attended, a far cry from the handful of stalwarts who had kept the organization going on the sly for the past year. Many of those who attended were McCall's good friends, but there were many others who weren't there whose voices could now count by proxy. That night Brackett was elected vice president and McCall was elected to a term on the executive board. Now that the reformed guild was applying to Washington to be recognized as the screenwriters' official union, Brackett and McCall had two priorities: increasing membership, so that they could justify eclipsing the rival Screen

Playwrights, and the articulation of the contract terms. They concluded the meeting by planning an all-out party for Thursday, July 22, at the Fiesta Room of the Ambassador Hotel. Considering how writers had been given the runaround by their studio bosses, it seemed appropriate that they hired ventriloquist extraordinaire Edgar Bergen and his pal Charlie McCarthy as entertainment for the night. Alongside Dorothy Parker, Harry Tugend, and Dudley Nichols, McCall wrote six "satirical blackouts 'kidding' the film industry."[14] Guests from the Screen Actors Guild performed the skits. SAG members had been officially recognized by the studios on May 9, and producers signed their contract on May 15. The writers used some of the night to ask their actor friends how they managed it.

Although it had been over a year since Warner Bros. fired McCall, the studio was still churning out projects she'd worked on back in 1935 and 1936 (without giving her credit). But she and Franklin were in good financial shape; he continued working for DeMille, and in the summer of 1937, the trade papers highlighted Franklin, screenwriter Jeanie Macpherson, and technical advisor William G. Beymer as "noted experts on the customs and costumes of the nineteenth century" who were part of a new wave of historical filmmaking. Franklin's miniatures were "likely to become a popular Hollywood fad."[15] Chodorov commissioned a Shakespearean group, writer Jo Swerling had ordered a miniature Samuel Johnson, and Fredric March posed as a curly-headed Jean Lafitte for the new DeMille pirate epic *The Buccaneer*. DeMille had been a fan of Franklin's pirate miniatures from the 1920s, and though the filmmaker was notoriously free and easy with historical details, Franklin supported his employer in the press for *The Buccaneer*: "The flavor of the period is the most important quality for which to strive in historical films; exact duplication of all details is obviously not always possible or desirable."

McCall briefly joined her husband and Charles Brackett for a stint at Paramount in the fall, and *Film Daily* reported that she and Franklin were in New York to research an American Revolution story. Perhaps they hoped to create a DeMille-esque historical action drama on which they could both work. But nothing came of it. When they returned to the West Coast, producer Emanuel Cohen hired her to "prepare the screenplay of *Eight Hours* for George Raft."[16]

Though she lunched with Brackett in the studio commissary, they weren't paired on any scripts. Brackett was caught up in projects with Billy Wilder. That November, studio journalists reported that McCall would adapt Rose Franken's magazine story "Call Back Love," (actually a novel by Franken and W. B. Meloney) and an original script cowritten with Leonard Q. Ross (the pen name for Leo Rosten), called *Free Woman*, for Cohen.[17] Her friend Allen Rivkin collaborated with her on *Call Back Love*. *Free Woman*, about a good wife who leaves her husband when she discovers that he has been cheating on her, had possibilities, but Cohen's productions stalled, and she left Paramount without getting any credits.[18]

Agent Mary Baker then arranged a deal at RKO to write *Breaking the Ice*. The film promoted the talents of two child stars, singer Bobby Breen and figure skating protégée Irene Dare. Rather than write a saccharine juvenile success story, McCall looked at the darker side of child star exploitation. In deciding to hire her for the project, RKO executives may have thought that a mother of three children would have a greater stock of cute scenes and dialog. But McCall never wrote straight sugar. Actress Dolores Costello's specialty in the mid-1930s was the winsome mother (*Little Lord Fauntleroy*, 1936), yet her maternal role in *Breaking the Ice* is disturbing in its ineffectual passivity. She fails to save her boy from venal relatives and promoters (Charles Ruggles) who pocket the proceeds from the protégé's singing gigs. Despite its darker Dickensian aspects the production did well at the box office, with reviewers praising the two young stars.[19] But McCall didn't like working at RKO any better than she had enjoyed her stint at Paramount. When a *Daily News* feature on women screenwriters came out in January, McCall's name was still linked with Columbia.[20]

Though Jane Murfin, Wanda Tuchock, and Sarah Y. Mason had done well at RKO earlier in the decade when David O. Selznick was in charge of production, more and more of that studio's productions were being written by men. After Selznick formed his own company, he refused to promote his ambitious secretary, Silvia Schulman, and Barbara Keon to his list of writers. In retaliation, Schulman began writing an exposé of the film industry with an "old-school feminist" streak: *I Lost My Girlish Laughter*.[21] It would end her chances of becoming a contracted screenwriter.

But McCall gave Selznick a try in early 1938.[22] The project was more to her liking: developing Helen Grace Carlisle's popular novel, *The Merry, Merry Maidens* (1937). It was the story of six high school girls who are friends but go their separate ways after graduation in 1917. Ruth, the narrator, is the most conventional of the group and ends up a relatively happy housewife. Carol is a sedate career woman, Lisa abandons her professional career in music after bearing an illegitimate child and teaches music, political activist Bertha marries a Russian engineer, Maida steals Lisa's beau and becomes a rich and unhappy wife, and the poor but brilliant Wanda (she bobs her hair even before Irene Castle) becomes a famous but lonely actress. In the novel marriage generally makes women miserable, and no one's life turns out exactly as she planned it back in 1917. Its feminist theme fit in with some of the projects Selznick had focused on since the early 1930s (*Little Women*, 1933; *A Star Is Born*, 1937), and McCall, being of that generation of New York women, seemed a good choice to develop the material. She was one of the few writers on salary not roped in to do rewrites on his adaptation of Margaret Mitchell's *Gone with the Wind*.

She wrote quickly and that January met up with Arzner. Over drinks, Arzner asked her what her new script was about. When McCall proceeded to give mini-biographies of each of the women, Arzner became impatient. There really didn't sound like there was a coherent theme, just a collection of character sketches. McCall commented: "I was brought up short, because I realized that it really was about nothing!"[23] Arzner remarked, "I don't care how corny the theme is—that 'home-keeping hearts are happiest' or you never know till you try or anything else—but what is the basic theme of the story?"

Arzner recognized the thorny issue of narration in Carlisle's novel. Having the housewife with the pack of kids and mundane existence narrate endorsed and normalized this kind of life choice above the others. The other women's lives (many of them career-oriented) were more exciting but less romantically fulfilling. Wanda was a vivid character, years ahead of her time, but Carlisle dwells on her barren existence without a husband. It was unsettling for both Arzner and McCall to contemplate this kind of "message" film. McCall, upon reflection, felt that Carlisle's understanding of American women and the age-old conflict between career and marriage was both muddled and regressive. As she later wrote, "I'm afraid the author of the book . . . hadn't thought it out, just kind of grabbed a thin idea from, maybe, her own high school days. It had no substance." McCall didn't feel she had the creative support from Selznick to restructure the material.

It's interesting to speculate on the varied, messy lives of these women and Carlisle's and Hollywood's inability to find a workable plot for a modern woman. Hollywood's stock in trade at this time was the women's picture, but most plots were riven with ambivalence about reconciling independence and traditional values. Although McCall reshaped Shelby's story in *The Woman in Red*, Carlisle's multiple heroines and disparate experiences muddled narrative and message. Since, as *Time* magazine reviewed it, it was just "an ordinary novel about six ordinary maidens," there was nothing outstanding about any of the individual stories.[24] Selznick by that time was obsessed with the adaptation of *Gone with the Wind*, a novel that needed only one unordinary female protagonist.

McCall found out she wasn't the only writer to get a headache from the project. Back in 1937, Sonya Levien and Elizabeth Meyer had done a fulsome adaptation with no clear storyline.[25] Budd Schulberg had even less success working on it after McCall, though his solution was to turn Wanda into a mentally disturbed aviatrix and kill herself over love in the manner of *Christopher Strong* (1933).[26] McCall eventually decided to focus on Wanda's rise from poverty to celebrity and Lisa's blighted romantic hopes, which she later realizes vicariously as a single parent to a musical son.[27] The other women in the original novel faded into the periphery as McCall focused on the difficulties facing working women and the stigma of single parenthood.

Selznick's reputation for indecisiveness and employing legions of writers on a single script was not something that endeared him to McCall. As she confided to Baker, she had MGM in her sights, the richest major studio in town—and the one with the most female stars and screenwriters. Even though she would be a comparatively small fish in a big pond, her salary would be exponentially higher. She wanted to break the $1,000-a-week barrier.

After Franklin finished with *The Buccaneer*, the couple decided that they needed a party. Rather than focus on a depressing milestone like Franklin's upcoming fiftieth birthday, they threw a ten-year anniversary bash on January 28, 1938, at the Swedish Three Crowns. The guests included all their old and new friends, the Cagneys, of course, the Frank McHughes, the Chester Morrises, the Jimmy Gleasons, the Robert Montgomerys, the Pat O'Briens, and Doug Jr., going stag. Given that McCall was fishing for an MGM contract, a female journalist was invited to report on McCall's enviable list of high-profile friends. Grace Wilcox noted in *Screen and Radio Weekly*: "When Dwight Franklin, film character actor, and his wife, Mary McCall Jr., screen writer, celebrated their tenth wedding anniversary with a dinner for 100 film celebrities, they sent out invitations in tin—tin being the symbol for the tenth year."[28] In keeping with the ten-year "tin" gag, the guests all brought tin presents, from tins of sardines to pencils and sunglasses. Franklin was almost used to the notes in the columns that referred to him as "Mary McCall's husband" or misrepresented his actual job in Hollywood. The marriage had survived Doug Jr., Leslie Howard, and three kids.

Bogart was the only close friend conspicuous by his absence. He too had married back in 1928 (on April 3, the day before McCall's birthday), and he and his

wife, actress Mary Philips, had tried to emulate McCall and Franklin's open marriage. But Bogart found he couldn't handle Philips's affair with actor Roland
Young any more than Philips could tolerate the rumors about Bogart's woman-
izing. Though Bogart would always quote McCall and say that life in Hollywood
was "a goldfish bowl," journalists covering his marital difficulties had him under
pressure.[29]

McCall had tried to help the couple back in 1937, recommending Philips to
Dorothy Arzner for a small role in the director's most recent production at MGM,
The Bride Wore Red. She hoped that if Philips had more film work in Hollywood,
Bogart and she might reconcile. But in February 1937 *Variety* had reported Philips would return to New York City to "start divorce proceedings."[30] On the same
page, the actress Mayo Methot announced she was divorcing her husband Percy
Morgan for "too much interference in her career." The timing of the announce-
ments was no coincidence; Bogart and Methot had started their affair on the set
of Warner Bros.' *Marked Woman,* and when Philips found out she called time on a
marriage that had run its course.

In the midst of the melodrama Bogart still seemed to want to patch up the
marriage, claiming to *Photoplay* journalist Katherine Albert as late as July, "Right
now we're—well, I guess you can call it a 'trial separation.' "[31] But on August 18,
1937, *Variety* reported their divorce.[32] McCall and Franklin liked the witty, easy-
going Philips and were sorry to see their friends divorce. They weren't as comfortable with Methot—especially McCall. Methot was jealous of Bogart's female
friends and accused McCall of having an affair with Bogart.

After celebrating her thirty-fourth and Bette Davis's thirtieth birthdays at a
Jezebel-themed party (where Davis's brother-in-law Robert Pelgram dressed up as
Scarlett O'Hara), McCall and Dwight made another effort for Bogart at the Tri-
Guild Ball at the Cocoanut Grove on April 21, 1938.[33] McCall invited Methot to
be a special guest at their table. Bette Davis and her bandleader husband Ham
Nelson; Bogart, McCall, and Bogart's agent, Mary Baker; Baker's husband Mel;
Hugh Herbert; the irrepressible Mischa Auer (*It's All Yours*); McCall's New York
society cousin Dorothy McClave; and Methot made up the table. It was one of
the big social events in the Hollywood calendar. Though McCall always swore
that she and Bogart didn't sleep together (allegedly because the actor was "mal-
odorous" and it put her off), Mayo maintained her suspicions about McCall, and
allegedly the actress hurled "a silver coffee urn at her out of jealousy."[34] Although

Bogart's and McCall's agent Mary Baker was certainly Bogart's type of woman, allegedly she was "the only woman Mayo wasn't jealous of."[35]

When Bogart finally got around to setting the date with Methot, he insisted that Dwight and Mary and Sheila and the boys all be invited to the wedding. The ceremony was held at the Bakers' on August 20, 1938—after more than one delay—and was memorable for more than one reason.[36] David Niven recalled that Auer danced naked at the wedding reception.[37] Methot didn't throw anything at McCall, but seven-year-old Sheila was wary of annoying her, since Bogart usually bear-hugged the little girl and swung her up on his shoulders when they met at the McCall-Franklin house. When Sheila reached Bogart in the reception line, she made everyone laugh when she "asked Mayo's formal permission" to kiss him, fearing this would cause jealousy.[38]

Meeting Cagney was less dangerous. Though McCall didn't go out regularly with him on his Irish mafia drinking bouts (those were strictly for the boys), their guild work brought them closer.[39] For her part, she had been a little jealous that the actors' guild had full union status when the Screen Writers Guild was still struggling to receive legal backing from Washington. But finally the guild's luck changed.

On June 7, 1938, after a nearly five-year struggle, the guild leadership learned that it had federal protection to unionize under the Wagner Act. In its examination of the guild's case against the producers, the National Labor Relations Board concluded that the producers' premeditated "plan of interference" with labor organizing among writers (which included blackmail, propaganda, and firing) was unlawful and that the producers had "conspired" with the Screen Playwrights when the organization clearly was a minority group and did not have a mandate.[40] Another formal election was held on June 28 to reconfirm the Screen Writers Guild as the official union. When, smarting from their defeat at this election, the Screen Playwrights and producers threatened to take the action to court, the infamous Paramount antitrust suit against the studios was filed on July 20. The Supreme Court decision would eventually force the studios to deaccession their theater holdings ten years later. Given the close proximity of the case filing and the crippling of the Screen Playwrights, executives put two and two together and blamed their writers for undermining the system. However, the studio heads would have their revenge with another and more lasting blacklist that would claim the careers of some of Hollywood's most prominent and political writers, including McCall. In 1938 she had little time to count the cost of her involvement in the guild, her feminism, or vengeful producers—because that summer, she finally reached the top.

Mary Baker negotiated a deal with MGM that gave her client an enviable weekly salary of $1,250. McCall would work for several weeks on one major project, to be determined, and then the studio would exercise its option to sign her to a longer contract. She would continue to write independently for New York magazines, and only her screenwork would be exclusive to MGM. It was a coup; only a handful of writers in Hollywood crossed the $1,000-a-week threshold in the 1930s. According to guild records, the average weekly wage for a guild-affiliated writer in 1938 was $356. McCall and Franklin moved into a fancier New England colonial-type house at 10449 Bainbridge Avenue in West Los Angeles near UCLA.

Her first picture at MGM was a rewrite of Ernst Vadja's *Dramatic School* (1938), the story of a group of aspiring theater actresses in Paris starring Paulette Goddard, Lana Turner, and two-time Academy Award-winner Luise Rainer (*The Great Ziegfeld*, 1936; *The Good Earth*, 1937). The theatrical material was familiar territory for McCall; she knew Broadway women and all-female environments back to her Vassar days.

McCall kept a few elements of class-ridden grime amid the regulation MGM chiffon (perhaps she was remembering some of Wanda's struggle in *The Merry, Merry Maidens*). In fact, the opening text dedication celebrates the connection between writers and actors: "The Producers dedicate this play to the actors, that is to those people who step before the footlights heroically, night after night, in order to proclaim the power of the word and of the idea to a world, in which ideas meet defeat day after day." In McCall's guild work, she realized that her fellow writers' best allies were not studio executives or directors but actors who depended on those great parts to attract their fans. Naturally she wanted the alliance between the Screen Actors Guild and the Screen Writers Guild to continue to flourish.

In the script Rainer's working-class dramatic student Louise works nights in a factory to pay for school tuition. She is easily the most sympathetic character in the cast, and clashes instantly with Goddard's rich girl. She does meet and fall for a rich marquis, but he drops her, and Louise continues to work her day and night jobs to attain success on her own terms. An older actress competes with her for a role in a new play about Joan of Arc, but eventually they reconcile, and Louise becomes a great star. She celebrates her success not with the marquis or with her new fans, but with her old pal from the factory.

McCall enhanced the clash between working-class and wealthy students and teachers in her script rewrites for producer Mervyn Leroy and his assistant, Jack Ruben. Very early on in the script she even manages to convey Louise's new, realistic way of approaching her role as Marie Antoinette mounting the scaffold, as opposed to her old teacher's way. Naturally, the "old school" view is to have the queen always act like a queen, regal and untouched by her circumstances, whereas Louise recognizes the historical context of her part: "I've been in prison for weeks. I am tired. And frightened of the guillotine. All those nights, waiting in that cell with the dirty straw—not knowing when they'd come. Trying to comfort my little boy—keeping the rats from him. Oh, she'd keep her head up, remembering that she's a queen—but she'd be so weary!"[41] McCall echoes her perspective from the *Screen Guilds Magazine* article on lifelike acting and writing, but when Louise tries to quote Sarah Bernhardt to support her argument, her teacher cuts in angrily. The Establishment fears realism.

McCall was invested in showing that this theatrical world was focused on the study of great female roles. The young actresses aspire to be like the great Bernhardt, and they have role models in teachers who were once great actresses. But they also study the lives of famous women—such as Marie Antoinette and Joan of Arc—and the dramatic roles they afford the profession. Their art, focused on keeping the memory of women's heroism circulating in contemporary culture, is imbued with feminism. And, of course, the young women's personal narratives are about becoming, in their smaller ways, part of that female pantheon, harnessing emotion and resilience to become great actresses. Acting was the most popular profession for women in the nineteenth and early twentieth centuries, with far more opportunity for public recognition than writing, teaching, or office work.[42]

Although she didn't mix with the cast, McCall respected Rainer as an actress and realized how out of place the Viennese star felt in Hollywood.[43] *Dramatic School* was Rainer's final film for MGM. After starring in a biopic of Broadway's most famous showman, Florenz Ziegfeld (*The Great Ziegfeld*) and a best-selling Pearl Buck adaptation (*The Good Earth*), and wining two Oscars, her champion, MGM producer Irving Thalberg, died, leaving her to the untender mercies of Louis B. Mayer. A succession of less impressive "wife" roles with Spencer Tracy wrecked her career. Louise in *Dramatic School* was one of her few non-long-suffering girlfriend or wife roles. But despite good reviews, the film was too like RKO's *Stage Door* (1937), starring Hepburn and Ginger Rogers, and barely recouped its $600,000 production costs.[44] Rainer would leave Hollywood soon after the film's release.

Rainer's case was an extreme example of how foreign female stars' careers could be ruined by misogyny, xenophobia, and mismanagement. Homegrown American stars did far better in Hollywood, particularly at MGM, which specialized in glamorous pictures starring and aimed at women. Being at MGM meant more to McCall than a high salary and some prestige. MGM has been called "the pivotal studio in the writers' war," since, in part, it employed twice as many writers as the other studios. Many of MGM's writers were women. In the 1930s and 1940s the studio's writing roster was composed of 23–26 percent women and was a *Who's Who* of screenwriting (Frances Marion, Anita Loos, Lenore Coffee, Salka Viertel, Ruth Gordon, Isobel Lennart, and Frances Goodrich all worked there).[45] As screenwriter Dorothy Kingsley recalled, MGM's women tended to support each other.[46] McCall's rising status as an adaptor of prestige literature, her knack for creating contemporary women's stories about work, sex, and love, and her friendship with MGM writer and fellow Vassar alumna Goodrich (*The Thin Man* franchise) sweetened the contract further.

Many of MGM's top female screenwriters had been in the business for decades, including Frances Marion. By the late 1930s Marion had taken on more of an administrative role at MGM, and most of the studio's scripts passed through her hands for her approval. Together with colleagues Loos and Coffee, she represented a strong, powerful bloc of screenwriters who began their careers in the silent era and flourished in the early years of the studio system. Marion in particular created and nurtured a network of Hollywood women during the 1910s and 1920s and used her influence with Thalberg to help the careers of other women.

These networks had become tenuous by the 1930s. Marion, though fond of executive secretary Ida Koverman, "the real power behind [Mayer's] throne," was nonetheless wary of Mayer. She sensed a growing hostility to women's power as writers and was careful not to use her own work as an example of a perfect screenplay when she published the successful *How to Write and Sell Screenplays* (1937). Though Marion briefly agreed to serve as vice president of the fledgling writers' guild in 1933, she functioned more as a figurehead than as an advocate for unionization and quickly withdrew her membership when an irate Thalberg demanded it.

Marion's colleague Bess Meredyth was hostile to the guild, something that endeared her to Mayer.[47] She, Pickford, and conservative Jeanie Macpherson were, significantly, the only three female founders of the Academy of Motion Picture Arts and Sciences. The conservative producer-controlled organization did what it could in its early years to crush the emerging guilds and unions, and as McCall put it later in her 1948 history of the Screen Writers Guild, it "had fallen into disrepute among workers in the industry, because it had been used by the producers in their efforts to institute a fifty per cent salary cut."[48] McCall's presence at MGM politically reinvigorated its ranks of female writers while ensuring that she could organize new or undecided colleagues to join the guild and put further pressure on the producers to accept a high shop percentage (meaning the studios would be obliged to hire guild writers in most cases).

On September 21, 1938, *Variety* reported that the guild's committee had submitted the first tentative agreement to the producers. They wanted as high a guild shop percentage as possible, and 85 percent was considered good. The response was that they "were unwilling to grant a complete guild shop to the scriveners because of a prior contractual agreement" with the Screen Playwrights, which would run well into the next year.[49] This was a sticking point, since the National Labor Relations Board had recognized the Screen Writers Guild as the union with negotiating credentials. McCall and her colleagues mentioned obstruction and stated that they would complain to the board. Furthermore, McCall, Brackett, and the executive committee reiterated that a blanket pay raise from $40 to $125 a week for all writers was nonnegotiable. According to *Variety*, producers were not against this salary for veterans but wanted "some provision made for employment of beginners" at a much-reduced rate. This, McCall stated, was unacceptable.

Talks at the Brown Derby restaurant broke down. Boris Ingster, who attended many sessions, remembered, "Mary McCall and I were both very militant, very demanding . . . the other producers would get so furious they would really go insane."[50] At one meeting Y. Frank Freeman screamed, "I'll go back to selling Coca-Cola first" before signing such a contract. At another, Freeman and Eddie Mannix had to carry out Harry Warner, who was literally frothing at the mouth in another rage about ungrateful writers. McCall rallied broad moderate support around Brackett and "beset" him over several months with arguments in favor of his campaign for guild leadership. After several persuasive liquid lunches at Lucey's and the Cock and Bull, Brackett ran and was elected on November 9, 1938.[51]

While these negotiations were running on, McCall and Baker were experiencing their own issues with the MGM contract. The studio liked McCall's work on *Dramatic School* and wanted to exercise its option to prolong her employment, but McCall was appalled to find something in her contact stating that she was held to screen credit arbitration by the Screen Playwrights. She complained to the guild and the National Labor Relations Board. As *Variety* reported, the guild "has clashed with executives of major film companies over the form of contract the scriveners are required to sign."[52] Screen Writers Guild leaders "have instructed members to ink contracts when renewals are offered, but to attach a rider stating that they are signing under protest with reference to [a] clause requiring arbitration by Screen Playwrights, Inc. if [there are] any disputes over screen credits." McCall confronted Mannix and demanded that the clause be "eliminated," but she told the executive board of the guild that studio "executives refused and stated that if she did not care to sign there were plenty of writers who would and who also would be 'friendly to the Playwrights.'" According to *Variety*, "Miss McCall" appeared before the executive board of the guild and "recommended that some action be taken to protest the clause." But, the trade paper noted, "formal protest has been lodged with producers and situation called to attention of the National Labor Relations Board." MGM was publicly embarrassed; the federal government was on McCall's side.

That fall, while her future at MGM seemed in doubt, she and Baker tapped into the lucrative trend in historical films. In October she and Stanley Rauh sold their original story of Victorian feminism, "The First Co-Ed," to Samuel Goldwyn, which allegedly was intended for Andrea Leeds and Joel McCrea.[53] It was postponed until 1943, when Don Hartman and Teresa Wright were attached to the property, before it was again shelved. McCall then was assigned to adapt an Edna Ferber story, *Nobody's at Home*, for Goldwyn.[54] Then, in November, it was announced she would write additional dialogue for Republic's big, million-dollar prestige picture, *Westward the Wagons*. Renamed *Man of Conquest*, it starred Ferber alumnus Richard Dix (*Cimarron*, 1931) as Texas legend Sam Houston and was a big hit for the studio.[55]

MGM caved into McCall's demands that December, again offering her $1,250 a week and a new project on her own with producer Jack Ruben.[56] But she won an even bigger victory for her guild colleagues across the industry, since executives could no longer include the Screen Playwrights in any future contracts. When columnist Sheilah Graham profiled Hollywood's powerful women writers in a major article in December 1938, McCall was among them. She claimed, "There are only two ways for a woman to make big money in Hollywood—to act for the movies and to write for the movies."[57] Although "any woman" can act in them, Graham wrote, "It takes something more" to join the cohort of women who make from $750 to $3,000 a week. She praised her lover F. Scott Fitzgerald's friend

Dorothy Parker and mentioned Levien, Coffee, Bella Spewack, and Frances Goodrich in a club started by the legendary Frances Marion, but "pretty little Mary McCall" was singled out in the $1,000 a week bracket, working on *Midsummer Night's Dream*, *Babbitt*, and *Theodora Goes Wild*. Graham didn't dare mention McCall's work for the guild, but everyone in town knew the story of how she had brought MGM to heel.

Among all the writers Graham singled out, only McCall acted in the interests of all writers rather than for her own job security. The studio could have dropped her over the contract dispute, but McCall used the press, her colleagues, lawyers, and the Washington establishment to force the producers to fall in line with the guild's labor negotiations. During this tense period, McCall also turned to her friends in the Screen Actors Guild. By now SAG had obtained its contract, and McCall worked to cement relations with her acting colleagues. Prominent SAG members Lucile Webster Gleason, Montgomery, and Cagney continued to lend moral support and advice to McCall, coming over for dinner for union powwows. In another show of solidarity McCall wrote the first Screen Guild Theater play for the CBS Gulf Oil Program, *Can We Forget?*, for friends Bette Davis, Montgomery, George Murphy, Louise Beavers, and Basil Rathbone. It was an adaptation of her own story "Yesterday Was a Dream." The show aired on WABC on January 22, 1939.[58]

That month, she was at work drafting her new assignment for Jack Ruben, the adaptation of popular novelist Wilson Collison's *Dark Dame*. The heroine, like McCall, would go on to become one of the most influential women of the next decade. She wasn't a glamorous debutante or an heiress or a queen. She was a homegrown woman of the people, and her only assets were the blonde head on her shoulders, a smart mouth, and the courage to go toe to toe with all types of men—cheap bosses, cheating boyfriends, bullies, and creeps.

CHAPTER 8

The Invention of Maisie

After ten years of dodging the Great Depression, working from story to story and from studio to studio, McCall finally made it to the top. The year she started working for MGM, Hollywood publicists went into overdrive, claiming that 1938's lineup of new films would be the industry's best ever.[1] But the best was yet to come. Years later, critics proclaimed 1939 the high point of "classical" Hollywood production and style before the impact of the Second World War broke the spell with realism, independent production companies, star directors, percentage deals, bigger union disputes, and the blacklist.[2] In 1939, after ten years of hard times, American cinemagoers finally believed they saw light at the end of the tunnel—just as the rest of the world was on the brink of war. It was the best of times and the worst of times, but for Hollywood, the last days of the Thirties were golden.

A deluge of westerns hit the box office (*Jesse James*, *Stagecoach*, *Dodge City*, *The Oklahoma Kid*, *Union Pacific*, *Destry Rides Again*, *Drums Along the Mohawk*), but Hollywood offered a range of literary adaptations (*Wuthering Heights*, *Gunga Din*, *Beau Geste*), society romances (*Love Affair*, *Midnight*, *Ninotchka*), and melodramas (*The Old Maid*, *Dark Victory*, *In Name Only*). It was also the year of *The Wizard of Oz* and *Gone with the Wind*, two films that would define twentieth-century American cultural history. The stories of Dorothy Gale (Judy Garland) and Scarlett O'Hara (Vivien Leigh) also marked the conventional high tide of women's presence in Hollywood cinema. They matured from pampered girls to women unafraid of pulling back curtains and exposing charlatan men or lying, cheating, stealing, and killing to protect their homes. But there is another film, unnamed in most histories, that deserves to be remembered, one that became the sleeper hit of the year. It was a film about a woman, but she didn't grow up on a quaint Kansas farm or on a rich

Georgia plantation. She was a working-class girl from Brooklyn who became a Hollywood golden girl for ten films and eight years. Her name was Maisie.

When studio story editor Edwin Knopf assigned McCall to Wilson Collison's *Dark Dame* (1935), he hoped he was getting rid of a problem that had plagued his department for the last few years. In 1932 the studio had optioned another Collison novel, *Red Dust* (1928), which became one of MGM's biggest hits, ensuring its stars, Jean Harlow and Clark Gable, lasting fame. The studio executives had then begged Collison to write more stories in this vein for Harlow, but, as McCall remembered, "he sold them two stories that were exactly the same... there was always the big, rough, tough guy who didn't want to get married and the girl who looked and talked like a floosie but had a heart of gold."[3] *Dark Dame* had a different setting and characters, but, as McCall pointed out, it had the same old storyline as *Red Dust*. Critics dismissed it upon publication as "readable trash," a slender tale of a cowboy torn between an evil married woman and a New York showgirl.[4] It might have proved a lucrative sequel, but Harlow had died in 1937 at the age of twenty-six, and the property was shelved until McCall arrived.

She felt the irony of the situation. *Red Dust* had been adapted by one of her conservative adversaries in the Screen Playwrights, John Lee Mahin. But however detestable Mahin was on a personal level, McCall had to admit he was still a good writer. Even so, McCall couldn't replicate *Red Dust*'s brand of racy humor in 1939. Not only was Harlow dead, but her trademark frank sexuality, perfect for bringing Mahin's script to life, had been outlawed. The Production Code silenced many of the wisecracks and double-entendres that were the stock in trade of Harlow and Mae West. Harlow's kind of woman—blunt, working-class, hard-loving—could no longer compete in a world of sheltered heiresses, glamorous showgirls, powerful queens, and sexual hypocrisy. The star's nearest competitor, West, had cowritten many of her scripts at Paramount but had been forced to remove the sexual overtones from her jokes, so that by the end of the Thirties she seemed a bowdlerized relic of a bygone age.

McCall realized that she was brought in to work on a project that, minus Harlow and hamstrung by censorship, was distinctly "B" in quality.[5] In many ways, it was just a retelling of *Red Dust* in the modern American West. But since MGM wasn't attaching major stars to the project (and had no intention at the time of developing it as a series of films), it meant that McCall could do whatever she liked with Collison's flimsy "Broadway to Wyoming" yarn—including a complete rewrite and title change.

So, what's in a name? As far as *Maisie*'s status as a film about a working woman is concerned, plenty. Collison's "Dark Dame" is an alluring, dangerous, sexualized type, an image for the consumption of men. "Maisie" isn't a birth name but one that the main character, born Mary Anastasia O'Connor, created for her professional self. No man chose it for her. But "Maisie" was also a popular name for girls in the first half of twentieth-century America, so it was homegrown and familiar, not fancy. Of course, McCall was partial to it since a variant had been her mother's nickname (Mazie), and Sheila, Jerry, and Alan addressed their grandmother as "Granmazie." Mary Jr. often went by Mazie too.

When her Screen Writers Guild colleague Dashiell Hammett heard about the *Maisie* films, he assumed that MGM was adapting the magazine stories of his ex-lover, Nell Martin, which featured a heroine called Maisie St. Claire.[6] Martin's heroine started life in show business as a circus girl (her father was an acrobat) before taking a job as a stenographer in a law firm. She's always getting her boss, a judge, out of a jam. A "blithe and opinionated" flapper, she appeared in "The Hand Is Quicker Than the Eye" (January 1928), "All Is Not Wasted That Leaks" (February 1928), and "Move the Whole House" (June 1928), among others.

Despite Hammett's assumptions, McCall was freely adapting from Collison's novel rather than Martin's stories. That said, in an interview with critic Irene Thirer, producer Jack Ruben claimed that back in 1927 he had thought of writing a story about "a girl who'd been kicked around, but who was emotionally good, who managed to get other people's lives to rights without being an obvious Miss Fixit."[7] This was, of course, when Martin started writing her Maisie stories, and it is possible that Ruben remembered this Maisie too when he was put on the project with McCall.

But McCall was arguably more inspired by another "Mazie"—Mrs. Harriet Craig's outspoken maid in *Craig's Wife*. In cleverly combining George Kelly's "Mazie" with Collison's showgirl, McCall was able to access a working-class perspective and voice in her comic narrative. In all her many incarnations, Maisie would be the quintessential working-class girl in search of a job. Things don't always break her way, but Maisie's tough humor and Irish American good sense are her armor against any adversary. In McCall's first *Maisie*, written in January 1939, the heroine masquerades as Mrs. Ames's new maid to land a job and stay close to her cowboy love interest, Slim. Throughout much of the story it is her "servant's perspective" in the swank household that injects this run-of-the-mill modern western with some spirit. And so, rather than keep Collison's original title, *Dark Dame*, which referred to Mrs. Ames, the adulteress who drives her rancher husband to suicide, McCall retitled the script *Maisie*.

While Harlow's showgirl in *Red Dust* was spurred on her travels in search of the wealthy man who could keep her for a while (in exchange for sex), Maisie is her own lady and likes everything, as she puts it, "on the up and up." She wants a legit paycheck rather than a man to cover her next meal. Though Harlow mined all the nuances on the spectrum from gold digger to call girl in her brief but spectacular career, Maisie will do "anything . . . within reason" for a job, as she tells a crooked fairground barker. For Maisie, the operative phrase was always "within reason."

When we encounter Maisie in McCall's first script, she's swaggering down the main street of a small Wyoming cow town, with her gaudy showgirl's clothes, a suitcase, and a telegram promising her $75 a week to appear in "Frawley's Frolicks" review. Of course, the show has folded, and the unscrupulous manager has skipped town, leaving her jobless and penniless (she's spent her last dollar on the fare to Wyoming). Though she quickly talks her way into another job as an assistant in a fairground shooting gallery, her salary is a lowly $5 a week. And her boss is a creep.

Maisie hails a tall cowboy as he passes her stand, calling him "Slim"—as generic a name for a cowboy as "Bud" or "Tex," but McCall had a sense of humor. It turns out it's his real name. Men, Maisie knows all too well, always live down to women's expectations. When Slim refuses to pay for a round in the shooting gallery, she cajoles him: "Doing what you don't like to do strengthens your character. Look at me, I don't like the Wild West and I don't like this cheesy carnival . . . but I'm doing it, ain't I?" A job's a job. Was that too subtle for her former bosses at Warner Bros. to read between the lines? Was it too cheeky for her current bosses at MGM? McCall's Maisie might have done quite well as a studio executive, as she remarks later to Slim that she understands two languages: "English and double-talk."[8] It also more than qualified her to communicate with men.

Most of the action in *Maisie* takes place on a cattle ranch that is trying to pay its way in a modern economy, but the Brooklyn-born heroine isn't sentimental about the Old West. When ranch hand Shorty tries to interest her in the scenery by pointing out the last herd of buffalo roaming the western plains, Maisie responds coolly, "I like my buffalos on nickels." Later, after her romance with her cowpoke has been soured by the two-timing ranch owner's wife, Maisie tells the unsuspecting Mr. Ames that she's leaving the West: "I just don't belong out here where the spaces are wide and the minds are narrow."[9] But romantic disappointment doesn't faze Maisie; in her words, "I always bounce back." As a mythical place for fresh starts and a pioneering attitude, the West would serve the franchise well over the next decade. In addition to *Maisie*, McCall would set *Gold Rush Maisie* (1941), *Swing Shift Maisie* (1943), and *Maisie Goes to Reno* (1944) in the modern frontier. Still, Maisie never finds any dime novel heroes in the sagebrush.

McCall gambled that women wanted to see someone like themselves onscreen rather than another typical studio glamor girl of the period. Maisie doesn't wear gowns by Adrian or have her hair done by Sydney Guilaroff. She came of age in the Depression and is a shrewd survivor. As she points out to Slim, life "has prepared me for a right upper-cut and a double-cross, but up till now I've never been caught off balance." When Slim tries to disparage Maisie's efforts to finagle a job, saying the ranch doesn't need "pickpockets" or "strippers," she belts him in the face. When he patronizes her, saying she should be a "good little girl" and read a book, and asks, "You can read, can't you?," Maisie responds she could *write* one (meaning she could write a book about all the creepy men she's lost money over). But women are not always straight either, as she finds out from working with Mrs. Ames. When Maisie accidentally discovers Mrs. Ames with her handsome young lover, she says contemptuously, "You better put him back in his box." Maisie is dead honest, something which endears her to Mr. Ames. In fact, at the end of *Maisie*, after the cuckold Mr. Ames shoots himself and leaves his ranch to Maisie in his last-minute will, she offers Slim "a job"—as her husband.

As McCall remembered, she and producer Jack Ruben "were in such a small way of business that no one paid us the slightest attention, and we had great fun. We used to read the scenes over to each other and laugh and laugh."[10] She wrote the script in six weeks. While MGM really didn't care who played Maisie, Ruben, who had directed Harlow in *Riffraff* (1936) and understood the connection between the character and Harlow's legacy, allegedly refused to hire just any studio ingénue and said, "This is a part for a comedienne. Comedy is very hard to play. I would much rather put an inexperienced ingénue into a drama or tragedy than attempt to have her do comedy."[11] His blonde wife Virginia, who had starred in *The Great Ziegfeld* and more recently in McCall's *Women of Glamour*, had undoubted comic abilities, but was typecast as a languid society beauty. They needed someone with too many rough edges to be a conventional star, someone who would remind the public of Harlow . . . but with more scrubbed Irish honesty. Maisie was a woman who wore down-market costume jewelry and bargain basement clothes because she'd rather buy stuff she liked and could afford than to have some man pick them out for her in exchange for something she wasn't willing to give.

One night, Bruce and Ruben went to a double feature and saw Ann Sothern in a screwball comedy directed by a young Otto Preminger: *Danger—Love at Work*. "Immediately I knew she was Maisie," Ruben confessed. There was initial studio "opposition," and some trade papers had already announced that Virginia Grey, a director's daughter who made her film debut as Little Eva in *Uncle Tom's Cabin* (1927), would head the cast.[12] But with Ruben's constant pressure, the executives caved in.[13] Robert Young (Slim), Ruth Hussey (Mrs. Ames), Ian Hunter (Mr. Ames), and adorable, wide-eyed Cliff Edwards (Shorty), who would voice Jiminy Cricket in Disney's *Pinocchio* in 1940, rounded out the cast.

Ann Sothern had started life as Harriet Lake from Valley City, North Dakota, and worked for Florenz Ziegfeld in New York, but in the 1930s she was hired by Columbia and headed back West. It was Harry Cohn who changed her name to Ann Sothern. She played a collection of forgettable ingénues and second leads at Columbia and later RKO. Frustrated by career setbacks, according to Louella Parsons, Sothern married Roger Pryor and more or less dropped out of Hollywood until a good part came along. *Maisie* was her salvation. As Parsons remarked, *Maisie* is "the surprise movie of the year, a picture that no one on the lot knew or even cared was being made and which is better than the majority of pictures."[14] Critics gave McCall a lot of the credit, awarding *Maisie* the top award for the "Screenplay Which Most Completely Disregarded Its Source Material."[15] *Maisie* also represented a type of double bill "B" picture usually farmed out to the less affluent small town theaters of America, but one that became so popular with mainstream audiences that it achieved A status with the studios and got superb reviews. As one journalist put it, "Maisie is definitely a word-of-mouth picture."[16]

Sothern would become one of the biggest stars of the 1940s playing Maisie, and her comic timing, the result of endless hours of practice alone and with McCall, Rubin, and later cowriter Betty Reinhardt as an audience, made the "trenchant and humorous lines of Mary C. McCall Jr." some of the best-known one-liners during the war years.[17] Sothern, unlike McCall, was a political conservative, but the two women responded to what they did have in common: humor, a formidable work ethic, and loads of experience dealing with dismissive, patronizing, or handsy men. As the streetwise performer, Sothern embodied the modern American pioneer woman who had every curveball thrown at her but dodged each one with aplomb and a good clapback. As an article in *The MGM*

Studio News noted, "18 months ago, after 8 years of assorted ingénue roles in which she had little more to do than look nice while the hero rescued her, or the comedian used her as a stooge, she announced that she never would play another straight leading role in motion pictures." Sothern said enthusiastically, "I've had the time of my life playing these different characters. Maisie the honkytonk girl who found love in the wide-open spaces was such a far cry from straight leading roles that I reveled in her."[18]

From the beginning, Ruben and McCall knew that Maisie's wisecracks and sound advice for women, authored by McCall, would be the big selling points for the franchise. Film posters and lobby cards promised "Everybody's crazy about Maisie," and included some of her typical quips: "You're a big shot, but Maisie will whittle you down to size!" and "I've been thrown down before but Maisie always bounces back!"[19] Although McCall did appear on the one-sheet poster, publicists did not always include McCall in smaller advertisements or pressbooks. Only the main cast members and director Edwin Marin and producer Ruben regularly made the cut. It's possible these omissions were studio payback for her contract dispute in 1938. In the first *Maisie* pressbook, there were articles on Marin and Ruben, stars Sothern, Young, Hunter, and Hussey—even features on how Cliff Edwards got a case of sunburned feet—but nothing about the woman who wrote the script. If McCall wanted recognition she had to get it from the likes of Louella Parsons.

At least MGM hired her to write another Maisie script as soon as the good reviews began to roll in. Hollywood had experimented with female-led serials and franchises before (*The Perils of Pauline*, 1914), but, more recently, Warner Bros. had no masterplan to make a film series starring Torchy Blane (Glenda Farrell) when *Smart Blonde* (1937) was released to surprise acclaim. Subsequent films followed with little financial or story investment on the studio's part. Farrell was even recast twice, and the second unpopular recasting (Jane Wyman) killed off the series for good. The studio's other youth series, *Nancy Drew*, starring blonde Bonita Granville, lasted only a couple of years. Columbia's slightly longer-lived series, *Blondie* (Columbia, 1938–42), based on Chic Young's comic strip, was another story of a clever young woman (but the bane of her existence was her bumbling husband rather than incompetent cops). Only MGM's male-centered *Andy Hardy* pictures for Mickey Rooney (1937–46) could compete with *Maisie*'s longevity and box office.[20] Maisie was even a trend-setter. Ginger Rogers's Academy Award–winning performance as Irish American working girl *Kitty Foyle* (1940) owes a lot to Maisie's never-say-die attitude, and Marsha Hunt's comedic turn in Isobel Lennart's satire *The Affairs of Martha* (1942) also has a touch of Maisie's class consciousness and humor.

Unfortunately for McCall, the studio still had unused options on Collison material and told her to adapt *Congo Landing* (1934), a rehash of the novelist's *Red Dust*. Collison's ubiquitous blonde is a low-grade entertainer called Dolly who is stranded in Africa with her partner. Over the course of improbable events, Dolly helps a local doctor perform an operation, and in return he lets her stay with him. His wife, perhaps understandably, leaves. McCall did the best she could and finished *Congo Maisie* that July. In her story Maisie, broke again, is trying to reach her next engagement in a nightclub in Africa. She stows away on a boat before realizing it's going in the wrong direction. The boat breaks down and she treks through the jungle in heels in search of the nearest settlement. Her companion, a bad-tempered rubber planter and former doctor, is a less attractive version of Slim. The white compound in the jungle is a stand-in for the ranch. The trouble is, while Maisie's ranch had harmless buffalo and cattle (and no Indians), *Congo Maisie* is riddled with derogatory portrayals of local Africans, who appeared mostly as hostile or childlike savages to be manipulated by white plantation owners and Maisie. Many of the African men (there aren't any women or children) are under the influence of voodoo priests and threaten to wipe out the white settlements. If it weren't for Maisie's presence in the compound, it's hard not to wish them luck.

Although the film got good reviews, the rest of the *Maisie* films would stay stateside and avoided *Congo Maisie*'s mixture of exoticism and racism.[21] But the second film established the franchise's rule that Maisie would never stay with the same guy or get married: Maisie "loves 'em and leaves 'em."[22] The men in her life were as impermanent as her jobs. And while losing a job when she was down to her last nickel was devastating, audiences learned that getting rid of a guy isn't always so sad. To Maisie men are replaceable like cars, and, like cars, there's a new model coming around every minute. When the matron in *Congo Maisie* (Rita Johnson) falls for the cranky, single rubber planter, Maisie advises her to stick to her husband. As for the other guy? "Oh, he's a kind of special job. A *de luxe* model of what he is—white wall tires, two horns and fog lights, but leaving out the gadgets—it's the same old car! You'd have a great six months. And when I say six months, I'm allowing for shrinkage. Three's nearer."[23]

Away from the studio, McCall and Jack Ruben were an equally formidable team. As members of the Hollywood Anti-Nazi League, they broke with some of their fellow members over the German-Soviet Non-Aggression Pact of August 23.

Unlike many of her communist screenwriter colleagues and Anti-Nazi League members, McCall would not find any excuses for the Soviet Union's alliance with Hitler's anti-Semitic regime. She also reminded her colleagues very pointedly that fascism was not purely a European disease. At a meeting of the Hollywood Anti-Nazi League on October 21, she and Ruben exposed more than four hundred Hollywood workers as members of the resurgent KKK (including an MGM extra). *Boxoffice*, covering the scandal, commented that fascism "came uncomfortably close to home."[24]

A week later she made even bigger waves with her first bid for the presidency of the guild. It was the first time a woman had run for the office, and many of the male writers were shocked at the possibility of a woman in charge. She was more than qualified, having spent four years in the top ranks of guild management pursuing the contract and keeping the organization alive during the crisis of 1936. But politics were against her. She was strongly anti-Nazi and pro-British, and her criticism of the Soviet Union's alliance with Hitler was not popular with her communist colleagues. So it was no surprise when her ex–Warner Bros. colleague Sheridan Gibney (*The Story of Louis Pasteur*, 1936) won. He was male and a member of the communist League of American Writers, which was then following the Soviet Union's peaceful stance toward Germany.[25] McCall's good friend, writer Harry Tugend, recalled being utterly appalled when he returned to Los Angeles to find the Hollywood Anti-Nazi League had been renamed "The American Peace Mobilization," thereby removing any criticism of Germany in deference to the Soviet Union's new ally.[26] After the Soviets invaded Finland on November 30, McCall resigned her membership in protest.

Writers, actors, and other filmmakers opposed to Hitler faced another uphill battle against conservatives in Hollywood and in Washington, from McCall's former bête noire Charles Lindbergh to Y. Frank Freeman, who viewed the many British foreigners in Hollywood as a threat to American jobs. "We should take care of Americans first," the producer proclaimed in the press.[27] McCall, acting as president in Gibney's absence, disagreed and offered "a welcoming hand": "Writing and directing are unique talents," she stated. "It isn't as if one hundred carpenters and electricians arrived to take the jobs away from Americans. With 52 pictures a year at each major studio, there aren't enough writers to supply original ideas, so we welcome the refugees."[28]

McCall continued to offer her public support to the many actor refugees from Europe who had fled the Nazis. She wrote a story of an Anglo-American love affair, "Second Hand Ghost," which became the New Year's radio broadcast for CBS's Silver Theater, starring Conrad Nagel and Wendy Barrie.[29] While back in her grandfather John A. McCall's day it was fairly common for wealthy American heiresses to head across the pond as financial bait for impoverished English lords, McCall reversed the gender roles, putting the wealthy American man on the marriage market for the highborn Wendy Barrie. It was a new twist that gave the woman the historic power and land and made the American man the handsome title hunter. Her sympathy with Britain made her a whole new group of allies, many of them concentrated in the acting and writing professions.

In early 1940 MGM thanked McCall and Ruben for their successful work on the Maisie series by assigning them to a distinctly "A" feature for Joan Crawford: Louis Bromfield's *Night in Bombay*. At the time, Bromfield, another Pulitzer Prize-winning novelist, was popular with middlebrows, but McCall was dismissive, suspecting that the poorly researched novel was written "on the porch of the hotel in Bombay." She hired an Indian woman to assist her with language and wrote a strong first and revised draft called *Bombay Nights* that the top brass felt "had taken a rather formless novel and given it form."[30] When the studio then assigned it to a new writer, Ruben protested that McCall should remain the sole writer on a project in which she had invested so much creative energy. Then he was removed from the project too. It felt almost like Warner Bros.

One afternoon a couple years later, her friend Jane Murfin telephoned to ask McCall to translate some Hindi, since she remembered that she'd worked on an "Indian picture." McCall, instantly realizing what had happened to her old assignment, told her there was a glossary at the front of her second script. Murfin was stunned; no one had ever told her McCall had worked on the project, and she did not have access to any previous scripts. It was McCall's turn to be stunned. "What stage of the work are you in?" McCall asked. "I am reading the book aloud to Hunt Stromberg," she replied. They sat in the producer's office each afternoon, she read, and he listened. "Of course," Murfin admitted, "the telephone rings 18 or 20 times an hour, and it makes it a little confusing, but that is what we are doing!" The picture was never made.

Something similar happened to Elizabeth Pickett Chevalier's *Drivin' Woman*, a best-selling historical follow-up to *Gone with the Wind* serialized and optioned by the studio in 1941 but eventually shelved due to serial studio mismanagement and lethargy. McCall was one of several women writers at MGM who worked on the ill-fated female-led historical drama.[31]

Fortunately, in lieu of *Bombay Nights* or *Drivin' Woman*, she and Ruben were given the green light for the third *Maisie* film. There was some more good news: The studio finally agreed that it had run out of Collison material, and Ruben told her to do what she wanted. Delighted, she revisited one of the few things she had liked about the original—its western setting. In developing *Gold Rush Maisie*, she played upon the accelerating interest in frontier film narratives, the rising numbers of women who now headed West in search of financial security, and Maisie's own tendency to be labeled a "gold digger" by the men she rebuffs. *Gold Rush Maisie* opens with a shot of the wide-open spaces of the Southwest, and Maisie sputtering down the road in an old jalopy. There's no Slim, but instead there's a bad-tempered prospector she calls "Tex" (Lee Bowman) whom she persuades to help her with her car to she can get to her singing gig in the next town. The job has already been taken, so Maisie joins up with some itinerant sharecroppers who have heard of a nearby gold strike.

Ruben shrewdly chose Betty Reinhardt to collaborate with McCall. Reinhardt was a newcomer to MGM and the Screen Writers Guild, and the women became close friends and such great collaborators that even Ann Sothern was fooled by which writer wrote which gag. She and Reinhardt reteamed for *Maisie Was a Lady* (1941) and *Maisie Gets Her Man* (1942), both set in New York. McCall, who always felt guilty that Reinhardt never got "the recognition that she deserved" on the series, mentored her at the guild and was delighted when Darryl F. Zanuck later assigned Reinhardt to adapt Vera Caspary's noir thriller *Laura* in 1943 after she left MGM.[32]

Sothern was, in McCall's estimation, "the most professional, the most rewarding actress to work for."[33] They had one disagreement. Sothern wanted McCall to write Maisie a drunk scene for *Gold Rush Maisie*. McCall insisted that Maisie was always in control, and a central part of her character was her abstemiousness: "She is too embattled against the world to weaken her defenses by getting drunk," she argued. Sothern suggested that she be "tricked into drinking." McCall cautiously agreed, but she wasn't going to make it a cute drunk scene, where Maisie simply becomes an innocent figure of fun for the in-control hero.

Early in the film Maisie's car has broken down, and she seeks shelter at Tex's cabin. He thinks Maisie needs to pay him that night for his assistance, but not with money. When she doesn't warm to the idea, he tries to make her more sexually compliant by getting her drunk on hard lemonade. But Maisie is tougher and smarter than any prospector; she fends off Tex's heavy-handed pass and locks him out of the bedroom. She had already dealt with sexual harassment in her first two films, but this scene was franker in its portrayal of potential sexual violence against women.

Sothern loved the scene and telephoned McCall so she could run her lines with her and practice the timing, so that, within three pulls on the lemonade, the inexperienced Maisie is distinctly "fuzzy." As McCall later remembered, "I went over to the set.... She had worked it out the way you would work out a piano exercise with a metronome, and yet, when she played it, you would swear that it had never been rehearsed before.... So I want to go down as one of Ann Sothern's great fans."[34]

With the unpleasant Tex out of the picture for a while, Maisie hooks up with a family of ex-Arkansas sharecroppers who have been picking fruit at various farms over the past two years. Their two older children have had no chance to go to school, and money is nonexistent. Maisie's early scenes with them put her own job troubles in perspective, and, as they all head toward a rumored gold strike in the mountains, she does her best to prevent the family from being scammed by squatters who've taken all the good land with water and another grocer who is charging extortionate prices for pork and beans. The only solidarity in the film exists between Maisie and her family and the film's other working women. There's a brief scene between a weary waitress and out-of-work, out-of-luck Maisie that is very effective in conveying the bond between two broke girls in a shithole town. Jubilee, or Juby, the sharecroppers' daughter (played by Virginia Weidler), is in awe of Maisie, and is delighted when the showgirl trades her gaudy dress and heels for some trousers and a pickax. As Maisie tells the family, she remembers the day when she got mad at some fellow for calling her a gold digger! Now she is proud of the name.

But *Gold Rush Maisie* is best known for expounding the Maisie philosophy of life. As they wearily trudge toward the gold site, Maisie advises Juby: "Well, anyway, if you work for what you get, it can be anything and you don't have to apologize for it. But if you ever take anything from anybody, be sure it's the best.... Listen, as soon as you take something from somebody, you've lost part of your right to tell 'em to go jump in the lake and that's awful important for a girl on her own. So you gotta be sure that what they're offering is tops. If it's a fur coat it's gotta be the genuine article.... And if it's jewelry? 14 carats or no thanks. And if it's love? Well, if he gives you his whole heart, grab it quick cause there's nothing better than that. But don't ever go shares."[35] Juby replies she wants to be exactly like Maisie when she grows up. But Maisie wasn't just a role model for young girls.

In 1941 *Photoplay* profiled the impact the films had on American women, who had been writing in droves to Ann Sothern, asking her advice on love, career, and marriage.[36]

Maisie Ravier may have been a distillation of the never-say-die, working-class, Depression-era woman of McCall and Reinhardt's generation, but she also wasn't above poking fun at the New Deal. Though many praised *The Grapes of Wrath* (1939) for bringing up the plight of Dust Bowl migrants, Steinbeck's chronicle of the sharecropping Joad family was set in 1934. By 1940, when Twentieth Century-Fox produced the film adaptation, the Joads were part of a recent, painful, past. The family eventually reaches California, and, thanks to Nunnally Johnson's clever script, the Joads look like they've found their feet in a government-run camp. *Gold Rush Maisie*, in contrast, is set in 1940 and shows hundreds of ex-sharecropping families still without steady work. Owning their own land and striking it rich in a gold rush are unattainable frontier fantasies, and the Depression has never gone away. Maisie feels the pain and embarrassment of the nomad family she rides with but tells them, "Listen, I'd like to have a dime for every dollar I've got on credit! It's a wonder I haven't got a government job!" As one reviewer argued, "The plight of the migrants is realistically presented, and the film contains an unmistakable plea for a deeper understanding of their needs" without sacrificing entertainment.[37] *Motion Picture Herald* asked "why more pictures like this and fewer historicals, biographicals, and extravaganzas, are not produced."[38] The answer lay in the studios' basic conservatism and preference for men's "great lives." Maisie was focused on a modern woman of the working class and her struggles came closer to mirroring the average American's.

If the New Deal turned out to be a raw deal for some Americans, Maisie also knew that women usually got a raw deal from men. In fact, in all of Maisie's films it is men who are responsible for making her lose her jobs. Maisie's attitude is simply, "When Heaven forgets to protect the working girl, she has to do the best she can on her own." This might also have been a motto for Hollywood's many female writers in their dealings with producers. Look out for yourself, cultivate your own career, and make the best choices you can under the circumstances. Being a screenwriter at MGM was one of the best paid jobs available to women in the 1930s and 1940s. Anyone else might have just taken the money without complaint. But Hollywood writers still did not have a signed and sealed contract with their employers. And McCall, like Maisie, was unafraid of tangling with the big boys, no matter the personal cost.

1. Mary C. McCall Jr.'s mother, Mazie Burke (1902), McCall-Bramson Collection

2. McCall with her father Leo (1910), McCall-Bramson Collection

3. McCall (center) with her Vassar College newspaper colleagues (1924), McCall-Bramson Collection

THE ·· 1·9·2·5 ⬭ V·A·S·S·A·R·I·O·N

MARY C. McCALL
Lydecker St.
Englewood, N. J.

4. McCall's yearbook photo in *The Vassarion* (1925), Vassar College archives

5. Dwight Franklin aboard the *Arcturus* (1925), McCall-Bramson Collection

6. McCall in the family garden in Englewood (1926), McCall-Bramson Collection

7. With Dwight Franklin at
the Beaux Arts Ball (1930),
McCall-Bramson Collection

8. Publicity photo for
The Goldfish Bowl (1931),
McCall-Bramson Collection

9. With Douglas Fairbanks Jr. on the set of *It's Tough to Be Famous* (1932), McCall-Bramson Collection

10. The key creatives of *Craig's Wife* (1936), left to right: Viola Lawrence, Rosalind Russell, McCall, and Dorothy Arzner, author's collection

11. With Dorothy Arzner
(1936), author's collection

12. Dwight Franklin discussing *Captain Blood* with director Michael Curtiz (1935),
Academy of Motion Picture Arts and Sciences

13. With Leo Carrillo on the Columbia Pictures lot (1937), author's collection

14. Lighting up between scripts (1938), McCall-Bramson Collection

15. *Maisie* (1939), author's collection

16. With Donald Ogden Stewart and Dorothy Parker at a Hollywood Anti-Nazi League meeting (1940), McCall-Bramson Collection

17. With Eleanor Roosevelt in Los Angeles (April 1941), McCall-Bramson Collection

18. The two Maisies (1942), Academy of Motion Picture Arts and Sciences

19. Presenting at the Academy Awards (1943), Academy of Motion Picture Arts and Sciences

20. With Michael Kanin at the Academy Awards (1943), Academy of Motion Picture Arts and Sciences

21. Bette and Bobby Davis, the Academy Awards (1943), Academy of Motion Picture Arts and Sciences

22. A birthday present from Bette Davis (1943), author's collection

23. Jerry, Sheila, Mary-David, and Alan (1947), McCall-Bramson Collection

24. A Screen Writers Guild group photo (1952), Writers Guild Foundation Library

25. Ella Raines in action in *Ride the Man Down* (1952), author's collection

26. On the Radio Free Europe trip (1961), McCall-Bramson Collection

27. At daughter Mary-David's wedding (1968), McCall-Bramson Collection

28. Mary-David and McCall's granddaughter at Freedom of Choice Day (1981), McCall-Bramson Collection

CHAPTER 9

Golden Girls and Brass Rings

In early 1941 *Los Angeles Times* film critic Philip K. Scheuer gushed that Maisie was "first in the hearts of the Fox-West Coast people" and could do no wrong.[1] With the franchise well established, McCall and Reinhardt took Maisie back to McCall's New York roots and decided to take a chance with the content, creating scenarios where the heroine experienced the realities of sexism in America. In *Maisie Was a Lady*, a rich playboy (Lew Ayres, in a reprise of his 1938 *Holiday* role) gets drunk and ruins Maisie's circus act but, feeling contrite, lends her his car to get back to the city. Of course, the police pick her up on suspicion of grand theft, and the next day the judge is quick to assume Maisie's guilt based on her gender and class (he sneers at her working-class Brooklyn accent and the number of jobs she's lost). Edwin Schallert took note that since *Gold Rush Maisie*, Ann Sothern's wisecracking golden girl had become "a decidedly sociological heroine," but figured "no doubt, MGM has found that surrounding the so-spontaneous and adventurous heroine with current problems pays."[2]

In McCall's *Ringside Maisie*, she's fired from her dancing gig when her male partner sexually harasses her. Jobless, she ends up being a caretaker to the ailing mother of a rising professional boxer and makes friends with his cynical manager, played by George Murphy. In *Maisie Gets Her Man*, Sothern is teamed with bashful comic Red Skelton, and the two fail in everything but their friendship. In each of these cases Maisie faces what most working-class women in America faced: a succession of temporary or unstable jobs that could be lost through a man's carelessness, if they didn't agree to have sex with their bosses, or through plain bad luck. Whatever the 30 percent female component of the American workforce had seen over the years, Maisie had seen too. She complained when she could, even though she knew it rarely did any good. But in her personal life and at work

Maisie was honest and unafraid of challenging the status quo. Like the women who came to see her films, she continued to wear off-the-rack clothes, several years out of date. Her heels were worn down and her jewelry wasn't understated, because she couldn't afford understatement. Her speech was even blunter, and she didn't apologize for that.

There were hierarchies everywhere at MGM too. McCall's old *Screen Guilds' Magazine* adversary, Donald Ogden Stewart, was now a studio colleague. But he continued to pen top adaptations about the rich and famous (*The Philadelphia Story*, 1940) and had fawning male admirers hovering around him in the commissary. McCall, author of the studio's cut-rate woman-of-the-people saga, must have felt the irony of the writers' political situation. In January 1941, as Sidney Skolsky reported in his column, Stewart and McCall were lunching at the writers' table with another writer, Tom Jenk. "When Martha [the waitress] asked Tom Jenk at the far end of the table what he wished, the writer looked toward Stewart's plate and asked, 'what's that Stewart's having?' Martha answered, 'a veal cutlet.' 'I'll have that,' said Jenk. Then Martha asked, 'what'll it be to drink?' Tom Jenk looked toward Stewart, and asked, 'what's Stewart drinking?' Martha answered, 'tea with cream.' 'I'll have that,' said Tom Jenk. It was then that Mary McCall interjected, 'Tom, that isn't how you become a writer.'"[3]

Maisie never made the big time in any of her stories, though offscreen she earned dividends for MGM. Edwin Marin, who directed the first, third, fourth, and fifth installments of the Maisie franchise, was nevertheless quick to downplay the Maisie phenomenon. As he remarked in an interview, "She's a born fixer-upper of other people's problems, often at the expense of patching up her own, but she should never become the center of any sociological problem or attempt to solve any serious large-scale difficulties. . . . When she becomes involved in any legal or technical thinking she's out of her depth and loses her entertainment value. Let her battle on the basis of intuition, instinct, and her own experience, and she's good for another fifteen rounds.'"[4] For Marin, Maisie was essentially a good-hearted but dumb blonde with some entertainment value. But as far as McCall was concerned, even among Hollywood's hack directors, Marin wasn't particularly bright. Years later, she couldn't even bring herself to mention him by name in her memoirs: "The directors, since these were low-budget pictures, were not the most talented in town."[5] When she first met Marin on the set of *Maisie*, he announced he "had a great idea to contribute." McCall worried this would involve extensive rewrites, but "it turned out to be that when a Chinese manservant said, 'Mr. Slim plenty glad to get away,' Marin wanted him to say the same line but *add a whistle*! And that was his sole contribution." She saved the ultimate putdown for last: "This man shot whatever you wrote, including the typographical errors."

McCall was aware that while she wrote gags in which Maisie deflects harassment and fights assault, things were not as easy for the rest of America's working women—including those who worked in Hollywood. The star of her next film, *Kathleen* (1941), was Shirley Temple. During the Depression Temple had been the top box-office draw and was a key factor in keeping Twentieth Century-Fox in business. For years, screenwriters at Fox had rewritten old Mary Pickford hits for Temple and fellow studio star Janet Gaynor. The actresses' fresh appeal gave this tired star packaging some life, but when the stale plots continued and both actresses aged outside of Zanuck's comfort zone, first Gaynor and then Temple were fired. Temple had worked since she could walk and, with her ringlets and dimples, had been the country's favorite little girl. But in 1940, after the lackluster *Susannah and the Mounties*, Zanuck terminated her contract.[6]

Things went from bad to worse for her at MGM. In her first meeting with her prospective producer, Arthur Freed, the older man exposed his penis in his office and invited her to become his next star in exchange for sex. Temple, paralyzed, could only giggle nervously and fled the office.[7] Then Freed started spreading rumors about her, saying her career was finished. Temple's mother's concurrent meeting with Louis B. Mayer was equally ominous. The mogul began: "Never forget...at MGM we are a family"—and then sexually assaulted her. Temple's contract was reworked from two films to one, and for months the actress fretted over just what that one film might be.

Virginia Weidler was about Temple's age, and before she became a juvenile star at MGM and was assigned to *Gold Rush Maisie* she played Kay Van Riper's poor little rich girl "Kathleen" in an April 1939 radio broadcast for the Star Theatre. Once *Gold Rush Maisie* boosted Weidler's career, someone sympathetic to Temple attached McCall and Temple to *Kathleen*. The writer had a knack for creating material for young actors. Around the same time her short story "Fraternity," purchased by Fox, became the basis for Roddy McDowall's first starring role after *How Green Was My Valley*.[8] Both *Kathleen* and "Fraternity" explored the loneliness and jealousy experienced by preteen children and were inspired by McCall's troubled relationship with her eldest child.

McCall's adaptation of *Kathleen* was in some ways a reworking of an earlier Mary Pickford vehicle, *Poor Little Rich Girl*, the story of a lonely girl who dreams of having a loving family. Herbert Marshall was cast as Kathleen's distant father, with Gail Patrick and newcomer Laraine Day playing versions of Hollywood's bad girl and good woman (though McCall's "good woman" is a child psychologist hired to look after Kathleen). Temple worked hard on her lines and characterization; she knew she had to make a success of the role but never learned that her part was based on the writer's daughter.[9]

Sheila was now an articulate ten-year-old but had never had much of a relationship with her mother. Although in the early 1940s the press played up McCall's role as a parent, it was canny studio publicity to soften her image as a professional woman. One item by her friend Skolsky described him walking through the commissary, where he was drawn to the writers' table by the sound of laughter. McCall and Betty Reinhardt were doing Sheila's geography homework, giving it a Maisie-esque touch. As Skolsky reported, the two women, with colleague Mark Connelly chiming in, helped make "a map of a mythical country" and provided Sheila with a unique set of names for cities, mountains, streets, and geographical features.[10] These are some of the names they came up with: "Silver Fox Cape, Moot Point, Jello Sea, Estuary Politely, Rudy Vallee, Great Kitchen Range, Hositt Bayou, Peak Aboo, East Inks, Cecil Rhoades, Julian Street, Priscilla Lane, Widow's Peak, Grape Harbor, and Stag at Bay." It was a map of Hollywood, but, as Skolsky commented, "The teacher, it is needless to add, was bewildered."

This little news item did nothing to counteract the very real, long-term effects of absentee parenting. Sheila wanted to dance, but her mother pushed her into acting. The girl was sent to camp in Maine on the other side of the country rather than having to spend the summer with her parents. The boys got even less parental time. Sheila doted on her father but was too in awe of her mother to have a close relationship with her. "All she had to say was: 'I'd rather you didn't' to one of my suggestions, and I would freeze," Sheila remembered.[11] She certainly didn't experience the warm relationship Juby had with Maisie. Her governess, Georgia Chapman, raised Sheila, and the girl felt her school friend Pamela Herbert (writer F. Hugh Herbert's daughter) got along better with her mother than she did. It is true that Pamela and McCall had a bond that went beyond their shared birthdays. Temperamentally, the "quite centered and pragmatic" Pamela had a lot more in common with McCall than Sheila. Even at a young age Pamela aspired to be a writer like McCall and her father. (She went on to work for television legend Norman Lear.)

McCall never revealed whether she felt guilty about her distant relationship with Sheila and the twins Jerry and Alan. Whatever parenting experiences she remembered became grist for her writing. According to her younger daughter Mary-David, McCall also worked stories about Franklin's childhood as a prankster into Kathleen's attempts to get her father's attention. Franklin, of course, had grown up an only child, fatherless as Kathleen is motherless, but Jean Franklin had been an engaged, loving single parent.

Thanks to Mary Baker, Franklin had also joined MGM in 1939 as part "of the Metro research staff," but it wasn't the sort of job he enjoyed. He was massively overqualified, and since the studio was Cedric Gibbons's domain there was no chance that Franklin could become a studio art director in his own right. James Cagney wanted Franklin back at Warner Bros. so the two could develop a John Paul Jones biopic together. According to Cagney, "my friend, Dwight Franklin, the sculptor" said, "not only did I resemble Jones very strongly in facial characteristics, but that our physical measurements, general attitude, personality, everything, seemed to be identical. He urged me to play Jones on the screen."[12] When the project fell through, Franklin became depressed. It didn't help matters that his mother Jean was seventy and still living alone in Manhattan. When her health started to deteriorate in the fall of 1940, Franklin told McCall he wanted to go back to New York.

Although McCall was normally too busy with the studio and Screen Writers Guild work, she accompanied him. While in town, *Variety* claimed that it was rumored Franklin was "negotiating for a post with a New York museum."[13] They returned the first week in December. Franklin didn't get the job—very likely the replacement for the current president of the Museum of Natural History, aviator and politician F. Trubee Davison, who remained director until 1941, when he became assistant secretary of war.[14] Franklin returned to work with DeMille and Cooper on *The Story of Dr. Wassell* (1941) and *Reap the Wild Wind* (1942) with Ray Milland and John Wayne, but it was a time of massive personal and professional disappointment for him.

McCall might have looked like the devoted wife accompanying Franklin to New York during his mother's illnesses, but while in town she had begun another affair. Nickolas Muray was born in Hungary of Jewish parents and moved to New York as a young man, establishing a successful photographic portrait studio in

Greenwich Village from 1920. He made his name photographing gorgeous celebrities but was rather fit himself, having twice been on the Olympic fencing team. Today Muray is perhaps best remembered for his ten-year relationship with Mexican artist Frida Kahlo, which began in 1931 and continued through her marriage to Diego Rivera. But in 1940 he moved on to McCall, and things became serious enough for her to bring Sheila along to see whether "they could make it together" as a family. It must have been serious if Muray was considering marrying a woman who had three children and wasn't simply going to leave them with the father. He took McCall's portrait in 1941, a bold and sultry glamor shot where white hands and layers of pearls contrast with shadowy eyes and lips. According to her daughters, Franklin urged McCall to see as much of Muray as possible to get him out of her system. He had other things to worry about: Jean Franklin died on August 26, 1941, in her home in Manhattan.[15] She was seventy-one.

Over the years, McCall and Franklin had amassed powerful friends across all parts of the industry. Their three kids, handsome home, and successful lifestyle made them a good advertisement for the Hollywood film industry and worked to offset any danger incurred by her association with the Hollywood labor movement. Even when she had affairs in the past or had ignored her children in the interests of work, she and Franklin remained a united front. Contemplating divorce just as she was beginning to wield significant power in the industry appears, with hindsight, strikingly self-destructive. Perhaps it was madness to risk everything for a stunning new lover. But her male colleagues did it all the time, and McCall was, after all, a firm believer in equal rights.

Her relationship with Muray also had a political edge, since it occurred at a time when anti-Semitism in the United States, sometimes masked by calls for nonintervention in the Second World War, was at its height.[16] The rise of an anti-Semitic Ku Klux Klan and a series of immigration acts targeting Eastern Europeans in the 1920s was followed in the 1930s by popular radio stars such as Father Coughlin praising Hitler and Mussolini while denouncing communism and the Jews. McCall's old bête noir Charles Lindbergh headed the anti-Semitic America First Committee (1940–41), which aimed to keep the country out of war.

As an industry dominated by Jewish producers and film executives, Hollywood was an obvious target for anti-Semitic attacks. But as the labor movement gained traction in town during the 1930s, a cabal of right-wing political critics denounced the film industry as a hotbed of communist activism. Since 1938 various

Washington representatives of the House Committee on Un-American Activities (HUAC) had grilled Hollywood stars suspected of communism; McCall's friends Humphrey Bogart, James Cagney, and Melvyn Douglas had to clear themselves the previous year with committee head Martin Dies.[17] Anyone active in the guilds, supportive of the New Deal, or opposed to fascism was a potential target. Jean Muir was the only actor brave enough (or foolish enough) to ignore Dies. While Dies, California Senator Jack Tenney, and Democratic Senator from Montana Burton K. Wheeler made headlines attacking Hollywood's support of labor and antifascism, McCall was one of the few to go on the offensive against Dies and his colleagues in the press. In March 1940 she drafted a resolution on behalf of Hollywood's screenwriters calling for Dies's "removal" from the House committee, since, in his criticism of Hollywood film plots, he was nothing more than "a political censor."[18]

Although in August 1940 Wheeler announced he was moving beyond questioning individuals and was now investigating Hollywood's pro-Allied propaganda, singling out *Confessions of a Nazi Spy* (1939) and *The Sea Hawk* (1940), the tide was turning against him and other conservative extremists.[19] Roosevelt and Churchill signed the Atlantic Charter that same month, and the House of Representatives passed a draft extension by one vote. By 1941, perhaps because Hollywood producers rather than mere actors and writers were now subjected to their own political investigation for subversive film content, the industry's response was more robust and bipartisan (Republican Wendell Willkie represented the studios in the inquiry). That fall McCall and Melvyn Douglas got up on stage for the "Film Art Fight for Freedom" rally in Hollywood. Sidney Skolsky reported in the *New York Post* on October 25, "There will be sketches in which Charles A. Lindbergh and Sen. Wheeler will be kidded."[20] McCall wrote them.

As McCall was assigned to Ann Sothern's rare non-Maisie vehicle *Panama Hattie* that November, U.S. relations with Japan worsened and Roosevelt stepped closer to the war in Europe, granting the Free French Lend-Lease on November 24. On December 7, two days after McCall handed in her script, the Japanese attacked Pearl Harbor and America declared war, joining Britain in the fight against Germany, Italy, and Japan. It was probably not the time to break up a picture-perfect family image. McCall was forced to spend the next couple of weeks working out the kinks in her December 5 script with new director Roy Del Ruth (a replacement for Norman McLeod), but according to Sidney Skolsky's column, she "fled to New York" when "she discovered two other writers were also working on the rewrite of *Panama Hattie*."[21] It was reasonable cover for a quick trip to square things with Muray.

Kathleen was filling theaters while she was in town. Although *Variety* and the *New York Times* critics had disliked the film, most trade papers and audiences enjoyed it, and *Variety* had to eat its words when the film turned out solid box office that winter and spring.[22] *The Hollywood Reporter* hailed it as "one of the most exciting movies of the season" and promised audiences, "No better story could have been devised" for Temple's return to the screen "than this screenplay by Mary McCall Jr."[23] It was "a brilliant, inspired piece of writing—a striking penetrating analysis of a child's mind." McCall's script helped Temple reassert herself as an actress and star. After her horrible experience with Freed, Temple had been convinced *Kathleen* "was destined to bomb" and was pleasantly surprised when the good reviews appeared after the premiere, praising her transition into "an engaging juvenile actress." A few years later, she confessed to *Los Angeles Times* critic Edwin Schallert that in comparison to her other work she "quite liked" the film, since she wasn't playing a perfect, "sweet" little girl.[24]

McCall returned to Los Angeles, where, in addition to being vice president of the Screen Writers Guild, she served on the Motion Picture Relief Committee and was soon asked to serve on the Hollywood Mobilization Committee.[25] With notable Democrat friends Dorothy Arzner, Helen Gahagan Douglas, and Dorothy Parker, she was also part of the Women's Speakers' Bureau, which helped with women's efforts for the USO in Los Angeles.[26] She also returned to another Maisie script and the almost daily grind of meetings with producers to finalize the guild contract.

As their birthdays approached, she met up with Bette Davis for their annual party. They both had problems to discuss. After resigning from the presidency of the Academy over the Christmas holidays, Davis lost her bid for a historic third Oscar, playing Lillian Hellman's Regina in *The Little Foxes* (1941). Warner Bros. still didn't pay her enough. But her personal life was in better shape. After divorcing her first husband, bandleader Ham Nelson, she had married businessman Arthur Farnsworth in 1940, and they seemed happy. Davis was glamorous and powerful and over thirty—and living proof that if a woman got a divorce, her life could change for the better. Bette's birthday gift to Mary was an engraved silver cigarette case.

At thirty-eight, McCall's confidence and poise were rock-solid, and though she never cared enough to choose her own clothes, the designer wear from I. Magnin selected by her personal shopper was always stylish. But she had started to go gray. Her mother Mazie's hair had turned snow white when she was just twenty-six, so McCall knew it was only a matter of time until she looked more white than dark brown. But she refused to dye it. She had more important problems to face, not least of them a crumbling marriage.

Although Davis's friendship was important, McCall credited a fictional woman for helping her keep it together in stressful times. Maisie's upbeat philosophy was not only a therapeutic balm for legions of women who felt pulled in too many directions but also therapy for her creator. McCall confessed that Maisie was essentially her alter ego: "When writing, I literally step into Maisie's gaudy garb and go sailing through adventures with her. . . . I know her as well as I know myself."[27] Up until *Maisie Gets Her Man* (1942), McCall and Reinhardt had Jack Ruben supporting their work and vision for Maisie. But in September Ruben died suddenly of a heart attack in the middle of *Assignment in Brittany* (1942).[28] McCall was devastated. The Maisie series was passed to producer George Haight, who had produced *Kathleen*. Then Reinhardt left for better pay at Fox, where her husband directed Spanish-language features. The invincible partnership of McCall, Ruben, and Reinhardt was over. Hollywood had a notoriously short memory, but McCall wanted some kind of memorial for her friend. She persuaded widow Virginia Bruce and others to contribute toward a bungalow in Ruben's name at the new Hollywood Country House in Calabasas, the longtime plan of the Motion Picture Relief Fund for retired or financially straitened members of the film community.[29]

A few weeks later Davis, now the new president of the Hollywood Canteen, called to ask if McCall would volunteer as a hostess to entertain the troops stationed at nearby bases. McCall was already involved in just about every wartime industry committee, but this was the only one that might get her a free drink and a dance. She was overworked, creatively adrift, and grieving. The thought of disappearing in a crowd, meeting men who didn't know who she was and whom she'd never see again, was attractive.

But when McCall walked into the Hollywood Canteen that night in October, Davis was waiting for her with a blind date: the Army's chief public relations officer for nearby Fort MacArthur, Lieutenant David Hitchcock Bramson. Tall, bronzed, and handsome, he was perfect Hollywood casting for an army officer. But Bramson hadn't been in uniform all his life; ironically, he not only knew who McCall was but was more of a Hollywood insider than she. Born in Los Angeles in 1911 to

Goldie and Theodore Bramson, he was a true Hollywood baby. Family legend claimed that Lillian Gish had "changed his diapers on a movie set." Later, as a cute little boy in a sailor suit, he appeared in a series of Christie Comedies. But as with most child stars, his fame was on a timer. So was family life. His parents were divorced, and his father disappeared. His mother Goldie worked as an engraver and traveling salesperson. She had to leave David and her other son Herb home alone while she worked. Eventually she married her brother-in-law, known as Uncle Bill to the boys.

His film career over, young David decided he wanted to be a writer. Luckily he met the legendary Ida Koverman when he joined MGM's junior writers' program in the 1930s. Koverman had a reputation for helping the careers of handsome young men from Clark Gable to Robert Taylor and did what she could to introduce Bramson to the right people.[30]

Koverman recognized he was a natural for public relations and pushed work his way. After working at in the studio's publicity department, he opened his own office. Bramson worked for actors William Boyd and Anthony Quinn at the start of his career and wrote several profiles of the actor to build his image. The articles may not have been screenplays, but at least he was writing something. He joined the Guild of Screen Publicists and in 1940 was the chairman of the guild's publicist bureau. At one point he was behind a search for a new young star, a "Cinemarella." As Louella Parsons reported, "Any girl now in Hollywood, 16 or over, with or without screen experience" could enter the contest.[31] Of course, the judges were just men—a committee of executives, producers, directors, cinematographers, and Bramson.

With war talk becoming more ominous, Bramson quit the business and revisited his early desire for a military career. In 1940 he enlisted in the California National Guard and was commissioned as lieutenant in the infantry in August 1941. He was at Fort MacArthur in nearby San Pedro on maneuvers when his superiors discovered his Hollywood background and assigned him to handle press relations after a general was stabbed with a bread knife in "suspicious circumstances."[32] Army brass worried the press would suggest that the officer had committed suicide or had been murdered by his wife. Bramson handled it.

Much to his frustration, the army kept Bramson in their publicity department throughout 1942. According to the *Los Angeles Times*, he shared an office with "a publicity hound," his English bulldog Mulligan, who was "PFC [Private First Class] in charge of the Complaint Department."[33] But Bramson had plenty of complaints of his own, and he didn't go through Mulligan. In early 1942, not liking the look of Olivia de Havilland in trousers, he had waged his own private battle against Hollywood women wearing "masculine" attire. In his "one-man drive against women in uniforms," he claimed the actress looked "like a boy" in a uniform. Feeling "unmanned," he wrote, "These women have no right to do this to us. . . . We wear the pants well enough."[34]

His commanding officer assigned him the task of writing the post's newsletter to massage his sensitive ego, but as much as he liked writing, it was not exactly how he imagined his army career. Rather than be sent into combat overseas, as he requested, he was coordinating events with the newly formed Hollywood Canteen and supplying entertainment for the troops at the Desert Training Center at Fort Irwin near Barstow.

Then he met McCall. According to family legend, it was love at first sight. Even when McCall was in heels, David Bramson towered over her. The corners of his blue eyes were always crinkling with laughter, and he had stories to tell about the idiocies of army life and growing up in Los Angeles. His curly, chestnut hair was clipped short, he was lean and athletic, and he was dazzling to look at in his uniform.

For McCall, Bramson was an escape from her routine marriage to an older man on the downward slope of his career. McCall always wanted to be at the center of things, and Bramson, despite his conservative masculinity and intellectual limitations, had sex appeal. In a club full of Hollywood's most beautiful starlets, Bramson's attraction to an older, married writer with three kids was unusual. But it was also practical: McCall was one of the most well-connected writers in town. If Bramson still had any postwar ambitions about becoming a writer, McCall was his best chance. He courted McCall, and she fell for him.

Over the next few weeks they met in upscale Los Angeles hotel rooms whenever Bramson could get off the base. One night, when he'd arranged for famed conductor Leopold Stokowski to appear at Fort Irwin, he invited her up. According to his daughter, "After she left, she got a telegram saying something to the effect of 'when you left, that warm thing in your hand was this soldier's heart.'"[35] Even McCall was susceptible to PR corn. When she admitted the affair to Franklin as per their longstanding marital policy, he shrugged Bramson off as the West Coast-Jewish version of Muray. She disagreed, telling him, "This is no fling."

Always the diplomat, her husband advised her to see as much as possible of Bramson to get him out of her system.

But the more she saw of Bramson, the more she wanted him. Then, with her marriage and everything she had built in Hollywood for the past eight years at stake, with Hollywood and the rest of the world in the chaos of war, overnight she became Hollywood's most powerful screenwriter.

CHAPTER 10

A President at War

On the evening of November 12, 1942, the Screen Writers Guild held its annual election at its headquarters, 1655 North Cherokee Avenue. Back in August President Sidney Buchman had stepped down, allegedly to take a job as an executive producer at Columbia.[1] That was only part of the truth; Buchman was thoroughly worn out by the lengthy contract negotiations with the producers, and so Vice President McCall had unofficially taken over. The annual November meeting made it official: McCall was elected with 177 votes and no competition.[2]

Many decades later it still astounds some members of the Writers Guild of America West to learn that their union's first female president was elected in 1942, but at the time no one was very surprised by the election result. McCall had proven herself to be one of the guild's most committed and astute advocates since first paying her dues in 1934. She was also shrewd enough to realize that her ability to negotiate for all Hollywood writers was based in part on the relationships she fostered with filmmakers across Hollywood and the greater Los Angeles community.[3]

Through Charles Brackett she had met Hedda Hopper, a well-known actress who embarked on a new career as the *Los Angeles Times* gossip columnist on February 14, 1938. Although not politically aligned, both women believed in supporting the careers of other women—and loved hats. Hopper covered events in McCall's career, and as far as politics was concerned, they had an armed truce for a few years.

Brackett and Screen Actors Guild colleague Lucile Webster Gleason recommended cultivating more sympathetic, high-ranking members of Hollywood's producer class and the wider community of committee workers who supported unemployed or retired filmmakers. So, back in 1938, McCall joined the Motion Picture Relief Committee, an organization founded in the 1920s by Mary Pickford to support unemployed or retired members of the film community.[4] She helped arrange a star-studded polo benefit for the fund in 1940 that brought producers such as Zanuck, writers, actors, and executives together, and fostered Hollywood community spirit—courtesy of the Screen Writers Guild.[5]

At the relief fund, McCall developed her relationship with another friend of Hedda Hopper, executive secretary Ida Koverman, who was instrumental in developing the *MGM Studio Club News*, a monthly community newsletter highlighting the achievements and charitable causes of the studio's workers. McCall not only contributed articles about current affairs in the writers' building but also encouraged members to commit to charitable donations. Regardless of whether they supported intervention in the European war, McCall reminded them that their contributions to the Motion Picture Relief Fund helped the Community Chest. "There's one cause we're all united in—the survival of our free, democratic United States in this world holocaust," she wrote. "The spirit, the very soul and essence of our America, is embodied and functioning in the Community Chest. If we let that spirit die, we've defeated ourselves more overwhelmingly than we could be defeated on any battlefield."[6]

McCall was the force behind the Screen Guild radio show in January 1939, which she, fellow relief fund board member Bette Davis, and their SAG colleagues did for CBS for free.[7] All the money generated from the show went to fund Motion Picture Relief, and she received a special testimonial from the organization's president, actor Jean Hersholt, expressing "our appreciation and gratitude for the unselfish service you contributed."[8] Working for the Motion Picture Relief Fund also brought her closer to MGM's managerial fixer, Eddie Mannix. In 1940 and 1941, when she served as chairman of the executive committee, she and Mannix met not only in the studio commissary but also at planning meetings for the Motion Picture Relief Home in the Valley—and at more cantankerous guild contract meetings over the closed shop.

But McCall's most ambitious strategic expansion of her contacts came outside of Hollywood in the early 1940s. Melvyn Douglas's wife, former actress Helen Gahagan Douglas, had moved on from starring in Rider Haggard's *She* (1935) to serving as Democratic National Committeewoman for California and as vice chairwoman of the Democratic State Central Committee. McCall campaigned vigorously for Roosevelt's reelection and served alongside Gahagan Douglas as a party delegate in 1940.[9] That November First Lady Eleanor Roosevelt wrote "Miss McCall" a special thank-you note: "It is heartening to my husband to know that you supported him and his policies so loyally and so well."[10] When the First Lady headed to California in April 1941 for a well-publicized visit, it was natural that Douglas would involve McCall in the planning of key events.[11] Although McCall arranged for Brackett and his wife Elizabeth to attend the larger reception, only McCall and a few intimates were invited to the dinner. She and Roosevelt were photographed together, with McCall later remembering the whole event as "a great treat."

Roosevelt later wrote about meeting McCall in her popular syndicated column, "My Day," but the two had a private conversation in which Mrs. Roosevelt proposed that the two of them work together on "stories of other Americans" she had met on her travels and "thought other Americans should know about them."[12] When McCall praised the First Lady's gifts as a writer and encouraged her to write them herself, McCall recollected that Mrs. Roosevelt said she wrote "only factual" things and thought McCall "was the person to write their stories." It was one of McCall's biggest professional regrets that they never found the time to develop the project. But the national papers covered their meeting, and the event had special symbolic value, since Franklin D. Roosevelt's administration had swung in favor of the Screen Writers Guild. When she met the First Lady, McCall was in the process of finalizing the details of the Screen Writers Guild contract.

Two months later, in June, the guild voted unanimously in favor of the seven-year contract, but the producers wouldn't officially sign it for another ten months. It was particularly infuriating since writers were still coming to the guild with horror stories about routine exploitative practices. Many of these victims were women who were paid less money than their male counterparts. A case in point was Elizabeth Beecher. Since 1939, she informed the guild on November 22, 1941, she had been writing screenplays for the Range Busters western series at Monogram (her first was about Billy the Kid) for producer Sigmund Neufield and another screenwriter, Oliver Drake. Drake had paid her $50 per script and promised her screen credit, which she never got. He did. Her pay went up slightly over time, but, she added, "After learning what is usually paid for original screenplays, etc., I am considerably 'burned up' over the way I have been taken in—all because I really needed the money and was a trusting 'sucker.'"[13] Now, she reported, even her male agent "seems to agree with me that even ghost writers are entitled to some breaks . . . and that established writers should not take advantage of less known ones by paying them 'buttons' when they consider the latter's work sufficiently competent to entitle them to credit on the screen."

McCall had been behind calls to curb producer-writer members who denied screen credits of less-known screenwriter "collaborators" who were responsible for writing the scripts. This was a big election issue for the November 1941 meeting, where Brackett stood for president against Sidney Buchman and "a close vote" was expected between McCall and her frenemy on the extreme left, Ralph Block, for the vice presidency. Buchman edged out Brackett, but McCall won.[14] By the time McCall was serving as president in 1942, Beecher, a guild member, got credit on *The Lone Rider in Cheyenne*, produced by Neufield. But she soon left Neufield and Drake for better jobs, writing *The Silver Bullet* (directed by Joseph Lewis) and countless other westerns such as *Cowboys in the Clouds* and *Bullets and Saddles* where she not only got screen credit but also had her name on film posters and associated publicity.

Even as the guild handled Beecher's case, producers were still refusing to sign the contract, and a writers' strike was more than a possibility. Many of the guild's left-wing members advocated a wage freeze to show wartime solidarity, keep production costs down, and bring the execs to the table. McCall spoke for the moderate members in the Screen Writers Guild who were strongly opposed to what effectively was "freezing the contract" before anything had been formally signed. But as it turned out, the producers began the meeting by agreeing to McCall's demand for a minimum wage of $125 a week before the left could propose their own "generous" offer of a wage freeze. Guild leadership announced that contract would be signed that spring.

The chief advocates for the freeze—guild president Sidney Buchman, Lester Cole, Dalton Trumbo, John Howard Lawson, and Ralph Block—had, as McCall's friend Richard Maibaum would later remember, "egg on their faces," and McCall was regarded as a heroine.[15] Her three most important contractual commitments had always been the elimination of speculative writing, guild-supervised credit arbitration, and a decent minimum wage for all guild members (unlike SAG leadership, which focused on stars and did not advocate for the rights of extras). For years, many writers had been making do on $40 a week—if anything. Winning the wage war earned McCall complete loyalty from a young, impoverished writing membership who would be more than willing to support her "moderate" policies over any extreme proposals that would end up hurting their weekly take-home pay. Believing they had won the contract war with the studios, Hollywood's unionized writers set to work to win the other war against Germany, Japan, and Italy.

Having proved herself more useful to members than Buchman, that summer McCall took over the reins of power. However, her ally and confidante Charles Brackett was forced to resign from the executive board after Paramount made him a writer-producer. (A writer who employed another writer in any capacity could still hold membership but was not eligible for a governance position.) Brackett, who had taken McCall out for an ice cream soda to celebrate in August, now left her to an uncertain fate. As he put it, though "feeling quite a pang" as he resigned, "I've grown more and more angry with the dewy-eyed New Dealism and frank Leftism of the group."[16]

The two reunited in late September 1942, when both were elected to the Board of Governors of the Academy of Motion Picture Arts and Sciences.[17] Brackett joked that he would now force Billy Wilder to call him "Cher Maître" and that he would "wear a snip of typewriter ribbon in my buttonhole."[18] It was a historic moment, because for nearly ten years, the Screen Writers Guild had been at odds with the Academy; many writers had resigned Academy membership in order to pursue the goal of an independent contract.

In October, several months after the contract was in place, McCall was in Washington "to discuss the proposed freezing of high Hollywood salaries" for the duration of the war.[19] The committee involved actors, producers, and writers. When producers proposed to go along with a potential five-year wage freeze (they could afford it, after all), McCall remembered, "I sucked air" and waited for "some of these handsome actors with good voices" to "come awake and say something," but they "didn't say a bloody word."[20] So McCall told them point blank: "The Screen Writers Guild could not go along with this because a contract is a two-way street and if one party, for any reason, is unable to fulfill his part of the bargain, the bargain is off." With the eventual support of James Cagney, the Screen Actors Guild president, she dodged a bullet that would inevitably have hurt writers and actors on lower salaries. But not everything worked out for her while she was in town. Columnists reported that she had been considered as head of the film division of the Office of War Information, but ex-journalist Lowell Mellett hung onto the job.

McCall was given "a heroine's welcome" upon her return to Hollywood.[21] She more than earned her election in November, and nationwide the press highlighted the historic importance of President McCall. She, Jane Murfin, Gladys Lehman, and Marguerite Roberts (who joined her on the executive board), as well as Molloy, Hellman, and Parker, had served on numerous committees and meetings with producers who saw the writers' efforts to improve pay and normalize working conditions as the end to executives' control of the studio system. They were the frontline of the struggle and represented hundreds of female writers.

In her first postelection address to her colleagues, McCall didn't call obvious attention to herself as the Screen Writers Guild's first female president. The press had already done that. As an Equal Rights Amendment feminist, she didn't *have* to draw attention to her gender. But since there was a war on and no shortage of disgruntled older male colleagues unused to a woman in charge, she began her speech diplomatically, listing the names of the many men now "in service" overseas or in intelligence work. While some 172 were in branches of the armed forces, "to all of us," she said, "the war has brought a heightened sense of responsibility."[22] Both men and women were involved in the war effort, and writers, regardless of gender, were more important than ever. Although during the First World War, journalists, historians, and screenwriters had written false and malicious propaganda for the government, this time around, she promised, the government was not going to censor Hollywood. This time "the ideas are ours." Through the Hollywood Writers Mobilization, McCall noted that guild members already accrued a "fine record" of accomplishments "as *writing* men and women to the cause of freedom." McCall had also addressed the Hollywood Writers Mobilization earlier that spring "about the part women might play" in the war effort.[23]

If Washington was going to respect Hollywood's creative and patriotic boundaries, the film industry had to grow up too. She hoped that in this new context "the pictures we write will be better pictures, more entertaining, more exciting, and quite possibly more profitable, because the war has demanded from us that the screen shall not be used to tell vapid stories, meretricious stories."[24] She had argued that Americans did not need heavy-handed propaganda on screen. They were too intelligent, she claimed, to be manipulated by false messages and race prejudice. In a CBS Pacific Network forum with Dalton Trumbo and the Academy's Donald Gledhill the press quoted her at length, drawing attention to her definition of honest pictures as "those that don't misrepresent races, that don't cater to race prejudice, that are free of all jingoistic nationalism, that don't glorify rascality, that don't set getting ahead at any cost as a goal."[25]

For the first time in Hollywood's history screenwriters had status: "It's become almost natural for writers to use the front stairs." Even better, "Nowadays when the story editor inquires whether a writer is a member of the guild, he no longer winces and puts up his hands in instinctive self-defense." Wages had risen, while the agreement had given "protection from having our brains picked by predatory producers" and longer notice periods between jobs.

It had been a long fight to get their contract, and there was much to be proud of, but McCall was focused on the future. "You must not let yourself be cajoled, wheedled, browbeaten, coaxed, kidded or stalled into speculative writing," she warned. "Every member can help the guild live up to the contract, every member can help the guild see to it that the producers live up to the contract." With income going up for everyone (and thanks to her, no wage freezes for workers on lower salaries), the first order of business was to establish a clear basic agreement with agents, so that writers weren't impoverished by the system. She imagined a day when even the fees writers paid their agents would be treated as work-related tax deductions, but the first step was drafting a basic agreement between writers and agents.

More than anything she wanted colleagues to become involved in committee work and to raise the profile of all writers: "We need hard workers on a great many tedious committees. The grievance committee of the guild has a vitally important job to do." She continued, "The guild must have conscientious representatives on the Motion Picture Relief Fund Case Committee, on the board of the Hollywood Writers Mobilization, the Permanent Charities Committee, the Industry War Bond Committee. We need replacements on many studio shop committees." She appealed to the room: "Board members can't do it all. They shouldn't do it all. I decline to believe the list of names on the ballot tonight, fine a list as it is, is the complete roster of men and women of good will in this guild."

The key to the Screen Writers Guild's future, she believed, lay in its next generation of screenwriters. She hoped, she said, to "live long enough to see the guild establish its own school of screen writing. The training and developing of new writing talent should certainly be the job of the Screen Writers Guild." She concluded the historic speech: "By nominating me unopposed for the presidency of the guild you have given me the greatest honor which I've ever received. I'll work hard for you."

McCall's plea for others to come forward to organize and lead committees was a veiled cry for help from an overstretched and exhausted woman whose personal life was hanging by a thread. That winter, she told Franklin that she wanted a divorce.

It was a difficult Christmas for everyone. Her parents, Mazie and Leo, were not happy that she was divorcing a son-in-law they both loved to marry Bramson; unfortunately, the family anti-Semitism that had hurt Tod and Rose Burke years before hadn't diminished. Bramson's Los Angeles family was more welcoming; being connected to McCall had its perks. Bramson's mother Goldie was always calling up, asking to borrow the chauffeur and car McCall had on hand as president of the Screen Writers Guild. Bramson had applied for active duty and expected to be shipped overseas, but for now, remained at nearby Fort MacArthur. Because McCall was busy with the guild and under contract and "couldn't leave town to establish residence in Reno, as divorcing people of the day did," Franklin went to Nevada. When he told her he "couldn't say bad things about her," she told him to say she "was spending too much time at the studio."[26]

The hearing was on the fourth of February. When he returned a few days later, having had, by his own admission, "fun," her daughter admitted: "My mother was extra convinced that the passion for their marriage was justifiably pronounced Over." She had already told the papers that "differences in temperaments have caused the breach," but the media's take was "here's a case of where two careers in a family didn't work out."[27] McCall's career was the dominant one, they acknowledged, citing "plenty of publicity" over her guild presidency. She seemed, the *Los Angeles Examiner* said, "to be in every movement in our town." Hopper, for her part, preferred Franklin and misspelled Bramson's name "Branson" in her coverage of the marriage. And though she got the groom's army ranking correct, it was also clear whose career she valued. McCall was "one of our top writers for many years," and had "no time for a honeymoon," since "Mary's working on *No Surrender* at Metro."

On the night before her remarriage, McCall told twelve-year-old Sheila all about her extramarital affairs and even admitted that she had had premarital sex with Franklin. It was a lot to learn at twelve, but Sheila had accompanied her mother to New York only a year and a half ago to shop around for a prospective new daddy. Years later she could remember with some humor how right her mother was when she gave advice about getting married: "Before you buy the shoe, you have to try it on first."[28] Sheila was more outraged when she found out her mother had given her best friend Pamela Herbert the diamond engagement ring from Franklin.[29]

The next day McCall married Lieutenant Bramson. The ceremony was performed by Municipal Judge Alfred A. Paonessa at McCall's home in West Los Angeles and was attended by a few of their close friends. There was no engagement ring, no fancy party, and "her wedding ring was a thin gold band with a line around it that cost about $20, tops." But he did give her a "chunky silver I.D. bracelet, engraved 'Mazelah' on the front," with "More Than Yesterday, Less Than Tomorrow" on the inside.[30] Ironically, the announcement in the *Los Angeles Examiner* on February 4 was titled "Film Writers Plan Wedding." If Bramson was still feeding journalists his own press, then this item was a nice touch for his post-Army career.

When she stood up at the Cocoanut Grove on Oscar night a few weeks later, Hollywood was still buzzing about her new marriage. McCall's name was in the trade papers several times a week—only two days before the Oscars, she'd made the front page of *Motion Picture Daily* as the newly appointed chairman of the Hollywood Branch of the War Activities Committee (WAC). She headed an industry-wide, ten-person executive board "in a general effort to focalize the industry's war efforts."[31] It was a huge deal, and McCall's good relationships with columnists Parsons, Graham, and Hopper meant that she could count on them not spilling the details about her personal life until after her terms in office were well underway.

She was still credited as the creative force in the Maisie franchise, and after reading the script for *Swing Shift Maisie* (1943), OWI reader Lillian Bergquist praised "the now renowned showgirl" for her patriotism. Maisie was no longer searching for a showbiz job but was working alongside other young women in a Los Angeles aircraft factory. Bergquist continued, "Maisie, in her own way, can set an example to all Americans—and especially to those millions of young women who are so urgently needed in all our war industries."[32] Contemporary fans tend to cite *Swing Shift Maisie* as their franchise favorite, since it puts the heroine in the position of "Rosie the Riveter." Writing in the 1990s, critic Marsha McCreadie, one of the few to mention McCall, focused on *Swing Shift Maisie* to the exclusion of McCall's other *Maisie* scripts.[33] But viewing the 1943 film as a Hollywood-made feminist intervention is a stretch. Although many popular histories of women's employment in America have given the impression that women only entered the workforce during the Second World War, this is fundamentally incorrect.[34] At the end of the 1930s, women made up over a quarter of the workforce.[35] Maisie, like many American women, worked through the 1930s; she didn't just get a job because she wanted to be patriotic toward Uncle Sam or some male soldier serving overseas.

Not everyone in Hollywood thought patriotism was a good excuse for an "average" film. *Variety* thought the script was "loosely written" and the direction was "lackluster."[36] As another critic wrote, "There appears to have been a lull in the *Maisie* series, and this shows it. Maybe the producers have lost their enthusiasm."[37] Perhaps McCall's workload at the Screen Writers Guild was taking its toll and she was writing less than her new cowriter, Robert Halff. Or perhaps her new fascination with alpha male Lt. Bramson had changed her and Maisie's attitude toward the male sex.

In *Swing Shift Maisie*, Sothern's character is routinely duped, manipulated, laughed at, and rendered stupid by men. She also gets stress-related illnesses on the job as a riveter in a war plant, proving she can't do what men do, presumably. Although in *Ringside Maisie* she combatted sexual harassment, in the later film, she seems to welcome the wolf whistles and come-ons from men at the plant and is duped by another woman for the first time (one of her skiving co-workers, played by Jean Rogers). Also, *Swing Shift Maisie* does not begin with the usual shot of the heroine looking for work. Instead it opens with action scenes of the bland male lead testing his airplane. Maisie's experiences onscreen were rendered of secondary importance.

The dismissive treatment would continue in *Maisie Goes to Reno*, a film that in a series first acts as a sequel to *Swing Shift Maisie*'s war work. Having been excused from work due to stress on the job, the heroine goes to Reno—not to recover, but to help a soldier whose young wife mysteriously wants a divorce. She has developed a facial tic that makes her wink at every man she sees, a seemingly humorous touch that subjects her to repeated and unwanted sexual harassment. When she becomes involved with the details of the couple's marriage, she discovers that crooks are trying to fleece millions from the wife while the husband is in camp and later overseas. No one, including her new love interest, a card dealer at the casino (John Hodiak), will believe her. They routinely tell Maisie that she's delusional, hysterical, and insane. It may come as no surprise that McCall's cowriters on these last two Maisie films were men. Though the *Maisie* series' post-1943 studio ad campaign stressed its bigger production values, even trade reviewers evaluated the new work as just "average entertainment."[38]

But as McCall's and the public's interest in Maisie waned, she moved on to bigger spheres of influence within Hollywood. Despite her snubbing by Mellett back in the fall of 1942, she had been busy in her role as chairman of the Hollywood War Activities Committee. She oversaw industry participation in the Hollywood Victory Committee for radio shows, benefits, personal appearances, war bond drives, and camp shows in the United States and overseas; coordinated work on the Hollywood Writers Mobilization, which supplied work for camp shows and broadcasts; and helped raise money via the West Coast's Permanent Charities Committee. For a few years the research council for the Academy of Motion Picture Arts and Sciences and the Signal Corps had collaborated on training films for the War Department. But she had her eye on more war film production in Hollywood. She was a shrewd supporter of the OWI and as head of the War Activities Committee did what she could to promote its reputation.

OWI director Elmer Davis endured a group of obstructive military censors who withheld information for alleged "public safety" and public perception that the agency was spinning truth in the Roosevelt administration's favor. In the spring of 1943 members of the House of Representatives attacked the OWI as an expensive propaganda machine for Roosevelt's administration, and former employees complained in the press about the "slick salesmanship" that trumped "honest information."[39] McCall was staunchly with Roosevelt but only telegrammed her support to Davis and Vice President Wallace in June 1943, when domestic budgets for films were on the line. On behalf of the Screen Writers Guild, she urged that they "do all in your power to insure the continuance of the domestic branch of the OWI" and stressed "the enormous value of the OWI in facilitating the organization of motion pictures and to the war effort."[40] When quoted in the press, McCall had always carefully referred to films promoting the war effort as "information films" rather than "propaganda films." But she wanted Hollywood to have control over the production of these films, not the U.S. government.

Even before war was declared, Washington had accelerated production of defense and citizenship-themed short films for exhibition in studio-owned theaters. In the first phase of cooperation between the government and Hollywood, the year before Pearl Harbor, there were twenty-five films made for National Defense; indeed, the War Activities Committee (WAC) was then called the Motion Picture Committee Co-operating for National Defense. In stage two, from Pearl Harbor to June 1942, when the OWI was established, there were thirteen films produced by Roosevelt's "general handy man" Lowell Mellett as coordinator of government films.[41] Mellett then became head of the Film Bureau of the Domestic Branch of the OWI in stage three, from July 1942 to July 1943. This period saw thirty-five war information films produced, but only about half were produced by the OWI film unit.

This wasn't an impressive track record, and Hollywood knew that it could do better than the government. McCall, as head of the guild, the WAC, an Academy governor, member of the Hollywood Democratic Committee and the Labor Management Committee, and executive of Motion Picture Relief Fund, was in many ways the professional voice and face of the Hollywood studios. Even colleagues such as Y. Frank Freeman realized how good she made them look to the American public and to the Allies.[42]

In 1943 Hollywood's war machine was humming. In January exhibitors revealed that *Casablanca* had topped even *Mrs. Miniver* at last year's box office, and a range of war films including *Air Force* (February), *Edge of Darkness* (April), *Action in the North Atlantic* and *Swing Shift Maisie* (May), *Bataan* and *So Proudly We Hail!* (June) continued to make money for the studios. Then a media story broke that threatened McCall's plan for a complete Hollywood takeover of the OWI's cinematic war effort. In July the well-known *Chicago Tribune* journalist Marcia Winn published a series of exposés on contemporary Hollywood, challenging the industry's good wartime reputation. Her front-page headlines ("City of Magic, Fantasy and Filth: It's Hollywood" and "Hollywood Vice Swallows 300 Girls a Month") attracted a wide readership from the *Tribune*'s anti–New Deal base.[43] Winn targeted agents and publicists who arbitrarily broke stars' careers and sexual predators such as Darryl F. Zanuck, Errol Flynn, and Charlie Chaplin. It wasn't a new media approach. Hollywood exposés had thrived since the days of Fatty Arbuckle, William Desmond Taylor, and Clara Bow, but raking up many of the old stories at a time when Hollywood's image was playing for such patriotic high stakes spelled a potential public relations disaster.

Everyone in Hollywood was talking about the articles, but on July 28 McCall took a few days off to be with Bramson, now a captain, who had been posted to Columbus, Georgia.[44] While she was away, her industry colleagues held a committee meeting on July 29, where "plans were laid for concerted action to counteract these articles with the course of action gradually taking shape even at the initial huddle on the subject." On August 4 *Variety* announced that Charles Francis Coe, vice president of the Motion Picture Producers and Distributors of America (MPPDA), would go after Winn for her anti-Hollywood screeds at a talk with Eastman Kodak workers in Chicago: "The Marcia Winn bylined articles have aroused considerable comment in the film business, and a definite reply to the stories is figured to highlight Coe's Chi address."[45] But most agreed this was not enough. The public needed to read something forceful and convincing—and from another woman. Upon her return McCall agreed to write a riposte, even though she may have been sympathetic to Winn's attacks on lecherous producers. But on August 1 her schedule became far busier.

Mellett had resigned from his job as head of the film bureau (the job McCall had initially wanted) and on August 1, 1943, Hollywood officially took over the government's war film production. Under McCall's stewardship as War Activities Committee chair, Hollywood oversaw the development and production of all war information films and their quick distribution in more than fifteen thousand theaters within eight weeks after release. Two of her first projects were a war bond drive film with her old *Craig's Wife* colleague, Rosalind Russell, and another on nurses. There would be nearly fifty films produced under her yearlong term as chair of the War Activities Committee-Office of War Information film program. Films varied from thirty seconds to twenty minutes in length and were made on a voluntary basis for the Army, Navy, Marines, Red Cross, Treasury, Woman's Army Corps, and the National War Fund.[46] As she later remarked in a report for *Film Daily*, "In the past year, this Division has become a healthy, smoothly-functioning branch of the industry's aid to the war effort."[47]

McCall continued to promote opportunities for women in Hollywood and material that dramatized women's potential in the war effort. When Lieutenant Commander Dorothy Stratton was due to visit as head of the women's division of the Coast Guard on August 27, 1943, Lieutenant Lea Burke wrote McCall asking if "you or one of the guild members" would be interested in interviewing Stratton.[48] Perhaps "an interview or story for one or more of the motion picture magazines would be particularly affective [sic] in stimulating interest in this branch of the Women's Reserve," she added. McCall was seen as a natural advocate for women's equal opportunities and employment. By 1943 she was so well known nationally that journalists were drawing attention to her as a role model for girls and women of any age. In his "Life with Salt on the Side" syndicated column, E. V. Durling drew attention to McCall's unusual moniker, suggesting to parents of new girls, "How about naming your first daughter after her mama and having a female junior at your home?"[49] That fall Hedda Hopper announced that McCall was writing a Red Cross drama for Shirley Temple and that the actress was said to be "learning every angle of the picture business" from Selznick so that when her star days were through, "she'll be prepared to move in as a director-producer."[50] Although McCall sold Goldwyn a story entitled "The First Co-Ed," which told the story of a mid-nineteenth century undergraduate at a formerly all-male college, way back in 1938, the producer announced that fall that he was finally gearing up for production. Louella Parsons commented that it was timely, "because a number of our schools, heretofore only open to males, are taking in women because there are not enough male students to keep them going."[51]

At the War Activities Committee she commissioned cross-studio shorts, including a script by Tess and Frank Slesinger entitled *What If They Quit?* (Twentieth Century-Fox) and RKO's war bond drive short, *Ginger Rogers Finds a Bargain*, slated as a Woman's Army Corps release. McCall's two OWI/WAC film commissions for *Box-Office Maisie* (MGM), tied into the release of McCall's *Swing Shift Maisie*, and *Reward Unlimited* (Selznick's Vanguard) were also aimed at female audiences.

Her own script, *Reward Unlimited*, directed by Jacques Tourneur, focuses on the Cadet Nurse Training Corps as part of a major recruitment push and resonated with David O. Selznick's *Since You Went Away* (1944), a women's home front drama, starring Claudette Colbert, Jennifer Jones, and Shirley Temple, involving a young woman's decision to become a nurse's aide.[52] In the WAC short film, Peggy (Dorothy McGuire) wants to marry her sweetheart before he goes overseas, but when he refuses she decides to change her old job for a war job. A professional nurse, played by McCall's former colleague from Warner Bros., Aline MacMahon, convinces Peggy to start a training course funded by the U.S. government. As Peggy learns, "it's not just a job, it's a profession," and one that, the male government-official voiceover tells audiences in a departure from most wartime propaganda, she is free to continue after she is married.

Most Pearl Harbor war propaganda added official approval of gender equality in the workplace—but only "for the duration," as long as it took to win the war.

From 1942 American women moved into war jobs and were photographed working in glossy magazines and put in Hollywood documentaries.[53] But McCall wanted it understood, whether she was addressing her guild colleagues or the paying customers in the cinemas, that working women weren't going to disappear when the war against the Axis was over.

CHAPTER 11

A Woman in the Establishment

She may have been Hollywood's most famous labor leader and on practically every major committee in town, but Mary C. McCall Jr. was still a screenwriter looking for the breakthrough project where she had complete creative control. To her delight, she found it in 1943. Ironically, it was a war story with only two significant roles for women. But rather than adapt another MGM screenwriter's work or the latest doorstop-sized bestseller, she was offered the chance to develop an original story with an independent producer. The head of her agency, the "quiet, almost professorial" Sam Jaffe, turned producer with former Warner Bros. director Lloyd Bacon, and the inspiration for their film was in the headlines the day after McCall's election as guild president.[1]

On November 13, 1942, five Irish American brothers—George, Frank, Joe, Matt, and Al Sullivan—from Waterloo, Iowa, all died when their ship, the USS *Juneau*, was torpedoed in the naval battle of Guadalcanal. The thought of parents losing five children touched the nation, and journalistic attention focused on the Sullivans.[2]

When Jaffe approached McCall with the idea of dramatizing the Sullivan tragedy, she was initially appalled at the thought of commercializing the deaths of five young men: "I do not think to watch a small child run over by a steam roller is drama; I think it's disgusting. You want to turn your face away."[3] She also felt there were problems with shaping the material into a drama that would hold audience attention. There was nothing "dramatic" about a torpedo killing thousands in a few seconds. While hand-to-hand battlefield combat might yield some suspense, for these heroes, she remarked, "there was no time when they and their fate were equally matched."

But after doing some research on the family and reading the factual story Jaffe had optioned about their background, McCall agreed. Rather than follow the template of the typical macho-patriotic war film, with a heroic soldier (*Sergeant York*, 1941) or a lovable, ragtag company defying the odds and fighting to the death (*Bataan*, 1943), McCall delivered a richly textured emotional biopic of the Sullivan family from the boys' childhood to the day they died. The final scenes of combat only last a few minutes on screen.

Her script recreated a "full-blooded mongrel family," with eight people competing for one bathroom, a father perpetually cutting himself shaving, gang fights, black eyes, and smoking corn silk.[4] Though the boys outnumbered the girls in the house, life lessons came from both the mother and father. Rather than the more conventional heroism on the battlefield, McCall would look at the heroism of the everyday, the durability and courage of an average, working-class family unit. Though the boys' stories would be prominent, McCall spent significant time on family relationships, the bonds between the parents, and the romance and pain of a young married couple, and, afterward, daughter Genevieve's decision to become a WAVE. As McCall explained: "These young men had so lived in their country and in their family that when their time came to die and when the parents and the young wife and the small baby learned the news that the five were gone, they were able to rise and fill a heroic frame without losing a step."[5]

McCall explained at length how she imagined the final scenes when the man who recruited the boys had to break the news of their deaths to the parents. It was easier for McCall to imagine the reaction of the father and the young wife, but the mother required the most thought. "I decided that, probably, she would be concerned for her husband, she would be concerned for her daughter-in-law— she would be, really, in a state of shock, and her personal grief would come at a later time—so I had her offer the poor Navy man, played by Ward Bond, a cup of coffee, as she would be thinking how hard it must be for *him*."[6] McCall took a lot of time developing the mother's character and dialogue. Genial Irish patriarchs were easy sells to a public who wanted a strong father figure in a time of war, but presenting the mother's own qualities of strength, endurance, and daily self-sacrifice was as important to her. She remembered her grandmother Katie Green Burke and wanted to convey something of her memories of the gentle dreamer who quietly managed a large household (Mrs. Sullivan and Katie shared the same brood of mostly boys and one girl).

The writer did not want major stars playing the Sullivan brothers or other family members; she wanted to reach American audiences through the power of ordinary and extraordinary new faces. Eventually, the only known faces Jaffe hired were character actors Thomas Mitchell (Mr. Sullivan) and Selena Royle (Mrs. Sullivan). Usually a screenwriter wouldn't have had any say in production development or casting; it was the norm to be one of several writers on any project. But when Baker and Jaffe negotiated McCall's leave of absence from MGM, McCall insisted on $15,000 up front plus 5 percent of the producers' profits if they used 75 percent or more of her script. They used 100 percent of her script.

McCall's percentage deal was not that unusual for a Hollywood actor in 1943. After breaking away from their studio contracts, stars James Cagney and Gary Cooper formed their own production companies, and more and more actors were following in the freelance footsteps of pioneers Constance Bennett, Barbara Stanwyck, Irene Dunne, and the late Carole Lombard—but were demanding percentages of the gross and even production credits in addition to salaries. Some writers had done very well, usually by combining writing with producing jobs or directing. Preston Sturges, Nunnally Johnson, Joseph Mankiewicz, and Virginia Van Upp turned writer-director and producer. But almost no full-time writers had broken into this lucrative percentage market (unless they combined writing with directing and producing). McCall's deal was a significant gain for Hollywood screenwriters.

In a 1945 article for the Screen Writers Guild's new monthly magazine, *The Screen Writer*, McCall would remember writing *The Sullivans* as "one of the happiest and most profitable experiences of my working life."[7] She was thrilled to be away from the studio, finally developing a project where she had creative control and no budgetary limitations. Jaffe took it to Twentieth Century-Fox and arranged a deal for the production to be shot and released through the studio, free from interference. It was lucky that the studio's West Coast boss, Darryl F. Zanuck, had joined the Army Signal Corps and was too busy in Washington and London to order any script rewrites or reassign the screenwriter. As head of Fox, Joe Schenck admitted, "When I originally concluded the deal with Sam Jaffe, giving him a cut in the profits of the picture and permitting him to be the producer of the picture . . . we were short of pictures and ready material for pictures."[8] McCall's script was so good that after "a few minor changes" they "immediately put it into production."

Bacon followed McCall's narrative lead and shot the story without the fancy camera angles, dramatic lighting, and oral narration that were slowly becoming the vogue in many Hollywood productions of the 1940s. As she commented on *The Sullivans* in 1970, "In connection with that picture, this is something which I believe very strongly: that a good motion picture gets from the audience a suspension of disbelief. The audience is absorbed in it and believes that it is happening before their eyes. When you do 'tricks,' director's tricks, cameraman's tricks . . . you jar the audience out of that state of suspended disbelief and make them conscious that they are watching a motion picture."[9]

The only sour note during production was Jack Warner, who still hated McCall for bringing a screenwriters' union to his studio. He dug around for anything he could find to attack the film and wrote to Joe Schenck that they hadn't acknowledged in the film that Mrs. Sullivan's grandfather had been of Jewish descent. When Zanuck found out Warner was attempting to criticize his studio's big picture of 1944, he slammed his colleague with a long letter: "All members of the family were clearly identified as Irish Catholics" and "if anyone had suggested that we put in a few lines or a scene to show that one of Mrs. Sullivan's ancestors was Jewish, I would have strongly objected."[10] He continued, "Audiences throughout the world, not knowing the true facts in the case, would immediately accuse the so-called 'Jewish producers in Hollywood of again trying to stuff propaganda down their throats.'"

Critics seemed to agree and praised *The Sullivans* for its lack of heavy-handed wartime propaganda or crude patriotism. The bimonthly *Motion Picture Reviews*, produced by the Los Angeles County branch of the American Association of University Women, wrote that it was a "must-see" film, and that "no film has pictured the best American traditions with greater fidelity, genuineness and warmth than this simple story of a family group with the inarticulate loyalty to each other and their sense of responsibility to the country which means Home to them."[11] *Modern Screen* opened its review with the claim that it was "the funniest, saddest, truest, most human picture you've ever seen."[12] *Film Daily* was even more complimentary: "In creating this inspiring monument to the memory of the five Sullivan brothers who fell together in a naval engagement in the service of their country, Twentieth Century-Fox has enriched the world with a film possessed of a universal appeal that has not often been matched on the screen."[13] It was "a human document . . . not a war picture." There weren't any fantastic special effects or over-the-top heroism or stars or even a "formal plot." Instead, it was a "study of family life—a study rich in detail and warm with feeling. Its picture of an American family of modest means is painted with laughter and tears, plus a bit of romance."

Because *The Sullivans* focused on what was most treasured about everyday family life, audiences were left realizing the country's social and cultural losses in wartime—not just the men and women who would never come back, but the family memories, the slower pace of life, and the lessons of the gritty 1930s, when so many Americans survived poverty and loneliness thanks in part to the sense of community in their small towns and city streets. Many critics considered *The Sullivans* a rare cinematic achievement, since it represented these perspectives in such an unadorned way—and contrary to both Hollywood's slick production machine and the government's other forms of wartime propaganda.

According to *Film Daily*, "Mary C. McCall Jr. rates raves for her screenplay."[14] Others came right out and said "Mary McCall Jr., writer of some of Hollywood's best screen plays, should win an Academy Award for the script of *The Sullivans*."[15] But it was Edward Doherty and Jules Schermer who were nominated for an Academy Award for Best Story, a category discontinued in 1956 and replaced with adapted and original screenplay awards. If McCall felt the snub, she didn't acknowledge it. MGM wasn't about to campaign for her nomination for a script she had done with an independent production company. Although her work on *Maisie* had been successful, the studio spent comparatively little on the franchise. *The Sullivans*, in contrast, challenged even more of the norms of studio production, casting, and traditional genre.

In her article for *The Screen Writer* McCall tried to be absolutely candid in order to help other writers negotiate similar deals. As she noted, "when the picture has played out its world market, it seems likely that I will receive in all about eighteen thousand five hundred dollars, with the possibility of some small amount from a re-release in the future."[16] It was the most she had ever made on any film. She had wondered initially why she had the luck to get such an offer, saying her screen credits were "respectable but not impressive." McCall also acknowledged that being president of the Screen Writers Guild and known to all the studio heads gave her clout in the industry that she had not had from mere screen credits. She also credited Jaffe for supporting writers and being willing to let them escape the confines of studio employment to write something truly great. Diversifying the producer pool could only help writers in the future, she concluded. Writing for the left-leaning *New Masses*, journalist Marjorie de Armand praised McCall's article "with a frankness too infrequent in such matters" and stated that *The Screen Writer*'s editors "hope her article 'will establish a precedent for candor.'"[17]

McCall's rise in the industry continued that September when she was reelected to the board of the Academy of Motion Picture Arts and Sciences.[18] She would continue to serve on the board through 1948. In November 1943, her reelection as Screen Writers Guild president attracted a fair amount of press, with Leonard Lyons reporting that the guild happily "draft[ed] Mary McCall Jr. for a second term as president."[19] Her second term represented a high tide in women's executive positions in guild leadership. Betty Reinhardt joined Gladys Lehman and Jane Murfin on the main executive board.

Becoming part of the Academy establishment had a price tag, and her rebuttal to Marcia Winn's attack on the industry had to be robust and convincing. Her response in the November issue of *Motion Picture-Hollywood* was a tough and unapologetic defense of Hollywood.[20] Since the drug and sex scandals of the 1920s, Hollywood had been blamed for practically every evil in American society from communism to war mongering and prostitution, and McCall fired a broadside at all of the detractors, highlighting an industry that had rebuilt its reputation through war service, improved negotiations with the various guilds and unions, and successful star-oriented press campaigns. While she occasionally drew upon metaphors of the studio "family" (an expression popular with everyone from the predatory Louis B. Mayer to charitable work of the Motion Picture Relief Fund), McCall argued that Hollywood was neither a benign nor a predatory patriarchy but a place where women and men had an equal chance of success.

If McCall felt uncomfortable with writing a piece defending studio moguls against charges of sexual impropriety, Winn made it easy for her by blaming other women for this systemic abuse in the entertainment industry: the dreaded stage mothers. Her attack on Hollywood moms was not so far removed from Philip Wylie's recent vituperations on "Momism" in *Generation of Vipers* (1942), and McCall turned the tables on the journalist by praising the strong mother-child relationships that nurtured so many careers, including Mary Pickford, Shirley Temple, and Mickey Rooney and their mothers. Without the matriarchy, McCall argued, the Hollywood star system would not be as powerful. It was her studio colleague Ida Koverman who had been instrumental in developing a studio school and child welfare initiatives, models copied at RKO by the likes of Lela Rogers. McCall's discussion of the studios' careful education and labor protection of child stars might appear as fake as anything coming from studio public relations chief Howard

Strickling's office—just propaganda from a highly placed insider—but it also adds another dimension to Hollywood's aspiring image as a family-oriented organization.

When Winn complained about the industry's exploitation of unknown starlets, McCall replied that both Ginger Rogers and Joan Crawford were working-class actresses who had used the Hollywood system to escape punishing careers in dance halls. And Hollywood's women weren't just actresses, she reminded readers. "It wasn't an acting role I was avid for as a young girl. It was a writing job. Hollywood gave it to me and freed me from the eviction notices and the shame of borrowing money from friends." She also pointed out that she wasn't the only woman in Hollywood to work on the other side of the camera. Winn targeted Hollywood's "soiled-faced," handsy agents, but McCall responded that her agent, Mary Baker, always had a clean face—"except when she's spading up the back yard to enlarge her Victory Garden."

Although from Terry Ramsaye's *A Million and One Nights* (1926) onward histories of studio-era Hollywood have given the impression that women were on one side of the camera and men on the other, McCall told a different story of an industry that supported women in many branches of filmmaking. This perspective had appeared in coverage from the 1930s about Hollywood as "a generation ahead of the rest of the world" in terms of its commitment to women's careers.[21]

McCall, however, did not mention Freed's treatment of Shirley Temple or the countless starlets and top actresses whose careers were destroyed by sexual abuse, alcoholism, drugs, and age. She herself had been chased around desks and had seen other women, perhaps less emotionally resilient, financially protected, or well-connected, buckle under the abuse and the slights from older, wealthier, more powerful men. Mentioning specifics would have been career suicide for McCall. She acknowledged at least, "Right now the going may be tough." But, she continued, "I believe that genuine talent has a greater chance of being recognized in the motion picture business than in most large industries." If McCall wanted to continue to improve the standing of women in the industry (as well as enhance her own), using her position to work with Hollywood's more amenable men would reap more long-term rewards than relentless criticism. Her defense of Zanuck, one of Winn's prominent nasty men, would pay off for her personally within months when he hired her on a long-term contract.

But before that could happen, just as *The Sullivans* was released in early February 1944, McCall became involved in another cross-industry project, the

Academy Foundation. Although her dreams for a studio screenwriting school never came to fruition, McCall discovered other members of the Hollywood community who were interested in preserving the history of motion pictures and encouraging their study by funding scholars and providing a library and archive. McCall, Cary Grant, Donald Crisp, Eddie Mannix, Howard Hawks, James Hilton, Walter Wanger, and Y. Frank Freeman announced that "a non-profit educational institution concerned with the cultural and technological advancement of motion pictures had formed alongside, but not part of the Academy of Motion Picture Arts and Sciences." As William K. Weaver commented, "Mary McCall Jr., eminent in her field as a writer of scripts, is currently president of the Screen Writers Guild, an organization fervently and generously active on behalf of the war effort since, and before, Pearl Harbor. Her presence in the list of sponsors betokens the support and sympathy of her craft."[22]

The eight goals outlined by the nonprofit were the promotion of motion pictures in everyday life, the promotion of understanding between peoples and nations through motion pictures, the creation of a central film library, the establishment of graduate film scholarships, the sponsoring of research studies, showing films, sponsoring lectures, and publishing books on film. It was an ambitious beginning that would eventually lead to the Margaret Herrick Library, the Pickford Center for Motion Picture Study, the Academy Museum, and even financial support for this book. McCall became a trustee and secretary of the organization, working alongside Margaret Herrick, Brackett, Wanger, and longtime colleague in the Motion Picture Relief Fund, Jean Hersholt, who replaced Cagney as Screen Actors Guild president in 1945.

Although she and Cagney continued to work together as wartime presidents of their respective guilds, their friendship had not survived her divorce. (She had tried to build bridges in her *Motion Picture-Hollywood* article in November, citing Cagney's career and service to his industry and his country as one of the great Hollywood success stories.) Initially, things were easier with Bogart since he himself had gone through several marriages and wasn't hypocritical enough to snub McCall for doing something he did himself. In 1943, Bogart also met someone new, and like Bramson, Betty Bacall happened to be Jewish and younger than he was. He allegedly introduced his girlfriend to his old friend "McCall . . . Bacall."[23] After Bogart remarried the two old friends saw each other occasionally at parties. But Bramson's pretty-boy looks, PR background, and assertive alpha male vibe were all guaranteed to annoy Bogart. He preferred Dwight Franklin. From

McCall's perspective, Bogart had gone "full Hollywood" with his pretty, young, ex-model wife, fancy house, and designer dogs. The man she had known—the maverick, the intellectual, the outsider, the lacerating critic of Hollywood, and the epitome of the cynical hero—was gone. Hollywood accepted the Bogarts because "Bogie" was definitely head of his household, with the bigger career. Things were harder for McCall and Bramson.

In the final months of McCall's MGM contract, George Haight worked with her on a big-budget, star-studded project that seemed tailor-made for the head of the War Activities Committee. *Keep Your Powder Dry* (1945) began in the summer of 1942 as a potential Joan Crawford vehicle after her success with the wartime drama *Reunion*. Anita Loos drafted what was then titled *Women in Uniform*, but the project was shelved when Loos retired.[24] After the War Department requested that the studio make more pictures to boost Women's Auxiliary Army Corps recruitment, though, Haight asked McCall to write her version of the idea for a trio of the studio's top female stars. In between all her other committee work, she dashed off *Woman's Army*. A variation on the male wartime "buddy" drama, McCall's script focused on a group of women surviving training camp to become officers before being shipped overseas. It was one of a cluster of high-profile feature films about women's military contributions to the war and divided the critics.

Unlike Claudette Colbert's veteran medical officer in *So Proudly We Hail!* (1943) or Ann Sothern and Ella Raines in *Cry Havoc* (1943), the recruits played by Lana Turner, Laraine Day, and Susan Peters remain in a stateside training camp for the duration of the film. There are no shocking scenes of survival in Bataan and Corregidor, but McCall's script shows far more scenes of women managing the war from the home front and at army training facilities. Critics noted that unlike most war pictures that focus on women, "the romance element is so negligible that it might be said to be non-existent," but "this absence of romance in the usual sense is not missed."[25] McCall's "straight-from-the-shoulder presentation" is more critical of the male officers running the war than the patriotic *So Proudly We Hail*. After a particularly grueling training session, Val (Turner) complains, "Who was it said an Army travels on its stomach?" Another female recruit retorts, "Some general who rode a horse," taking a swipe at the male officers who see war from a comfortable position.[26] Later, when the trio spots a broken-down officer's jeep, Val sneers, "The chief of staff can't fix his car. He's waiting for mamma to come fix it..." Officers don't like getting their hands dirty. The women are told to get it working after the male chief of staff and general are unable to identify the parts of their engine. After a quick consultation, the jeep is up and running.

Louella Parsons advertised McCall's star-studded picture as the "story of three women in a man's world," linking it thematically to Maisie and many other of her female-centered scripts, but Office of War Information script readers found the unflattering depiction of the American home front, with its hoarders, racketeers, and shirkers, potentially bad for the national image.[27] One drew particular attention to Leigh Rand (Laraine Day), a backstabbing recruit from a famous army family who attempts to sabotage the career of Val Parks (Turner), an officer-in-training: "At a time when women all over the world are serving the United Nations war effort, the story's presentation of American women at war could mislead overseas audiences as to the real nature of their contribution."[28] Yet one could argue that Rand uses her family connections to powerful men in order to create an unfair hierarchy among the female recruits. McCall's point was that female solidarity should matter more.

It was all too confusing for *Motion Picture Herald*, which had hoped for a conventionally patriotic propaganda film. Though Lana Turner was "doing a little more acting than usual," the women's importance "to a nation at war, however, is not made clear in the film."[29] But Bosley Crowther and Eileen Creelman were scathing, with Creelman dismissing the characters as "so petty, the episodes so trivial, the atmosphere so filled with bickering that, although audiences may well have a good time, [Women's Auxiliary Army Corps recruiting] is not likely to be helped."[30] Crowther indulged in a little pettiness of his own, making fun of the "Jr." in McCall's name and claiming that she and cowriter George Bruce "must have dashed off" the script "on the doorsteps of the studio beauty shop."[31] Turner and Day's roles were "catty," and while grudgingly admitting that there were some "amusing" and "acid" wisecracks in the script, Creelman sniffed that the women's army "deserves more dignified and dramatic treatment than this." She had a point: only Agnes Morehead's lieutenant colonel character displays any gravitas or maturity, and even she is barely able to keep the bickering younger women in line. But what would have constituted dignified treatment for Creelman and Crowther—a more conventional romance, perhaps, or less obvious personal ambition? The removal of female criticism of male authority or the portrayal of a uniformly patriotic American public? Increasingly as the war drew to a close, conservative ideals of patriotism were restricting what women could do on screen and off. But MGM was happy enough; *Keep Your Powder Dry* more than doubled its earnings at the box office against a $1.3 million budget.[32]

McCall was not particularly interested in her next assignment, the adaptation of Rose Franken's play *Soldier's Wife*. A studio effort to repair Laraine Day's unsympathetic image in *Keep Your Powder Dry*, Parsons described the plot as a cute wartime romance where "the heroine, wife of a soldier, puts his letters in a book and presto, becomes famous overnight as an authoress."[33] Since McCall had spent her career proving that women could become famous authors writing their own words and not using those of their husbands, she was more than happy to leave it unfinished when her contract at MGM ended.

But for the first time in her adult life, she was discovering curbs to her independence at home. Over the years she had managed her "professional" image by keeping her kids at home, overseen mostly by a troupe of servants. This was fine with Dwight Franklin, who never wanted to be a househusband any more than McCall wanted to be a housewife. In the first year of their marriage, McCall found out Bramson was a different proposition. He was not only controlling; he was also increasingly verbally and physically abusive. However much he complained about her long working hours, whenever he was on leave, he willingly spent her money and attended star-studded events that were inevitably printed in the papers.

In early May, before Bramson was shipped overseas, they were guests at a testimonial dinner at the Ambassador Hotel's Embassy Room for actor Joe E. Brown, in recognition for his work entertaining the armed forces.[34] Along with Brown's son, who was serving in the armed forces, Ida Koverman, *Maisie* alumnus Robert Young, and comedian Henny Youngman were in attendance. Such friendly, cross-industry social events were numbered. Already the Hollywood coalition she helped to broker was crumbling under the impact of a new committee: the Motion Picture Alliance for the Preservation of American Ideals.

CHAPTER 12

The Party Is Over

It is one of the great ironies of Hollywood politics that within days of McCall and the Board of Governors announcing the inclusive social and educational aims of the Academy Foundation, the Motion Picture Alliance for the Preservation of American Ideals (MPA) sent out its own, very different, press statement. On February 4, 1944, a group including director Sam Wood, Walt Disney, John Wayne, and Spencer Tracy met at the Beverly Wilshire Hotel, where they declared their opposition to "a rising tide of Communism, Fascism, and kindred beliefs" spreading throughout Hollywood and the United States.[1] There was no hard evidence to support their claims unless a national minimum wage, the right to strike, and increased presence of women and other minorities in the workforce were communist or fascist. Most of the MPA members were solidly right-wing Republicans fed up with over a decade of a Democrat in the White House. Increasingly as the year rolled closer to the November election, anyone who supported the New Deal, working people, and labor unions was vulnerable to their accusations of "subversive activities" in the pages of industry trade papers and the national press. *Anyone* included McCall: two groups she belonged to, the Hollywood Writers Mobilization and the Hollywood Victory Committee, were singled out as "Communist Front" organizations.

At the Screen Writers Guild's April meeting, conservative writer and member of the MPA executive board James McGuinness recommended that a guild committee meet with the MPA "to discuss the aims and purposes of the organization." Guild members voted down the resolution and instead adopted one denouncing "as untrue the inference of the Motion Picture Alliance that this industry (motion picture) is dominated by Communists, radicals, and crackpots."[2] Guild members, including McCall, thought they had swatted their reactionary colleagues away. On June 24 she joined Walter Wanger, James Hilton, and other Academy officials hosting a luncheon for Gregor Irsky, the chief engineer of the Soviet film industry. Irsky hoped that Hollywood would take the lead in efforts "to rebuild the Leningrad and Kiev studios after the war."[3] It was just the sort of Allied war event that made the MPA see red.

When the MPA directly targeted Hollywood's guilds and unions as un-American and politically subversive that summer, McCall swung into action. Going after unions meant going against the New Deal and the administration that had stood against the Axis since 1941, and the MPA's actions were to her an unconscionable betrayal of the country in wartime. It was alarming that that the MPA appeared to be "masterminded by a group of reactionary writers and producers concentrated mainly in the Metro-Goldwyn-Mayer studios"—her home studio.[4]

On June 28, 1944, she and representatives from seventeen Hollywood guilds and unions launched a "counterattack" from the Hollywood Women's Club, organized by the Emergency Committee of Hollywood Guilds and Unions.[5] The Emergency Committee united liberal workers across the film industry and included the Brotherhood of Electrical Workers, Screen Cartoonists (who loathed the anti-union Disney), the Screen Publicists Guild, the Society of Motion Picture Film Editors, the Story Analysts Guild, the Brotherhood of Carpenters and Unions, the Songwriters Protective Association, and the Screen Writers Guild.

At the meeting, McCall "flatly accused MPA members of union-busting intentions." She was widely quoted in the national press: "We don't believe union-busting is an American ideal."[6] Although the groups invited members of the MPA "to attend and present their viewpoints," no one responded to their invitation. Then, on June 29, the Council of Hollywood Guilds and Unions turned the tables on their conservative foes, accusing the MPA of being "a subversive and dangerous organization."[7]

When her ex-husband's boss, Cecil B. DeMille, added his voice against the unions, McCall, with her mid-Atlantic drawl, took his arguments apart on the radio. She quoted Hollywood's excellent war record and stated, "We've got to win as much attention for the truths as for the smears. We're late in telling the truth about ourselves, late in meeting in unity to plan the most effective way of telling it. But we have met. We are united. We know the story, and it's a proud story.

Let's spread it on the record."[8] But for McCall it wasn't just a proud story of American labor, the solidarity of writers, and free speech: it was also a proud story of women and the way they shaped Hollywood's product.

Since the mid-1930s, McCall had advanced the rights of all screenwriters and maintained her position in Hollywood by pursuing a pragmatic, frequently middle-of-the road strategy appealing to colleagues across the industry—a strategy uncannily like President Roosevelt's, who maintained a shifting but broad coalition in Washington and among the electorate.[9] Although not from a working-class family, writing was McCall's labor, and her aim was to put an end to economic exploitation for all writers and improve Hollywood's production system. Through a complicated mesh of political, gender, cultural, and ethnic links, she bridged the radicalism of Dorothy Parker and Dalton Trumbo, the Democratic feminism of Bette Davis and Helen Gahagan Douglas, and the conservatism of Charles Brackett and Eddie Mannix, Ann Sothern, Hedda Hopper, and Ida Koverman. It's worth remembering that she became the first woman president of the Screen Writers Guild and oversaw expansion of the number of women in governance at a time when women were not a majority of Hollywood screenwriters or guild members. But this individual power wasn't achieved through compromising core beliefs. In her day-to-day work supporting equal treatment for all writers, in her activities for the War Activities Committee, and in scripts, McCall revealed her commitment to expanding women's independence in the Hollywood workforce during and after the war.

As this battle with the MPA unfolded, the national media talked of the Democratic Party's endorsement of the Equal Rights Amendment in its 1944 platform and women's employment across the industries soared.[10] In Hollywood, Sam Goldwyn put McCall's historical script about women's education at Oberlin into production and MGM assigned her to write an epic women's film for Greer Garson.[11] Women's history, content, and stars were still valued.

There was growing resentment, however. In 1944 Zanuck spoke to his employees at Fox about how the war had changed "the boys" and how Hollywood needed to adapt and make "vital, thinking-men's blockbusters." He continued, "Although I recognize there'll always be a market for Betty Grable and Lana Turner and all that tit stuff," when the boys came back, a newer, more masculine Hollywood would supplant the saccharine melodramas and sex pictures focusing on women.[12]

While McCall advocated greater realism and attention to social issues in films, something that Zanuck had also addressed in the 1943 Writers' Conference at UCLA, she did not share Zanuck's dismissal of women's pictures or the Hollywood that had supported them.[13] That summer of 1944 she called upon members of the Emergency Committee of Hollywood Guilds and Unions to work with producers "in reabsorbing returning Hollywood servicemen and *women*."[14] McCall vowed that this was one industry where women's employment gains were not going to be purged with the peace.

But just as she was pushing back against the MPA and staving off potential attacks on women's postwar employment in the industry, McCall, six months pregnant, caved into pressure from Bramson to stop working. On August 4, 1944, Hollywood was shocked to read that McCall had resigned as president of the Screen Writers Guild.[15] She did retain the chair of the Hollywood branch of the War Activities Committee through her pregnancy and the birth of her daughter on November 9, but she turned over those duties in early 1945 to the new chairman, director John Cromwell, and vice chairman, Eddie Mannix.[16] At this meeting, a nine-member all-male committee of was appointed, the flavor of things to come.[17]

It's very possible that Bramson stood to gain from McCall's resignation in more ways than one. He had a connection with his wife's replacement as head of the guild, Lester Cole, through their army service at Fort MacArthur. Given Bramson's ambitions as a writer and his dislike of women being assertive in public and private, future patronage from another man such as Cole would be far more acceptable to his ego than continuing to receive favors from his wife. Years later, in his memoirs, Cole's misogyny manifested itself when he described his election to the presidency "following the pregnancy of Mary McCarthy."[18] His attempt to diminish McCall's importance later in life by mixing her up with another Mary masked gendered resentment of a woman having so much power.[19]

With McCall away, other women writers looking for help from the guild suffered. In mid-1944, Cole received an application for membership and plea for help from Thelma A. Prescott.[20] In 1939 Prescott was appointed NBC's first producer-director but was fired after eight months and began writing film scripts.[21] One of the producers she worked for did not give her any credit for extensive script rewrites and dialogue she did on *Since You Went Away* (1944). The producer was David O. Selznick. The guild went through the motions of contacting Selznick, but he deflected the claims, and the investigation fizzled. Prescott quit screenwriting.

Cole lasted only a few months as president, and in October 1944 he withdrew his candidacy in favor of Emmet Lavery, a comparative newcomer to guild party politics. This was an advantage because Lavery appeared to be a left-of-center political moderate like McCall. He also shared her Irish American connections, which was an advantage among the profession's considerable population of former Chicago and New York journalists. But he had two advantages over McCall at first—he was a man, and he was an unknown quantity in an increasingly divisive political climate. McCall always made sure people knew exactly where she stood. He was elected unopposed on November 8, with James Hilton, Howard Estabrook, and Michael Kanin rounding out the vice president, secretary, and treasurer roles.[22]

The only women in this new administration were executive board members Frances Goodrich and Betty Reinhardt. Though McCall returned to work only a few months after the birth of Mary-David and rejoined the executive committee throughout 1945 before serving as a vice president in 1946-47 under Lavery, the Screen Writers Guild would elect fewer and fewer female members to top positions after she left the presidency.[23] It was part of a gradual but relentless phantom lady syndrome in Hollywood as more and more women were muzzled and pushed to the margins of power. Frances Marion, for many years one of the most highly paid writers in Hollywood, would retire from MGM in the mid-1940s, commenting that screenwriting had become like "writing on sand with the wind blowing."[24]

McCall had no intention of quitting to play a stay-at-home mother for more than a few weeks. At the start of 1945 she raised money for Jewish orphans in Palestine with Eleanor Roosevelt and her son Elliott's new wife, Faye, and organized a fundraiser with Paul Robeson at the Mocambo that February.[25]

Then in March, just as one war was drawing to a close, she was faced with another, which had the potential to damage the guild and undermine her credibility as its most popular leader. The United States was rocked by some of the largest strikes in its history in 1945-46, and they started in Hollywood. In the 1930s, many studio painters, carpenters, electricians, set decorators, and screen cartoonists were represented by the Conference of Studio Unions (CSU). Producers stalled over negotiating with additional set decorators who had left the rival union, the International Alliance of Theatrical Stage Employees (IATSE) to join the CSU, and then refused to comply with the War Labor Board's independent arbitrator, which sided with the CSU.

More than ten thousand members of the CSU and Local 1421 went on strike over wages, picketing Disney and Warner Bros. And on March 2, 1945, McCall was elected chair of the Hollywood Council of Guilds and Unions by its fifteen thousand members.[26] She worked with the National Labor Relations Board to side with the CSU strikers and ignore the rival IATSE. Many workers across the industry, including screenwriters, wanted to join the picket. Inflation was up, wages had less earning power, and the studios were raking in record profits. Instead of joining the picket, McCall advised the guild to donate $25,000 to the CSU strike fund. Many on the left felt it was the easy way out, or, as writer John Bright put it, "putting a price tag on our conscience."[27]

It was a tricky situation, not only because it split the left (the Communist Party members of the guild were still abiding by a wartime no-strike pledge and would not support the strikers) but also because had McCall and other trade unionists gone with their first instinct and struck with the CSU, it would have violated the guild's minimum basic agreement with the producers by siding with the other union.[28] As historian Miranda Banks has pointed out, "Officially, a sympathy strike was not an option; contractually, writers were obliged to cross other employees' picket lines."[29] Acting as a negotiator with the National Labor Relations Board kept the Screen Writers Guild contract safe while helping the CSU strikers get public government backing. But the last remaining bastions of New Deal liberalism were under threat. The studios had successfully pitted unions against each other and sat back for months, refusing to negotiate. They could afford to with a backlog of more than a hundred films that they could release during the conflict. By October, Warner Bros. used tear gas on the picketers after a fight between strikebreakers and strikers broke out. Outside of Hollywood, Democrats were losing their hold on Washington as right-wing politicians stoked public antagonism to the unions and Hollywood, calling anyone even remotely to the left a "Red." There was no room in the middle anymore.

McCall was old enough to remember the context for America's isolationist stance after the Great War, the xenophobia, the antagonism toward unions, and consequences of the country's failure to engage with other nations and feminists' struggles to build upon the momentum from the Nineteenth Amendment. She continued to speak out. On March 8, International Women's Day, she addressed the Russian War Relief women's committee at the Beverly Hills Hotel, appearing alongside the much-decorated Soviet war veteran Raissa Potanina, a tank commander; actress Michele Morgan, who spoke of women working in the French Resistance; Dame May Whitty, who discussed women's work in British War Relief; and *New York Times* Moscow Bureau writer Jeannette Reisbord, who reminded her largely American audience that Russian women "work side by side with men, their work evaluated equally."

McCall concurred and went further in her address: "It is the women's battle from now on for a world peace . . . women in America must teach their children not to be against minority groups or against the religious views of others. It is the job of the mother, not the father. American women should wake up still more to their responsibility."[30] She cautioned the audience, reminding them of anti-Semitism and white supremacy in the United States, of the riots and internment that had marked the war years. The solution, she argued, was for women to think internationally and take control of education and the peace negotiations.

But there were unfriendly spies in the audience: FBI agents transcribed her speech and put it in her growing FBI file, which claimed she was "active in Communist Party front organizations, especially those having to do with women."[31] Her work in Black civil rights initiatives was also suspect, and local newspapers reported her working alongside Atlanta University President Rufus E. Clement and Bette Davis on the Los Angeles Division of the United Negro College Fund that spring.[32]

Motivation for the growing anticommunist "witch hunts" aimed at Hollywood not only centered on film workers' prominent role in the strike waves but also reacted to the industry's prominent New Deal Democrats, civil rights advocates, and leaders of international wartime coalitions. McCall was arguably the most prominent of these women, deeply committed to Roosevelt's policies, including his pragmatic alliance with the Soviet Union.[33]

A month after her International Women's Day speech, Roosevelt was dead. McCall, like millions of Americans, saw FDR as one politician she could love and respect without reservation. He had become part of the household of every American family that owned a radio since his first Fireside Chat in 1933. He was hope, he was continuity, and, as one working man memorably put it, "Mr. Roosevelt is the only man we ever had in the White House who would understand that my boss is a sonofabitch."[34] No other leader or politician would dare to attack the wealthy, big business, and bankers as he had done in his famed Madison Square

Garden speech: "They are unanimous in their hate for me—and I welcome their hatred."

Shortly after the president's death, MGM producer Dore Schary wrote to secretary of the Hollywood Writers Mobilization, Pauline Lauber, asking if McCall would write a speech for an event in the Hollywood Bowl. She, Helen Deutsch, Emmet Lavery, Ring Lardner Jr., and Dudley Nichols were among those members of the Hollywood Writers Mobilization approached to write speeches in tribute. Members of all branches of the Hollywood community lined up to participate. Ingrid Bergman recited the late president's favorite prayer, Frank Sinatra sang, and James Cagney closed the event with a community "pledge of support to President Harry S. Truman."[35] But with the MPA still denouncing the Hollywood left in the papers, this was arguably the last moment that Hollywood worked together.

For the time being, McCall retained the industry's respect as a prominent wartime image maker and power broker. But MGM wouldn't match Zanuck's $3,000-a-week contract offer, and so McCall bid the *Maisie* series farewell and moved to Twentieth Century-Fox.[36] Zanuck had a long-standing reputation for supporting those writers he liked to the hilt. As screenwriter, humorist, and contemporary media historian Leo Rosten commented, "A writer or director at Universal does not 'rate' with a writer or director at Twentieth Century-Fox."[37] McCall, having begun her Hollywood career with Zanuck in 1931, could expect to "rate" high at the studio.

Assigning McCall to adapt Rosemary Taylor's 1943 memoir *Chicken Every Sunday* reveals traces of Zanuck's often dormant sense of humor.[38] It was the story of a hardworking wife who has supported her feckless dreamer husband's string of failed businesses over the years—and who finally wants a divorce. Although the heroine merely adds another room to her house to take on more boarders to cover her husband's debts, she had more than a few things in common with McCall and her habit of cranking out popular short stories to pay the bills back in the 1920s and '30s—and now, cranking out more scripts to support her growing family.

She began her new job with her new husband at home full-time. But if Bramson wanted to play the conquering Hollywood war hero, the *Los Angeles Times* wasn't about to let him off the hook for his heroic "war record." In his August 19 column, Art Ryon noted that Major David Bramson had recently been awarded the

Bronze Star in Italy for "meritorious achievement in connection with military operations."[39] "What did he do?" Art Ryon asked his readers. Bramson the "real hero" was a "public relations officer of the replacement training command in Italy" who arranged for articles about the achievements of *real soldiers* to reach publications in the United States. "The typewriter may not be mightier than the Garand rifle," Ryon sneered, "but it nevertheless is a potent and important weapon." Bramson's macho self-image was, like so many things manufactured by Hollywood publicity offices, airbrushed.

When Bramson returned to his wife's house on Bainbridge Avenue, he met his nine-month-old daughter for the first time and took over as stepfather to Sheila and the twins. Bramson may have charmed McCall in their Hollywood Canteen days, but he couldn't handle anyone disagreeing with him, even children. He assaulted the boys. Sheila tried to get on her stepfather's good side but couldn't find one.

The three older children looked forward to visits with their father, but they were infrequent, since Franklin had taken up with a pretty, divorced, and monied architect, Eliza Moultrie. They would marry on Eliza's birthday, February 20, 1947, according to Dwight so that he "would have only one major date to remember." At least Sheila and the boys were able to spend Christmas Day with their father, but there was never enough time with him. Bramson made them dread coming "home."

Bramson spent his wife's money lavishly on nights out, cars, and, as it turned out, other women—some of whom he would even bring to the house, claiming they were interior decorators or secretaries. He endlessly picked over McCall's appearance, complaining that she was no longer attractive, had terrible taste in clothes, and "combed her hair with an egg-beater."[40] He also hit her repeatedly.

McCall, a lifelong boxing fan, was still tough enough to swing back at him, but she put up with his abuse of her and her children. How could she have put up with it? Was she just worn out, tired of always calling the shots in her own life? Did she fantasize about letting someone else make the decisions? Was she prepared to put up with anything for a pretty face and good sex?[41] Unfortunately, this kind of marriage was not uncommon, even among the toughest of Hollywood feminists. Bette Davis was in a similarly abusive relationship with her third husband, artist William Grant Sherry. As Davis later revealed in *The Lonely Life*, "It is not unusual for the husband of a famous woman to be insulting to her in public."[42] Bramson was abusive in public and in private. It was the beginning of a trend that would split up her family more irrevocably than her divorce from Franklin. In her *Maisie* series, her heroine is always cautioning other women against throwing everything away for a good-looking man, and yet McCall ended up being a woman who couldn't take her own advice.

In a career first, McCall even played the role of the domesticated wife. "When she and my father were first married," her daughter Mary-David recalled, "she bought herself a chintz pinafore and went to cooking school. She made popovers, Hollandaise, baking powder biscuits, Angel Food cake, gingerbread, broiled chicken, roast beef, omelets, sweet and savory." It became a kind of proof of her abilities as a mother to "serve Eggs Benedict on a school day." But McCall's performance failed to convince Bramson: "My father never appreciated either the pinafore or her cooking."[43]

Bramson soon made his reasons for marrying McCall crystal-clear: Rather than remain in the military, he wanted a career as a Hollywood writer. But even McCall couldn't force a producer to hire him. Zanuck was too much of a professional to hire an untried writer, even if he was McCall's husband. McCall suggested Broadway as an alternative. She had been involved in financing plays in the past, including *Angel Street*, in 1941–42, alongside her other "angels," producer George Haight, actress Rita Johnson, and writer Charles Lederer.[44] The U.S. theatrical version of British playwright Patrick Hamilton's *Gaslight* (1938) starred Judith Evelyn (later immortalized as Miss Lonely Hearts in *Rear Window*, 1954) in her breakout role as a young wife manipulated into thinking she was insane by an evil husband (Vincent Price).

In early 1946, soon after leaving the army, Bramson tried to interest Tallulah Bankhead in a stage play by L. Bush-Fakete and Mary Fay, *The Big Two*. According to Louella Parsons, "Later it will be made into a movie. . . . It's the story about the US and Russia and Bramson's wife, Mary McCall, is already working on the movie script."[45] The topic, however timely it seemed in 1946, soon went out of fashion. It was not a year to make a romantic play on words out of the former U.S.-Soviet alliance.

The Canadian government indicted twenty-two communist agents in February, and in March visiting dignitary Winston Churchill warned of the descending "Iron Curtain" and the threat of communist Russia at a speech in Missouri.[46] Americans took up their own anticommunist cudgels that summer. Billy Wilkerson, publisher of the *Hollywood Reporter*, started his own war, accusing Emmet Lavery, Ring Lardner Jr., and several other prominent Hollywood writers of being "Red Commissars" on the front page of the tradepaper.[47] McCall wasn't mentioned, but the redbaiting would get worse.

McCall also recognized that the current political climate was pushing women of experience out of public life—and out of her industry. Together with Lillian Gish, Muriel Wright, Dr. Wendy Stewart, and K. Alexandra White, McCall formed the "Frankly Over Forty" organization, "which aims at greater maturity in motion picture entertainment."[48] It was the first prominent organization in the U.S. culture industries to tackle society's unfair double standards for working women "above breeding age." For McCall, continuing to employ professional women over forty had obvious advantages for Hollywood. They had experience in production and were more interested in making pictures "that will reflect life as we know life really is." There was no need to train such women; they had connections, initiative, and confidence. But women over forty in front of the camera in 1940s Hollywood were as little wanted as they are in the twenty-first century, and increasingly McCall found that Hollywood's men weren't interested in keeping them behind the camera either.

In steadfastly refusing to dye her gray hair to hide her age, McCall was one of the most prominent women to resist ageist hypocrisies. But many of the great stars of her era were retiring or going through rough patches, including Rainer, Garbo, Shearer, Davis, and de Havilland, and offscreen, Loos, Marion, and Murfin were winding down their Hollywood careers. Men returning from the war were getting the plum writing jobs. Frankly Over Forty argued that older women should embrace their power and own it rather than retreat silently into the kitchen.

Bramson wasn't interested in the guild's problems or the wider political situation. His only interest in women was in younger ones susceptible to a quick affair; the problems of the over-forties (including his wife) did not matter to him. But as his wife still had some influence in Hollywood, he wanted her to get him a job with prestige. That May, McCall was reelected to the Academy Board of Governors. The position carried some influence, so on September 7, 1946, she pulled strings and got Bramson a job as the organization's "director of public relations."[49] Although Bramson put out a lot of positive material about the Academy and the film industry to his press contacts, the political climate was against him. The rising tide of anticommunist attacks on the Hollywood community made good headlines hard to promote. Bramson resigned in November, and Donald Black took over. It was a thankless job, and in April 1947 the Academy accepted Black's resignation after Wanger, William Dozier, and McCall proposed "to take charge . . . of passing on all publicity releases, promotional undertakings, and related matters in advance of their execution."[50]

His Hollywood career going nowhere, Bramson pushed his wife to sell her cherished Bainbridge Avenue house. They moved to 523 North Beverly Drive, on the corner of Beverly and Carmelita, to a house Charlie Chaplin had built for his second wife, Lita Grey.[51] But Bramson also wanted a ranch where he could play cowboy and remove McCall from her urban seat of power. McCall still had her Fox salary, so they bought a house in Morro Bay, several hundred acres near San Luis Obispo, and some stock and horses. Bramson had McCall buy some rabbits that he raised for meat. The children, committed lovers of all little fluffy animals, were horrified. As Mary-David recalled, "I think this was my mother's way of letting my father have his dream of being away from the Hollywood scene." Given Bramson's abuse of her and the children, it was also a convenient way to isolate them from friends and colleagues, and to reassert control over the family in a western fantasy.

Morro Bay, to put it mildly, "was not a great fit" for McCall. As Mary-David joked, "She just could not hang there. The local residents were mostly dairymen who did the morning milking and then hung out in the town square for the balance of the day, until evening milking time."[52] One day the principal of Alan and Jerry's junior high called in McCall to tell her that her boys were liars. When McCall asked for more detail, he complained that the boys told classmates that they knew Jimmy Durante and the Marx Brothers. When McCall responded that "they did indeed know these celebrities" since they were former neighbors from Beverly Hills, the principal was open-mouthed. They used to ride their bikes past the Durante house, and very often they would stop and chat when he "would be outside watering his lawn with zinc on his schnozz."[53] Harpo Marx was a next-door neighbor.

But this was all in the past, and Bramson had alienated most of McCall's old friends before he forced her to relocate to Morro Bay. Brackett was one of the few who continued seeing her after her remarriage, and, given his wife Elizabeth's tendency to get plastered when they were out with friends, he sympathized with McCall's spousal tribulations.[54]

She took refuge in work, driving into Los Angeles, staying late at the studio, and running for leadership positions, catching up with Brackett on guild matters when she could. She was elected to the Academy again in May 1947, this time serving as secretary under Jean Hersholt, who headed both the Academy and the Motion Picture Relief Fund. Writer Delmer Daves acted as McCall's assistant.[55] Though McCall would later confess to her daughter that "Careers for women are the shits," there were some compensations working for Zanuck again.[56] McCall had a sweet deal at Twentieth Century-Fox: one picture a year, with a ten-week guarantee and, as she gloated, "I was free to work outside the rest of the time but not for less money."

But Zanuck soon had a stable full of male screenwriters returning from the war and lost interest in developing McCall's material. After she completed her treatment of *Chicken Every Sunday* in the fall of 1945, the film project was shelved. Then Zanuck put her on a musical, his default move for his remaining female screenwriters.[57] McCall's musical was a "rewrite" of "a story property of the studio originally titled, *Star Dust*." Linda Darnell had starred in the picture, but Darnell was no longer making the big box-office dividends. The remake was symbolic, and when Zanuck retitled McCall's script *Dancing in the Dark* and gussied it up with color and a $2 million budget, according to *Variety*, most at the studio assumed it would be for one of Zanuck's new moneymaking ingénues, either Jeanne Crain or Betty Grable.

Zanuck's crony Gregory Ratoff had been attached to the project as director when it was at Columbia (Arthur Schwartz was also attached to write some new songs) before the project and Ratoff moved to Fox.[58] Then Broadway legend George Jessel came west to produce, replacing William Perlberg. Jessel, Zanuck's "court jester," would maintain his position at the studio largely through flattering his boss. He is credited with only half-jokingly saying, "When I die, I want to be cremated, and have my ashes sprinkled on Mr. Zanuck's driveway so his car won't skid."[59] McCall was a longtime expert on handling Hollywood's difficult male egos and managed to get along well enough with both king and jester.

Luckily, *Dancing in the Dark* was also planned to showcase the legendary Clifton Webb "dancing for his first time in a film."[60] McCall adored Webb. As the suave, poisonously witty Waldo Lydecker in Betty Reinhardt's *Laura*, he had become a major Hollywood star in 1944. She was equally delighted when she found out the "wonderfully pretty" brunette Jeanne Crain (the former Miss Long Beach) was to play the female lead. But then Crain got pregnant, and the project was shelved.

Jessel, getting restive, asked McCall to write a script for another Fox star, singer Dick Haymes, who was then playing at the Copa nightclub in New York. Haymes announced that "Jessel will produce his next movie, *New on Sunday*, by Mary McCall and he'll only sing one song in it."[61] It was planned as a big acting break-through for him, but McCall shrewdly took orders only from Zanuck, who told her that fall and winter "to re-write" *Dancing in the Dark* "for a much more 'hep chick,'" namely Betty Grable. As she recalled, "The day I finished the revised script, in which we gave this girl much more of a show business background, I bought a trade paper on my way to lunch." A column in the *Hollywood Reporter* announced that Grable and husband Harry James were expecting their second child. "I looked up and Darryl Zanuck was coming in from lunch, and I said, 'Is it true?' and he nodded his head." That's Hollywood, she thought. "These are some of the things which come between a writer's hopes and their realizations."[62]

Until this point, Zanuck had been committed to a light song-and-dance comedy for Webb and some other un-pregnant Fox actress, but then McCall met Webb in the Fox commissary and received some bad news. After telling the actor "how excited" she was to be writing a picture for him since she'd seen him dance in so many of his New York shows, he told her that he didn't want to appear in *Dancing in the Dark* since he was now so much older than his glory days on Broadway. He "didn't want to appear second best" to Fred Astaire, Gene Kelly, and James Cagney.[63] McCall conveyed the news to Zanuck and suggested that she work on a more dramatic story with some entertainment history background to give it depth. She had always loved Selznick's *A Star Is Born*, released ten years back, and wanted to pursue a variant of the fading-rising star genre that would create solid dramatic roles for Webb and one of Zanuck's many younger starlets. Instead of focusing on *Dancing in the Dark*'s romance between the ingénue and her boyfriend Bill, or a variant of the Esther Blodgett-Norman Maine romance, McCall's script would explore a father-daughter relationship, where faded star Emery Slade helps propel his daughter Julie to stardom. With McCall still on $3,000 a week and no workable production schedule in sight, Zanuck agreed. She started over, calling the story *Julie*.[64]

She had an original western in reserve called *On to Oregon* in case the musical didn't work out. Hers had a novelty aspect: the only stars were children.[65] It was based on the seven famous Sager kids, who in 1844 traveled westward on the

Oregon Trail with their parents. After their parents died en route, missionaries Marcus and Narcissa Whitman adopted them. The Whitmans weren't liked by their Native American flock and were massacred in 1847, along with two Sager brothers.[66] In 1860, the eldest girl, Catherine, wrote a memoir but was unable to find a publisher in her lifetime.[67] McCall focused on the two eldest children, offering a different kind of western derived from an authentic female account.

Zanuck, aware that westerns and films for the family market sold more tickets, greenlit her script and assigned Sam Engle, who had worked with John Ford on *My Darling Clementine* (1946), to produce. She went on research trips to Oregon, where she read Sager's story in context, and visited the Snake River in Idaho with Engel and the director Louis King (Henry King's brother), who'd had a good run with family-oriented westerns such as *Thunderhead, Son of Flicka* (1945) and *Smoky* (1946). Engel planned a $100,000 search for the teenaged leads, and the story was to be filmed on location over three seasons "to catch the real colors."[68] Everything was ready . . . and then Zanuck abandoned the project. He allegedly said, "Well, after all, this is a costume picture, location picture, color picture—and the lead is a 14-year-old boy."[69] He of course neglected to mention Catherine's leading role, but then, she was a girl.

Writing for the guild magazine *The Screen Writer* in 1946, McCall was able to air some of her frustrations with writing for the studios. "I grant that writing is a chancy line of work, that few writers earn as much as stenographers, that it's painfully hard to create with the gun of debt pressed against one's temple," she wrote. "I've lived by free-lance, unsubsidized writing, and a meager and worried life it often was. But I dared it, I risked it, and whatever security I achieved, I got by writing stories of my own, and selling them in an open and competitive market."[70]

She had no illusions about being a great artist, but she had worked hard as a highly paid contract writer and put her disappointment aside when projects were abandoned by producers or reassigned to someone else. Her work for the Screen Writers Guild had improved conditions for writers and eliminated the worst abuses by producers, and yet she acknowledged that the studio system and the contract did not necessarily encourage great writing. "To me, an annual guaranteed wage for writers who are still potent, still creative, working in a field where there is and always will be a market for capably-written material, is retrogression, not progress."

But the days of comfort and security for any screenwriters were fading fast. Away from the studio, McCall's battle with the conservative MPA continued; in

March 1947 she spoke at the Olympic Auditorium in Los Angeles in protest against the ongoing "attacks on labor." Representing Lavery, she was the only woman present in the March 18, 1947, meeting at Perino's between the representatives of the Hollywood guilds and the head of the Motion Picture Association of America (MPAA), Eric Johnston.[71] At that meeting she suggested that Hollywood "use its own medium to tell the true Hollywood story" since Johnston was so concerned about improving "the standing of our industry at home and abroad." They planned a series of short films about the various branches of the filmmaking profession, and the actors, remembering McCall's long-standing support of their guild, chose her to write the script for their documentary film.

She took another tack as an Academy governor, proposing new initiatives connecting Hollywood to a wider film community. During the war she had been a passionate advocate of British cinema and was instrumental in getting filmmakers such as David Lean and Emeric Pressburger Academy recognition. In March 1947 she and Charles Brackett fought "a bloody battle" with other Academy governors to give Laurence Olivier's *Henry V* (1945) a special Academy Award.[72] McCall, it must be said, relished this fight, since conservative director Frank Capra was the most violently opposed to the idea. She had never forgiven the way he had courted the Screen Writers Guild in the days when the Screen Directors Guild was in its infancy and contractless, only to abandon his writer allies after directors got their deal.

McCall still had plenty of allies among the other governors. In May, with Jean Hersholt and Walter Wanger, she was involved in plans for an international film festival in Hollywood to be held in 1948.[73] She and Hersholt hoped that a less provincial film gathering in Hollywood would make some of its more vociferous, xenophobic, and anticommunist members realize not only that foreign films were not all communist propaganda but also how innocuous international audiences and filmmakers found Hollywood scripts. Unfortunately, it was to be a joint enterprise between the Academy and the MPAA represented by Eric Johnston. It never happened.

Her reforms at the Motion Picture Relief Fund were more successful. In 1947 she arranged for 1 percent of all writers' salaries to be sent to the charity.[74] Soon other guilds and unions followed this policy, and the MPRF remained the industry's most successful example of social care. The fund was able to expand the country house bungalows and add new hospital wings for elderly and sick members of the film community. But the Motion Picture Relief Fund was about the only Hollywood organization protected from overt political discord and revenge.

If McCall ever truly believed that Hollywood was a community of filmmakers who cared about the future of their industry and that screenwriters were essential members of this community, she was in for a reality check. When Hollywood went to war again, this time against itself, McCall was caught in the crossfire.

CHAPTER 13

Scarlet Woman

O nce the Democrats lost control of Congress after the 1946 elections, Republican senators pushed a bill through limiting the power of the unions, forbidding wildcat strikes and political donations, and ordering leaders to sign noncommunist membership affidavits. It was sweeping anti-union legislation designed to hamstring the Wagner Act's protection of the right to strike and an incursion on First Amendment protections. The Taft-Hartley Act, passed on June 23, 1947, over President Truman's veto, threatened everything that McCall and her Screen Writers Guild colleagues fought for.

At the same time the Motion Picture Alliance for the Preservation of American Ideals approached conservatives in Washington, demanding that Hollywood be purged of allegedly communist screen content and the left-wing writers responsible for it.[1] The House Committee on Un-American Activities, originally formed in the 1930s to investigate right-wing fascist groups, returned with a vengeance with Hollywood liberals in its sights.

Political tensions exploded over the summer; forty-three names were added to HUAC's list as it opened investigations into alleged communist infiltration of Hollywood. For HUAC and its informants the hearings were an opportunity to settle political scores and bask in the limelight. As Victor Navasky put it, "The HUAC hearings were degradation ceremonies. Their job was not to legislate or even to discover subversives . . . so much as it was to stigmatize."[2] The committee hunted academics, labor leaders, scientists, and military figures, but Hollywood was its preferred hunting ground—not because it was a den of communists intent on overthrowing the government but because attacking showbusiness people generated media headlines for politicians.

Many of the filmmakers called to testify before the committee were not only McCall's colleagues, they were also her friends, including Lardner and her former Warner Bros. and Columbia colleague Dalton Trumbo. Even her former vice president on the Guild, Lester Cole, was subpoenaed. But Jack B. Tenney's California Legislative Committee investigating un-Americanism had also targeted an organization McCall had been a member of during the war, the Hollywood Writers Mobilization.[3] Soon even the Hollywood Bowl memorial for Roosevelt was smeared as a communist event.

McCall could read the writing on the wall: most of those called before the committee were writers. HUAC was after the guild, and the producers were doing nothing to stop the coming purge. In the spring and summer McCall was head of the labor committee at Twentieth Century-Fox and presided over meetings on May 28 and July 17, 1947, to maintain the terms of the 1942 contract and commit to the stabilization of salaries and credit arbitration.[4] If the producers could be kept to the terms of the contract, the guild would be able to shield most of its members. But the Taft-Hartley Act stated that labor union leadership had to sign affidavits proclaiming their noncommunist affiliation, or they would no longer have the protection of the National Labor Relations Board in labor disputes. McCall didn't want to sign anything, but the guild was boxed in by the new legislation. One, should disgruntled members on the right break away from the guild, angered at any perceived gestures of protection for communist members, Taft-Hartley would encourage them to break the power of the writers' hard-won company union and form their own. Two, since only noncommunist-declaring groups would make any potential ballot for a new union, outraged members of the left fleeing a more compliant guild would have no protection at all and wouldn't even be eligible to appear on a selection ballot. And three, should its members not declare themselves, then the Screen Writers Guild couldn't appear on any future ballot to compete as the screenwriters' union.

Lavery announced to the papers that he would file an affidavit of noncommunist affiliation with the NLRB, and later "severely criticized" screenwriters who refused to say that they weren't communist.[5] This didn't sit well with writers who knew that the Constitution protected the right to avoid self-incrimination. However much President Lavery liked to portray himself as the savior of the guild during the great purge, it was actually McCall, as his vice president, who managed day-to-day matters while Lavery did publicity in New York for his new play. In early November 1947, finally realizing how much respect he had lost from members opposed to his conciliatory policies, Lavery declined to run for a third term.[6] His *Gentleman from Athens*, starring David Bramson's old client Anthony Quinn as a roughneck politician, was a complete flop in New York; it didn't exactly help that Hedda Hopper said it was a communist tract.[7]

A few weeks later, president of the MPAA Eric Johnston released a two-page press release stating that the nine screenwriters (Adrian Scott, Cole, Bieberman, Trumbo, Jack Lawson, Albert Maltz, Sam Ornitz, Lardner, and Alvah Bessie) and one director (Edward Dmytryk) recently charged with contempt of Congress for not cooperating with HUAC would no longer be hired by the industry. This document created the blacklist. Soon, more than the Hollywood Ten would be out of a job; even with the guild protected by its executive board affidavits, individual writers were at the mercy of producers for assignments.

McCall scaled back her public presence during the crisis. She maintained her work at the Academy through the end of her term and agreed to write the first "history" of the Screen Writers Guild for the fifteenth anniversary issue of *The Screen Writer* that April.[8] As someone who had friends and enemies on both the right and the left, McCall was chosen as the best objective historian in a tense and polarized era. She matter-of-factly reconstructed the origins and aims of the guild from the early meeting in March 1933 through the creation of the constitution and the first negotiations by Jack Lawson, the early days of intimidation by producers, and the rise of the conservative Screen Playwrights and on to dissolution and reformation in 1936-37. She downplayed her own role in negotiations for the contract, merely noting the dates of success and the fact that in the guild's early days the membership numbered only 470. She highlighted August 8, 1938, as a "red-letter day"—the day the NLRB "certified the SWG as collective bargaining agent for all screen writers"—and May 1942, when the contract was finally in place.

In referring to her own power as a uniting force within the industry, she was so self-effacing she didn't even name herself: "The guild cooperated with all other industry groups in the War Activities Committee of the Motion Picture Industry. In 1943, the president of the guild became the chairman of the Hollywood Division of that all-industry committee." She predicted, "In the next fifteen years, big winds will blow on us, but when they subside, we will still be on our feet and moving forward, still fighting for the dignity and security of those who have chosen motion pictures as their field of writing, within the constitutional sense." But by 1947 some worried that if writers of good faith didn't take a stand soon the Screen Writers Guild would be history.

The March 25 Report of the Senate Fact-Finding Committee on Un-American Activities on Communist Front Organizations didn't mince words. According to the committee, the Screen Writers Guild was "a Communist dominated organization."[9] Although McCall was not denounced as an out-and-out Red like former president Jack Lawson, whose name peppered the three-hundred-odd-page document, she was listed as a member or sponsor of several organizations deemed to be communist-infiltrated, including the Hollywood Democratic Committee and the Hollywood Writers Mobilization, for whom she wrote the Los Angeles mayor's speech at Franklin Roosevelt's memorial service back in April 1945. But her most terrible offense was attending a Hollywood Democratic Committee meeting with "such outstanding fellow-travelers and Communists" as Orson Welles and Albert Dekker on the night of Thursday March 4, 1943, at the Hollywood Roosevelt Hotel. It was a complete fabrication; that night she had been presenting the Oscars at the Cocoanut Grove and had photos and more than a thousand witnesses to prove it.

Zanuck stood by her but work on *Dancing in the Dark/Julie* stalled again. Although he found McCall's characters Julie "completely believable, sympathetic, and delightful" and Slade "a minor masterpiece," Zanuck and others worried that the father-daughter story was "too melodramatic" for audiences who just wanted color and showmanship.[10] Grable was back at work after giving birth to her daughter Jessica but was busy with other projects.

Clifton Webb, meanwhile, had a hit that March playing the eccentric Lynn Belvedere in the social comedy *Sitting Pretty*. The dapper and opinionated Belvedere makes a reluctant living as a nanny to a wealthy family (he detests children), while on the side he writes a best-selling satire about his employers' lifestyle. The film, which pokes fun at middle-class suburbanites, became one of the studio's top grossers of 1948 and convinced Webb that he wanted "to follow his tremendous success with . . . another successful comedy." Although writer Jerry Cady, who loved McCall's script, commented that "it seems unlikely that Mr. Webb can continue to confine himself to the character of Belvedere [for] the rest of his life" and pleaded that "the present *Julie* script is too excellent to cast aside without very serious thought," Zanuck put McCall onto writing the sequel to *Sitting Pretty*.[11]

Two years into her contract and without any new credits, McCall had few options except continuing to ingratiate herself with Zanuck. She persuaded her fellow Academy governors to give Zanuck the Thalberg Award for producing *Gentleman's Agreement* (1947) in March. The film, starring Gregory Peck, was an unusually liberal offering from the studio about postwar anti-Semitism in America, and it possibly resonated with McCall's experience of her mixed marriage to Bramson. It may have been convenient for Bramson's ego to believe his exclusion from the film industry was due in part to being Jewish, but in historically Jewish Hollywood—where all the key executives save Zanuck and Winfield Sheehan were Jewish—it seems unlikely Bramson's career was stalling due to anti-Semitism. Brackett, sensing the mix of personal and office politics, was a bit irritated with her "emotional and over-passionate speech" for Zanuck, but Walter Wanger cast the deciding vote.[12]

She dashed off a treatment for Zanuck's sequel and called it *Mr. Belvedere Goes to College*. Although she hadn't been involved with any aspect of *Sitting Pretty*, which was written by her friend F. Hugh Herbert, she knew Webb's comic abilities and devastating stares. Her story opens with the new best-selling author walking across the country to pick up a literary award, since he lost all his money on libel suits over his novel. McCall had him meet a pair of attractive college alumnae on their way out to visit a friend. They pass him several times en route, only to need his scathing assistance when their car breaks down on more than one occasion. Once on the West Coast he is stunned to find out he needs a college degree to qualify for the award. His solution is to get a four-year college degree in one year. Belvedere ends up enrolling at a UCLA-lookalike college with the intention of speeding through the curriculum.

While in a journalism class he meets a "very sharp" fellow student, Ellen McIntyre, who writes a controversial article about him for the school newspaper. As McCall writes, "Their bright minds and their arrogance—she driven by ambition, thinking only of getting a good news story—he not caring whose toes he steps on when he gives forth his caustic criticism of the collegiate world—clash from the start." But he okays Ellen's interview transcript and "is secretly tickled by its impudence and competence." They argue again in a child psychology class. Belvedere, of course, thinks he knows better than anyone about children, and the professor "is a dope." Ellen, it turns out, is a single mother with a young child and knows even more than these two men about looking after kids. But of course, embarrassed about admitting her circumstances to her fellow students (it is unclear at this point whether she is married or widowed), she hesitates about explaining the true source of her knowledge.

Ellen needs a successful career in journalism to support herself. At first things go well. Her interview is published in a large Los Angeles daily paper. She is offered an additional $500 for the Sunday feature, but although her career is now in full swing, all the publicity unintentionally hurts Belvedere when the "mossback" foundation men say they don't want their chosen author to have any more publicity of this sort.[13]

In order to "muzzle" Ellen, Belvedere finds out about Ellen's child and attempts to blackmail her before changing tack and advising her how to get her husband back. Belvedere states that Ellen "has been too tense and career-minded to pay proper attention to her looks or to soften her manner" and gives her a makeover. Eventually all the college girls in a sorority want him to make them over. The before-and-after pictures of the sorority girls create great publicity for the university, and parents write letters to the administration saying, "if they could be assured that their daughters could be improved like that, in deportment and appearance, they would send them to this university above all others." Belvedere is offered a "Chair of Euthenics" (instead of eugenics—perhaps a passing snipe at the right), and Ellen wins back her spineless husband.

McCall's college looks like a middle-class finishing school for wealthy parents more interested in seeing their daughters dress properly than achieve great careers. From the opening scene in which two Mount Holyoke women can't fix their own car, McCall sets them up as inept and brainless. Using women's college graduates as patsies for Webb's comic abilities is a cheap shot—and an odd one for McCall, once a proud graduate of Vassar. But she deploys countless other gender stereotypes: Ellen's "appearance and deportment" suffer when she is doing well at school; when she is career-minded she is not a successful "woman." Finally, it is Belvedere, the persnickety man, who gets to judge standards of female beauty. The film is an exercise in derailing Ellen's career ambitions and furthering Belvedere's. Perhaps some of Bramson's misogyny had rubbed off on McCall, or perhaps she accurately gauged mainstream America's growing dislike of intelligent career women. But would promoting these stereotypes for Zanuck prolong her career?

Zanuck endorsed McCall's May 19 script as "an excellent basis for a sequel to *Sitting Pretty*. Mary McCall has done a good continuity job."[14] But he turned the script over to Hugh Herbert, arguing that he "can state Mr. Belvedere's problem even more convincingly and logically than Mary McCall has done." In a memo written two days later, producer Michael Abel said he hated both McCall and her script. The story of Ellen's baby was "trite," the characters "stereotyped, wooden, unbelievable," and key comedy sequences as "absurd."[15] He also disliked Ellen's assertive attitude as a reporter, arguing that she assumed responsibilities that should really have been at her editor's discretion. Zanuck kept Abel at arm's length, fired Herbert, and brought in Anita Loos's niece and her husband Richard Sale to write their own versions. Eventually Zanuck disliked all their rewrites and used most of McCall's original continuity for the shooting script.[16]

By now McCall was used to being bounced from project to project at Fox, but she was well paid. In 1948 she was on the studio's rich list, making $106,000 (writer Philip Dunne made only $83,810).[17] But her lack of screen credits since leaving MGM, combined with the publication of the Tenney report, made it increasingly unlikely that Fox would renew her $3,000-a-week salary. McCall called Hedda Hopper, ostensibly to discuss the big lie about her in the report. Hopper was too far right to attack the committee findings, but she did put a good item about McCall in her May 6 column. She stated that McCall was creating her own production company with her new husband. They would produce three of McCall's stories, "Cardboard Heaven," "The People's Choice," and "Wife of the Whiffenpoof."[18] Nothing developed but a rumor in late 1949 that Mel Ferrer would star in their jointly written *Golden Slippers*.[19] Despite their political differences, Hopper was annoyed that so many male actors and writers were climbing the ladder ahead of McCall and other qualified women.

Bramson was neither the writer nor producer he thought he was, and Zanuck was uninterested in making another deal. McCall saw his point. "You can only maintain a salary as high as I had been making—$3,000 a week—if smash credits keep on coming, and they weren't forthcoming."[20] Her agent Mary Baker told her that "it was getting harder and harder to sell her" and recommended that McCall adjust the contract to extend the guarantee of work and lower the salary. It was a reasonable measure in difficult times, but McCall objected that on the basis of her current contract, she was earning $30,000 a year and had everything budgeted. (Bramson was her biggest expense, but unfortunately he wasn't tax-deductible.) And McCall knew but may not have wanted to admit to Baker that she couldn't be sold outside of the studio. The offers just weren't there. She refused to renegotiate, but Baker had already made the offer to the studio. Since Zanuck had "eagerly accepted," Baker had to go back and say her client wasn't interested in changing the contract. "This, of course, put me in the Fox doghouse," McCall admitted. Zanuck was furious. The writer left the Jaffe Agency soon afterward under a cloud.

Hopper knew McCall's status was slipping, and on August 9, 1948, she revealed "Mary McCall, a fixture at Metro for years, has retired to a ranch to write fact and fiction for slick magazines."[21] A little tartly, she wrote, "Mary's been called an Irish liberal." Hopper took a slight dig at Bramson: "She and her husband should do mighty well. Mary's got enough story material to last her for years; and all Hollywood will be watching her yarns with great interest—to see if they can recognize the characters." It was Hopper's way of saying that McCall knew where a lot of bodies were buried in Hollywood, but McCall did not end up writing a Hollywood exposé, since she still valued her career. While she was stuck at the ranch and out of touch with day-to-day matters at the guild, Brackett did his "poor best" to keep McCall "caught up on the SWG thing,"[22] and she stayed on at Fox for the remainder of the term Baker had initially negotiated for her—the spring of 1949. She reported to Sam Engle on the development of *The Jackpot*, based on a *New Yorker* story that had caught Zanuck's eye as a potential addition to the Belvedere franchise.[23] But the project went nowhere; Zanuck was just letting McCall's wheels spin and he did not give her screen credit for *Chicken Every Sunday* when it appeared in theaters in January 1949. This might have been for the best, since according to the critics Valentine Davies's rewrite had turned her script into "standard patterns of burlesque" with characters that were "not so much human beings as professional types."[24]

But *Mr. Belvedere Goes to College* was a bona fide hit. The film raked in over $3.5 million at the box office, making it the seventh most popular film at the box office in 1949, and some critics swore it was "even more hilarious than *Sitting Pretty*."[25] Critics praised the "lively sequel" that "comes close to demolishing the old saw about sequels never matching the model that inspired them."[26] The scene in which Belvedere calls J. Edgar Hoover from a police station at a "pay-station without a nickel—and gets a return call" was notably droll. However, critic Mildred Martin despised Shirley Temple's Ellen, "the war widow student," as a "soggy" distraction from the sparkling Webb. Ironically, Temple's other comeback role that year was a schoolgirl who campaigns for women's rights in *Adventure in Baltimore* (RKO). Critics panned it. Soon after Temple divorced and retired from the screen.

McCall's *Julie* (retitled *Dancing in the Dark*) might have been a good vehicle for Temple—or even Crain or Grable, as Zanuck had originally hoped—but it never worked out. After shelving McCall's dramatic meditation on fallen stars and second chances and returning to the original song-and-dance libretto, studio politics persuaded Zanuck to cast Cary Grant's lackluster wife, Betsy Drake, in the lead. Grant's popularity was accelerating given his association with Alfred Hitchcock (*Notorious*, 1946), and signing Drake would potentially sweeten any future film deals with Grant. Years later McCall remembered, "Not only could Miss Drake not sing a note, but she could not dance at all, and explained at the start that she did not even do ballroom dancing with her husband. Every step of the dancing had to be doubled, so the dances were all shot in extreme long shots, and all the singing was doubled."[27] William Powell, who in McCall's opinion "lacked Mr. Webb's acid, biting quality," was the studio's eventual choice for the male lead.

Zanuck incorporated some of McCall's original thoughts about *A Star Is Born* by casting Adolph Menjou in the role of a sympathetic Oliver Niles-style producer. Jean Hersholt, McCall's friend on the Motion Picture Relief Committee, had a role—as himself. The film premiered in December 1949, and although it was critically acclaimed, it made only $1.3 million. McCall's observations about Drake were correct. As Hedda Hopper put it, Drake did talk Grant "into giving up liquor and cigarettes," but the actor "subsequently gave up Betsy" as well.[28] Although some critics praised the "good writing," McCall's name was rarely mentioned in reviews.[29] The *Hollywood Reporter,* run by notoriously right-wing editor and publisher Billy Wilkerson, mentioned everyone else in the cast and crew but omitted McCall's name entirely.[30] It was Wilkerson's way of blacklisting her.

McCall's family was living off the remainder of her Fox salary throughout 1949 and 1950, but matters weren't helped by Bramson, who was doing his best to spend it on girlfriends and fancy cars. He was unemployed but had a Duesenberg and a Rolls-Royce. They had a small tract house in Reseda, part of a new development in the San Fernando Valley. Bramson's temper was short, and he continued to physically abuse McCall and the children. Since they couldn't afford any "help" now, McCall was working, cleaning the house on Vanowen Street, making all the meals, and "schlepping over the hill" to Los Angeles in her old Plymouth for guild meetings (there was no highway to shorten the drive back then). When Bramson didn't like her cooking or her conversation, he used to throw the plates of food against the dining room wall. McCall's border collie Lex would lap up the food, and she would try to diffuse the tension, saying to the children, "Well, at least I won't have to wash that plate."[31]

Yet despite his abuse, Bramson continued to hold his "most favored" spot with McCall and mercilessly rubbed it in with Sheila, Jerry, and Alan, even signing Christmas gifts to her "from Mamie [Sheila's name for McCall] and Murdstone [the evil stepfather from Charles Dickens's *David Copperfield*]."[32] Things were better for Sheila at UCLA, where she mixed with fellow students and developed her own taste for writing.[33] She also worked part-time in the Westwood Bookstore, where she met writer Ray Bradbury. "Much taken" with McCall's daughter, and sympathetic to her need to earn extra money, the writer offered Sheila a babysitting job for his kids.[34] She accepted and started to salt money away for an escape to New York.

One night at dinner in Sheila's sophomore year, Bramson butted in on McCall and Sheila's conversation, yelling at them, "Everyone talks too goddam much in this family." As Mary-David recalled, there was dead silence at the table, and then Sheila, forgetting the latest patriarchal order, asked her mother a question. Bramson jumped out of his chair, stomped around the table to Sheila's place, grabbed her and her chair and tipped her upside down on the floor. Her brothers were aghast, Mary-David was too terrified to cry, and their mother made no effort to curb Bramson.[35]

Sheila packed her stuff in a cardboard box, got in her second-hand jeep, and drove to her father and Eliza's house in Rustic Canyon that night. Sadly, things were no better for Mary-David and the boys after their sister left. But in 1950, reacting to the "size" issue of their one house—and the fact that Jerry and Alan hated Bramson, disliked their mother, and were getting too big to be hit with a belt—McCall bought a second tract house through the Federal Housing Association and sent the boys there to live with a housekeeper. Hollywood gossip columnists reported that there was "much talk" about McCall's new living arrangements.[36] They didn't last; even in another house, the boys were too close for Bramson. He sent them to military school. Jerry, sensitive and clever, survived to graduate from law school and become a highly regarded district attorney in Santa Barbara.[37] Alan, after leaving the school and enlisting in the military, drove an ambulance in Los Angeles.

Because of the Hollywood blacklist and slowing film assignments McCall had more time on her hands, and as Mary-David acknowledges, her mother took much more of an interest in her than she had in Sheila, Jerry, and Alan. Apart from her attendance at guild meetings she was free to cultivate her image as a perfect housewife and mother. Years later, reflecting upon their lonely childhoods and her mother's dedication to the guild, Mary-David mused, "children of parents who dedicated themselves to a 'Higher Purpose' unanimously feel that they, the kids, got the short end of the stick." McCall had unimpeachable values in private too, and once "walked from Hollywood Boulevard and Laurel Canyon back to Sunset and Fairfax to repay the butcher at the A & P who had undercharged her for lamb chops."[38] The family could have used that extra bit of meat at the time, but McCall doggedly took the receipt and the package back on foot to correct the cashier's error.

She may have been counting nickels and dimes for the family shopping, but in 1950 she was back in the news, although it wasn't because of film credits. McCall was once again elected to the Screen Writers Guild executive board, the only other woman except Virginia Kellogg, and participated in the film and television writers' strike that winter over the payment of writers' residuals for televised films.[39] She continued to rebuild links with members that had been neglected during her marriage to Bramson while laying out a more acceptable anticommunist writing strategy for producers. In March 1951 the *New York Times* announced that McCall was adapting a "spy melodrama" called *Eye Street* for MGM producer Robert Thomsen. The drama allegedly concerned "an 'Iron Curtain' embassy in Washington," but ironically the real Eye Street in the U.S. capital was the new home of the Motion Picture Association of America![40] Were agents uncovering a spy ring at the MPAA rather than the Screen Writers Guild?

Nothing came of it, and a new round of HUAC hearings defined the term of guild president Karl Tunberg. More screenwriters and members of the guild, including William Pomerance, executive secretary under Lavery, were subpoenaed. Tunberg's practical response was to rebuild the union's credibility in the press. The organization's signature was put on a Motion Picture Industry Council letter supporting HUAC, and Tunberg made no secret of the fact that he wanted to run communists out of the Screen Writers Guild. But he offered an olive branch to some of his more powerful colleagues. In his voluntary testimony on September 25, 1951, he defended McCall, Brackett, Allen Rivkin, George Seaton, and Valentine Davies as members of an "Anti-Communist front" and described how McCall and Brackett had thwarted the communist leadership over proxy votes.[41]

Tunberg was too compliant with HUAC to appeal to the whole membership, and after he indicated his decision to run for reelection, McCall quietly launched her own campaign. Rather than go public through the guild secretary with her campaign letter, she contacted members through her own index card file. When Tunberg discovered the identity of his political rival, a woman he'd actually defended in front of HUAC, he was livid.

The *Los Angeles Examiner* put it mildly: It was a "controversial election."[42] Communist writer Michael Wilson and conservative Adele Buffington wrote their own campaign letters to the membership criticizing Tunberg's leadership, and

Tunberg charged them both with disloyalty. He wanted them censured at the next meeting, when he assumed he'd be elected. McCall called out Tunberg's reference to the Radio Writers Guild "as an external pressure group through which Reds were attempting to disrupt the Screen Writers Guild" and criticized him for "having suggested legislation to the congressional committee without 'mandate from the membership.'" Tunberg argued that he had gone after radio writers who refused to sign loyalty affidavits and only wanted "to outlaw the communist party." Sneered Tunberg, "Evidently Miss McCall is against this."[43] Normally conservative Oliver H. P. Garrett sided with McCall ("I find myself curiously allied to some strange bedfellows") and argued that free speech mattered more.[44] She was elected 263 to 194.[45] Doris Gilbert, who worked closely with McCall during her first two terms, sent her a congratulatory wire on November 23: "Couldn't be happier— you're the president and I was right!"[46] McCall tried to remain diplomatic in her acceptance speech: "We represent many shades of opinions here, but in this we are not divided: Each of us seeks according to his lights to further the welfare and the dignity of the screen writer."[47]

She celebrated her third election as president with a photo shoot. Posing surrounded by books and a large stuffed St. Bernard, McCall perched debonairly on her desk wearing a man's tweed blazer. A replica of Sherlock Holmes's pipe was wedged between her teeth, and she clutched a pint of beer in one hand. It was a humorous sendup of the traditional sexist image of the great writer as a tweed-wearing, pipe-smoking Anglophile man in his study. In an age of hardening conservatism, and when Hollywood was closing its doors on so many women, McCall defiantly projected another image.

Her term began with a joint seminar between the American Cinema Editors and the Screen Writers Guild arguing for "a closer pre-production relationship"— modeling the kind of productive, cross-industry image she wanted for Hollywood's guilds and unions. Nearly two hundred writers and editors attended the seminar "Where Shall We Cut—on Film—or on Paper?"[48] Women led the discussions, including editor Eda Warren, McCall, and screenwriter Virginia Kellogg.

However, things quickly turned sour in the new year. A credit dispute that had arisen under Tunberg's leadership in September 1951 between screenwriter Paul Jarrico and the new head of RKO Pictures, Howard Hughes (a nephew of McCall's adversary on the MPA, Rupert Hughes), had resurfaced when a guild committee ruled in Jarrico's favor. The producer got nasty. The younger Hughes was the son of a millionaire inventor of a rotary drill for petroleum and had been involved in motion pictures since 1930, when he produced *Hell's Angels*. His production company also made *Scarface* in defiance of censorship strictures, and the producer again courted controversy with *The Outlaw* (1943). Back in the early 1940s McCall had made fun of Hughes's reputation as a womanizer who stashed starlets all over town, promising to make them famous.[49] He took over RKO in 1948 and proceeded to cut the staff to the bone. That said, he kept the only female member of the producers' guild, Harriet Parsons, on salary, and was even backing Ida Lupino's independent content from 1949.

Jarrico had first met McCall at Columbia Pictures in 1937. In the early 1940s he joined her at MGM and was nominated for an Academy Award for his work on a Ginger Rogers's vehicle, *Tom, Dick, and Harry* (1941). During that period, McCall wasn't particularly friendly with Jarrico, but like many in Hollywood she enjoyed his wife Sylvia's company. By 1951, when Jarrico signed a contract with Hughes for $2,000 a week to write *The Las Vegas Story* (1952), it seemed like just another picture. The first wave of investigations in 1947 had passed, and even though Jarrico had written the notorious *Song of Russia* (1943), he was still working. The Hollywood Ten had been called to testify, cited for contempt, jailed, and released after serving their time. But the 1951 investigations were in many ways more damaging than the ones in 1947. Some of those affected, like McCall's colleague and editor on *The Screen Writer*, top MGM earner Isobel Lennart, were persuaded to name names that were already known to the committee. In exchange Lennart kept her lucrative career at MGM.[50] McCall's ally on the guild, MGM veteran Marguerite Roberts, was called to testify, and blacklisted for refusing to name names.

Jarrico was also subpoenaed. When Hughes found out, he fired Jarrico before he testified, hired new writers, and purged Jarrico's name from the credits. The writer then contacted the guild, and an arbitration committee sided in Jarrico's favor in October 1951.[51] When Hughes released the film in February 1952 without Jarrico's name listed in the credits, the Screen Writers Guild wrote to Hughes and sought arbitration. Hughes responded, "any arbitration of this matter would be without meaning . . . RKO will not yield to Jarrico's demands."[52] For his part, Jarrico filed for $350,000 damages against Hughes in a separate suit.

Though undoubtedly wary of supporting Jarrico at the height of the blacklist, McCall later explained her position with characteristic humor: "I did not intend to permit Mr. Hughes to trample on a labor agreement with muddy tennis shoes."[53] Once she approached Hughes in her official capacity as guild president, the producer expanded his vicious press campaign to include McCall. He also released copies of his responses to her correspondence to the conservative Hearst papers before they reached her and publicly criticized "Miss McCall and the organization she purports to represent" in an attempt to smear McCall as a communist and a factionalist rather than a president elected by the membership and presiding over an executive board composed of more than twenty other members.[54] McCall responded firmly: "The Basic Agreement states, 'The decision of the Guild Arbitration Committee with respect to writing credits ... shall be final and the Producer will accept and follow the designation of screen credits contained in such designation and all writers shall be bound thereby."[55] Hughes's action was in violation of a fundamental right of the Minimum Basic Agreement, active since 1942 and affirmed ten years later, which outlined the guild's prerogative to arbitrate and award screen credit on all productions. She went on, "This is clearly a labor dispute. It does not involve the political beliefs of Mr. Jarrico, however repugnant they might be to you or us." She reminded him, "By terms of our corporate charter, by terms of our agreement with RKO-Radio and all major motion picture studios, we are obligated to extend guild membership to, and protect the rights of, any writer you choose to employ. You chose to employ Mr. Jarrico. We have no choice but to protect his professional rights."[56]

Hughes replied that if they didn't like his firing Jarrico, then the Screen Writers Guild could boycott RKO and go on strike. "My conscience cannot be changed by a committee of arbitrators," he wrote to McCall, so "is it or is it not the intention of the Screen Writers Guild to call a strike against RKO?"[57] McCall acknowledged, "such action at this time might suit your purposes, since it is a well-known fact that production at RKO is at a virtual standstill." But, she concluded, "Under no circumstances will a strike be called at your suggestion or for your convenience."[58] She and the Screen Writers Guild's attorney Gordon Stulberg petitioned to the state superior court to get the arbiter to progress matters, but the motion was denied by Judge Roy L. Herndon on the grounds that "the controversy is between the writer and the producer ... and the rights of the union are not primarily involved."[59] McCall, stunned by this failure to recognize the guild's jurisdiction, told journalists that "the decision is shocking and incomprehensible" and stressed that the court was confusing Jarrico's $350,000 damage suit against Hughes with the issue of the contract.[60] She appealed the decision in early May. But Herndon noted that an ambiguity of language in the new minimum basic agreement contract written and implemented during Tunberg's tenure as president (drafted and overseen by Stulberg) left a loophole for the producer to slip through.[61]

In May, while the appeal was still under review, McCall appealed to a center-left base beyond Hollywood, writing an article for the California-based *Frontier* magazine. She gambled that her frankness might win her some allies. She began bluntly, "I hate Communism" anywhere in the world, and particularly "as demonstrated in the criminal assault on the sciences and the arts in the Soviet Union."[62] She then offered some context for what she considered was a long-term fight for the right to free speech: "I remember one night at the Screen Writers Guild, during the dark days when the carelessness and lethargy of the dominant majority of the membership had permitted the election of six extreme Leftists to the Executive Board." They received a letter from a right-wing member of the guild, intended for inclusion in the new guild magazine. After some discussion, "The Comrades, thinking as one, as usual, voting as one, as always, made the point that the letter was fundamentally anti-guild, and there was no obligation on the Board to print in our official magazine anything which might destroy the organization." But then, "a gifted and curmudgeonly writer"—not named by McCall but later identified as James Cain—said: "I think this is an execrable letter . . . I disagree with every sentence in it. And I say to you that unless you print it in its entirety, you'd better shut up shop. There's a lot of prattle here around here about free speech. What you really mean is freedom of speech for people who agree with you." But if she hoped California's silent majority would rise up in outrage after reading her account of the Jarrico case, she miscalculated.

McCall didn't give up and spoke to other California papers, stressing that the Screen Writers Guild was "a huge organization" with a thousand members who became members when studios hired them and paid their dues; the guild didn't accept them first.[63] But her attempts to scrub the organization's reputation and hand herself and other moderates halos of tolerance didn't work. On May 16, 1952, the California Supreme Court denied the guild's last appeal; Hughes was within his rights to sack Jarrico for his political beliefs regardless of the Minimum Basic Agreement.[64] The contract for which she and her colleagues had fought so hard was nothing but a slip of worthless paper to the courts. McCall soon grew bitter against Jarrico and "the communist minority in Hollywood" who, she fumed, "are against blacklists only when they are being blacklisted."[65]

Rather than be forced to oversee the rewriting of the contract to exclude the rights of communist members, on September 2 McCall announced that she would not run again for the presidency. "Three times around is enough for me . . . the job is too time consuming."[66] But she didn't just clock off in despair. That summer was taken up with a punishing strike against the Alliance of Television and Film Producers, who, among other things, were trying to steal writers' residuals when their works appeared on television. And as a television writer, McCall had a stake in the fight.

CHAPTER 14

Smaller Screens

Mary McCall was one of many women in the culture industries to experience a career decline during the blacklist.[1] She was convinced that because of her role in the Jarrico case Howard Hughes had destroyed her career by denouncing her as a communist and persuading other producers not to hire her. "As a consequence of my . . . back and forth with Mr. Howard Hughes," she explained in 1979, "I was unable to find work."[2] But the FBI had been noting her comings and goings long before her confrontation with Hughes. They had kept tabs on her since she was first elected president of the Screen Writers Guild in 1942. Although in the early 1950s failed playwright turned anticommunist pamphleteer Myron C. Fagan, one of several "freelance" blacklisters, claimed she was a "fellow traveler," she was in good company—just about every liberal star and writer in the business, including Bogart and Davis, made his little blacklist.[3]

Despite her need to cast herself as the victim of a Hughes-engineered anticommunist conspiracy, it is more likely that McCall was penalized for being the dominant guild leader in the 1940s and early 1950s. Producers didn't refuse to hire her in the 1950s because of her alleged political affiliations, but because she had sued a studio and publicly confronted one of their colleagues (and one of the country's richest men).

Following her split from Zanuck and Mary Baker, she signed with agent Ingo Preminger, who had lots of experience with blacklisted or graylisted Hollywood talent (he also repped Ring Lardner Jr.). But McCall's career problems were not as clear-cut as those of the notorious Hollywood Ten. McCall had been a member of the establishment, and during the 1945–46 strike waves, unlike her left-wing writing colleagues, she had favored caution over supporting the strikers. She also didn't join the Committee for the First Amendment protesting the hearings in Washington in 1947.[4] As head of the Screen Writers Guild she had publicly defended Jarrico, but only because she had to uphold the Minimum Basic Agreement. In the media she was loud and clear in her hatred of communism. McCall argued she was acting to defend the guild and its protective contract for its members—she was acting for the good of the many rather than the few. But there was undoubtedly self-interest in her actions: in defending the contract, she was also defending her own legacy and the bridges she had built with producers and executives.

Her declining offers of work and financial difficulties predated her involvement in the Jarrico case. In August 1951, when McCall wrote to J. Edgar Hoover, long-term head of the FBI, to explain her "case history," it was not because no one at the studios would hire her. It was because her brother Leo Jr. had recently been denied employment at a Hughes plant because McCall "was listed as a member of many Communist Front organizations."[5] She explained that she was never subpoenaed by HUAC or fired from a project, unlike her colleague Jean Muir, who had lost her job in *The Aldrich Family* after sponsors threatened to withdraw their backing over her casting in 1950.[6] Stating that she was "against both Communism and Fascism and was for Democracy," McCall described herself to Hoover as "among the middle-of-the-road people who believed sincerely in the principles of collective bargaining and craft unions, and who were willing to take the boredom and hard work of attendance at guild meetings and of office-holding in the guild."[7] Hoover replied that he was unable to do anything, since, as he put it, the FBI was "strictly an investigating agency and at no time injects itself into employer-employee relationships."[8] But behind the scenes, Hoover was well aware that McCall had never been a party member. The two principle male informers, both disgruntled male writers who called McCall "a political opportunist" for becoming guild president, admitted as much in their "confidential reports."[9]

McCall eventually signed a two-picture deal with Herbert J. Yates of Republic. Perhaps for someone who'd once made $3,000 a week working at Twentieth Century-Fox it was a comedown. Yates, born in Brooklyn, was a former executive at American Tobacco who moved into film finance in the 1920s, formed Republic in 1935, and turned cowboys Gene Autry and Roy Rogers into stars. It wasn't a major studio, but it wasn't Poverty Row either. "Lowly Republic"[10] distributed *Rio Grande*, John Ford's western with Merian C. Cooper, in 1950, as well as *The Quiet Man* (1952), and later produced Nicholas Ray's cult western starring Joan Crawford, *Johnny Guitar* (1954).

Although in 1950s Hollywood the overall number of women writers declined as the studios cut their budgets and male director-producers took over the task of creating independently produced content, women writers continued to be well represented in the western genre.[11] McCall was one of many women to write westerns in the 1950s because westerns were plentiful and cheaply paid—perfect for those who had increasingly limited options in a tightening film market. As writer Elizabeth Wilson remarked in her HUAC testimony September 21, 1951, women were hired to write westerns because they could be paid less for westerns than for other material.[12] Although she would joke that she worked for "Repulsive Pictures," McCall later conceded, "I had a very happy time at Republic."[13]

Maisie series collaborator Betty Reinhardt, after leaving the comfort of Twentieth Century-Fox, wrote a small-budget western for Elmo Williams in his directorial debut (*The Tall Texan*, 1953). McCall's Vassar sister, Frances Goodrich, was somewhat protected from postwar misogyny since she wrote in collaboration with her husband Albert Hackett, creating a range of material, including *The Virginian* (1946) and *Seven Brides for Seven Brothers* (1954). After she left her studio contract to freelance, Lillie Hayward, McCall's former Warner Bros. colleague, specialized in westerns, from *Heart of the Rio Grande* (1942) to *Bronco Buster* and *The Raiders* (both 1952). Until she was blacklisted, Marguerite Roberts used her real western background to write *Honky Tonk* (1941) and *The Sea of Grass* (1947).[14]

When McCall signed with Yates, her only credit in the genre consisted of her handful of *Maisie* dramas that were set in the modern, twentieth-century West. Her big "traditional" western for Fox, *On to Oregon*, had been shelved. But Yates handed her the studio's most prestigious western property to develop: Luke Short's *Ride the Man Down*.[15] Short's complex psychological westerns were as much about what was thought as about what was done. RKO produced an adaptation of Short's *Blood on the Moon* (adapted by Lillie Hayward from *Gunman's Chance*), and Enterprise produced *Ramrod* (adapted in part by another western specialist, Cecile Kramer).

Published in 1942, *Ride the Man Down* remains among the most respected novels in the western canon. McCall's adaptation was faithful to Short's narrative structure and dialogue, and as McCall admitted, "Although I cannot say that I am a westerner, I have always been an admirer of the work of Luke Short."[16] She also liked the novel because it had a female protagonist, ranch owner Celia Evarts.

Though it focuses on the family legacy of a domineering pioneer, *Ride the Man Down* isn't a conservative western, endorsing big business and the patriarchy.[17] The ranch belongs to Celia, and the story's dramatic conflict is her struggle to retain her inheritance. The male squatters, the men in the saloon, the corrupt sheriff conspiring to break up the ranch, and even other women in the area all want to write her off, saying once Celia is married her future husband will run things.

But Celia is different, as McCall's script highlights. When her uncle is confronted with the survival of the ranch, she joins the foreman Will in discussions over its future. When her fiancé Sam advises that they knuckle under and let the rival rancher have Indian Springs, the best water around for miles, she reacts angrily, challenging him: "Are you out of your mind?" She won't concede an inch, realizing that just as with blackmail, the blackmailers are never satisfied. When Sam, embarrassed at being outthought by a woman, attempts to recover some dignity by telling her to "go to bed," she replies, "I'm not sleepy; I've got too much to think about." Instead, she tells him, "run along to bed, darling," and sits down for a smoke with her foreman. Of course, she rolls her own.

McCall's additions to the story enhanced Celia's presence in the script. She wears trousers, throws a man to the ground, and punches another out while pointedly drawing attention to herself as "the female owner" of Hatchett Ranch following her father's death. Though veteran actor Brian Donlevy, playing the villain, was at the top of the bill, the story focused on the power and love triangle between Celia (Ella Raines), foreman Will (Rod Cameron), and Sam (Forrest Tucker). Raines was a calm and steely Celia. Though she tries to be "feminine" when she wants to take her mind off things, she doesn't look or act the conventional part. When Red Courteen (Jim Davis) comes to smash up the ranch house in an act of retaliation for holding maverick cattle, she throws Courteen on the ground, punches another rawhide assailant, and kicks the hell out of the third. "I don't believe in anything you do," she finally tells Sam, realizing he is working with the very people who want to steal her ranch. Sam's reaction is to hit Celia, in an echo of Bramson's treatment of McCall.

Despite a game performance by Raines and some spectacular photography, the film was just another western to the critics, apart from a nod to its "top-notch personnel" by McCall's longtime admirer, *Los Angeles Times* critic Edwin Schallert.[18] But McCall's former advocate Mildred Martin dismissed it as a "long-winded" script and a "confused, soporific western."[19] Martin also savaged McCall's final project for Yates and producer John Auer, *Thunderbirds*. The period

World War II drama involved two National Guardsmen (John Derek and John Barrymore Jr.) who love the same girl, tellingly named Mary Caldwell, McCall's two Christian names. The love triangle unfolds from 1940 to 1941, when the two young men are shipped overseas to Sicily, where Bramson served, and one goes missing. Mary (Eileen Christy) declares her love for Tom (Barrymore) and Gil (Derek) consoles himself with a nurse, Lt. Ellen Henderson (Mona Freeman). The similarity to McCall's wartime romantic mess with Franklin and Bramson a decade before is glaringly obvious. McCall claimed in 1970 that she and Bramson "were going to write the script together, but he had to go on active duty. I guess they figured that since I had consorted with an infantryman so long, I would do all right by myself. Technical advice consisted mostly of my phoning him at night."[20]

Martin was scathing. "Seemingly convinced that what the screen needs is still another Second World War drama," she lamented in her opening salvo, she proceeded to skewer the ponderous, "blow-by-blow" story of the two heroes' war service ("The war never seemed so long as it does in this cliché-ridden celluloid concoction").[21] Although some were undoubtedly bored by the glut of war pictures in the late 1940s and early 1950s, the genre was still relatively popular with audiences in the early 1950s; only a few months later, Columbia's *From Here to Eternity* (1953) would successfully combine location shooting, combat footage, and romantic melodrama. Bogart scored another hit with *The Caine Mutiny* (1954), and in 1955 Emmet Lavery would make something of a comeback with his Oscar-nominated biopic of a World War I hero, *The Court-Martial of Billy Mitchell*, starring Gary Cooper. But these war films had an edge and dared to be critical of the military establishment; McCall's unqualified endorsement of the armed forces when the United States was involved in an unpopular war in Korea made *Thunderbirds* tame and out-of-date.

Her judgment of the television landscape was more astute. Even as she handed in her scripts for Republic, McCall had laid the groundwork for a new career. Her old studio films were only ever seen on television, and over the summer of 1952 she had spent the last months of her presidency pushing back against television producers for screenwriters' residuals in other media.[22] She was also pitching television dramas, and luckily for her not all her powerful friends ran for cover at the mention of her name.

Will Rogers Jr., son of the beloved American humorist and film star, worked as a newspaperman before enlisting as a private in the Second World War. While on active duty, he ran for the California House of Representatives (as a Democrat, naturally) and served in Congress from 1943 to 1944. He lost the race for the Senate, but he played his father in the Marilyn Miller biopic written by McCall's friends, Phoebe and Henry Ephron and Marian Spitzer, *Look for the Silver Lining* (1949). His acting career looked over until McCall wrote him a thirty-minute, tailor-made television script: *Life, Liberty, and Orin Dooley*, the story of "a GI back from Korea, who takes up his schooling back where he left off—the fourth grade."[23]

The script "lured him out of retirement," and the show, produced by a young Jules Bricken, who subsequently worked on the series *Alfred Hitchcock Presents* and produced John Frankenheimer's classic *The Train* (1964), was seen on repeat on several networks throughout 1952. It became the first episode of *The Ford Television Theatre*. As Dorothy Manners reported, McCall's script was "a 'natural' for Rogers Jr." and led to other offers with the series.

Hedda Hopper once said that Hollywood "treated television the way a maiden aunt treats sex—if she doesn't think about it, maybe it will disappear."[24] But after the war, when television sales went domestic, the young networks quickly became cinema's media rival.[25] Hollywood stars let go from their studio contracts were now eager to work in television, and McCall's colleagues, from Lucille Ball (*I Love Lucy*, 1951–57) to Ann Sothern (*Private Secretary*, 1953–57), became top names in the industry. Good writing was at a premium for the half-hour primetime shows, and many writers, from old-time Hollywood pros to newcomers, lined up to work for the television industry.[26]

Although many of her screenwriting colleagues continued to look down on television as a debased medium, their perspective was losing credibility. Writing in 1954, critic Erskine Johnson disputed what "Hollywood writers have been screaming to me" about television—namely that "there's no time, they say, for good writing in a 30-minute show." He brought in McCall to support him.[27] She commented, "Some of the world's great masterpieces of dramatic writing are one-act plays. Bad writing is bad writing in any time limit. . . . Could it be that the approach to the medium of some Hollywood writers is one of condescension? They don't take the trouble to really do a job?" McCall recognized the drawbacks of writing for a television industry that depended on conservative corporate sponsorship to pay for production and competitive primetime spots. Content that was too politically challenging or cerebral or complicated ran the risk of censorship. But this wasn't a surprise for any writer who'd worked in the Hollywood studio system. And with the film industry's audience figures on a steady downward spiral,

McCall changed her Screen Writers Guild membership to the radio-television division of the Writers Guild of America West.

Bramson made his own attempt at a career shift. That year he ran for city council in the San Fernando Valley. There were an unusually high number of candidates in the race in 1953, sixteen in the Third District race alone, "calculated to give any political picker a headache."[28] Reseda, Canoga Park, Tarzana, Northridge, Woodland Hills, and Van Nuys all had favored candidates. McCall knocked on doors for him, distributing the campaign literature that her television scripts paid for. Bramson ran against a funeral director, a rancher, a mailman, and a former FBI man—and lost. It didn't improve his temper. Although Bramson enjoyed spending her money, creating a little fiefdom in the Valley, McCall worried about making enough to pay their bills. Despite her few scripts for *The Ford Television Theatre*, most pitches weren't working out.[29]

Things went from bad to worse. Betty Reinhardt died of cancer on January 21, 1954. She was forty-four. Seven decades later, Mary-David still remembers her mother's rare show of extreme grief. In her loneliness, McCall did reconnect briefly with Bette Davis, whom she hadn't seen since the star's marriage to Gary Merrill. She and Bramson had dinner at the Merrill house, and Mary-David was sent, much against her will, "to dine upstairs with the children."[30] While Merrill kept Bramson busy, Bette and Mary discussed a project they could work on together. Over the next few years she and Davis saw each other occasionally, and Mary-David was invited to a few of Bette's daughter B. D.'s lavish parties, but both older women were in career trouble. During the late 1940s a number of women, including Davis, had formed production companies to further their careers; most of these had dissolved by 1950. Only Harriet Parsons and Ida Lupino were still producing films. Soon even they would quit.

McCall, Bramson, and Mary-David downscaled further and moved to a rented house in the Hollywood Hills, at 6200 Mulholland, built by *Los Angeles Times* publisher Harry Chandler. Their landlord was Norbert Miles. Miles had acted in silent films since 1913 and later directed a couple of westerns in the 1920s (*The Daughter of Dawn*, 1920; *Walloping Wallace*, 1924). When this line of work dried up, he reinvented himself as a makeup man, working with Barbara Stanwyck (*The Miracle Woman*, 1931), Bette Davis (*The Little Foxes*, 1941), and Laurence Olivier (*Hamlet*, 1948), among many others. In the 1950s, he was doing makeup for comedian Jack Benny (*The Jack Benny Program*, 1954–62). Niles knew a thing or two about pulling his career back from the brink, so he sympathized with McCall and kept the rent low for her. But soon McCall couldn't pay even the discounted rate.

Their three cars were repossessed by the bailiffs, and the bank account was frozen. The bailiffs didn't want her books or her Royal typewriter, so she still spent as many hours each day as she could in her study, writing pitches. Sometimes, to get away from the bill collectors, as Mary-David recalled, "she'd go to the library and sit in an abandoned corner, face to the wall, so that no one would see her lips moving as she spoke the dialog to herself."[31] McCall had stopped writing material for the magazine trade ten years before when her career at the Screen Writers Guild hit its peak, and now it was hard enough for her to get a story in the *Philadelphia Inquirer Magazine*.[32] In the years since, the public demand and the pay for such magazine stories had waned, and McCall focused her creative resources on film. But in spite of her efforts, she was able to wrangle only a "a polish job on the script" of Marilyn Monroe's new vehicle, *There's No Business Like Show Business* (1954).[33] She was corpse rouging again and wasn't on a long-term contract. She didn't even rate screen credit. The guild "contract" was no more, and producers knew how to rub salt into wounds. McCall was philosophical. With typically black humor, McCall later quipped of Monroe, "She needs dialog?"[34]

Even with her occasional break they were always just one paycheck past insolvency, and Bramson complained that the amorphous allegations about her political history were destroying his career too. He was relieved of his reserve commission and could no longer attend the officers' club in town. At his urging, she had met with an FBI special agent in Los Angeles on March 23, 1954, to restate her hatred of communism and communists.[35] But when this wasn't enough for Bramson, McCall asked to testify before the California State Committee in the summer of 1954, hoping that a public exoneration might regenerate his career and produce a few more writing offers for her. After some effort and string-pulling from Brackett, it was arranged that she would speak before the committee on July 27. Mary-David accompanied them, but the morning of the hearing Bramson was so short-tempered with the nine-year old that he punched her in the face. She later had to have one of the front teeth he'd loosened replaced.

At the hearing, McCall was calm, collected, and ready to spout her anticommunist creed. She refused to take the Fifth Amendment, stating baldly that she "would rather be dead than be a Communist" and had never been "a fellow traveler in my understanding of the term."[36] She declined to name names and stated that the "listing of her name in a 1948 committee report had adversely affected her reputation and damaged her economically." The notorious Tenney report placed her in a Hollywood Democratic Committee on the night of March 4, 1943, when, as McCall pointed out, she was at the Academy Awards ceremony. She also explained that although she and others were members of many committees during the war including the Hollywood Democratic Committee, she "did not regret" her membership, since at the time "she believed they had worthy aims."[37]

She was armed with a character reference from Brackett that she read to the committee. In it he explained his and McCall's political dilemma in the 1930s: "In those years there was an attempt by certain well-organized communist members to take over the guild. A number of anti-communist members of the guild and I became aware of that attempt and put all our energies into fighting it." Brackett concluded: "Of all the fighters on our side, of all the ardent and aware anti-communists, Mrs. Bramson was the most ardent and the most effective. She was my right hand in the fight, and in later years, when she became president of that guild, she carried on and spearheaded that fight. That it should be necessary to write this letter for anyone with her magnificent public record shocks me profoundly."[38] She also mentioned that when she asked an alleged Communist Party member what the members thought of her, he replied, "They loathe you."

She got her headlines. *The Los Angeles Times* led with "Ex-Head of Screen Writers Guild Denies Ever Being Red" and praised the "gray-haired screen-writing veteran" and her career of over twenty years.[39] The paper quoted McCall at length when she charged "extremists from the Right . . . have done a great disservice to the good, solid, middle-of-the-road people who have been combatting communism in an orderly, sensible American way." She explained that television sponsors had "refused to accept a teleplay" she'd written due to her suspected communism, and her colleague Howard Estabrook, who had also moved on to work in television, was called to comment on the "real mess" the political backstabbing had created for workers and sponsors in the television industry. It was, Estabrook stated, "a jungle."

Hedda Hopper's response three days later in her column of July 31, 1954, was unforgiving. A lot of water had passed under the bridge since her last favorable mention of McCall in 1948. In the 1950s, Hopper had become a fervent anticommunist and had no tolerance for moderates, even if they were once women she considered friends. "Mary McCall, ex-President of the Screen Writers Guild," she began, "said she'd rather be dead than a communist but she didn't regret joining seven subversive groups and doing nothing while the rest of us were trying to stem the tide and save our industry from creeping communism."[40] In Hopper's mind, those individuals who weren't for her beliefs were now her enemies, and New Deal and labor moderates were her favorite marks.

Other papers deliberately misrepresented McCall's testimony to give the impression that she had been a communist. For example, the *Los Angeles Examiner* coverage of McCall's testimony also included her quote, "I would rather be dead than be a Communist," but led with a very different and inaccurate headline: "Mary McCall Admits Having Been in Seven Red Fronts."[41] Obviously this was not a headline that would make a headline-skimming producer ask for her agent's phone number. In the article McCall acknowledged she was a wartime member of the Actors Lab in 1942, the Writers Congress Advisory Committee in 1943, the Hollywood Democratic Committee in 1944, and the Independent Citizens Committee of the Arts, Sciences, and Professions, but "I do not regret joining any of the organizations. I thought they were all clean and decent at the time."

Something similar was done in a series of syndicated news features in the mid 1950s, profiling communism in American society. In the Hollywood issue of "Blueprint for Destruction," published in the *Syracuse Post-Standard* on February 15, 1956, McCall's famous ironic swipe at left-wing "cause" meetings was quoted out of context, making it seem as if she were one of "those middle class professionals attracted by the Communist Party," a Hollywood bleeding-heart liberal who lived "in an unreal world of images."[42]

But following her ordeal before the committee, George Seaton at Paramount and her former nemesis, Y. Frank Freeman, not only put McCall on the studio payroll but also "put Paramount's Washington lawyers at [her] disposal" to quell the persistent rumors she was a "fellow traveler."[43] McCall continued to make occasional pitches for the big screen, and though her name wasn't in any credits, at least she was in the trade papers again. Ann Sothern, now a top television star, indicated interest in collaborating with McCall on a feature project. In February 1955 her former MGM colleague, producer Jack Chertok, announced that McCall was tipped to develop Herb Baker's *The Easterner* for Sothern.[44] Unfortunately, nothing came of the Vegas-themed story. Then in April it was announced McCall was working on *Hamlet and Three Eggs* for the Ritz Brothers' next film.[45] Over the summer the trade papers claimed that silent film legend Marshall "Micky" Neilan (*The Lotus Eater*, 1921; *The Awful Truth*, 1929) was directing "a new picture down in Crystal Springs, Tennessee, *The Adventures of Davy Crockett, Boy*

Pioneer, from a script by Mary McCall Jr. in October."[46] Chad Kendall, a fourteen-year-old actor, was signed for the lead. Neilan supposedly was closing a distribution deal, but nothing more was heard about the picture. Though players from different stages of the film industry's past, neither she nor Neilan had a place Hollywood's "brave new world" of the 1950s.

Although Cagney's and Bogart's film careers were thriving, they didn't reach out to her with work. Instead, one of McCall's younger friends from the war years, actor Guy Madison (conveniently a Republican), wanted to form a production company with McCall at Columbia using her stories as material for a suite of films. Madison had been earmarked for stardom in *Since You Went Away* (1944), but apart from *Till the End of Time* (1946) he hadn't made much of an impact. His agent, Helen Ainsworth, named McCall's Civil War story "Seven Watchmen" as the basis of their first big film.[47] The press took note of the new partnership, since Madison was in the middle of a long-running television series about western icon and unlucky card player Wild Bill Hickok (1951–58) and was appearing in big-budget hits for just about every studio in town. If Madison couldn't bring McCall in on a deal, then no one could.

The deal stalled. In 1957 Ainsworth, now a producer at Columbia, persuaded the actor to drop McCall's material.[48] But her two intriguingly titled pictures starring Madison—*The Hard Man* (1957) and *Bullwhip* (1958)—failed to stir the box office, and soon Ainsworth also dropped Madison. He left Hollywood for Europe.

That year Miles decided to sell his house on Mulholland and offered McCall first option at a reduced price. Although touched by the gesture, she knew they couldn't afford it. The Bramsons moved to another rental near Nichols Canyon, "a tiny cottage" on Montcalm Avenue owned by Broadway producer Paul Gregory, who'd recently made a splash in film with Charles Laughton's *The Night of the Hunter* (1955) and television with *The Ford Star Jubilee*, 1955–56. McCall kept pitching and tapped the Motion Picture Relief Fund for some money.

Finally she got a break that fall when CBS producer Don Fedderson hired her for *The Millionaire*, where she wrote vignettes about what a different ordinary American would do with an out-of-the-blue gift of a million dollars. It was an easy daydream for her, given her current financial situation, and McCall wrote the first episodes of seasons one and two and most of the better episodes in those seasons, where a mix of working men and women find their lives changed for the better or worse by the money.

McCall lucked out with the top-rated *Millionaire*. Although its final season was in 1960, the show employed more than a hundred writers (including her old friend Doris Gilbert). McCall wrote more episodes than anyone else, fifteen of them, and was instrumental in shaping the working-class dynamics of the show. In 1955 *TV Guide* focused on McCall as the show's "spender-in-chief," praising one of her episodes, "The Margaret Browning Story," as "the best study of Hollywood yet seen on TV."[49] But the staff writer was also patronizing: "It will come as no surprise to the show's male fans that the author who proved most adept at spending the green stuff was a woman."

Like Jack Ruben so many years before, Don Fedderson was a supportive producer who not only hired McCall and Gilbert, but several other women to develop material. While popular shows of the 1950s and 1960s increasingly hired women for just under 10 percent of their episodes (*The Twilight Zone*, *Maverick*, and *Gunsmoke* were part of these statistics), nearly 20 percent of Fedderson's writers were female. He let McCall develop her stories as she saw fit. When she and Fedderson had one of their rare disagreements about story points, her daughter recalled that "in apology, he sent a lovely gift basket of Irish whiskey, enveloped in emerald cellophane." Working on the series was especially fun for McCall because in addition to hiring Gilbert for a handful of episodes, she persuaded Fedderson to hire her old Warner Bros. friend Al Green to direct.

Then, on May 24, 1956, McCall's episode for NBC's Ford Theater aired and attracted good ratings. Adapted from the story by Carol Warner Gluck, "Sheila" was the story of how two young women, Katherine and Laura, abuse the trust of Katherine's "Aunt Sheila" so Laura can visit her boyfriend. Irene Dunne, in one of her last screen performances, played Sheila. McCall knew a thing or two about clashes between older and younger generations of women, parenting angst about teenagers, and the sexual mores of the middle class, and Dunne brought a sensitivity to McCall's script that elevated it above even Ford Theater's usual prestige fare.

Produced by Fred Briskin, Joseph Hoffman, and Irving Starr and directed by James Neilson, the episode didn't earn her an Emmy, but that fall Father James Keller wrote to McCall informing her that she'd received a Christopher Award.[50] Founded by Keller, the semiannual awards paid tribute to those in the film and television industries for using "their God-given talents in a positive and constructive manner" —in other words, producing good, clean family shows that didn't offend America's legions of easily offended Catholic critics. Charles Brackett received an award for his work producing *The King and I*. McCall, Helen Cotton, and Bridget Boland (screenwriter, *War and Peace*, 1956) were the only women among thirty-three award winners.

McCall couldn't afford to fly to New York to attend the award ceremony on November 12, but, ever polite, she wrote to Keller, "I am proud that the Christophers, whose motto sets forth with such simplicity the aim in life of millions of men and women of good will, found my work worthy of a citation."[51] She explained that she couldn't attend because, "my husband and I are at work here at Universal on a screenplay based on a story we wrote together, and we're trying to make it good enough so that people who think like the Christophers will enjoy the picture." She was also at pains to explain that George Haight, her old *Maisie* producer, deserved some of the credit for developing "Sheila." In 1950 Haight was another casualty of postwar Hollywood downsizing. He moved to the East Coast that year and, thanks to his relationship with mutual friend Robert Montgomery, became a television producer, first for NBC's *Robert Montgomery Presents* and then for the landmark advertising firm McCann-Erikson in 1953, first as West Coast director of programming and then, in 1955, as vice president of radio and television programming.[52] His work with McCall was a side hustle. The episode was originally pitched to Four Star Theatre, but the company passed on it, even though Irene Dunne liked it. Three years later Screen Gems bought it, but "since Mr. Haight made a major contribution to the shaping of the screenplay," he accepted the award on her behalf on November 12. It was typical of McCall that she always gave credit where even a small bit was due.

McCall's success may have prompted others to reconsider the viability of one of her old big-screen hits for the small screen: *Maisie*. Though she was running her own television show, Ann Sothern, now in her late forties, was considered too old to reprise her iconic role as the explosive blonde from Brooklyn. But on New Year's Eve 1956 Louella Parsons was delighted to announce that MGM had signed McCall to do the TV pilot for a new Maisie series starring Janis Paige.[53]

It took over three years for the pilot it to reach the small screen, but MGM refused to develop it as a series. McCall's decision to insert Maisie peripherally into the contemporary military world, though a wifely tribute to Bramson's excareer, was less appealing than her earlier scenarios had been.[54] But producer Richard Maibaum learned a few things from Maisie's past serial success. After Maisie failed to attract a sponsor or audience interest, he turned James Bond into the most successful male-led franchise in history, beginning with *Dr. No* in 1962. Stories of resourceful, independent women just weren't as popular anymore.

While MGM's television branch briefly resurrected and buried *Maisie*, McCall continued her collaboration with Bramson on a new western for Universal. Over Christmas they had come up with an idea based on his memories of working as a publicist for William Boyd (cowboy legend Hopalong Cassidy). As their daughter recalled, "Hoppy" was an alcoholic and was told to "clean up his act, which he eventually did when he realized the impact his image had on young children."[55] The treatment had some connections to McCall's novel *The Goldfish Bowl*, exploring the media's construction of a hero and the disappointing reality. Now older and a little nostalgic for heroes after over a decade of living with Bramson, McCall was intrigued with the idea of a man who pulls himself together for the younger generation and in the process rediscovers his self-respect. *Slim Carter* was imbued with a sense of Hollywood's glory days, its faded and half-forgotten past, and the need for a new generation to remember and continue to create good work.

Whatever Bramson's contribution in the early stages, the approved script, dated January, has only McCall's name on it. Montgomery Pittman, the future wonder-boy of television directing (*Maverick*, 1958-59; *77 Sunset Strip*, 1959-62; *The Twilight Zone*, 1961-62), handled the rewrites with her and Bramson, producing a composite script in February. But the story doesn't begin with the man's story; it opens on Hollywood insider "Clover," a press agent who was practically born on a film set. Her father was a western star, and she herself is "an authority on the old West." The script shows her efforts to turn hack actor Hughie Mack into Slim Carter. Mack is not exactly a born horseman, and McCall staged a comic scene where Clover tries to teach him to ride. In a reversal of the Pygmalion and Galatea relationship, Clover "creates" her western hero. In the end the publicist and manufactured western star become parents to an orphan boy. Although many westerns over the years explored the divide between mythical and factual heroes, McCall's approach, which put a woman in charge of shaping the cowboy hero image, was unusual for 1950s audiences. It would still be unusual today.

Producer Howie Horwitz (*Appointment with a Shadow*, 1957) was not interested in a potentially feminist take on the western, and "so butchered [the script] that they considered taking their names off altogether."[56] Horwitz and director Richard Bartlett edited many of McCall's gender critiques and evocations of old Hollywood and classic westerns and focused on the development and transformation of a romantic couple into the parents of a winsome orphan. Shot in seventeen days, starring ex-stuntman and William Boyd protégé Jock Mahoney (*The Range Rider,* 1951) and young Tim Hovey, *Slim Carter* charmed most critics as a bit of lightweight schmaltz.[57] The following year Pittman and the same cast were hired for *Money, Women, and Guns* (1958). The Bramsons, however, were shut out.

McCall did what she could to make the money last: $5,000 for the story and a little over $7,000 for eleven weeks of development.[58] She also kept pitching, even collaborating with her teenaged daughter. She was always on the lookout for new ideas and commissioned Mary-David to write a *Leave It to Beaver* story in exchange for a bicycle. Although the pitch didn't work out, Mary-David did get the bike. A contract was still a contract to McCall. "It was a used, slim tired, boys' bike with hand brakes, painted British racing green. I was thrilled," she recalled.[59]

Although she still attended guild meetings as a private member, McCall had been out of the loop of union governance for several years while she rebuilt her career. But in 1957 she was encouraged to return, this time to lead writers in the television and radio branch of the Writers Guild of American West. She made an unsuccessful bid for the presidency against incumbent Edmund L. Hartmann in 1957.[60] But many younger television writers, from Christopher Knopf to Ray Bradbury and Rod Serling, respected McCall and appreciated her support for young and struggling writers, especially when she herself was so hard up. Her perspectives on guild history and politics were always razor-sharp. In late 1960 McCall was elected to the Television-Radio board of the Writers Guild of America West alongside Barry Trivers and Knopf.[61]

Her bank balance almost nonexistent, she accepted Columbia's offer to coscript *Juke Box Rhythm* with another old-timer, Earl Baldwin. The forgettable teen pic, a desperate studio attempt to capture the pop music market, was to be her final script. Both McCall and the old studio system were tone-deaf, but *Film Bulletin* seemed to regard the picture, the debut of Jack Jones, the lookalike son of actor-singer Allan Jones (*Show Boat*, 1936), as a "mildly amusing mixture of comedy, romance, and rock 'n roll music."[62] McCall avoided discussing the film in career reminiscences; perhaps it was a little embarrassing to wind up a Hollywood screen career as a librettist for juvenile pop tunes. The critics preferred the music: "The screenplay by Mary McCall and Earl Baldwin is a complicated throwback to the old days when Graustarkian plots were popular, but the treatment by director Arthur Dreifuss is light and never permits the plot to intrude too heavily on the musical numbers."[63]

Television had snatched Hollywood's stars, writers, and audiences. Fewer film productions were greenlit, and those that did make it to the cameras were hamstrung with delays and out of place in a new media world. McCall must have realized her Hollywood film comeback was never going to happen when, at the end of the 1950s, she was invited to teach some screenwriting extension classes at the University of Southern California. Long before McCall had shunned the teaching profession as a dead-end for women writers. But, as with McCall's kindness to young William Ludwig and her articles in *The Screen Writer*, McCall proved again that she was a born mentor who honestly cared about helping young writers succeed.

In "The Bespoke Script," her contribution to an anthology for the Writers Guild of America, *TV and Screen Writing*, McCall warned prospective young writers against speculative writing, especially when they were adapting content "not owned by him but a producer."[64] Writers needed to study the series thoroughly and meet with the producer: "Before he cuts his dramatic cloth, the writer must know his customer's measurements; he must know whether that customer is willing to place an order with him; there must be an agreement on price. This is bespoke writing." Television writing for these series was skewed in favor of old, reliable hands rather than new talent. Producers "may deprive themselves of being the discoverers of genuine writing talents, but they protect themselves against plagiarism suits."

Television writing might seem glamorous but required stern discipline and technique, she warned. Television budgets were "limited in size" and the format was rigid. It took thirty-four pages to tell a story with well-known characters in fresh situations, and the length was "as absolute as the length of a sonnet." "Against the whetstones of the musts and must-nots of a series," she wrote, the writer "can sharpen his technique." But even though television series were on tight budgets and under time constraints, the writer had to be as disciplined and polished as possible since everybody would want to change the material. "Though no one thinks he could fly a plane, raise sheep, or tat with no experience, no aptitude, no training, nearly everybody believes he could write if he just took the time to do it," she warned. "In television, producers, directors, players, sponsors, and account executives are all ready, willing and believe themselves able to write, or rewrite."

McCall's career path, like her marriage to Bramson, was one of disasters and setbacks. She fought back as best she could with words—words to defend her guild, pitches and scripts to prop up her crumbling Hollywood career, and the words of her friends and allies who still believed in her. In the past her imagination and freelancing skills kept her solvent. But now, after one too many battles at home and in the trade papers, she was weary.

She used to go walking alone in the early morning to think. Even in the 1950s, few Angelinos braved the sun to go for long walks. But when the family cars were repossessed, she didn't have many options. Mary-David remembers her mother telling her a story about one of these walks. McCall was moving slowly along the side of a parkway, occasionally stopping to kneel, her eyes on the grass, her fingers searching. A police patrol car slowed and stopped, and a patrolman got out of the car and approached her.

"May I help you, ma'am?" he asked.

She had looked up and smiled at his puzzled, concerned face—he obviously thought she was either drunk or had lost her keys. As Mary-David told the story, I tried to picture the effect of McCall's brilliant light-blue eyes, the short, curly, undyed white hair, pale Irish skin free of makeup, and the plain, neatly pressed, but rather faded housedress.

"Oh, no thank you, officer," she replied. "I'm just looking for four-leaf clovers."

"Four-leaf clovers?" he repeated slowly, bewildered.

"Yes, for good luck. I've found a few over the years. Even in Beverly Hills."[65]

CHAPTER 15

The Stuff That Dreams Are Made Of

When Mary C. McCall Jr. began her career as a short fiction writer back in the 1920s, she fantasized about having a story published in *The Saturday Evening Post*, which, at the time, was the most widely circulated and distinguished middlebrow magazine in the United States.[1] But no matter how well she was paid by other magazines, no matter hard she worked, no matter how many stories she submitted, she always got the dreaded rejection letter. Being McCall, she kept trying. Then, after more than thirty years as a writer and making and losing her Hollywood reputation, she got the letter informing her they were publishing "The Friday Girl."[2]

McCall got the idea for the story when she visited one of her rich Manhattan cousins on a rare trip back East. Day McClave lived on 242 East 72nd Street and was living the kind of life McCall might have had if she'd stayed in New York with Franklin all those years ago. One morning over breakfast, McCall admired Day's spotless kitchen and lamented the amount of time she had to spend cleaning house when she'd rather be writing. Day told McCall that she'd had a cleaner for many years but "had never actually seen her." McCall was appalled at the invisible treatment given to working-class women.

Back in the 1940s, when she'd had the money for servants, McCall always "felt very guilty having to hire people to do what she felt she should be doing, was ill equipped to do and had no interest in doing."[3] Screenwriter Phoebe Ephron's beliefs that a woman measured her career success by the ability to keep another woman in domestic slavery and that "to be a housewife was to be nothing" were shared by high-earning women in the Hollywood studio system.[4] As a writer, McCall knew she had a great job while other women were suffering in low-paid, unfulfilling work; as a labor leader she knew it was doubly important for her not to be an exploitative boss—especially in her own home. So she always had paid the top salary for domestic service, gave "lavish gifts and bonuses," and provided regular days off. And, of course, she talked with employees; no one was invisible in her household.

In "The Friday Girl," a New York cleaning lady matchmakes for two of her lonely single clients behind the scenes, having learned enough about them through working for them over the years. Too bad the studios never optioned it. It would have been a perfect vehicle for Thelma Ritter (*All About Eve*, 1950; *Rear Window*, 1954) and was ideal for the *Post*, which by the late 1950s had become one of the last outposts of middlebrow Americana—and one of the last magazines that paid freelance writers well. Later that year the magazine published an edited collection of the best stories to come out in 1959, and McCall's made the list. As Amelia Bean wrote in the *San Bernadino Sun* in May 1960, "'The Friday Girl' might almost be overlooked because of its quiet lack of impact. But it sneaks into your memory, you realize that the story and the characters have been delineated in most expert dialog and the finish leaves you smiling with satisfaction."[5]

It was on one of these infrequent visits to Day's that McCall left a purple capsule by the guest sink. When Day saw it, she was convinced McCall was "dying of a dread disease" and the pill was medication. (It was only her purple hair rinse, which McCall had used for years to keep her gray hair from yellowing.) After she learned of Day's suspicions, McCall considered writing a science fiction story using this vignette. These sorts of incidents delighted the writer, who, as her daughter recalled, "was the least vain person on the planet"—although she hated it when people "mistook her for Bramson's mother" when they were out together.[6] Bramson's contribution to their marriage was to give all the gray hair to his wife; his stayed the same chestnut brown until the day he died.

Going occasionally to the movies was as extravagant an evening out as McCall could afford. Mary-David remembered going to *The Apartment* with her parents when it appeared in theaters in the summer of 1960. Director-writer Billy Wilder had long since moved on from his partnership with Charles Brackett, and while she appreciated the film's clever dialog and take on modern New York, the film's leading lady, suicidal elevator operator Miss Kubelik (Shirley MacLaine), was indicative of the decline in roles for women. Maisie wouldn't have known what to do with her. But one of Bramson's old war buddies, Jack Kruschen, played the doctor who saves Miss Kubelik's life after her suicide attempt. As Mary-David recalled, "When they mustered out, Jack or Yankele, as my dad called him, stayed at our house in Beverly Hills until he got on his feet."[7] He told them his dream was to be an actor, and they tried to convince "this lovely, warm, rotund, unmade bed of a fellow that his chances for success as an actor were slim and he none. Fortunately, he ignored their advice." He was later nominated for Best Supporting Actor for his role.

Around that time, her friends George Bradshaw, who wrote regularly for *The Saturday Evening Post*, and ex-Broadway actor ("Let Freedom Ring") and writer Robert Thomsen commissioned McCall to write a play based on the life of Jane Addams of Chicago's Hull House. Hollywood had never given Addams, a titan of America's Progressive Era, the "great woman" biographical treatment accorded "great men" such as Alexander Graham Bell, Buffalo Bill, or Abraham Lincoln. McCall "worked long and hard on it" from 1960 to 1962. It was always possible that it could be a vehicle for her return to big screenwriting, but by the 1960s, biopics of formerly famous women were out of favor. The advance check was welcome, to say the least, so the night before a writers guild meeting "she decided to treat herself to dinner" at Don the Beachcomber's. Frank Sinatra was a regular, and when he saw McCall alone, he came over to say hello. Both had been committed Roosevelt Democrats and activists who had since been burned by their political convictions. Both had had their separate acrimonious encounters with Howard Hughes. A few years earlier Sinatra had been consumed by jealousy over Ava Gardner's relationship with Hughes, and after the Sinatras married, Hughes hired private detectives to spy on the couple. But Sinatra had the last laugh. He was now an even bigger star than he had been as a bobbysoxer's crooner back in the 1940s. McCall had not been so lucky.

Sinatra sat down and told her that he and Bette Davis had just been speaking about her. Lately Sinatra had been involved with Davis on *Pocket Full of Miracles* (he eventually left the project over creative differences with director Frank Capra, and Glenn Ford took his role). McCall's current project on Jane Addams would have been a perfect vehicle for Davis, since it resonated with Davis's own political background and her role as a nurturing schoolteacher in *The Corn Is Green* (1946). They chatted, Sinatra rose to leave, and McCall ordered dinner. When she called for the bill, "she was told that Mr. Sinatra had picked up her check."[8] He had slipped away before she could protest at the gesture.

Though Davis was intrigued by the project, McCall's work was never developed or given credit.[9] As her daughter recalled, the advance from Bradshaw and Thomsen just "paid the rent until it didn't."[10] But while her writing assignments dried up, McCall continued to give her time to the guild. In March 1961 she ran for the presidency against Charles Schnee (*The Bad and the Beautiful*, 1952) but lost. She was nominated following the withdrawal of Fenton Earnshaw, who faced a conflict of interest when he was appointed producer of Warner Bros. Solitaire Series. That same year her friend Christopher Knopf ran for the vice president slot of the radio-television branch. Curtis Kenyon was Writers Guild of America West president at time, and he had to resign (and McCall stepped up) when it was revealed he had a conflict of interest, being the new head of the Paramount Pictures story department.[11]

When the guild was on strike in May, a column in the *Hollywood Reporter* linked "their activities to those of Communists." McCall and three other writers sued publisher Billy Wilkerson, columnist Mike Connolly, editor Don Gillette, and business manager George H. Kennedy, for $350,000 in damages.[12] Then, like clock-work, Myron C. Fagan's right-wing Cinema Education Guild published yet another pamphlet naming her as a communist, and McCall again appealed to friends in government to exonerate her.[13] The harassment was unrelenting.

In the California Legislature's eleventh report of the Senate Fact-Finding Sub-Committee on Un-American Activities, members discussed "The Case of Mary McCall" as a separate item in June 1961. The committee members agreed with her criticism of Fagan, deploring this particular manifestation of witch-hunting. The *Los Angeles Times* and *Daily Variety* went out of their way to exonerate her, and there was sympathetic coverage throughout the United States warning people of the "sheer nonsense" published by the Cinema Education Guild about McCall and Gregory Peck, Myrna Loy, and Melvyn Douglas.[14] McCall followed up on the press coverage, addressing the Hollywood Democratic Club on "The Writer in Politics" that June.[15]

But the great irony was that while McCall devoted time and energy to defend-ing her name and reputation, real former-and-otherwise-communist writers were working for the studios again and writing some of their top box office hits. Dalton Trumbo made a triumphant return to Hollywood with *Exodus* and *Sparta-cus* in 1960, but Hollywood producers did not offer McCall any pictures after *Juke Box Rhythm*. As Hollywood's hard left returned to cultural acclaim in the 1960s, in some sense reborn on the ashes of the old studio system, McCall's status as a loyal woman warrior of a bygone age was out of sync and unmarketable.

That summer she contemplated writing a novel about her political experi-ences in Hollywood. She wrote to literary agent Ted Loeff, but her pitch merely recapitulated what had happened to her and Bramson since "the case" with Hughes and Jarrico.[16] Perhaps a novel about the current political situation and the polarized culture of Hollywood from a moderate perspective would have been a novelty in blacklist literary fiction, but Loeff showed no interest, and she never got around to writing it. Meanwhile Hollywood men claimed the lion's share of moral high ground in the blacklist. In the increasingly liberal Hollywood of the 1960s, McCall's public anticommunist self-defense appeared retrograde. Her perception of "the case" had eaten her up from inside, and Bramson's anger and her guilt kept her in a cycle of unproductive bitterness.

A few radio and television colleagues in the guild came to her aid and nominated McCall to represent them on an "inspection tour of Radio Free Europe" in Lisbon, Berlin, and Munich that October. They wanted to send two representatives from the motion picture industry, and as she recalled, "someone thought it might be a good idea to send a writer."[17] Network "big shot" Hubbell Robinson also went along, but Bramson and Mary-David remained in Los Angeles. She and Bramson were "dead broke," and it was just an all-expenses paid trip for one. It was her first trip back to Europe since her school days, and she enjoyed it, though, according to Mary-David, McCall was too "serious" about her "inspection tour" to go to Oktoberfest. That November she gave a talk at Temple Isaiah about her experience in Germany.[18] At the time McCall sincerely believed what the guild and the government said of Free Radio's alleged purpose: to combat Soviet censorship of the air waves with "free" content. As her daughter later remembered, McCall was "devastated" to learn it was just a Cold War propaganda outlet.[19]

She remained a force in the Writers Guild of America West in the early 1960s. In 1962, when the organization created the Valentine Davies Award for service to the guild, there was only one name that came up as the first recipient—hers. That March, she accepted the medal at the annual banquet at the Hollywood Palladium.[20] She was three weeks shy of her fifty-eighth birthday. But no matter how hard she fought back with pitches, her screenwriting career was over. She didn't have the money to send Mary-David to Vassar that fall, despite her daughter's top grades. Instead, like Sheila, Mary-David took classes at UCLA and lived at home for a while. McCall was still trying make ends meet, but the assignments, apart from a handful of episodes on *The Third Man*, shot on the Twentieth Century-Fox lot, were sporadic. Paul Henreid (*Casablanca*), a liberal survivor from her days at the top of the guild heap, directed one of the episodes.

McCall continued to attend guild meetings with another fellow golden age relic, Doris Gilbert, but much of the spirit that had motivated their generation of writers had vanished. They laughed when the otherwise charming Ray Bradbury would "dematerialize from any meeting" after a few minutes. Though *Twilight Zone* creator Rod Serling took a more active part in meetings, McCall was less than thrilled with his youthful pomposity. He broke up one dispute by asking the membership to "behave like ladies and gentlemen." She preferred people who could stand a good fight.

In the fall of 1963 McCall was still trying for a pitch breakthrough. One of her old friends on the guild, Ellis Marcus, was a story editor for MGM's *The Eleventh Hour*, a Wednesday prime time show managed by Irving Elman and executive producer Norman Felton. The medical drama featuring Wendell Corey and Ralph Bellamy explored lurid stories about women's mental health and treatment. Of course, women were the victims and men were the doctors. But McCall, remembering a tabloid story from her twenties, decided to provoke this stereotypical gender formula with a script based on the life and death of Starr Faithfull, an American socialite who had been sexually abused as a child by a friend of her parents, the former mayor of Boston, Andrew James Peters.[21]

Faithfull had been beaten and sedated before she was found drowned on the south shore of Long Island in 1931. Although Peters was accused of killing her, the jury ruled an open verdict. Peters was rich and well connected, and at the time of the murder was a friend of the governor of New York, Franklin D. Roosevelt. James O'Hara's 1935 novel *BUtterfield 8* (adapted as a film for Elizabeth Taylor in 1960) was based in part on the case, but no one had ever looked in depth at the horrors of child abuse and society's protection of rich pedophiles.

McCall pitched "She Called Him 'Uncle Hugh,'" and Marcus fought for the story. McCall's script renamed Starr Faithfull "Prudence Joy," and it investigates her mental breakdown and the inept mother and stepfather who allowed the sexual abuse.[22] Like Starr, Prudence turns to alcoholism, but, departing from the truth (and avoiding a potential libel suit with Peters's heirs), she eventually kills herself when her stepfather is too embarrassed to allow her to undergo therapy. Prudence's mother, much older than the stepfather, won't acknowledge feelings or problems or anything to distract her from surface normality. Her stepfather still insists in the end that "Uncle Hugh's passing was a great loss to Prudence." At one point Prudence talks to a doctor about why she never talked with her mother about "Uncle Hugh": "Anything 'Uncle' Hugh did was okay with them. . . .

A dirty old man raped me when I was twelve. . . . You can't talk about things like that when you're a kid. My mother would've . . . I don't know . . . washed my mouth out with soap." Prudence wasn't the only child to have felt her mother wouldn't support her in such a situation. But even with some censorship taboos loosening in the early Sixties, the network refused to risk shooting the story.

The atmosphere at the McCall-Bramson house hit rock bottom. According to Bramson, UCLA was too expensive. He kicked Mary-David out of the house, a replay of what had happened to Sheila years before. Thanks in part to her mother's connections, Mary-David got a job as a script reader in the last days of MGM. McCall knew Samuel Marx, a longtime story editor at the studio, and had even adapted one of his stories for the Ford Television Theatre when she was just getting back on her feet after the Jarrico case. His son was the assistant of legendary Hollywood musical guru (and alleged child abuser) Arthur Freed (*Kathleen*, 1941; *Meet Me in St. Louis*, 1944; *Singing in the Rain*, 1952). In another of life's ironies, Mary-David ended up working in Freed's office in 1964. For a while she "basked in the nostalgia" with the other young women in the office. But then one day his secretary Helen Auer opened his mail and showed them what the boss had ordered. "It was child porn."[23] So much for nostalgia. Things evidently hadn't changed since Freed attempted to assault Shirley Temple in 1940.

While her daughter began her career, McCall wrote her final credited television episode for the popular comedy *Gilligan's Island*, "Hi Fi Gilligan," in 1965. The script had an amusing gimmick: Gilligan swallows a radio and loses his voice. He can only say what the radio tells him. Whether it was a metaphor for the television screenwriter's relationship with her producer or not (or the wife's relationship with her husband), the ventriloquism was funny. McCall could have used extra laughs that year; in 1966 she and Bramson left Los Angeles for what she hoped would be a cheaper life in San Francisco. McCall and Bramson had an apartment at Greenwich and Lyon, across the street from the Presidio Officers' Club, where Bramson, now a retired colonel, could soak in the atmosphere.

McCall passed the time thinking up new pitches but returned briefly to Phoenix to attend her mother's funeral that March. She took her mother's debutante portrait by Irving Wiles back to the apartment in San Francisco and hung it near her desk. Though it would have fetched a little money at auction, she would not sell it. Mazie, along with her grandmother Katie, had always been McCall's staunchest supporter as a writer. Under the confident gaze of the portrait, she started writing again. She still hadn't given up on a comeback film idea, and in

June 1966 she approached her old lover and friend Douglas Fairbanks Jr., asking him if he would be willing to collaborate. Like many Sixties filmgoers, she had fallen for the James Bond franchise and Sean Connery's license to thrill. Ironically, it was her old friend Richard Maibaum, the producer of the failed *Maisie* television pilot, who wrote the scripts for *Dr. No* (1962), *From Russia with Love* (1963), *Goldfinger* (1964), and *Thunderball* (1965), ushering in the age of male-dominated action franchises.

In an attempt to emulate his success, she wrote what she hoped was an on-trend, international spy-themed story, tailored with a good role for Fairbanks, called "Who Played the Ace?" But in the mid-1960s, everyone was trying to reproduce Bond's success for MGM, and Fairbanks knew he was too old to play the lead, too proud to play a supporting role, and too rich to care about renewing his Hollywood career. "If I were ever again to be tempted to put my ageing shoulder to the cinematic wheel, it would be, I am sure, due to your undiminished persuasiveness," but, he said, "mundane interests" kept him far from Hollywood. He reminded her, "34 years at my job and then sliding away while all was still going well is enough I think."[24] But McCall had neither the luxury to say no nor his house at 10 Park Place, St. James, in London.

In the spring of 1968 Mary-David called to say she was getting married to comedy actor David Sheiner (*The Odd Couple*, 1968). Bramson grilled her with a few pointed questions. When he learned she had known Sheiner only three months and that her intended was forty years old, sixteen years older than Mary-David, his daughter recalled, "My father hung up on me." He may also have realized that in choosing a man fifteen years her senior, she was doing exactly what her mother had done with Dwight Franklin exactly forty years ago. McCall was more welcoming. Their mutual friend Ray Bradbury had never learned to drive, and so Sheiner, who knew Bradbury from their health club, had often volunteered to ferry the author around town. McCall also was grateful for her future son-in-law's generosity. He paid for the reception and for McCall and Bramson to stay in a hotel for the wedding. Although Mary-David had asked only Gerry to come to the wedding, Alan showed up anyway, still wearing his ambulance driver's uniform. They all dutifully posed for photographs, with Sheiner, beaming on all of them, keeping the mood light for the camera. Sheila was noticeably absent. She had remained in northern California with her husband and children.

As Mary-David remembered, "David thought it would be nice for my parents to be close." He paid for them to return to Los Angeles and found them an apartment at 150 South Spalding Drive in Beverly Hills. Knowing McCall's writing assignments had dwindled to nothing, he gave them a stipend each month. Bramson's small army pension and McCall's meager WGAW pension plan (which she'd help create decades before) made up the rest of their income.[25] McCall reactivated her Academy membership, which enabled her to attend screenings. Some old-timers were still around to say hello to, and occasionally some writers of her daughter's generation would recognize McCall at the screenings and come to shake her hand.

But within two years of moving back to Hollywood she suffered two crippling losses. Charles Brackett had had a stroke in the mid 1960s and had been in poor health ever since. McCall was still blindsided when she heard of his death in March 1969. While others may not have seen Brackett as a natural advocate for the guild, out of place among the Hollywood left, he once wrote that his memories of "the old meetings at their best" were when "I was at one with the Leftists." As he wrote in his diary, "democracy . . . is really my Lady."[26]

Then, in January 1971, Dwight Franklin died. He had continued to work in Hollywood through the 1950s, but after his retirement he had not returned to his native New York. He and McCall had stayed in contact in the years since their divorce, and things were "always civilized" when they discussed their children. If McCall ever had doubts about her divorce and remarriage, Franklin did not. Eliza Moultrie's low-key personality was worlds away from the dynamic, workaholic McCall, and, according to Sheila, Franklin's final decades were calm and happy. For years Hollywood believed that McCall and Franklin had the perfect marriage. Looking back on the traces of their joint careers and home life in the trade papers and in the surviving anniversary notes and presents, it seems as close to perfection as a modern woman could wish. But McCall always wanted more and was driven enough not to count the cost or her losses. Although Cagney had visited his old friend Dwight while he was ill in a nursing home, McCall hadn't had time to say goodbye.

Time passed. Sheila, divorced from photographer Chuck Ashley, remarried Marin County property developer Walter "Spike" Benson and turned into the perfect mother and domestic goddess that McCall never really wanted to be. Mary-David made her mother a grandmother in 1970 and 1974, and McCall learned to knit and babysit. But the marriage was not going well. Sheiner tried to get Mary-David, an aspiring television writer, to sign a letter saying she would never have a career. "My career is the only one we will discuss in this house," he stated. At first, Mary-David thought he was joking. He wasn't. In September 1977 she left Sheiner and, with friend Sheila J. Weisberg (who had just divorced her husband) got an agent, Ingo Preminger's son Jim, and started pitching and selling television scripts. As Mary-David put it, "We figured stupider people than we wrote sitcoms." McCall watched her grandkids while her daughter went to pitch meetings.

Though Mary-David and Weisberg worked hard to get their handful of credits on *Happy Days*, *The Jeffersons*, *The Mary Tyler Moore Show*, and *The Love Boat*, dozens of other projects didn't happen, including a Marilyn Chambers biopic and another spoof of men's casual misogyny, "Ignorant Sluts," a riff on a *Saturday Night Live* skit. After leaving Preminger for Marty Shapiro's "high-powered" agency in the early Eighties, their careers dried up. In Mary-David's words, as women their work was "palmed off on legmen and languished."

McCall had been somewhat resistant to the establishment of a "women's committee" at the Screen Writers Guild in the 1970s, since she remembered how much power and influence women had enjoyed in the 1930s and 1940s, long before "second wave" feminism made women's issues fashionable in the 1960s and 1970s.[27] Seeing her own daughter's talent squandered by a cruder generation of Hollywood men convinced her that the best days for women were back in her day when the Equal Rights Amendment was a creed, not just a lost cause. When she held forth on her brilliant career, it irritated David Sheiner. But she emphasized her kind of feminism in the mid-1970s when she organized a major tribute to "her dear Dorothy Arzner" at the Directors Guild. Alongside actress Margaret Lindsay, McCall sat with Arzner and read tributes from stars Joan Crawford (*The Bride Wore Red*, 1937) and Katharine Hepburn (*Christopher Strong*, 1933). There were tributes for her, too, and *Craig's Wife* was taken out of the vaults and shown again to a new generation of women.[28]

McCall received more substantial recognition when she was feted at several tributes to Hollywood women in 1978, including the Writers Guild of America West women's committee tribute on April 20 and the second annual Women in Film Crystal Awards on June 9. Second wave Hollywood feminists had rediscovered some of their industry's leading women, and for a while McCall was in the limelight again. However, there were no film offers from Hollywood's next generation of male producers, and the developing discourse of Hollywood history, popularized by Robert Sklar's *Movie Made America* (1975) and Richard Schickel's *The Men Who Made the Movies* (1975), ignored her career and the careers of countless other behind-the-camera Hollywood women. Even feminist film critics such as Molly Haskell focused on actresses.[29]

The accolades his wife received from other Hollywood women were too much for Bramson's ego. He died of a burst aneurysm that August, aged sixty-six. Mary-David moved McCall to a smaller apartment in Beverly Hills and thence to the privacy of the Park La Brea development. Sheila, who had succeeded Charles Champlin as the Los Angeles *Times*'s film critic, was in town for screenings, and the sisters met more frequently.

At the guild event honoring McCall, Christopher Knopf asked Mary-David and McCall's guild colleague, science fiction writer Harlan Ellison, to give the tribute speeches. Ellison and McCall were "birds of a feather" who liked each other's "feistiness" and outrageous banter. Ellison and Mary-David started dating, occasionally going out to lunch or the movies with McCall and Ray Bradbury, whose gentlemanly behavior was always a welcome contrast to Ellison's unpredictability. But one day Ellison was late to dinner at The Nibblers. They were all to attend a WGA screening afterward, and McCall, fed up with his bad manners, "ripped him a new one." Although it had been one of his favorite watering holes, Ellison "could never bear to go back to that restaurant, so deep was his shameful memory of that night."[30] It was perhaps the one time he didn't dare to talk back to someone.

In the early 1980s Mary-David started to notice her mother's erratic behavior and forgetfulness. One-off incidents became an alarming pattern: "She decided to put $300 cash in an envelope and mail it to the guild to help indigent writers (of which I was one—LOL). She called me at two in the morning to say that if I wanted anything from the local market, it was closed." In a sad parody of Maisie grown old and helpless, McCall "continued to wander, script case in hand, supposedly en route to a pitch meeting."[31] Sheila was divorced, busy with work, so McCall's care fell to Mary-David. Finally, in one of life's many ironies, Mary-David got her mother into "a ten-bed, locked Alzheimer's ward" at the old Motion Picture Country Home. It was McCall's long-term work for the organization that had helped build the ward. In order to get her mother into a facility with this level of care at such a reasonable fee, Mary-David had to agree to donate McCall's brain for research. The deciding moment for the medical professionals about whether she was being genuinely afflicted with Alzheimer's came when the interviewer at the hospital indicated Mary-David and asked McCall to identify her. "A girl," she replied, after glancing at her daughter.

In the midst of her declining health, her guild colleagues gave her the Edmund H. North Award in 1985 for lifelong service. Mary-David showed her the award, but McCall's mind was elsewhere. Her daughter continued to visit and remembered one of their last conversations. "When I reminded her, in the late stages of her Alzheimer's, that Ronnie Reagan was President, she just said 'Oh, shit!'"[32]

Other liberals McCall had known in their prime besides Reagan, from Frank Sinatra to Jimmy Cagney, had changed their political stripes to Republican. But this wasn't McCall's way. She never knew that Cagney died on March 30, 1986. She died four days later, on April 3, just shy of her eighty-second birthday. In all the years since her divorce and remarriage, she and Cagney had never reconciled. But without its two most powerful Irish Americans, without Cagney's Tom Powers and George M. Cohan, without McCall's Maisie and the Sullivans, Hollywood would have lacked the grit and honesty and showmanship that defined the best of the studio system—and actors and writers might never have had fair contracts.

McCall's autopsy revealed that in addition to Alzheimer's, she had also been suffering from Parkinson's disease. There was no funeral, but Mary-David arranged a memorial service in Los Angeles. Christopher Knopf delivered one of the eulogies, and many Hollywood notables, old and new, attended, including Ann Sothern, who, Mary-David remembered, slipped in unobtrusively at the last minute. At the time Sothern was shooting her latest film, *The Whales of August* (1987), and one of Sheila's daughters was working as the film's publicist. Ironically, Sothern's costar in *The Whales of August* was none other than Bette Davis. It was the first time the two legends appeared together onscreen—only McCall, her memory hovering like a ghost over the set, connected their long careers and this tale of three women who had survived at great personal cost. Vincent Price, who had starred in a play about gaslighting women that McCall had helped bankroll back in the 1940s, and Lillian Gish, who had changed Bramson's diapers seven decades before, were also in the cast of this swan song for the women of old Hollywood.

McCall was buried alongside Bramson in the Sawtelle military cemetery, also known as the Los Angeles Military Cemetery, near the 405 freeway off Wilshire Boulevard, section 321, row E, site 12. The Academy of Motion Picture Arts and Sciences and the Writers Guild of America West weren't interested in the many boxes of guild records, scripts, and correspondence McCall had stored in her lit-tle apartment, and other materials, gathering dust in a storage facility in San Francisco, were damaged one night by a flood and were thrown out. Sheila, her daughter Ann, and Ann's current boyfriend had their pick of the remnants, including McCall's old mahogany desk and Wiles's society portrait of Mazie. Alone, Mary-David put the leftovers in her study to look over—photos, awards, books, copies of old scripts and television pilots and short stories, an engraved silver cigarette case in a familiar hand, and a whimsical bookplate inside a favor-ite volume of poetry, containing the words:

> And I shall have some peace there, for peace comes dropping slow,
> Dropping from the veils of the morning to where the cricket sings;
> There midnight's all aglimmer, and noon a purple glow,
> And evening full of the linnet's wings.

Unlike her grandfather John, Mary C. McCall Jr. got no *New York Times* obitu-ary. Only journalists on the West Coast remembered her in a series of tributes, some written by young writers who listed her career milestones with awe and puz-zlement.[33] On Sunday, April 6, Sheila published a memorial for Cagney in the *Los Angeles Times*—but she wrote no similar tribute for her mother.[34]

In her day McCall had led her profession and her industry in the fight for fair pay, freedom of thought, and defense of democracy. But beginning in the 1960s and 1970s, most film journalists and historians focused on pre-sold, branded, and mostly male names. Hollywood's bibliography grows longer every day, yet McCall's name appears in only handful of books.[35] Academic studies of Hollywood screen-writers focus overwhelmingly on the Hollywood blacklist in the late 1940s and 1950s—of the all-male Hollywood Ten, the heroes of the First Amendment, and the downfall of the film industry's political conscience—but skip over McCall.[36] As Larry Ceplair remarked after interviewing McCall for his first book on the blacklist in the late 1970s, "Her memories were more personal than political. It is hard to picture her as the leader of a union."[37]

In the 1980s film and television production in Hollywood moved even further into a period of backlash against successful working women and the tenets of fem-inism. Though a handful of women including Sherry Lansing and Dawn Steel forged careers as film producers and studio heads, their most popular releases were often critical of single women and fit right in with an antifeminist agenda.[38] And screenwriting? It had become even more of a man's profession. It's another tragedy that the nature of McCall's illness prevented her from publicly combatting the surge of media misogyny in the Eighties.

As the years passed, screenwriter histories and collections of interviews ignored McCall and—perhaps the cruelest cut of all—even the guild itself forgot her. A notorious publicity piece from the early millennium (allegedly written at the dictation of writer Victoria Riskin and her husband) claimed that Riskin, elected to the presidency at the end of the 1990s, was "the first woman President in guild history."[39] McCall was simply "purged" from Hollywood's annals, as Eric Hughes noted in *The Wrap*. McCall's family still fumes at the memory of this press release. Its claims were particularly insulting given that Riskin's tenure as the Screen Writers Guild president is considered one of the least distinguished in the organization's history. As Hughes pointed out, Riskin was indeed "an important part of guild history, but only as the first president in guild history who was forced to resign" when it was discovered that she had no legal standing to run it, having been unemployed for the preceding four years. Before that happened, however, Riskin had agreed not to pursue negotiations with the Alliance of Motion Picture and Television Producers for writers' residuals prior to 1960, thereby enabling film companies to claim them. McCall, who spent years fighting tooth and nail to protect writers' intellectual property, must have been turning in her grave. More recently, journalists failed to mention her in coverage of the 2023 strike over writers' streaming residuals and the threat of artificial intelligence.[40]

Mary C. McCall Jr.'s name is not studded on a film industry building or stenciled over the lintel of a library reading room or a movie theater. She is not part of the exhibits on view at the new Academy Museum in Los Angeles. There is no star for her on Hollywood's Walk of Fame. Although there is no grand archive for golden age Hollywood's most influential female labor leader and writer, there are Mayer and DeMille libraries, a Goldwyn theater, and bespoke collections for Darryl F. Zanuck, Orson Welles, John Ford, John Huston, Howard Estabrook, David O. Selznick, George Stevens—even for Mary Pickford and Bette Davis.

There certainly is no McCall biopic for us to watch; Hollywood still defines its screenwriting past through the lives of prominent men (*Trumbo*, 2015; *Mank*, 2020). McCall's own films are in danger of vanishing altogether; nitrate prints of several of her best films from the 1930s and 1940s are deteriorating past the point of restoration. Statues aren't exactly in vogue these days, but I can't help but wish for a life-size bronze figure of her outside the old headquarters of the Screen Writers Guild on North Cherokee—brandishing the guild's first contract in one hand and a briefcase full of pitches in the other, her frizzy hair hat-free, her chin lowered like a prizefighter. "In the beginning was the Word," she once reminded an audience on Oscar night. It's time to remember her and another era in Hollywood—not a dream, but a reality, however fleeting, for creativity and equality.

Acknowledgments

O ver the years, most of my research on film and media history has been conducted in archives in the United States, but when I began to uncover the thousands of women working for the Hollywood studio system I learned that archival research yields substantially less material about women's careers than about their male contemporaries. Because so many libraries and film and media collections have been established and developed through endowments, acquisitions, and bequests from powerful men (the Academy of Motion Picture Arts and Sciences' Margaret Herrick Library included), their contents focus on the achievements of men. Collections have grown around these great male lives, and over many years fellowships have encouraged students and writers to focus on their material. Because of entrenched gender and material biases in our culture, women's collections have not been accepted for acquisition or sourced or promoted. Many treasures—including the most important resources for understanding the life of Mary C. McCall Jr.—remain in private hands because archives simply didn't want them. I know of cases involving other famous Hollywood women who destroyed their own papers, thinking them worthless. The most heartbreaking of these cases is that of Twentieth Century-Fox "editor-in-chief" Barbara McLean (1903-1996), who, according to her interviewer, Tom Stempel, decided to junk her personal records in the 1980s.

There are established patterns in historiography, popular research, media consumption, and publishing that have encouraged a grand narrative about men's dominance and women's lack of power in the culture industries in the early to mid-twentieth century. These patterns have metastasized, like any algorithm that serves the status quo. Although within the past few years, things have begun to change, some losses to McCall's and other Hollywood women's archival remains are irreparable.

This book simply wouldn't have been possible without the generosity and phenomenal memory of Mary-David Sheiner, McCall's daughter. In long conversations and exhaustive emails, we discussed everything from what her mother really thought about her Hollywood colleagues to why she never bothered to dye her hair after she started turning gray. As Mary-David acknowledges, she and her older sister Sheila had "a *Rashomon*-esque view" of their time with their mother. Sheila, Jerry, and Alan grew up when McCall was a famous Hollywood insider. When they saw their mother at home, they called her "Mamie." But as Mary-David pointed out, she knew her mother when she was more frequently unemployed and saw a humorous, lovable woman who rolled with the punches as deftly as her cinematic alter ego, Maisie. Having grown up in the Eisenhower-dominated 1950s, Mary-David could never associate her mother with First Lady Mamie Eisenhower. McCall was "as patrician, acerbic, flinty, and strong" as Bette Davis and "as cocky as Maisie," she told me. She called her mother M.

Mary-David has inherited her mother's gift for a neat turn of phrase as well as her compassionate objectivity—the good and the bad are remembered with humor and sympathy. She granted me access to her mother's papers, which provide rare insights into McCall's work and family life. She also told me what her mother liked to drink and smoke, how she adored Bette Davis, Charles Brackett, and Betty Reinhardt, and however clever Rod Serling was, he could also be a pompous ass. One of her childhood friends, Judge Stephen Haberfeld, took me aside after lunch one afternoon and reminded me firmly, "Mary-David is a treasure." She is.

Sadly, death and illness prevented me from meeting with McCall's twin sons, Alan and Gerald "Jerry" McCall Franklin. McCall's elder daughter, the late *Los Angeles Times* film critic Sheila Benson, lived through what I like to describe as Hollywood's McCall Era—and she had the scars to prove it. It was sad for me to discover that Benson did not particularly like her mother (there can be no more damning assessment of McCall than Sheila's conviction that actress Estelle Parsons would have been "best casting" in any Mary C. McCall Jr. biopic). But her early childhood memories, which included charming stories of McCall's friends Cagney and Bogart, were invaluable in writing this book and uncovering a fuller picture of McCall's life. McCall left many tracks in the trade and newspapers of the day, but without her two remarkable daughters, I would never have been able to bring her—however partially—back to life.

For years, Ned Comstock sent me a steady supply of encouragement and research material. He was one of Maisie's loyal fans, and I was one of his. There was no one like him.

Hilary Swett of the Writers Guild Foundation provided access to guild records and sent me an audio recording of McCall's oral history. I'll never forget the first time I heard that inimitable voice. Academy of Motion Picture Arts and Sciences archivists Genevieve Maxwell, Kristine Krueger, Louise Hilton, and Warren Sherk were a great help to me, and I'm also indebted to Kevin Thomas of the Franklin Roosevelt Presidential Library; Jane Klain of the Paley Center for Media; and Annemarie van Roessel and John Calhoun of the New York Library for the Performing Arts. The Academy of Motion Picture Arts and Sciences generously supported this project with an Academy Film Scholars grant, which made all the difference. I want to thank Shawn Guthrie, Michael Santana, Hector Garcia, and the Academy Film Scholars committee. I've thoroughly enjoyed working with my editor at Columbia, Philip Leventhal, and I would also like to thank Columbia University Press's Susan Pensak and Gregory McNamee.

This book is for Zoe most of all, who from a young age chafed under the smug sexism in the media, at her primary school, and even from her relatives. Learning something about Mary C. McCall Jr.'s life taught her that girls can be anything. They can be a Jr. and a feminist. They can have short hair and avoid bras and hair dye. They can write for a living and be their own boss. They can be elected president of a labor union and take a film studio to court. They can work full-time and be moms. They can fail at motherhood and sometimes hit the mark. They can make personal and professional mistakes and keep on fighting. They can be loved, feared, libeled, blacklisted, hated, passed over, forgotten—and they can be remembered.

Notes

INTRODUCTION

1. Louella Parsons, "Bette Davis Quits Academy in Row Over Dropping Awards," *Albany Times-Union*, December 29, 1941, 7; Hedda Hopper, "My Own Super-Superlative Awards for 1941," *Photoplay*, March 1942, 42–43.

2. "WGA Honors Veteran Writer Mary McCall," *Hollywood Reporter*, April 24, 1978).

3. "Frank Freeman Again Named Producer Head," *Motion Picture Daily*, March 2, 1943, 1.

4. William R. Weaver, "Mellett Gives Gov't Award to Industry," *Motion Picture Daily*, March 3, 1943, 4.

5. Leonard Lyons, "The Lyons Den," *New York Post*, November 2, 1942, 5.

6. "Coast WAC Reorganizes; Mary McCall Is Chairman," *Motion Picture Daily*, March 3, 1943, 1, 7.

7. Hedda Hopper, "Screen Writer Mary McCall Will Be Wed to Lieutenant," *Los Angeles Times*, February 4, 1943, A3; "Film Writers Plan Wedding," *Los Angeles Examiner*, February 4, 1943; "Screen Writer to Wed Army Man," *Albany Times-Union*, February 5, 1943, 3.

8. "Clarence 'Tod' Burke," *The Berkshire Eagle*, Pittsfield, MA, April 11, 1956, 17.

9. Actress Frances Howard McLaughlin, raised Catholic, married Goldwyn in 1925. Actress Joan Perry (born Elizabeth Miller), the daughter of a railroad executive and another Catholic, appeared in McCall's *Maisie Was a Lady* and married Harry Cohn in 1941.

10. Carl Rollyson, *Lillian Hellman: Her Life and Legend* (New York: St. Martin's Press, 1988), 123.

11. Matthew Dessem, "Charles Brackett, Billy Wilder, and the Rise and Fall of Hollywood's Happiest Couple," *The Dissolve*, June 26, 2014.

12. Nicolas Beck states without references that Kit "was thought" to have been based on writer Tess Slesinger; however, Slesinger turned screenwriter only in 1935 and was not prominent in the guild's administration. *Budd Schulberg: A Bio-Bibliography* (Lanham, MD: Scarecrow Press, 2001), 23.

13. Charles Brackett, *It's the Pictures That Got Small*, ed. Anthony Slide (New York: Columbia University Press, 2014), 155.

14. Mason Wiley and Damien Bona, *Inside Oscar: The Unofficial History of the Academy Awards* (New York: Ballantine, 1987), 122–27.

15. Sidney Skolsky, "The Week in Review," *Hollywood Citizen-News*, March 6, 1943, 4; Skolsky, *Don't Get Me Wrong—I Love Hollywood* (New York: Putnam's, 1975), 184.

16. "Claudine West Dies: Was Academy Award Winner," *Film Daily*, April 13, 1943, 7; Obituary, *Variety*, April 14, 1943, 54.

17. J. E. Smyth, *Nobody's Girl Friday: The Women Who Ran Hollywood* (New York: Oxford University Press, 2018), 225–26.

18. Susan Ware, *Holding Their Own: Women in the '30s* (Boston: Twayne, 1983), 49–50; Alice Kessler-Harris, *Out to Work: A History of Wage-Earning Women in the United States* (New York: Oxford University Press, 1982), 254, 259.

19. Smyth, *Nobody's Girl Friday*, 28; Hubbard Keavy, "Hollywood Screen Life," *Poughkeepsie Daily Eagle*, June 19, 1934, 6.

20. Smyth, *Nobody's Girl Friday*, 23; Bob Thomas, "Film Capital Is Girls' Land of Opportunity in Variety of Callings," *Binghamton Press*, January 10, 1948, 12.

21. Mary C. McCall Jr. to Eleanore Francis Humphrey, April 23, 1970, transcript interview for "The Creative Woman in Motion Picture Production," MA thesis, University of Southern California, McCall-Bramson Collection, 39.

22. Mary C. McCall Jr., "The Unlick'ed Bear Whelp," *The Screen Writer*, August 1946, 27–30.

23. "Oscars Sans Victuals," *Motion Picture Herald*, November 20, 1943, 8.

24. Wiley and Bona, *Inside Oscar*, 131.

25. Wiley and Bona, *Inside Oscar*, 131.

26. Mary-David Sheiner to author, September 7, 2016.

27. Mary-David Sheiner to author, November 30, 2017.

28. Screen Writers Guild press release, 1951, Writers Guild Foundation Library.

29. "Finds Her Maisie Thoroughly Real," *Brooklyn Eagle*, August 2, 1942, E5.

30. Harry Tugend to Mary C. McCall Jr., June 23, 1961, McCall-Bramson Collection; Nancy Lynn Schwartz, *The Hollywood Writers' Wars* (Lincoln, NE: iUniverse, 2001), 208.

1. MARY JR.

1. "In the Social World," *New York Globe and Commercial Advertiser*, July 13, 1904.

2. Mary C. McCall Jr., "As Much as Mary McCall Bramson Knows About the Burkes and McCalls" (1975), McCall-Bramson Collection, 6.

3. "John A. McCall Dies Poor," *The Clinton Advertiser*, February 24, 1906.

4. McCall, "As Much as Mary McCall Bramson Knows," 8.

5. Sliwoccam passed from owner to owner, its Gaelic name misinterpreted and repeated as "Shadow Lawn." It even served Woodrow Wilson as a summer White House in 1916 before it burned to the ground. In 1927, the president of Woolworth rebuilt on the same site, but he had to sell in after he went bankrupt in 1939. Years later, writer-director John Huston used the site as Daddy Warbucks's mansion in the period musical *Annie* (1982).

6. "J. A. McCall Very Ill; His Family Near Him," *New York Times*, February 9, 1906; "John A. McCall Dying, Receives the Last Rites," *New York Herald*, February 14, 1906;

"John A. McCall Succumbs to Worry Following Insurance Exposures," *San Francisco Call*, February 19, 1906.

7. "W. M. Sanford Wins Cup," *New York Herald*, August 18, 1907, 26; "Travis and Kirkby Beaten," *The Evening Post*, August 12, 1912.

8. "Mr. F. W. Goddard Weds Miss Benjamin," *New York Herald*, June 5, 1910, 12.

9. McCall, "As Much as Mary McCall Bramson Knows," 12.

10. McCall, "As Much as Mary McCall Bramson Knows," 4.

11. McCall, "As Much as Mary McCall Bramson Knows," 11.

12. McCall, "As Much as Mary McCall Bramson Knows," 11.

13. McCall, "As Much as Mary McCall Bramson Knows," 11.

14. U.S. Department of Commerce, Bureau of the Census, Historical Statistics of the United States, Colonial Times to 1970; U.S. Department of Education, National Center for Education Statistics, Digest of Education Statistics.

15. Patricia Ann Palmieri, *In Adamless Eden* (New Haven, CT: Yale University Press, 1977), 262, 199–200.

16. "Child Labor Topic of Guild Address," *Poughkeepsie Eagle-News*, March 6, 1924, 10.

17. "Winner of Prize at Vassar," *Billboard*, May 17, 1924, 42.

18. McCall, "As Much as Mary McCall Bramson Knows," 12.

19. *Variety* obituary, April 7, 1986.

20. "WGA Honors Veteran Writer Mary McCall," *Hollywood Reporter*, April 24, 1979.

21. McCall, "As Much as Mary McCall Bramson Knows," 12.

22. Mary C. McCall Jr. to Eleanore Francis Humphrey, April 23, 1970, 7.

23. McCall, "As Much as Mary McCall Bramson Knows," 12.

24. "Founder's Day Plans Brewing at Vassar," *Poughkeepsie Eagle-News*, March 27, 1925, 5.

25. McCall, "As Much as Mary McCall Bramson Knows," 12.

26. "Louis Gold Will Build on West Side," *New York Evening Post*, July 13, 1925, 23.

27. McCall, "As Much as Mary McCall Bramson Knows," 12.

28. McCall to Humphrey, April 23, 1970, 8–9; McCall (1975), 13.

29. McCall to Humphrey, April 23, 1970, 38, 45.

30. Robert Lynd and Helen Lynd, *Middletown* (New York: Harcourt, Brace, 1929), 158, 231, 239.

31. McCall, "As Much as Mary McCall Bramson Knows," 1.

32. "Aquarium Reverie." *The New Yorker*, October 2, 1926, 80.

33. "Peek A Boo!" *The New Yorker*, December 11, 1926, 74–75.

34. McCall to Humphrey, April 23, 1970, 10.

35. McCall to Humphrey, April 23, 1970, 10.

36. McCall to Humphrey, April 23, 1970, 10; Ruth Artmonsky, *Designing Women: Women Working in Advertising and Publicity from the 1920s to the 1960s* (New York: Artmonsky Arts, 2013).

37. As Kathy Peiss demonstrates, after 1920, women's cosmetic companies were increasingly overtaken by men and male dominated ad agencies. *Hope in a Jar: The Making of America's Beauty Culture* (New York: Metropolitan, 1998).

38. John Caples, *Tested Advertising Methods* (New York: Harper & Brothers, 1932).

39. McCall, "As Much as Mary McCall Bramson Knows," 13.

40. Mary-David Sheiner to author, November 30, 2017.

2. THE PIRATE

1. Mary C. McCall Jr., "As Much as Mary McCall Bramson Knows About the Burkes and McCalls" (1975), McCall-Bramson Collection, 13.

2. Jean Dwight Franklin, "A New Year's Hymn," *Deaf Mutes Journal*, December 30, 1915; Jean Dwight Franklin, "The Thing That Gits Me Rattled!" *Evening News*, July 19, 1918.

3. McCall, "As Much as Mary McCall Bramson Knows," 13.

4. "Displaying Animal Life in Its Native Haunts and Colors," *New York Tribune*, December 15, 1912, 2:1.

5. McCall, "As Much as Mary McCall Bramson Knows," 14.

6. "American Toys and Dolls Fill Fifth Avenue Shops, Replacing German Goods," *The Evening Telegram*, December 10, 1918, 4; "A Great Array of Pictures from All Over the World Every Day for News Readers," *Buffalo Evening News*, October 27, 1923.

7. McCall, "As Much as Mary McCall Bramson Knows," 14. The miniature display was first shown at a formal reception at McCall and Franklin's house before being shipped to Annapolis "as a morale builder." The *Los Angeles Evening Citizen News* reported Bette Davis among the guests. "Dwight Franklin Holds Exhibition 'Preview,'" May 13, 1942, 5.

8. "Swimming Scene Big Feature of *Black Pirate*," *Long Island Daily Star*, November 17, 1926, 4.

9. *Motion Picture News*, January 25, 1919, 569; "A Great Array of Pictures," 2:1.

10. "Famous Polish Actress Arrives," *Motion Picture News*, September 23, 1922, 1481.

11. *Film Daily*, November 4, 1922.

12. *Shadowland*, February 1923, 55.

13. Barbara Little, "The Pirates Are Coming," *Picture Play Magazine*, March 1923, 46–47, 100.

14. *Picture Play Magazine*, March 1924, 64.

15. "A Full Page of Pictures from All Over the World Daily for 'News' Readers," *Buffalo Evening News*, August 3, 1925, 2:1.

16. *Film Daily*, October 25, 1925, 16; *Exhibitors Herald*, October 31, 1925, 26; "Swimming Scene Big Feature of *The Black Pirate*," *Long Island Daily Star*, November 17, 1926.

17. Broun, "It Seems to Me," *Buffalo Courier*, February 7, 1926.

18. McCall, "Sonnet for a Partnership" (1928), McCall-Bramson Collection.

19. Mary-David Sheiner, interviews with author (2016–18).

20. "Mary Caldwell McCall, Well Known Socially Here, Married to Dwight Franklin in New York City," *Albany Times-Union*, January 18, 1928.

21. Alvin J. Kayton, "In the Theatres on Broadway," *Long Island Daily Star*, March 27, 1928, 16.

22. Charles Driscoll, "New York Day By Day," *San Bernadino Sun*, June 23, 1938, 28.

23. Kayton, "In the Theatres on Broadway," 16.

24. "Beaux Arts Ball to Be Held Dec. 6 at the Waldorf," *New York Sun*, October 21, 1935, 24.

25. McCall, "As Much as Mary McCall Bramson Knows," 14.

26. Mary C. McCall Jr. to Eleanore Francis Humphrey, April 23, 1970, 12, 11.

27. "Large Tea Given for Miss Bogart," *The Hempstead Sentinel*, September 5, 1929, 8.

28. "The Persian Rug Mystery," *The New Yorker*, July 21, 1928, 60–64.

29. "Defeat," *The New Yorker*, March 8, 1929, 102–3.

30. "Sesame Lollard," *The New Yorker*, April 27, 1929, 21.

31. "Butterfly," *The New Yorker*, May 11, 1929, 45-46.

32. McCall to Humphrey, April 23, 1970, 11. Four of McCall's stories appeared in the *Pictorial Review*, beginning in January 1931: "Scandal," January 1931; "Second Choice," March 1931; "Cresseida Calls," May 1931; and "Going to Jerusalem," June 1931.

33. McCall to Humphrey, April 23, 1970, 13-14.

34. Mary-David Sheiner to author, November 30, 2017.

35. Mary C. McCall Jr., "Wooden Shoes," *Redbook*, July 1930.

36. Russel Crouse, "Magna Cum Laude," *New York Post*, July 26, 1930, 6.

37. Mary C. McCall Jr., "Subway Diamonds," *Redbook*, October 1930; "Mr. Nolan's World," *Redbook*, November 8, 1930.

38. Mary C. McCall Jr., "Crazy—Or Something," *Redbook*, July 1931; "Let's Not Pretend," *Redbook*, November 1931.

39. Mary C. McCall Jr., "The Horse with the Flaming Mane," *Collier's*, October 31, 1931.

40. McCall to Humphrey, April 23, 1970, 14.

41. Ben Hecht, *A Child of the Century* (New York: Simon & Schuster, 1954), 466.

3. IT'S TOUGH BEING FAMOUS

1. Lynn Dumenil, *The Modern Temper: American Culture and Society in the 1920s* (New York: Hill & Wang, 1995), 96-97.

2. Mary C. McCall Jr., "As Much as Mary McCall Bramson Knows About the Burkes and McCalls" (1975), McCall-Bramson Collection, 14.

3. Mary C. McCall Jr., *The Goldfish Bowl* (New York: Little, Brown, 1932), 62.

4. McCall, *The Goldfish Bowl*, dust jacket.

5. McCall, *The Goldfish Bowl*, 189-90.

6. McCall, *The Goldfish Bowl*, 117-18.

7. McCall, *The Goldfish Bowl*, 132.

8. *Pictorial Review* editors to Sanders, April 18, 1931, *Goldfish Bowl* Correspondence File, Warner Bros. Archive; McCall, "Sea of Glory," *Pictorial Review*, February-May 1932.

9. Mary C. McCall Jr. to Eleanore Francis Humphrey, April 23, 1970, 17.

10. McCall to Humphrey, 17-18.

11. A.D.S., "A Sea Coast Drama," *New York Times*, January 9, 1932.

12. Wilk to Ebenstein, November 2, 1931, *Goldfish Bowl* Correspondence File.

13. Sanders to Ebenstein, November 4, 1931; memo, Ebenstein to S. Carlisle, November 5, 1931; receipt from Sanders for $8,750 from Warner Bros., November 5, 1931; Morris Ebenstein to Sanders, November 6, 1931, *Goldfish Bowl* Correspondence File.

14. McCall to Humphrey, 18.

15. "Fairbanks Vehicle," *Standard Union*, November 11, 1931, 11.

16. Wilk to Ebenstein, November 5, 1931, *Goldfish Bowl* Correspondence File.

17. McCall to Humphrey, 18.

18. McCall would confide to both Sheila and Mary-David about their affair. Sheila Benson and Mary-David Sheiner, interviews with author, 2016.

19. McCall to Humphrey, 18.

20. Wilk to Ebenstein, December 9, 1931, McCall Legal Correspondence, Warner Bros. Archive.

21. McCall to Humphrey, 18.

22. McCall contract, Warner Bros., December 15, 1931, McCall Legal Files, Warner Bros. Archive.

23. Louella Parsons, "*Goldfish Bowl* Causes Stir at Warners, But It's Name of Film for Young Fairbanks," *New York American*, November 9, 1931, 10; Louella Parsons, "Warner Brothers to Give Douglas Fairbanks, Jr., Lead in *The Goldfish Bowl*, Darryl Zanuck Will Direct Picture," *Albany Times-Union*, November 9, 1931, 10.

24. Louella Parsons, "Champ Stars Slated for New Hit," *Syracuse Journal*, December 15, 1931, 19.

25. "Fairbanks, Jr. in New Picture for the Merrick," *Long Island Daily Press*, May 31, 1932, 14.

26. McCall, *The Goldfish Bowl*, 5.

27. Kenyon, *Street of Women*, December 17, 1931; McCall, *Street of Women*, February 2, 1932, Warner Bros. Archive.

28. But Francis was outclassed in the early 1930s by Ruth Chatterton ($8,000 a week) and Constance Bennett, who had a two-picture, ten-week contact at Warner Bros. for $30,000 per week. Emily Carman, *Independent Stardom* (Austin: University of Texas Press, 2015), 20, 45.

29. J. E. Smyth, *Nobody's Girl Friday: The Women Who Ran Hollywood* (New York: Oxford University Press, 2018), 95–96. Francis produced and starred in several Monogram films of the 1940s but never recovered her former prestige. She is briefly considered in Mary Desjardins's "Not of Hollywood: Ruth Chatterton, Ann Harding, Constance Bennett, Kay Francis, and Nancy Carroll," in *Glamour in a Golden Age: Movie Stars of the 1930s*, ed. Adrienne L. McLean (New Brunswick, NJ: Rutgers University Press, 2011), 18–43.

30. Steve Neale, "Revisiting *Waterloo Bridge*: Censorship, Representation, Adaptation and the Persisting Myth of Pre-Code Hollywood," *Film Studies* 12, no. 1 (2015): 62–81; "Nancy Carroll Wins Star Role in *Revolt*," *Long Island Daily Star*, June 11, 1932, 8.

31. Douglas Fairbanks Jr., *The Salad Days* (New York: Doubleday, 1988), 177.

32. Zanuck to Obringer, February 16, 1932; Obringer to Zanuck, February 19, 1932, *Scarlet Dawn* Correspondence File, Warner Bros. Archive; copy in *Scarlet Dawn* Story File, March 23, 1932, Warner Bros Archive.

33. Tino Balio, *Grand Design: Hollywood As a Modern Business Enterprise, 1930–1939* (Berkeley: University of California Press, 1996), 13–18; McCall, "We're Old Enough to Know," July 7, 1952, Writers Guild Foundation Library.

34. McCall, "As Much as Mary McCall Bramson Knows," 15.

35. McCall to Warner Bros. Pictures, Inc., March 8, 1932, *Goldfish Bowl* Correspondence File.

36. "Mary C. McCall Jr.," *New York Evening Post*, April 13, 1932, 11. Jay E. House, "On Second Thought," *New York Evening Post*, March 29, 1932, 9, calls it a "corking book."

37. "*Snoop and Peep* Now at Proctor's in Stage Program," *The Herald Statesman* (Yonkers, NY), May 25, 1932, 15; "At Smalley's," *Madison County Leader and Observer*, April 21, 1932, 6.

38. *The Morning Herald*, April 18, 1932, 11.

39. B. W. N., "*The Goldfish Bowl*," *New York Times*, April 9, 1932.

40. "The New Bills," *Buffalo Courier-Express*, April 3, 1932, 7; "State Theatre: *It's Tough to Be Famous* Here Today and Tomorrow," *Courtland Standard*, May 10, 1932, 10.

41. *Street of Women* headline, *The Daily Argus* (Mount Vernon, NY), July 7, 1932, 15.

42. "*Street of Women*," *Long Island Daily Star*, July 5, 1932, 8.

43. "Double Feature Now at Embassy," *Daily Argus*, August 10, 1932, 5.

44. "Notables at Premiere," *North Shore Daily Journal*, September 7, 1932, 1.

4. A SECOND CHANCE

1. "Writers Speak to Club Women in Bronxville," *The Daily Argus*, March 19, 1932.

2. Mary C. McCall Jr., "Unknown Master," *Redbook*, April 1932; "Handed Down," *Redbook*, May 1932; "As Cheaply as One," *Redbook*, February 1933.

3. Mary C. McCall Jr., "Lure," *Redbook*, March 1933.

4. Mary C. McCall Jr., "She Said What She Meant," *The American Magazine*, July 1933.

5. Mary C. McCall Jr., "Yesterday Was a Dream," *McCall's*, September 1933; "Bullet," *Collier's*, September 23, 1933; "The Penny Ha'penny Ride," *The Delineator*, October 1933; "Rank and File," with Charles Clifford, *Redbook*, November 1933; "F. X. Healy, '33," *Cosmopolitan*, December 1933; "White Blonde," *Collier's*, January 20, 1934; "Red Desert," *Collier's*, January 27, 1934; "I'll Give You a Ring Someday," *McCall's*, February 1934.

6. Mary C. McCall Jr. to Eleanore Francis Humphrey, April 23, 1970, 15.

7. Mary C. McCall Jr., "As Much as Mary McCall Bramson Knows About the Burkes and McCalls" (1975), McCall-Bramson Collection, 15.

8. McCall, "As Much as Mary McCall Bramson Knows," 15.

9. "Beery-Cooper Set in *Treasure Island*," *Hollywood Reporter*, April 26, 1933, 1.

10. McCall, "As Much as Mary McCall Bramson Knows," 15.

11. "Victor Fleming Set to Direct MGM's *Treasure Island*," *Hollywood Reporter*, February 23, 1934, 7.

12. McCall to Humphrey, 21.

13. Leonard J. Leff and Jerold L. Simmons, *The Dame in the Kimono* (London: Weidenfeld & Nicolson, 1999), 281–92; see also Jonathan Munby, *Public Enemies, Public Heroes* (Chicago: University of Chicago Press, 1999), for its impact on Hollywood production.

14. McCall contract, April 20, 1934, McCall Files, Warner Bros. Archive; memo Obringer to Wilder, May 14, 1934, and McCall payroll notice, effective April 23, 1934, Warner Bros. Archive.

15. Louella Parsons, "*The Lady Surrenders* Picked for Jean Muir's New Vehicle," *Philadelphia Inquirer*, April 30, 1934, 11.

16. Mary-David Sheiner to author, February 24, 2020.

17. Mary C. McCall Jr., "A Lady Surrenders" (1934), *Desirable* Story Files, Warner Bros. Archive.

18. McCall, "A Lady Surrenders," 6.

19. "Player Portrays Herself in Film on Two Screens," *Los Angeles Times*, October 8, 1934, 14.

20. Mary C. McCall Jr., "Circus Girl," *The Delineator*, April 1934; "Love Match," *Collier's*, May 19, 1934; "Wedding Present," *Redbook*, June 1934; reprinted *Collier's* March 27, 1937; "Nineteen Jewels," *The Delineator*, July 1934; "You're Fired," *Cosmopolitan*, September 1934;

"Incomplete Returns," *The Delineator*, October 1934; "First Call to Live," *Serenade*, October 1934.

21. McCall, payroll notice, effective June 27, 1934; McCall, payroll notice, effective August 13, 1934, Warner Bros. Archive.

22. "Signers of the Contract," and Mary C. McCall Jr., "A Brief History of the Guild," *The Screen Writer*, April 1948: 25–34.

23. James Gross, *The Making of the National Labor Relations Board* (Albany: SUNY Press, 1974); Christopher Tomlins, "The New Deal, Collective Bargaining, and the Triumph of Industrial Pluralism," *Industrial and Labor Relations Review* 39, no. 1 (October 1985): 19–34.

24. Leo Rosten, *Hollywood* (New York: Harcourt Brace, 1941), 318.

25. McCall to Humphrey, 15.

26. André Sennwald, "A Confused Adolescent," *New York Times*, September 14, 1934.

27. "Jean Muir Heads All Star Cast in New Dynamic Drama," *Ballston Spa Daily Journal*, October 11, 1934, 8.

28. "*Desirable*," *Daily Variety* (1934), USC clipping files.

29. Tino Balio, *Grand Design: Hollywood as a Modern Business Enterprise, 1930–1939* (Berkeley: University of California Press, 1996), 179–211; J. E. Smyth, *Reconstructing American Historical Cinema from Cimarron to Citizen Kane* (Lexington: University Press of Kentucky, 2006), 34–51, 91–95, 153–65.

30. Wallis to Bischoff, July 25, 1934, *Babbitt* Correspondence File, Warner Bros. Archive.

31. Mary C. McCall Jr., *Babbitt*, August 3, 1934; budget, *Babbitt*, undated, *Babbitt* Correspondence File.

32. McCall, *Babbitt*, August 15, 1934, and August 2, 1934, Warner Bros. Archive.

33. André Sennwald, "At the Roxy," *New York Times*, December 17, 1934.

34. "*Babbitt*," *Daily Variety* (December 1934), USC clipping files.

35. McCall to Humphrey, 4, 1.

36. Emily Carman, *Independent Stardom: Freelance Women in the Hollywood Studio System* (Austin: University of Texas Press, 2015), 41–44.

37. Victoria Wilson, *Barbara Stanwyck: Steel-True* (New York: Knopf, 2013), 405.

38. André Sennwald, "*The Secret Bride*," *New York Times*, February 2, 1935; *Motion Picture Herald*, September 29, 1934, 64.

5. BENDING THE CODES

1. "Club Members Guests at Home," *Los Angeles Times*, June 22, 1934, 9; Marion Simms, "Hollywood Takes to the Sport of Millionaires," *Screen and Radio Weekly*, 1935, 8–9.

2. Simms, "Hollywood Takes to the Sport of Millionaires," 8–9.

3. *Picturegoer*, September 15, 1934.

4. Louella Parsons, "Howard May Play Beau Brummel," *Philadelphia Inquirer*, October 12, 1934, 8.

5. McCall payroll notice, effective August 13, 1934, Warner Bros. Archive.

6. Hal Wallis to Mary C. McCall Jr., August 20, 1934; Victoria Wilson, *Barbara Stanwyck: Steel-True* (New York: Simon & Schuster, 2013), 410.

7. Mary C. McCall Jr. to Eleanore Francis Humphrey, April 23, 1970, 34.

8. Budget, *A Midsummer Night's Dream*, December 18, 1934, Warner Bros. Archive.

9.   Hal Wallis to Henry Blanke, October 19, 1934, *A Midsummer Night's Dream* Correspondence, Warner Bros. Archive.

10. McCall to Blanke, October 24, 1934, *A Midsummer Night's Dream* Correspondence; André Sennwald commented, "The play has been adapted with intelligence and affection." "Warner Brothers Present the Max Reinhardt Film of *A Midsummer Night's Dream* at the Hollywood," *New York Times*, October 10, 1935.

11. Sheila Benson, "Lessons from a Man Named Jimmy," *Los Angeles Times*, April 6, 1986.

12. *Los Angeles Examiner*, November 5, 1934.

13. Mary C. McCall Jr., "As Much as Mary McCall Bramson Knows About the Burkes and McCalls" (1975), McCall-Bramson Collection, 15.

14. *Los Angeles Examiner*, November 18, 1934.

15. McCall payroll notice, effective November 24, 1934, Warner Bros. Archive.

16. McCall, payroll notice, effective December 10, 1934, Warner Bros. Archive.

17. McCall, payroll notice, effective February 25, 1935, Warner Bros. Archive.

18. Louella Parsons, "Max Baer Gets $50,000 from Paramount," *Albany Times-Union*, February 19, 1935, 10; "Lucas Given William Role in New Film," *Long Island Daily Press*, September 4, 1935, 8.

19. Ralph Wilk, "A 'Little' from Hollywood 'Lots,'" *Film Daily*, October 8, 1934, 7; Ralph Wilk, "A 'Little' from Hollywood 'Lots,'" *Film Daily*, March 16, 1935, 6.

20. "The Realist," *The 20-Story Magazine*, December 1934, and "The Man Who Gave His Heart Away," *Cosmopolitan*, April 1935, were the last of the major stories she wrote and sold prior to her new Warner Bros. contract.

21. Mary-David Sheiner, interview with author, October 30, 2017.

22. Robert Lord to Hal Wallis, May 20, 1935, *Dr. Socrates* Correspondence, Warner Bros. Archive.

23. Mary C. McCall Jr., *Dr. Socrates*, May 28, 1935, Warner Bros. Archive.

24. Hal Wallis to Mary C. McCall Jr., June 8, 1935, *Dr. Socrates* Correspondence.

25. Wallis to McCall, June 8, 1935, *Dr. Socrates* Correspondence.

26. McCall to Wallis, June 12, 1935, *Dr. Socrates* Correspondence.

27. Carroll Nye, "Radio Bills Title Bout," *Los Angeles Times*, June 13, 1935, 10.

28. Lord to Wallis, June 22, 1935, *Dr. Socrates* Correspondence.

29. David Niven, *Bring on the Empty Horses* (London: Book Club Associates, 1976), 83.

30. Budget, undated, *Dr. Socrates* Correspondence.

31. McCall to Humphrey, 16.

32. Robbin Coons, "James Cagney Collects What Buccaneers Failed to Bury," *Greenfield Daily Recorder-Gazette*, August 27, 1935, 3.

33. Charles Driscoll, "New York Day By Day," *San Bernadino Sun*, June 23, 1938, 28.

34. *The Petrified Forest* ran at the Broadhurst Theatre in New York from January 7 to June 29, 1935.

35. McCall, "A Brief History of the Guild," *Screen Writer*, April 1948, 25–34.

6. BREAKING THE RULES

1.   Mel Gussow, *Don't Say "Yes" Until I Finish Talking* (New York: Doubleday, 1971), 39–40.

2.   Douglas Fairbanks Jr., *The Salad Days* (New York: Doubleday, 1988), 191.

3. Lenore Coffee, *Storyline: Recollections of a Hollywood Screenwriter* (London: Cassell, 1973), 126.

4. Tom Stempel, *Framework: A History of Screenwriting in the American Film* (New York: Continuum, 1988), 72.

5. Kevin Brownlow, *David Lean* (New York: St. Martin's Press, 1996), 313.

6. Open Screen Writers Guild letter, October 23, 1935, Studio Deputies, Writers Guild Foundation Library.

7. Mary C. McCall Jr. to Eleanore Francis Humphrey, April 23, 1970, 37.

8. Minutes of Membership Committee, May 2, 1934, Writers Guild Foundation Library.

9. Maya Montañez Smukler, *Liberating Hollywood* (New Brunswick, NJ: Rutgers University Press, 2018), 10; Hilary Hallett, "How Hollywood and the Oscar-Nominated *Mank* Have Written Women Out of the Picture," *Los Angeles Times*, April 24, 2021.

10. Sidney Skolsky, "The Gossipel Truth," *New York Post*, April 7, 1941, 9.

11. Jane Gaines, *Pink-Slipped* (Urbana: University of Illinois Press, 2018).

12. Larry Ceplair misleadingly claimed that women held "less than 10% of board positions" and that "McCall was the only woman officer between 1938–1960." *A Great Lady: A Life of the Screenwriter Sonya Levien* (Lanham, MD: Scarecrow Press, 1996), 128n34.

13. Jack Alicoate, *The Film Daily Presents a Guide to Motion Picture Production 1934* (New York: Film Daily, 1934), 149.

14. *Amarillo Globe-Times*, August 24, 1939, 15.

15. "55 Featured Players on Warner Roll," *Motion Picture Daily*, June 4, 1936, 6. That was still just under 10 percent female representation—the worst studio record in the business at the time.

16. Nancy Lynn Schwartz, *The Hollywood Writers' Wars* (Lincoln, NE: iUniverse, 2001), 73.

17. Mary C. McCall Jr., tribute speech, Writers Guild of America West, *WGAW News*, June 1978, Writers Guild Foundation Library.

18. *Film Daily*, November 1, 1935, 15.

19. McCall payroll notice, effective August 26, 1935, Warner Bros. Archive.

20. "Stories Bought in Year for Showman's Screen," *Motion Picture Herald*, September 28, 1935, 283.

21. *Motion Picture Herald*, September 14, 1935, 50.

22. McCall, off payroll notice, effective January 4, 1936, Warner Bros. Archive.

23. McCall, payroll notice, "Recalled from lay-off," effective February 13, 1936, Warner Bros. Archive.

24. "Out Hollywood Way," *Motion Picture Daily*, April 7, 1936: 12.

25. "News of the Screen," *New York Sun*, July 11, 1936, 8.

26. Jean Muir, "The Theatre Workshop," March 1936, and Bette Davis, "Where Did You Get That Hat?," April 1936, Writers Guild Foundation Library.

27. Mary C. McCall Jr., "Let's Have a Motion Picture Kindergarten," *Screen Guilds' Magazine*, June 1935, 9, Writers Guild Foundation Library.

28. *Screen Guilds' Magazine*, November 1935, 11, 24.

29. Schwartz, *The Hollywood Writers' Wars*, 51–54.

30. Schwartz, *The Hollywood Writers' Wars*, 69.

31. "Executives Board Unanimously Elected at Annual Meeting," *Screen Writers Guild Magazine*, May 1936, 15, Writers Guild Foundation Library.

32. The studio charged Columbia $500 a week for her services, her current salary. W. S. Holman to Columbia Pictures Corp., April 23, 1936, McCall file, Warner Bros. Archive.

33. Douglas Warren, *James Cagney* (New York: St. Martin's, 1983), 60.

34. George Kelly, *Craig's Wife* (New York: Limelight Editions, 1999), 302.

35. In addition to producing Kelly's *Torch-Bearers*, Stewart also handled *The Enchanted April* (1925) and *Daisy Mayme* (1926).

36. Bob Thomas, *King Cohn* (Beverly Hills, CA: New Millennium Press, 2000), 149.

37. Louella Parsons, "He Signs for Two a Year," *San Antonio Light*, June 9, 1936.

38. McCall to Humphrey, 2.

39. McCall to Humphrey, 2.

40. Mary C. McCall Jr., *Craig's Wife* (1936), 17–20, New York Public Library Archives.

41. McCall, *Craig's Wife* (1936), 2, 24, 79b. McCall's final shooting script opens with a comic exchange between the housekeeper Mrs. Harold and Mazie the maid, whereas Kelly's script Mrs. Harold chats with Mr. Craig's sister Miss Austen.

42. Without any sources or historical foundation, author Paul Buhle claims that Edward Chodorov "helped" McCall write the script. *Radical Hollywood* (New York: New Press, 2002), 27.

43. McCall to Humphrey, 3.

44. McCall to Humphrey, 3.

45. Thomas, *King Cohn*, 150.

46. McCall to Humphrey, 1.

47. McCall to Humphrey, 1.

48. Mildred Martin, "Camera Angles: *Craig's Wife*," *Philadelphia Inquirer*, October 18, 1936, 12.

49. Archer Winsten, "*Craig's Wife* Shown Up at Radio City Music Hall," *New York Evening Post*, October 2, 1936, 19; "It's a Woman's Picture from Start to Finish," *Modern Screen*, December 1936, 49.

50. "Feminine Technical Crew Works on *Craig's Wife*," *New York Post*, September 19, 1936, 9.

51. "It's a Woman's Picture," 49.

52. Frank S. Nugent, "The Music Hall Presents a Skillful Film Version of That Pulitzer Prize Play, *Craig's Wife*," *New York Times*, October 2, 1936, 29.

53. Victoria Wilson, *Barbara Stanwyck: Steel-True* (New York: Simon & Schuster, 2013), 145.

54. McCall to Humphrey, 36.

55. Thomas, *King Cohn*, 233.

56. McCall to Humphrey, 35, 36.

57. McCall release, Warner Bros. July 14, 1936, McCall file, Warner Bros. Archive.

58. Sheilah Graham, "Women Writers Draw Big Pay in Hollywood," *Buffalo Evening News*, December 5, 1938: 6.

59. H. T. S., "The Screen: *I Promise to Pay*," *New York Times*, April 26, 1937, 15.

60. "*I Promise to Pay*," National Board of Review, April 1937, 2; "*I Promise to Pay*," *Motion Picture Herald*, February 27, 1937, 58.

61. "*Woman of Glamour*," *Motion Picture Herald*, March 20, 1937, 52; Philip K. Scheuer, "*Glamour*," *Los Angeles Times*, February 19, 1937, 10.

62. Ralph Bellamy, *When the Smoke Hit the Fan* (Garden City, NY: Doubleday, 1979), 128, 130.

63. James Harvey, *Romantic Comedy in Hollywood from Lubitsch to Sturges* (New York: Da Capo Press, 1998), 234; Jane M. Greene, "The Road to Reno: *The Awful Truth* and the Hollywood Comedy of Remarriage," *Film History* 13, no. 4 (2001): 337–58.

64. Eileen Creelman, "*It's All Yours*," *New York Sun*, January 8, 1938, 18; "*It's All Yours* at Star Theater Sun," *The Evening News* (Tonawanda, NY), October 23, 1937, 10; "*It's All Yours*," *Buffalo Courier-Express*, September 17, 1937, 24.

7. INDEPENDENCE

1. Nancy Lynn Schwartz, *The Hollywood Writers' Wars* (Lincoln, NE: iUniverse, 2001), 77; Bob Thomas, *King Cohn* (Beverly Hills, CA: New Millennium, 2000), 142.

2. McCall, tribute speech, Writers Guild of America West, *WGAW News*, June 1978.

3. Schwartz, *The Hollywood Writers' Wars*, 96, 101.

4. Mary C. McCall Jr., *Screen Guilds' Magazine*, February 1937, 7, Writers Guild Foundation Library.

5. Donald Ogden Stewart, *Screen Guilds' Magazine*, March 1937, 18.

6. Donald Ogden Stewart, *By a Stroke of Luck* (New York: Paddington, 1975), 211, 227.

7. *Daily Worker*, May 8, 1937, 7.

8. Ian Hamilton, *Writers in Hollywood, 1915–1951* (New York: Harper & Row, 1990), 112.

9. The film made a $2.25 million gross from a $212,000 budget.

10. William Ludwig, "Mary C. McCall Jr.," *The WGAW News*, May 1986, 17, Writers Guild Foundation Library.

11. Mary C. McCall Jr. to Eleanore Francis Humphrey, April 23, 1970, 50.

12. Between contracts McCall was able to publish two more stories, "I Knew a Girl Like That," *Redbook*, May 1937, and "Fair Warning," *Redbook*, April 1938.

13. Read Kendall, "Around and About in Hollywood," *Los Angeles Times*, May 19, 1937, 17.

14. "Screen Writers' Party on Thursday," *Los Angeles Times*, July 18, 1937, D6.

15. "Film Men to Continue Historic Epics," *Rochester Times-Union*, June 3, 1937, 35.

16. Ralph Wilk, "A 'Little' from Hollywood 'Lots,'" *Film Daily*, October 27, 1937, 6.

17. Wilk, "A 'Little' from Hollywood 'Lots,'" 7.

18. "Notes of the Screen," *New York Sun*, November 20, 1937.

19. W. E. J. M., "Theater Review," *Buffalo Courier-Express*, September 2, 1938, 11; "To Aid Mother's Romance Bobby Breen Runs Away!," *Dansville Breeze* (Dansville, NY), October 11, 1938; "Two Talented Youngsters Shine in *Breaking the Ice*," *Tri-County Forum* (Thief River Falls, MN), November 17, 1938, 7.

20. Harry Mines, "Raves and Raps," *Los Angeles Daily News*, January 20, 1938, 20.

21. Jane Allen [Silvia Schulman], *I Lost My Girlish Laughter* [1938], introduction by J. E. Smyth (New York: Random House, 2019), xi.

22. "Mary McCall Jr. With S-l," *Film Daily*, January 27, 1938, 6.

23. McCall to Humphrey, 22–23.

24.   "Recent Books," *Time*, November 8, 1937.

25.   Sonya Levien and Elizabeth Meyer, *The Merry, Merry Maidens*, October 15, 1937, author's collection.

26.   Budd Schulberg, *The Merry, Merry Maidens*, June 20, 1938, author's collection.

27.   Mary C. McCall Jr., *The Merry, Merry Maidens*, February 1, 1938, author's collection.

28.   Grace Wilcox, "Hollywood Reporter," *Screen and Radio Weekly* (1938), fultonhistory .org.

29.   Lauren Bacall, quoted in Joe Hyams, *Bogie: The Authorized Biography* (London: W. H. Allen, 1971), 7.

30.   "Bogart and Philips to Divorce," *Variety*, February 10, 1937, 60.

31.   Katherine Albert, "Meet Humphrey Bogart," *Photoplay*, July 1937, 44, 109.

32.   "Philips Divorced Bogart," *Variety*, August 18, 1937, 78.

33.   "Spotlight," *Los Angeles Daily News*, April 9, 1938, 21; Chester Paul, "Fannie and Charlie to Entertain at Ball," *Los Angeles Times*, April 10, 1938, iv, 11, and April 17, 1938, D6.

34.   McCall's assessment of "smelly" (208) Bogart was backed up by David Niven several decades later in his memoir *Bring on the Empty Horses* (London: Book Club Associates, 1976). Bogart evidently liked wearing old clothes and the same worn tweed jacket to annoy society snobs. Unfortunately, it also put off some of his friends. As to the coffee urn, Mary-David Sheiner to author, November 30, 2017.

35.   Hyams, *Bogie*, 76.

36.   *Variety*, August 24, 1938, 34.

37.   Niven, *Bring on the Empty Horses*, 1976, 202.

38.   Sheila Benson, interview with author, March 16, 2016.

39.   McCall was friendly with Cagney's regulars Pat O'Brien and Frank McHugh, but, according to her daughters, she disliked the "mean drunk" Spencer Tracy.

40.   *United States of America, Before the NLRB in the Matter of MGM Studios and MPPA et al. and Screen Writers Guild, Inc.*, Cases R400 to R420 (June 4, 1938).

41.   McCall, *Dramatic School* rewrites, August 23, 1938, esp. 5-6, University of Southern California Cinema-Television Library.

42.   Albert Auster, *Actresses and Suffragettes* (New York: Praeger, 1984), 31. U.S. census records show that the number of women declaring "actress" as their profession between 1870 and 1880 went from 780 to 4,652 (a 596 percent increase). By 1910, 15,432 women were recorded (another 332 percent increase).

43.   Julie Gilbert, *Opposite Attraction: The Lives of Erich Maria Remarque and Paulette Goddard* (New York: Pantheon, 1995), 145.

44.   Ada Hanifin, "*Dramatic School*, at Paramount, Is Entertaining Film," *San Francisco Examiner*, December 16, 1938, 17.

45.   Schwartz, *The Hollywood Writers' Wars*, 128, 69.

46.   Patrick McGilligan, *Backstory 2: Interviews with Screenwriters of the 1940s and 1950s* (Berkeley: University of California Press, 1991), 120.

47.   Schwartz, *The Hollywood Writers' Wars*, 19.

48.   McCall, "A Brief History of the Guild," *The Screen Writer*, April 1948, 25-31, 27.

49.   "Writers Give and Take," *Variety*, September 21, 1938, 21.

50.   Schwartz, *The Hollywood Writers' Wars*, 158.

51. Charles Brackett diary transcript, September 28, September 30, and October 26, 1941, Academy of Motion Pictures Arts and Sciences.

52. "Scribe Pacts Draw Fire," *Variety*, December 14, 1938, 5.

53. *"First Co-ed,"* *Film Daily* (October 12, 1938); *Variety*, October 12, 1938, 19.

54. "Scripters," *Boxoffice*, October 15, 1938, 75.

55. *"Wagons Westward* for Republic," *Boxoffice*, January 14, 1939, 100; Wilk, "A 'Little' from Hollywood 'Lots,'" 11.

56. "Metro has given Gene Reynolds and Mary McCall new contracts"; "Mary McCall signs writing contract," *Boxoffice,* January 28, 1939, 42.

57. Sheilah Graham, "Women Writers Draw Big Pay in Hollywood," *Buffalo Evening News*, December 5, 1938, 6.

58. Jo Ranson, "Radio Dial Log," *Brooklyn Eagle*, January 17, 1939.

8. THE INVENTION OF MAISIE

1. Catherine Jurca, *Hollywood 1938: Motion Pictures' Greatest Year* (Berkeley: University of California Press, 2012).

2. André Bazin, *What Is Cinema? I* (Berkeley: University of California Press, 1967), 23–40; Ted Sennett, *1939: Hollywood's Golden Year* (New York: St. Martin's, 1989); Jack Mathews, "It Was the Greatest Year in Hollywood History," *Los Angeles Times*, January 1, 1989.

3. Mary C. McCall Jr. to Eleanore Francis Humphrey, April 23, 1970, 23.

4. *"Dark Dame,"* *Kirkus Reviews*, February 15, 1935.

5. Claims that Hollywood was scaling back on B pictures in 1938 need to be reexamined. See Maureen Rogers, "Remaking the B Film in 1940s Hollywood," *Film History* 29, no. 2 (Summer 2017): 142. The studios all cultivated a higher class of B that year, resulting not only in MGM's *Maisie* but also Warner Bros.' *Nancy Drew . . . Detective* (1938) and Universal's inaugural Sherlock Holmes film, *The Hound of the Baskervilles*, 1939). The Holmes series also bolstered women's presence by making them archvillains as well as clients. Amanda J. Field, "Feline, Not Canine: The Rise of the Female Arch-Villain in the 1940s Sherlock Holmes Films," *Clues* 26, no. 4 (Summer 2008): 49–62.

6. Robert Sampson, *Yesterday's Faces: Dangerous Horizons* (Bowling Green, OH: Popular Press, 1991), 155–56. The short stories appeared in the pulp magazine *Top-Notch* in 1927 and 1928.

7. Irene Thirer, "Hollywood Visitors," *New York Post*, January 13, 1941, 7.

8. McCall, *Maisie*, January 19, 1939, Turner-MGM, M218, 24, Academy of Motion Picture Arts and Sciences.

9. McCall, *Maisie*, 90.

10. McCall to Humphrey, 24.

11. McCall to Humphrey, 25.

12. "News of the Screen," *New York Times*, March 6, 1939, 11; *Boxoffice*, March 11, 1939, 49.

13. "Screen News Here and in Hollywood," *New York Times*, March 28, 1939, 20.

14. Parsons, *San Francisco Examiner*, June 21, 1939; Arthur Pollock, "Twin Bright Comedies Come to Do Us Good," *Brooklyn Eagle*, June 23, 1939, 11.

15. B. R. Crisler, "Circus of Superlatives," *New York Times*, January 7, 1940, 135.

16. *The Digest*, June 30, 1939, 5; *Film Digest*, June 7, 1939, 6.

17. Herbert Cohn, "*I Take This Woman* Shown at Music Hall," *Brooklyn Eagle*, February 16, 1940.

18. "Ann Sothern Sticks to New Resolution: No 'Straight' Roles," *The MGM Studio News*, November 7, 1939, 12, folder 65, Harold Bucquet Collection, Academy of Motion Picture Arts and Sciences.

19. *Maisie* (1939), *Gold Rush Maisie* (1940), *Maisie Was a Lady* (1941), *Ringside Maisie* (1941) pressbooks, University of Southern California Cinema-Television Library.

20. While the early films focused on the whole family, films in the series increasingly focused on Mickey Rooney's character. See Jeffery P. Dennis, *We Boys Together: Teenagers in Love Before Girl-Craziness* (Nashville, TN: Vanderbilt University Press, 2007), 94–112.

21. *Film Digest*, January 18, 1940, 5; "Ann Sothern Stars in Film of Love and Death in the Tropics," *Buffalo Evening News*, January 22, 1940, 6.

22. Erskine Johnson discusses some of the elements of the series which "next to the Andy Hardy pictures" have become "the most popular of Hollywood's series pictures" in "Hollywood Column," *Bakersfield Californian*, May 10, 1944, 1.

23. McCall, *Congo Maisie*, July 19, 1939, C-1172 Turner-MGM scripts, 93, Academy of Motion Picture Arts and Sciences.

24. "Renewed Reactionary Activities Exposed," *Boxoffice*, October 21, 1939, 31.

25. "Woman Would Head Writers," *Hollywood Citizen-News*, October 20, 1939, 1; "Labor Situation Is Again No. 1 Problem of Film Capital," *Boxoffice*, October 28, 1939, 35.

26. Nancy Lynn Schwartz, *The Hollywood Writers' Wars* (Lincoln, NE: iUniverse, 2001), 150.

27. Louella Parsons, "Hollywood at Odds Over Foreign Talent," *Albany Times-Union*, August 11, 1940, D5.

28. Louella Parsons, "Screen and Drama: Whirlwind Centers on Foreign Writers," *San Francisco Examiner*, August 11, 1940, 34.

29. "Wendy Barrie in Air Drama," *Buffalo Courier-Express*, December 31, 1939, 8.

30. *Boxoffice*, March 30, 1940: 84; "Name News," *Motion Picture Herald*, April 6, 1940, 34; McCall to Humphrey, 29.

31. Hedda Hopper, "Looking at Hollywood," *Los Angeles Times*, April 4, 1947, A2.

32. McCall to Humphrey, 26.

33. McCall to Humphrey, 26.

34. McCall to Humphrey, 27.

35. Mary C. McCall Jr., *Gold Rush Maisie*, C1179, "Selection of Changes out of Mary McCall OK Script, October 27, 1939," November 27, 1939, and December 2, 1939, 8C and 8D, 63.

36. Marian Rhea, "Maisie's Remedies for Heartaches," *Photoplay*, June 1941, 34, 84–85.

37. "*Gold Rush Maisie*," *Motion Picture Review*, August 1940, 4.

38. "Showmen's Reviews: *Gold Rush Maisie*," *Motion Picture Herald*, July 27, 1940, 34.

9. GOLDEN GIRLS AND BRASS RINGS

1. Philip K. Scheuer, "*Maisie* and *Mary Dugan* 'On Trial,'" *Los Angeles Times*, February 20, 1941, 11.

2. Edwin Schallert, Ann Sothern as Maisie Turns Domestic Referee," *Los Angeles Times*, January 4, 1941, 2:9.

3. Sidney Skolsky, "The Gossipel Truth," *New York Post*, January 13, 1941, 7.

4. *Maisie Was a Lady* (1941), pressbook, University of Southern California Cinema-Television Library.

5. Mary C. McCall Jr. to Eleanore Francis Humphrey, April 23, 1970, 28.

6. Shirley Temple, *Child Star* (New York: Headline, 1988), 316-19, 331-35.

7. Temple, *Child Star*, 319-20.

8. *Variety*, October 29, 1941, 9; "Fraternity," *Collier's*, February 1, 1941; *Boxoffice*, March 1, 1941, 86.

9. McCall's other story, "The Twins," *Collier's*, September 5, 1942, also drew upon her observations of her children.

10. Sidney Skolsky, "The Gossipel Truth," *New York Post*, June 2, 1941, 15.

11. Sheila Benson, interviews with the author, March 16, 2016, and September 23, 2019.

12. Frederick James Smith, "Checking on Their Comments," *Silver Screen*, February 1940, 14; Beth Brown, "Back to the Farm," *Hollywood*, March 1940, 32-34.

13. *Variety*, December 4, 1940, 61.

14. A. Perry Osborn, Henry Osborn's son, served as acting director until 1946.

15. *Variety*, September 3, 1941, 62.

16. Leonard Dinnerstein, *Anti-Semitism in America* (Oxford: Oxford University Press, 1994), 78-127. See also David W. Petergorsky, "The Strategy of Hatred," *Antioch Review* 1, no. 3 (Autumn 1941): 376-88.

17. Howard Suber, "Politics and Popular Culture: Hollywood at Bay, 1933-53," *American Jewish History* 68, no. 4 (June 1979): 517-33; Victor Navasky, *Naming Names* (New York: Viking, 1980), 79, 86; John Sbardellati, *J. Edgar Hoover Goes to the Movies* (Ithaca, NY: Cornell University Press, 2012), 75.

18. "Announcement of Dies Probe Doesn't Faze Film Colony," *Boxoffice*, March 2, 1940, 66; "Screen Writers Ask Ouster of Dies for Committee," *Los Angeles Times*, March 6, 1940, 28.

19. Michael E. Birdwell, *Celluloid Soldiers: The Warner Bros. Campaign Against Nazism* (New York: NYU Press, 1999), 155-74.

20. Sidney Skolsky, "Week in Review," *New York Post*, October 25, 1941. This was in part a response to Lindbergh's September 11, 1941, speech in Des Moines where he claimed the "Jewish race" was pushing the United States into war.

21. *Panama Hattie* payroll, Arthur Freed Collection, University of Southern California Cinema-Television Library; McCall, *Panama Hattie* (December 5, 1941), MGM Collection, University of Southern California Cinema-Television Library; Sidney Skolsky, "Hollywood," *New York Post*, December 26, 1941, 14.

22. "Shirley Temple "Kathleen" Booked for Loew's With *Pulham, Esq.*," *Syracuse Herald-Journal*, January 13, 1941, 18; *Motion Picture Herald*, November 15, 1941, 361; *Photoplay*, February 1942, 22; Edwin Schallert, "Tarzan's Secret Treasure' 'Kathleen' Spell Release," *Los Angeles Times*, March 27, 1942, 28; *Variety*, "solid," February 18, 1942, 9, and doing "sturdy box office," February 25, 1942, 9.

23. "Temple Delivers Top Performance," *Hollywood Reporter*, November 11, 1941.

24. Edwin Schallert, "Sweet Role Now Bores La Temple: Shirley Wants to Be Just a Little Bit Sophisticated," *Los Angeles Times*, June 25, 1944, C1.

25. *Motion Picture Relief Fund Guild Bulletin*, July 1941, Writers Guild Foundation Library.

26. "Leaders Map USO Drive," *Los Angeles Times*, April 2, 1942, 6. The USO (United Service Organizations) was created in February 1941 to provide servicemen and women and their families clubs for entertainment. Hundreds of Hollywood stars and prominent figures volunteered to entertain the troops during the war. See Julia M. H. Carson, *Home Away from Home: The Story of the USO* (New York: Harper & Bros., 1946).

27. "Finds Her Maisie Thoroughly Real," *Brooklyn Eagle*, August 2, 1942, E5.

28. "J. Walter Ruben, 43, Film Producer, Dies; Also Was a Director for MGM—Husband of Virginia Bruce," *New York Times*, September 6, 1942, 31.

29. "Motion Picture Relief Fund Elects and Reports," front page; "Relief Fund Dedicates New Hollywood Country House," *Motion Picture Herald*, October 3, 1942, 32.

30. Mary-David Sheiner to author, November 30, 2017.

31. Louella Parsons, "Hollywood to Look for Cinemarella," *Philadelphia Inquirer*, August 6, 1940, 18.

32. Mary C. McCall Jr., "As Much as Mary McCall Bramson Knows About the Burkes and McCalls" (1975), McCall-Bramson Collection, 16.

33. Lee Shippey, "Lee Side O' L.," *Los Angeles Times*, March 31, 1942, A4.

34. Frederick C. Othman, *Times-News* (Twin Falls, NY), February 18, 1942, 12.

35. Mary-David Sheiner to author, November 30, 2017.

10. A PRESIDENT AT WAR

1. Charles Brackett diary transcript, August 31, 1942, Academy of Motion Picture Arts and Sciences.

2. Final Report and Ballot for the Annual Election of Officers and Executive Board, Screen Writers Guild, November 12, 1942, Writers Guild of America West (WGAW) Writers Guild Foundation Library; "Name Mary McCall President of SWG," *Motion Picture Daily*, November 16, 1942, 2.

3. McCall's charity work in Hollywood began in 1934 with Bette Davis for the Los Angeles Assistance League, a nonprofit to help children in poverty (*Los Angeles Evening Citizen News*, June 27, 1934, 7.

4. *Boxoffice*, July 23, 1938, 72. See also Maureen Lee Lenker, "Hollywood Taking Care of Its Own: 100 Years of the Motion Picture and Television Fund," *Entertainment Weekly*, January 4, 2023.

5. Maxine Bartlett, "Cinema Polo Fans Await April Classic," *Los Angeles Times*, March 17, 1940, D10.

6. McCall, "War's Here—And Now!" *MGM Studio Club News*, May 1941; see also "Factions from Fiction," *MGM Studio Club News*, June 1941, University of Southern California Cinema-Television Library.

7. "Film Aid Fund Chiefs Renamed," *Los Angeles Times*, June 2, 1939, A12.

8. McCall-Bramson Collection.

9. "Film Figures to Attend 18th District Luncheon," *Long Beach Morning Sun*, November 1, 1940, A4.

10. Eleanor Roosevelt to Mary C. McCall Jr., November 19, 1940, the Anna Eleanor Roosevelt Papers, Series 100, Personal Letters, 1933–45; container 721, file McA-McC, FDR Presidential Library, Hyde Park, NY.

11. Eleanor Roosevelt, "My Day," *Buffalo Courier-Express*, April 30, 1941, 11.

12. Mary C. McCall Jr. to Eleanore Francis Humphrey, April 23, 1970, 49.

13. Elizabeth Beecher to Screen Writers Guild, November 21, 1941, Writers Guild Foundation Library.

14. "Screen Writers to Ballot on Membership Regulations," *Los Angeles Times*, November 12, 1941, A3.

15. Nancy Lynn Schwartz, *The Hollywood Writers' Wars* (Lincoln, NE: iUniverse, 2001), 172–73.

16. Charles Brackett diary transcript, September 15, 1941, Academy of Motion Picture Arts and Sciences.

17. "Academy Elected New Board of Governors," *Motion Picture Daily*, October 1, 1942, 1, 8; James Cagney (Screen Actors Guild), George Stevens (Screen Directors Guild), and Y. Frank Freeman (Screen Producers Guild) were also elected.

18. Charles Brackett diary transcript, October 5, 1941, Academy of Motion Picture Arts and Sciences.

19. Leonard Lyons, "The Lyons Den," *New York Post*, October 12, 1942; Vance King, "Talent to Fight Inequities Under Wage Fixing Order," *Motion Picture Herald*, October 10, 1942, 16.

20. Mary C. McCall Jr., oral history transcript for the Writers Guild of America West, recorded on March 7, 1979, 4, Writers Guild Foundation Library.

21. McCall, oral history transcript, March 7, 1979, 6.

22. Mary C. McCall Jr., presidential speech, November 12, 1942, Annual Meeting, Writers Guild Foundation Library.

23. James Francis Crow, "Preston Foster to Enact Philo Vance Role at 20th Century," *Hollywood Citizen-News*, June 10, 1942, 4.

24. McCall, presidential speech.

25. "Entertainment First," *Motion Picture Herald*, August 8, 1942, 8.

26. Mary-David Sheiner to author, April 12, 2017.

27. "Film Writers Plan Wedding," *Los Angeles Examiner*, February 4, 1943; "Film Writer Officer's Bride," *Los Angeles Examiner*, February 14, 1943; Hopper, "Screen Writer Mary McCall Will Be Wed to Lieutenant," *Los Angeles Times*, February 4, 1943.

28. Sheila Benson and Mary-David Sheiner, interviews with author, March 2017.

29. Sheiner to author, April 12, 2017.

30. Sheiner to author, April 12, 2017.

31. "Coast WAC Reorganizes; McCall Chief," *Motion Picture Daily*, March 3, 1943.

32. Lillian Bergquist, Report *Swing Shift Maisie*, November 25, 1942, RG 208, box 3527, Office of War Information Film Analysis, National Archives, College Park, MD.

33. Marsha McCreadie, *The Women Who Write the Movies* (New York: Birch Lane Press, 1994), 120–25.

34. William Chafe, *The American Woman* (Oxford: Oxford University Press, 1982), 132.

35. Susan Ware, *Holding Their Own: Women in the '30s* (Boston: Twayne, 1983), 49–50; J. E. Smyth, *Nobody's Girl Friday: The Women Who Ran Hollywood* (New York: Oxford University Press, 2018), 17.

36. *Variety*, May 3, 1943, 16.

37. Chester Bahm, "The Week in Theaters," *Syracuse Journal*, June 5, 1943, 21.

38. *Independent Film Journal*, August 19, 1944, 52. Eventually producer George Haight would assign his girlfriend Thelma Robinson (they later married) to write the last two Maisie films without any input from McCall.

39. Allan Winkler, *The Politics of Propaganda: The Office of War Information, 1942–1945* (New Haven, CT: Yale University Press, 1978), 47; Sydney Weinberg, "What to Tell America: The Writers' Quarrel in the Office of War Information," *Journal of American History* 55, no. 1 (1968): 87.

40. McCall to Davis and Wallace, June 5, 1943, Writers Guild Foundation Library.

41. Betty Houchin Winfield, *FDR and the News Media* (Urbana: University of Illinois Press, 1990), 88.

42. "Film Unions Select Members of Committee," *Los Angeles Times*, March 25, 1943, 7; "Hollywood Division," *Film Daily Yearbook* Report, 1943, 153. Mellett resigned from Roosevelt's government in 1944 and returned to journalism.

43. Marcia Winn, "City of Magic, Fantasy and Filth: It's Hollywood," *Chicago Sunday Tribune*, July 2, 1943, 1; Winn, "Hollywood Vice Swallows 300 Girls a Month," *Chicago Daily Tribune*, July 26, 1943, 9; Winn, "Blackmail King in Hollywood: Anything Goes," *Chicago Daily Tribune*, July 27, 1943, 7.

44. *Variety*, July 28, 1943, 47.

45. "Coe to blast at Anti-Pix Series by Marcia Winn," *Variety*, August 5, 1943, 4.

46. John C. Finn (McCall's secretary), to Lance Heath (PR Committee of the Motion Picture Industry), November 26, 1943, and December 30, 1943, Writers Guild Foundation Library.

47. "Handling War Information Pix a Highlight," *Film Daily*, January 14, 1944, 31, 34.

48. Lt. Lea Burke to McCall, August 27, 1943, Writers Guild Foundation Library.

49. E. V. Durling, "Life with Salt on the Side," *Albany Times-Union*, October 10, 1943.

50. Hedda Hopper, "Looking at Hollywood," *Buffalo Courier-Express*, September 6, 1943, 35; Cecile Hallingby, "Activities of Women: Skits and Talks to Tell Red Cross Work Scope," *Los Angeles Times*, August 17, 1943, A6.

51. Louella Parsons, "Comedy Purchased for Teresa Wright," *Albany Times-Union*, December 17, 1943, 13.

52. Leonard Lyons, "The Lyons Den," *New York Evening Post*, November 2, 1942, 53.

53. McCreadie, *The Women Who Write the Movies*, 123.

11. A WOMAN IN THE ESTABLISHMENT

1. David Niven, *Bring on the Empty Horses* (London: Book Club Associates, 1976), 112.

2. "Sister of Heroes Enlists in WAVES," *New York Times*, June 17, 1943; Dan Kurzman, *Left to Die: The Tragedy of the USS Juneau* (New York: Pocket, 1994).

3. Mary C. McCall Jr., "Facts, Figures on Your Percentage Deal," *The Screen Writer*, June 1945, 32–35.

4. McCall, *Sullivans*, script f32 (August 27, 1943), 19, Lloyd Bacon Papers, Academy of Motion Picture Arts and Sciences.

5. McCall, "Facts, Figures on Your Percentage Deal," 30.

6. Mary C. McCall Jr. to Eleanore Francis Humphrey, April 23, 1970, 30.

7. McCall, "Facts, Figures on Your Percentage Deal," 32–35.

8. Schenck to Jack Warner, February 12, 1944, Twentieth Century-Fox Collection, University of Southern California Cinema-Television Library.

9. Schenck to Warner.

10. Zanuck to Warner, February 16, 1944, Twentieth Century-Fox Collection, University of Southern California Cinema-Television Library.

11. *Motion Picture Reviews*, January–February 1944, 9–10.

12. *Modern Screen*, March 1944, 14–15.

13. *Film Daily*, February 3, 1944, 14.

14. *Film Daily*, February 3, 1944, 14.

15. "In Hollywood," *Gloversville and Johnstown Morning Herald*, February 17, 1944, 2.

16. McCall, "Facts, Figures on Your Percentage Deal," 32–35.

17. Marjorie de Armand, "Writing for Films," *The New Masses*, July 17, 1945, 31.

18. *The Exhibitor*, October 6, 1943, 13.

19. Leonard Lyons, "The Lyons Den," *New York Evening Post*, November 13, 1943, 14.

20. "Mary C. McCall Challenges the Chicago *Tribune's* Charges of Corruption," *Motion Picture-Hollywood* (November 1943): 34–36, 84–85, 88; see also J. E. Smyth, "A Woman at the Center of Hollywood's Wars: Mary C. McCall Jr.," *Cineaste* 41, no. 3 (Summer 2016): 18–23.

21. Paramount's head of publicity, Julie Hunt, quoted by Hubbard Keavy, "Tact, Patience, Ingenuity and Nest Egg Entres to Movie Industry Aspirants," *Utica Observer*, February 12, 1939, 6C.

22. William K. Weaver, "New Academy Foundation has Cultural Designs," *Motion Picture Herald*, February 5, 1944, 43.

23. Mary-David Sheiner to author, November 30, 2017.

24. "Screen News Here and in Hollywood; Anita Loos to Write 'Women in Uniform' as Vehicle for Joan Crawford at Metro," *New York Times*, July 22, 1942, 23.

25. "Ace Haight Prod.," *Hollywood Reporter*, February 15, 1945.

26. McCall, *Woman's Army*, May 15, 1944, K76, 37, Turner-MGM. Scripts, Academy of Motion Picture Arts and Sciences.

27. Parsons, *Rochester Times-Union*, May 23, 1945, 6A.

28. Sandy Roth, Report on *Woman's Army*, August 8, 1944, RG 208, box 3520, Office of War Information Script Review, National Archives, College Park, MD.

29. *Motion Picture Herald*, February 17, 1945.

30. Eileen Creelman, "*Keep Your Powder Dry*," *New York Sun*, March 12, 1945.

31. Bosley Crowther, "*Keep Your Powder Dry* Seen at the Criterion," *New York Times*, March 12, 1945, 22.

32. Most MGM releases of the period are listed in the Eddie Mannix Ledger, Academy of Motion Picture Arts and Sciences.

33. Louella Parsons, *Philadelphia Inquirer*, June 6, 1945, 15.
34. "Joe E. Brown Honored at Coast Testimonial," *The Exhibitor*, May 10, 1944, 15.

12. THE PARTY IS OVER

1. "Wood Outlines Aims of New Alliance," *Motion Picture Daily*, February 8, 1944, 4.
2. "Screen Writers' Guild Turns Down Parley," *Los Angeles Times*, April 11, 1944, 2:12.
3. "Russian Film Engineer at Academy Luncheon," *Motion Picture Herald*, June 24, 1944, 97.
4. "Guilds Attack Hearst-Based Film Alliance," *New York PM*, July 2, 1944, 17; "Hollywood Guilds Denounce Alliance, Create Council," *Motion Picture Herald*, July 8, 1944, 29.
5. "Coast Units Query Alliance Position," *Motion Picture Herald*, July 1, 1944, 42.
6. "Guilds Attack Hearst-Based Film Alliance," 17; "Hollywood Guilds Denounce Alliance," 29.
7. *Motion Picture Daily*, June 30, 1944, 1.
8. "Replies to De Mille," *Daily Variety*, 23 July 1945, 5. See ad for KHJ, "Hear Mary McCall Jr., Prominent Writer, Answer Cecil B. DeMille Tonight," *Hollywood Citizen-News*, July 21, 1945, 14.
9. William E. Leuchtenburg, *Franklin D. Roosevelt and the New Deal, 1932–1940* (New York: Harper & Row, 1963), 189–90.
10. J. E. Smyth, *Nobody's Girl Friday: The Women Who Ran Hollywood* (New York: Oxford University Press, 2018), 47-48, 91-93.
11. Louella Parsons, *Albany Times-Union*, January 1, 1945, 5.
12. Otto Friedrich, *City of Nets* (New York: Harper & Row, 1986), 179.
13. *Writers' Congress: The Proceedings of the Conference Held in October 1943 Under the Sponsorship of the Hollywood Writers Mobilization and the University of California* (Berkeley: University of California Press, 1944), 31.
14. "Guilds Attack Hearst-Based Film Alliance," *New York PM*, July 2, 1944, 17.
15. *Film Daily*, August 4, 1944.
16. "WAC Elections," *The Independent Film Journal*, December 9, 1944, 15; "Studios Make 45 WAC Films in 1944," *Motion Picture Herald*, January 20, 1945.
17. "John Cromwell New Hollywood WAC Head," *Boxoffice*, January 13, 1945, 69.
18. Lester Cole, *Hollywood Red* (New York: Ramparts Press, 1981), 201.
19. The backhanded references continue in Rocky Lang's and Barbara Hall's *Letters from Hollywood* (New York: Abrams, 2019), where the *only* document included about McCall is her resignation letter due to her pregnancy. Given all her professional service to the industry and the uniqueness of her work as guild president, using this of all documents to represent her diminishes her work and legacy.
20. Thelma A. Prescott to Lester Cole, n.d.; Exec. Sec. SWG [Ann Roth Morgan] to Thelma A. Prescott (July 25, 1944); Thelma A. Prescott to Ann Roth Morgan (August 2, 1944), in which she enclosed copies of her work from August 1943 to January 1944 working for Selznick (all documents from the Writers Guild Foundation Library).
21. "Names in the News," *NBC Transmitter* (January 1939), 4; see also Cary O'Dell and Jane Clain, "Thelma Prescott," May 24, 2017, https://blogs.loc.gov/now-see-here/2017/05/thelma-prescott-televisions-first-female-producerdirector/.

22.   "Lavery Unopposed for SWG Presidency," *Motion Picture Daily*, October 10, 1944, 5.

23.   "Screen Guild Elects Progressive Slate," *Los Angeles Eagle*, November 21, 1946, 22.

24.   Cari Beauchamp, *Without Lying Down: Frances Marion and the Powerful Women of Early Hollywood* (Berkeley: University of California Press, 1998), 355.

25.   "Youth Aliyah Opens Drive for Children in Palestine," *Daily News*, February 10, 1945, 3.

26.   "Mary McCall Jr. Heads Union Council," *Hollywood Citizen-News*, March 2, 1945, 13.

27.   Miranda J. Banks, *The Writers* (New Brunswick, NJ: Rutgers University Press, 2015), 83.

28.   Nancy Lynn Schwartz, *The Hollywood Writers' Wars* (Lincoln, NE: iUniverse, 2001), 221–27.

29.   Banks, *The Writers*, 82.

30.   Christy Fox, "Group Notes International Women's Day," *Los Angeles Times*, March 9, 1945, A5.

31.   McCall, Confidential FBI Report, 5. McCall's attendance at an American-Russian Friendship Concert at the Shrine Auditorium on May 16, 1945, was also noted in her file (6).

32.   "United Negro College Fund Campaign," *The California Eagle*, May 24, 1945, 3.

33.   McManus, "Speaking of Movies: Who's for Dewey, Who's Who for Film Daily," *New York PM*, September 22, 1944, 20.

34.   Leuchtenburg, *Franklin D. Roosevelt and the New Deal*, 189n73.

35.   "A Bow for Pres. Roosevelt; A Pledge to Truman," *Boxoffice*, May 5, 1945, 47.

36.   *The Adventures of Maisie* radio show debuted on July 5, 1945, on CBS, starring Sothern and scripted by Samuel Taylor. The two final films, *Up Goes Maisie* (1946) and *Undercover Maisie* (1947), were written by Thelma Robinson, who married the series producer, George Haight, in 1950.

37.   Leo Rosten, *Hollywood* (New York: Harcourt Brace, 1941), 173.

38.   Edwin Schallert, "Capra, Wyler Company Aligned with RKO," *Los Angeles Times*, August 23, 1945, A3.

39.   Art Ryon, "Southlanders with Occupation Forces," *Los Angeles Times*, August 19, 1945, 12.

40.   Mary-David Sheiner to author, February 9, 2017.

41.   After their epic fights, daughter Mary-David recalled that the sounds of "makeup sex were deafening. . . . He made all the bells ring for her." Mary-David Sheiner, interview with author, November 30, 2017.

42.   Bette Davis, *The Lonely Life* (New York: Putnam, 1962), 277. See also Stephanie Coontz, *The Way We Never Were* (New York: Basic Books, 2000), 279.

43.   Sheiner to author, November 30, 2017.

44.   Sheilah Graham, "This 'Angel Street' Is Paved with Gold," *Buffalo Evening News*, June 6, 1942, 3.

45.   "Louella Parsons Says," *Albany Times-Union*, February 8, 1946, 4.

46.   Henry B. Ryan, "A New Look at Churchill's 'Iron Curtain' Speech," *The Historical Journal* 22, no. 4 (December 1979): 895–920.

47.   William R. Wilkerson, "A Vote for Joe Stalin," *Hollywood Reporter*, July 29, 1946, 1.

48.   Edwin Schallert, "Drama and Film," *Los Angeles Times*, March 2, 1946, 2:5; "Women Select Guiding Group," *Los Angeles Times*, March 6, 1946, A2.

49.   *Motion Picture Herald*, September 7, 1946.

50. "Art by the Inch," *Motion Picture Herald*, April 12, 1947, 8.

51. Sheiner to author, November 30, 2017.

52. Sheiner to author, November 30, 2017.

53. Sheiner to author, November 30, 2017.

54. Charles Brackett notes in his January 20, 1948, diary entry that "Mary asked me to stop at their place for a drink," since "David was so low," Academy of Motion Picture Arts and Sciences.

55. *Motion Picture Herald*, May 10, 1947.

56. Sheiner to author, February 17, 2017.

57. Helen Logan wrote *Hello, Frisco, Hello* (1943), Sonya Levien wrote *State Fair* (1945), Marian Spitzer wrote *The Dolly Sisters* (1945), and Phoebe Ephron wrote *Look For the Silver Lining* (1949). It's a pattern.

58. "Jessel's *Band Wagon* Film Musical at 20th," *Variety*, November 28, 1945, 17.

59. Mel Gussow, *Don't Say "Yes" Until I Finish Talking: A Biography of Darryl F. Zanuck* (New York: Doubleday, 1971), 121.

60. Louella Parsons, *Philadelphia Inquirer*, January 16, 1947, 9.

61. Earl Wilson and Paul Denis, "The Midnight Earl," *New York Post*, August 19, 1946, 25.

62. Mary C. McCall Jr. to Eleanore Francis Humphrey, April 23, 1970, 19.

63. McCall to Humphrey, 20.

64. Mary C. McCall Jr., *Julie*, May 26, 1947, University of Southern California Cinema-Television Library.

65. McCall to Humphrey, 32; *Los Angeles Examiner*, October 22, 1946; McCall, *On to Oregon* (May 8, 1947), McCall-Bramson Collection.

66. Catherine Sager, *The Whitman Massacre of 1847* (Fairfield, WA: Ye Galleon Press, 1989).

67. Catherine Sager, *Across the Plains in 1844* (New York: Dodo Press, 2010).

68. Louella Parsons, "Claude Rains' Portrayal . . . ," *The Fresno Bee*, October 22, 1946, 6.

69. McCall to Humphrey, 32.

70. Mary C. McCall Jr., "The Unlick'd Bear Whelp," *The Screen Writer*, August 1946, 27–30.

71. Eric Johnston to Emmet Lavery, March 23, 1947, Writers Guild Foundation Library. Johnston was also a noted Republican activist.

72. Charles Brackett, *It's the Pictures That Got Small*, ed. Anthony Slide (New York: Columbia University Press, 2014), 306.

73. "48 Film Festival in Academy-MPA Talks," *Motion Picture Daily*, May 15, 1947, 1.

74. Ann Penneman to Milton Krims, April 15, 1947, Writers Guild Foundation Library.

13. SCARLET WOMAN

1. "Coast Probe Hits Pro-Red Writers," *Philadelphia Inquirer*, November 6, 1947.

2. Victor S. Navasky, *Naming Names* (New York: Viking), 319.

3. "Leftish Ghost-Writing Told on Coast," *Rochester Democrat and Chronicle*, November 4, 1947, 14.

4. Alice Penneman to Talbot Jennings, May 27 and July 16, 1947, Writers Guild Foundation Library.

5. Emmet Lavery, "Sitting Out the Waltz" [1948], Writers Guild Foundation Library.

6.   "Writers Who Dodged Red Query Hit," *Los Angeles Examiner*, November 7, 1947.

7.   Louella Parsons, "Million Dollar Damage Suit Filed Because Film Story Gets Communism Label," *Rochester Democrat and Chronicle*, September 18, 1947, 12.

8.   Mary C. McCall Jr., "A Brief History of the Guild," *The Screen Writer*, April 1948, 25–34.

9.   *Fourth Report of the Senate Fact-Finding Committee on Un-American Activities, 1948: Communist Front Organizations* (Sacramento, CA, March 25, 1948), 97, 252, 253, 255, 260–61, 279, 372.

10. Mary C. McCall Jr., *Julie*, May 26, 1947; *Julie* memos, March 16 and 23, 1948, Twentieth Century-Fox Collection, University of Southern California Cinema-Television Library.

11. Jerry Cady to George Jessel, March 16 and 23, 1948, Twentieth Century-Fox Collection, University of Southern California Cinema-Television Library.

12. Charles Brackett, *It's the Pictures That Got Small*, ed. Anthony Slide (New York: Columbia University Press, 2014), 340.

13. Mary C. McCall Jr., Outline treatment, March 15, 1948, Twentieth Century-Fox Collection, University of Southern California Cinema-Television Library.

14. Zanuck to Sam Engel and F. Hugh Herbert, May 25, 1948, Twentieth Century-Fox Collection, University of Southern California Cinema-Television Library.

15. Abel to Zanuck, May 27, 1948, Twentieth Century-Fox Collection, University of Southern California Cinema-Television Library.

16. Herbert's *Belvedere*, August 6, 1948; Loos and Sale's *Belvedere*, September 7, 1948; conference notes, Zanuck, September 9, 1948, Twentieth Century-Fox Collection, University of Southern California Cinema-Television Library.

17. "Top Industry Salaries Listed by US Treasury," *Motion Picture Daily*, July 7, 1948, 7.

18. Hopper, "Marion Cooper, John Ford to Make New Argosy Film," *Buffalo Courier-Express*, May 6, 1948, 14.

19. Edwin Schallert, "Zinnemann Discussing Teresa," *Los Angeles Times*, December 2, 1949, B9.

20. Mary C. McCall Jr. to Eleanore Francis Humphrey, April 23, 1970, 32.

21. Hedda Hopper, "Indian Prince Backs New Movie Venture," *Buffalo Courier-Express*, August 9, 1948, 6.

22. Charles Brackett, Diary Transcript, November 12, 1948 and November 17, 1948, Academy of Motion Picture Arts and Sciences.

23. *The Jackpot* (April 7, 1949), Twentieth Century-Fox Collection, University of Southern California Cinema-Television Library.

24. Bosley Crowther, "Celeste Holm and Dan Dailey Star in *Chicken Every Sunday*, New Bill at the Roxy," *New York Times*, January 19, 1949.

25. "*Mr. Belvedere Goes to College*," *Ballston Spa Journal*, June 9, 1949, 7.

26. Mildred Martin, "Mr. Belvedere Goes to College Is Fox Film," *Philadelphia Inquirer*, April 16, 1949, 8.

27. McCall to Humphrey, 19.

28. Hedda Hopper, *The Truth and Nothing But* (New York: Doubleday, 1962), 248.

29. "*Dancing in the Dark*," *Motion Picture Daily*, November 7, 1949, 3.

30. "*Dancing in the Dark*," *Hollywood Reporter*, November 4, 1949.

31. Mary-David Sheiner to author, November 30, 2017.

32. Sheiner to author, February 1, 2018.

33. Alvin Sargent, interview with author, April 15, 2018.

34. Sheiner to author, March 4, 2020.

35. Sheiner to author, November 30, 2017.

36. Whitney Bolton, "Looking Sideways," *Times Herald* (Olean, NY), August 22, 1950, 1.

37. Laurel Phillips, "Gerald 'Jerry' McCall Franklin," *Santa Barbara Independent*, March 3, 2021.

38. Mary-David Sheiner, "Mary C. McCall, Jr.," *Writers Guild of America West*, June-July 1986, 18-19.

39. "New SWG Officers," *Variety*, November 22, 1950, 9; Leonard Lyons, "Broadway Melody," *San Mateo Times*, December 23, 1950, 20.

40. Thomas F. Brady, "Metro Plans Film of Spy Melodrama," *New York Times*, March 7, 1951, 43.

41. Tunberg Testimony, September 25, 1951, *HUAC Hearings, Vol. II* (Washington, DC: U.S. Government Printing Office, 1951), 1837.

42. "Film Writers in Bitter Row," *Los Angeles Examiner*, November 11, 1951.

43. "Film Writers in Bitter Row."

44. Thomas M. Pryor, "Hollywood Writers' Wrangle," *New York Times*, December 2, 1951, 125.

45. "Film Writers Pick Mary McCall Jr.," *Los Angeles Times*, November 23, 1951; "Writers Guild Votes to Cancel Disciplinary Move," *Los Angeles Times*, November 24, 1951, 3; "Mary McCall Heads Screen Writers Guild," *Pomona Progress Bulletin*, November 22, 1951, 13.

46. Doris Gilbert to Mary McCall Jr., November 23, 1951, Writers Guild Foundation Library.

47. Pryor, "Hollywood Writers' Wrangle," 125.

48. "Film Seminar Draws Editors and Writers," *Los Angeles Times*, December 6, 1951, A30.

49. Sidney Skolsky, "Sidney Skolsky Wires," *New York Post*, June 21, 1941, 5.

50. See Navasky, *Naming Names*, 252-57; Larry Ceplair, "Isobel Lennart and the Dynamics of Informing in Hollywood," *Historical Journal of Film, Radio and Television* 27, no. 4 (2007): 513-29.

51. The guild ruled that Jarrico had written the requisite one-third of the final script to qualify for credit ("Hughes Broke Contract," *Hollywood Citizen-News*, March 28, 1952, 9; see also Barbara Hall, "Jarrico V. Hughes," *Written By* 19, no. 5 (September-October 2015): 38-39.

52. "Hughes Broke Contract," *Hollywood Citizen-News*, March 28, 1952, 9.

53. Mary C. McCall Jr., oral history transcript for the Writers Guild of America West, recorded on March 7, 1979, 9, Writers Guild Foundation Library. Ceplair's biography of Jarrico covers some aspects of the case but never mentions McCall. Ceplair, *The Marxist at the Movies: A Biography of Paul Jarrico* (Lexington: University Press of Kentucky, 2007).

54. McCall, oral history transcript, 8; see "Hughes Defies Film Writers," *Los Angeles Times*, March 28, 1954, no. 1.

55. "Arbitration Asked in Jarrico Case," *Los Angeles Times*, April 5, 1952, 3.

56. McCall to Hughes, March 27, 1952, Writers Guild Foundation Library; reprinted "SWG Says Strike Won't Be Called; Stirs Hughes Retort," *Los Angeles Examiner,* March 31, 1952. McCall's point was that as soon as a writer was hired by a studio, the contracting studio would pay the writer's guild membership fee. So Hughes bought his own trouble.

57.   "Hughes Puts Strike Issue Squarely up to Writers," *Los Angeles Examiner*, March 28, 1952.

58.   McCall to Hughes, March 29, 1952, Writers Guild Foundation Library.

59.   "Court Backs Howard Hughes in Firing Over Commie Row," *Los Angeles Mirror*, April 24, 1952, 14; "Howard Hughes Victor Over Jarrico on Appeal," *Los Angeles Times*, May 16, 1952, 2.

60.   "Court Backs Howard Hughes in Firing Over Commie Row," *Los Angeles Mirror*, April 24, 1954, 14; Thomas R. Pryor, "Hollywood Turmoil," *New York Times*, April 27, 1952, 5:5.

61.   The ambiguity in the wording seemed to be a typo, since the following sentence stressed the guild's protection of its members' credits through arbitration. Stulberg remained with the guild long enough to redraft the writers' contract to discriminate against communists and went to work for Columbia Studios, eventually becoming a high-ranking executive.

62.   Mary C. McCall Jr., "As a Matter of Fact," *Frontier*, May 1952, 9–11.

63.   Mary Davis, "Road to Film Writer's Career Was Indirect," *Sacramento Bee*, May 15, 1952, 19.

64.   The presiding justice was Clement Shinn. Jarrico also sued RKO and others for "obstructing the completion" of *Salt of the Earth*. "Paul Jarrico to File Damage Suit," *Monrovia Daily News-Post*, July 30, 1953, 12. His suit for damages was rejected in 1954: "RKO Wins Declaratory Judgment Against Jarrico," *Hollywood Citizen-News*, December 18, 1955, 1. The new discriminatory contract, rewritten in 1953, would remain in place until 1973.

65.   William H. Mooring, "Diluting the Decency Code," *The Tidings*, May 23, 1952, 22.

66.   "Mary McCall Won't Run for Reelection as Prexy of SWG," *Variety*, September 3, 1952, 11.

14. SMALLER SCREENS

1.   Twenty-three percent of urban married white women in the 1950s worked, though their jobs were "downgraded" to mostly secretarial work. Stephanie Coontz, *The Way We Never Were* (New York: Basic Books, 2000), 160. McCall, though a higher earner from 1928–1950, also saw declining prestige and earnings in television. See also Carol Stabile, *The Broadcast 41: Women and the Anti-Communist Blacklist* (Cambridge, MA: MIT Press, 2018).

2.   Mary C. McCall Jr., oral history for the Writers Guild of America West, Writers Guild Foundation Library, recorded on March 7, 1979, 10.

3.   Myron C. Fagan, *Documentation of the Red Stars in Hollywood* (Hollywood, CA: Cinema Education Guild, 1950), 86.

4.   Bogart did join and later regretted it as a career move. Victor S. Navasky, *Naming Names* (New York: Viking, 1980), 153–54. Davis did not join, yet her political circumspection did not lead to more roles.

5.   Mary C. McCall Jr. to J. Edgar Hoover, August 29, 1951, McCall Confidential FBI Report, FBI; American Business Consultants, *Red Channels: The Report of Communist Influence in Radio and Television* (New York: American Business Consultants, 1950).

6.   Merle Miller, *The Judges and the Judged* (Garden City, NY: Doubleday, 1952), 32–47.

7.   McCall to Hoover.

8.   J. Edgar Hoover to Mary C. McCall Jr., September 13, 1951, McCall Confidential FBI Report, FBI.

9. Names are redacted, but McCall's principal foes on the Screen Playwrights, including Rupert Hughes, Howard's uncle, are obvious suspects (McCall Confidential FBI Report).

10. Gaylyn Studlar and Matthew Bernstein, eds., *John Ford Made Westerns* (Bloomington: Indiana University Press, 2001), 6.

11. J. E. Smyth *Nobody's Girl Friday: The Women Who Ran Hollywood* (New York: Oxford University Press, 2018), 5, 11–12. See, among other reports, "Women's Job Statistics Oct. '73–Sept. '74," Newsletter, Writers Guild of America West, December 1974, 1; WGAW Women's Committee, "Employment Statistics for Male and Female Writers, Television and Feature Films," May 1984, Writers Guild Foundation Library.

12. Wilson, September 21, 1951, *Communist Infiltration of Hollywood Motion Picture Industry—Part V, HUAC Hearings, Vol. II* (Washington, DC: U.S. Government Printing Office, 1951), 1,717.

13. Mary C. McCall Jr. to Eleanore Francis Humphrey, April 23, 1970, 33.

14. Roberts would make her comeback writing *True Grit* (1969) for anticommunist star John Wayne.

15. *Los Angeles Times*, January 15, 1952, 17.

16. McCall to Humphrey, 33.

17. Mary C. McCall Jr., *Ride the Man Down* (March 11, 1952), McCall-Bramson Collection.

18. Edwin Schallert, *"Clown* Retells Rare Human Tale," *Los Angeles Times*, January 23, 1953, 11.

19. Mildred Martin, "Western Film in Trucolor at Stanton," *Philadelphia Inquirer*, March 23, 1953, 16.

20. McCall to Humphrey, 33.

21. Mildred Martin, *"Thunderbirds," Philadelphia Inquirer*, December 12, 1952.

22. "Screen Writers Prep Ultimatum on Telefilm Pact," *Variety*, July 30, 1952, 30. She argued that the "original payment to author is advance against percentage or royalties."

23. Dorothy Manners, "Rogers, Jr. Decides to Make 2d Film," *Philadelphia Inquirer*, August 21, 1952, 19.

24. Hedda Hopper, *The Truth and Nothing But* (Garden City, NY: Doubleday, 1962), 238.

25. The number of television sets sold annually jumped from 14,000 in 1947 to more than 32,000,000 in 1954. Navasky, *Naming Names*, 144.

26. Annie Berke, *Their Own Best Creations* (Berkeley: University of California Press, 2022).

27. Erskine Johnson, "Joan Crawford Specifies TV terms," *Saratogian*, March 1, 1954.

28. "123 Candidates File for Municipal Offices," *Los Angeles Times*, February 1, 1953, B1, B2; The Watchman, "Spirited Races Expected in San Fernando Valley," *Los Angeles Times*, March 17, 1954, 4.

29. McCall was contracted to write *The Taming of the Shrewd* for Irving Starr, but it didn't work out. "Coast Screenwriters Busy in Vidpix," *Variety*, November 18, 1953, 27.

30. Mary-David Sheiner to author, November 30, 2017.

31. Sheiner to author, April 14, 2020.

32. "Fortune Cakes," *Philadelphia Inquirer Magazine*, May 2, 1954.

33. "Briefs from the Lots," *Variety*, May 12, 1954, 22; Edwin Schallert, "Actor-Singer Keith Andes Wins New Setup; Johnson Hinted as Joey," *Los Angeles Times*, May 4, 1954, A11.

34. Mary C. McCall Jr. to [redacted], Paramount Pictures, February 8, 1955, McCall Confidential FBI File.

35.   A. H. Belmont to L. V. Boardman, November 9, 1954, McCall Confidential FBI Report.

36.   "Ex-Head of Screen Writers Guild Denies Ever Being Red: 'Rather Be Dead,' Mary McCall Tells Probers," *Los Angeles Times*, July 28, 1954. A1, 3

37.   "Ex-Head of Screen Writers Guild Denies." McCall participated in a number of cultural events sponsoring Presidents Roosevelt and Truman, including a two-hundred-person event for sculptor Jo Davidson (Bette Davis was also in attendance): "Jo Davidson, Sculptor, Reception Honor Guest," *Hollywood Citizen-News*, April 23, 1945, 1.

38.   Charles Brackett, copy, undated letter [1954], box 20, folder 2, Charles Brackett Papers, Academy of Motion Picture Arts and Sciences.

39.   "Ex-Head of Screen Writers Guild Denies"; "Rather Be Dead Than Red, Says Script Writer," *Knickerbocker News*, July 28, 1954, 10A. See also "Commie Hunters May Clear Names of Wrongly Cited," *Los Angeles Daily News*, July 28, 1954, 21.

40.   Hedda Hopper, "Wayne Considering Levi Strauss Story," *Los Angeles Times*, July 31, 1954, A2.

41.   *Los Angeles Examiner*, July 28, 1954; *Motion Picture Daily*, August 12, 1955, 2.

42.   "Blueprint for Destruction," *Syracuse Post-Standard*, February 15, 1956, 1, 5.

43.   McCall to Y. Frank Freeman [redacted], October 27, 1954; Paramount, Washington, DC offices to Louis Nichols (Assistant to Hoover), January 27, 1955 [redacted], McCall FBI File; Mary C. McCall Jr., "As Much as Mary McCall Bramson Knows About the Burkes and McCalls" (1975), McCall-Bramson Collection, 18.

44.   "James Mason Slates Duo of Productions," *Los Angeles Times*, February 26, 1955, 15.

45.   "Holden Will Carry Out Orient Project," *Los Angeles Times*, April 19, 1955, 25.

46.   "Neilan Set October Date for Crockett," *Motion Picture Daily*, August 12, 1955, 2.

47.   Louella Parsons, "Guy Madison Signs for 6 New Pictures," *Washington Post*, May 20, 1955, 78.

48.   Edwin Schallert, "Madison Outfit Aims at Six Films; Cagney Captures New Villain," *Los Angeles Times*, February 23, 1957, B3.

49.   "It's Not So Easy: How to Spend $1,000,000 a Week," *TV Guide*, October 29, 1955, 18.

50.   "33 Get Christopher Awards," *Rochester Democrat and Chronicle*, November 13, 1956, 18.

51.   Mary C. McCall Jr. to Father Keller (November 9, 1956), McCall-Bramson Collection.

52.   "McCann-Erickson Elects Haight," *Broadcasting Magazine*, November 28, 1955, 35; "Our Respects to George Haight," *Broadcasting Magazine*, April 21, 1958, 24.

53.   Louella Parsons, "Warner Busy on New Film," *Albany Times-Union*, December 31, 1956.

54.   Mary C. McCall Jr., "Maisie," January 2, 1959; "Missile Maisie," January 29, 1959, University of Southern California Cinema-Television Library.

55.   Sheiner to author, November 17, 2017.

56.   Sheiner to author, September 17, 2019.

57.   Material on *Slim Carter*, University of Southern California Cinema-Television Library; Edwin Schallert, " Mahoney, Hovey Costar in *Slim Carter*," *Los Angeles Times*, January 18, 1957, 23; reviews of *Slim Carter*, Ardis Smith, "*Tarnished Angels* Reunites Hudson and Dorothy Malone," *Buffalo Evening News*, January 23, 1958, D:43; Irene Thirer, "*Slim Carter* Satirizes a Film Oprey Hero," *New York Post*, September 29, 1958, 39; "*Slim Carter*," *Buffalo Courier-Express*, January 23, 1958, 6; "*Slim Carter*," *Harrison Reports*, September 28, 1958, 156.

58. *Slim Carter* budget and production schedule, Universal Collection, University of Southern California Cinema-Television Library.

59. Sheiner to author, February 29, 2020.

60. "Mary McCall Candidate to Head Writers Guild," *Motion Picture Daily*, February 28, 1959, 3.

61. *Weekly Television Digest*, November 7, 1960, 12.

62. "*Juke Box Rhythm*," *Film Bulletin*, April 13, 1959, 12.

63. "*Juke Box Rhythm*"; *Photoplay*, June 1959, 24: "nobody cares much about the plot" and W.G.H., *Motion Picture Daily*, March 30, 1959, 4: "routine story."

64. Mary C. McCall Jr., "The Bespoke Script," in *TV and Screen Writing*, ed. Lola Yoakem (Los Angeles: University of California Press, 1958), 83-86.

65. Sheiner to author, March 16, 2018.

15. THE STUFF THAT DREAMS ARE MADE OF

1. John William Tebbel, *George Horace Lorimer and the Saturday Evening Post* (Garden City, NY: Doubleday, 1948); Jan Cohn, *Creating America: George Horace Lorimer and the Saturday Evening Post* (Pittsburgh, PA: University of Pittsburgh Press, 1990).

2. Mary C. McCall Jr., "Friday Girl," *Saturday Evening Post*, February 28, 1959; reprinted in *The Saturday Evening Post Stories* (New York: Doubleday, 1960).

3. Mary-David Sheiner to author, November 30, 2017.

4. Nora Ephron, "Reunion" (1972), in *The Most of Nora Ephron* (New York: Random House, 2013).

5. Amelia Bean, "Great Variety in *Post* 1959 Best Shorts," *San Bernadino Sun-Telegram*, May 29, 1960, C10.

6. Sheiner to author, November 30, 2017.

7. Sheiner to author, March 21, 2016.

8. Sheiner to author, April 15, 2020.

9. Thomsen's *New York Times* obituary lists *Hull House* as one of his two play credits but does not give credit to McCall for writing it (October 31, 1983, B15).

10. Sheiner to author, November 30, 2017.

11. *Weekly Television Digest*, March 13, 1961, 8.

12. "Guild Writers Sue Magazine; Libel Alleged," *Chico Enterprise-Record*, December 21, 1960, 6. The three other writers involved in the $350,000 libel suit were Robert Yale Libbot, Samuel Newman, and Lee Berg. In 1963 Superior Court Judge Martin Katz accepted a retraction from the magazine and limited damages to "whatever monetary loss the petitioners could show." "Damage Suit Settled by Four Writers," *Los Angeles Times*, December 18, 1963, 53.

13. "Red Activity Is Predicted in CA," *Times News* (Twin Falls, ID), June 18, 1961, 3.

14. "The Case of Mary McCall," *11th Report of the Senate Fact-Finding Subcommittee on Un-American Activities*, California Legislature (1961): 202-4; "Erroneous Branding of Stars as Red Blasted," *Los Angeles Times*, June 13, 1961, 16; "State Legislature Punctures Some of Fagan's H'Wood Red Charges," *Daily Variety*, June 14, 1961, 3.

15. "Mary McCall to Address Demo Club," *Hollywood Citizen-News*, June 27, 1961, 3.

16.   Mary C. McCall Jr. to Ted Loeff, September 3, 1961, McCall-Bramson Collection.

17.   *Hollywood Citizen-News*, October 25, 1961, 13.

18.   "Mary McCall to Speak at Temple," *The Voice Evening Vanguard*, November 17, 1961, 4.

19.   Cord Meyer, "The CIA and Radio Free Europe," *Georgetown Journal of International Affairs* 1, no. 1 (Winter/Spring 2000): 127–30; Mary-David Sheiner, interview with author, October 14, 2020.

20.   Philip K. Scheuer, "Guild Presents Awards to Top Screen Writers," *Los Angeles Times*, March 16, 1962, 3:15.

21.   Jonathan Goodman, *The Passing of Starr Faithfull* (London: Piatkus, 1990).

22.   Mary C. McCall Jr., *She Called Him Uncle Hugh*, *The Eleventh Hour*, MGM (October 28, 1963), McCall-Bramson Collection.

23.   Sheiner to author, November 30, 2017.

24.   Douglas Fairbanks Jr. to Mary C. McCall Jr., June 21, 1966; Fairbanks Jr. to McCall, July 5, 1966, McCall-Bramson Collection.

25.   In 1979 McCall was getting $108.55 per month on the guild's pension plan and joked, "I try not to be too extravagant."

26.   Charles Brackett diary transcript, January 3, 1938, folder 1154, Academy of Motion Picture Arts and Sciences.

27.   Second wave feminism and the dominant feminist scholarship of the late twentieth century obscured the Equal Rights feminism between the so-called first and second waves. Nancy Cott, *The Grounding of Modern Feminism* (New Haven, CT: Yale University Press, 1987). For some exceptions, see Sharon Hartman Strom, "Challenging 'Woman's Place': Feminism, the Left, and Industrial Unionism in the 1930," *Feminist Studies* 9, no. 2 (Summer 1983): 359–86; Susan Ware, *Holding Their Own: Women in the '30s* (Boston: Twayne, 1983), 88; Barbara Foley, "Women and the Left in the 1930s," *American Literary History* 2, no. 1 (Spring 1990): 150–69; J. E. Smyth, *Nobody's Girl Friday: The Women Who Ran Hollywood* (New York: Oxford University Press, 2018), 17–20; Einav Rabinovitch-Fox, *Dressed for Freedom: The Fashionable Politics of American Feminism* (Urbana: University of Illinois Press, 2021).

28.   Sylvie Drake, "Achievement of Women in Arts," *Los Angeles Times*, October 14, 1975, 4:1.

29.   Molly Haskell, *From Reverence to Rape* (New York: Holt, Rinehart, and Winston, 1973).

30.   Sheiner to author, February 26, 2020.

31.   Sheiner to author, November 30, 2017.

32.   Sheiner to author, November 30, 2017.

33.   "Mary C. McCall Jr., Ex-WGA Prez, Dies," *Variety*, April 7, 1986; Mary C. McCall, Major TV, Film Writer, Dies at 81," *Los Angeles Times*, April 6, 1986, A24.

34.   "Lessons from a Man Named Jimmy," *Los Angeles Times*, April 6, 1986, R25; *Los Angeles Times*, April 6, 1986, 24; *San Francisco Examiner*, April 6, 1986, B9; *San Bernadino County Sun*, April 6, 1986, 3.

35.   In addition to a few entries in Englund and Ceplair's *The Inquisition in Hollywood* (New York: Doubleday, 1980), and Nancy Lynn Schwartz's *The Hollywood Writers' Wars* (Lincoln, NE: iUniverse, 1982), McCall appears briefly in Bob Thomas's biography of Harry Cohn, *King Cohn* (Beverly Hills, CA: New Millennium Press, 2000); Lizzie Francke's *Script Girls* (London: BFI, 2000), Marsha McCreadie's *The Women Who Write the Movies* (New York: Birch Lane, 1994); and John Sbardellati's *J. Edgar Hoover Goes to the Movies: The FBI*

and the Origins of Hollywood's Cold War (Ithaca, NY: Cornell University Press, 2012), and more extensively in Smyth, *Nobody's Girl Friday*, 2018.

36. Larry Ceplair and Steven Englund, *The Inquisition in Hollywood: Politics in the Film Community, 1930–60* (New York: Doubleday, 1980); Victor S. Navasky, *Naming Names* (New York: Viking, 1980), Paul Buhle and Patrick McGilligan, *Tender Comrades* (New York: St. Martin's, 1997); Rebecca Prime, *Hollywood's Exiles in Europe* (New Brunswick, NJ: Rutgers University Press, 2014).

37. Larry Ceplair, McCall interview notes (1972), sent to author March 23, 2022.

38. *Fatal Attraction* (1987) is perhaps the most notorious of these films. See Susan Faludi, *Backlash: The Undeclared War Against Women* (London: Chatto and Windus, 1991), 140–202.

39. "Carl Reiner and Victoria Riskin to Receive WGAW's Valentine Davies Award," press release, January 30, 2009, https://awards.wga.org/awards/awards-recipients/honorary -servoce-awards/valentines-davies-award/carle-reiner-victoria-riskin.

40. Scott Wilson, "A History of Hollywood Writers' Strikes," *Los Angeles Times*, May 4, 2023; Michael Schulman, "Why Are TV Writers So Miserable?" *New Yorker*, April 29, 2023.

Bibliography

Alicoate, Jack, ed. *The Film Daily Presents a Guide to Motion Pictures*. New York: Film Daily, 1934.
—. *The Film Daily Year Book of Motion Pictures*. New York: Film Daily, 1930–1954.
Allen, Jane. *I Lost My Girlish Laughter*. Ed. J. E. Smyth. New York: Random House, 2019.
Amador, Victoria. *Olivia de Havilland: Lady Triumphant*. Lexington: University Press of Kentucky, 2018.
American Business Consultants. *Red Channels: The Report of Communist Influence in Radio and Television*. New York: American Business Consultants, 1950.
Arnold, Rebecca. *The American Look: Fashion, Sportswear, and the Image of Women in 1930s and 1940s New York*. London: I. B. Taurus, 2009.
Artmonsky, Ruth. *Designing Women: Women Working in Advertising and Publicity from the 1920s to the 1960s*. New York: Artmonsky Arts, 2013.
Auster, Albert. *Actresses and Suffragettes*. New York: Praeger, 1984.
Balio, Tino. *Grand Design: Hollywood as a Modern Business Enterprise, 1930–1939*. Berkeley: University of California Press, 1996.
Banks, Miranda. *The Writers*. New Brunswick, NJ: Rutgers University Press, 2015.
Banks, Polan. *Street of Women*. New York: Jonathan Cape and Harrison Smith, 1931.
Barbas, Samantha. *The First Lady of Hollywood: A Biography of Louella Parsons*. Berkeley: University of California Press, 2005.
Barefoot, Guy. *The Lost Jungle: Cliffhanger Action and Hollywood Serials of the 1930s and 1940s*. Exeter, UK: University of Exeter Press, 2017.
Basinger, Jeanine. *A Woman's View: How Hollywood Spoke to Women*. Middleton, CT: Wesleyan University Press, 1993.
Baxter, John. *Hollywood in the 1930s*. New York, A. S. Barnes, 1968.
Baym, Nina. *Woman's Fiction: A Guide to Novels by and About Women in American, 1820–1870*. Ithaca, NY: Cornell University Press, 1978.
Bazin, André. *What Is Cinema? Vol. I*. Berkeley: University of California Press, 1967.
Beauchamp, Cari. *Without Lying Down: Frances Marion and the Powerful Women of Early Hollywood*. Berkeley: University of California Press, 1998.
Beck, Nicolas. *Budd Schulberg: A Bio-Bibliography*. Lanham, MD: Scarecrow Press, 2001.
Beebe, William. *The Arcturus Adventure: An Account of the New York Zoological Society's First Oceanographic Expedition*. New York: Putnam's, 1926.

Behlmer, Rudy, ed. *Inside Warner Bros., 1935–51.* New York: Viking, 1985.

—. *Memo from Darryl F. Zanuck.* New York: Grove, 1995.

Bellamy, Ralph. *When the Smoke Hit the Fan.* Garden City, NY: Doubleday, 1979.

Berg, A. Scott. *Goldwyn: A Biography.* New York: Random House, 1990.

Berke, Annie. *Their Own Best Creations: Women Writers in Postwar Television.* Berkeley: University of California Press, 2022.

Birchard, Robert S. *Cecil B. DeMille's Hollywood.* Lexington: University Press of Kentucky, 2004.

Birdwell, Michael. *Celluloid Soldiers: The Warner Bros. Campaign Against Nazism.* New York: New York University Press, 1999.

Brackett, Charles. *It's the Pictures That Got Small.* Ed. Anthony Slide. New York: Columbia University Press, 2014.

Briggs, Colin. *Cordially Yours, Ann Sothern.* New York: BearManor Media, 2007.

Brownell, Kathryn Cramer. *Showbiz Politics: Hollywood in American Political Life.* Chapel Hill: University of North Carolina Press, 2014.

Brownlow, Kevin. *David Lean.* New York: St. Martin's, 1996.

Buhle, Paul. *Radical Hollywood: The Untold Story Behind Hollywood's Favorite Films.* New York: New Press, 2002.

Burnett, W. R. *Dr. Socrates.* New York: O'Bryan House Publishing, 2007.

Cagney, James. *Cagney by Cagney.* New York: Doubleday, 1976.

Caples, John. *Tested Advertising Methods.* New York: Harper & Brothers, 1932.

Capra, Frank. *The Name Above the Title.* New York: Macmillan, 1971.

Carlisle, Helen Grace. *The Merry, Merry Maidens.* New York: Harcourt, Brace, 1937.

Carman, Emily. *Independent Stardom: Freelance Women in the Hollywood Studio System.* Austin: University of Texas Press, 2015.

Carson, Julia M. H. *Home Away from Home: The Story of the USO.* New York: Harper & Bros., 1946.

Ceplair, Larry. *A Great Lady: A Life of the Screenwriter Sonya Levien.* Lanham, MD: Scarecrow Press, 1996.

—. *The Marxist at the Movies: A Biography of Paul Jarrico.* Lexington: University Press of Kentucky, 2007.

—. *Trumbo.* Lexington: University of Kentucky Press, 2015.

Ceplair, Larry, and Steven Englund. *The Inquisition in Hollywood: Politics in the Film Community, 1930–60.* New York: Doubleday, 1980.

Clark, Danae. *Negotiating Hollywood: The Cultural Politics of Actors' Labor.* Minneapolis: University of Minnesota Press, 2008.

Coffee, Lenore. *Storyline: Recollections of a Hollywood Screenwriter.* London: Cassell, 1973.

Cohn, Jan. *Creating America: George Horace Lorimer and the Saturday Evening Post.* Pittsburgh, PA: University of Pittsburgh Press, 1990.

Cole, Lester. *Hollywood Red.* New York: Ramparts Press, 1981.

Collison, Wilson. *Congo Landing.* New York: McBride, 1934.

—. *Dark Dame.* New York: Claude Kendall and Willoughby Sharp, 1935.

Coontz, Stephanie. *The Way We Never Were.* New York: Basic Books, 2000.

Corkin, Stanley. *Cowboys as Cold Warriors.* Philadelphia: Temple University Press, 2004.

Corliss, Richard. *Talking Pictures: Screenwriters in the American Cinema.* New York: Penguin, 1974.

Cott, Nancy. *The Grounding of Modern Feminism*. New Haven, CT: Yale University Press, 1987.

Davis, Bette. *The Lonely Life*. New York: Putnam, 1962.

—. *This 'N That: A Memoir*. London: Pan, 1987.

Davis, Bette, and Whitey Stine. *Mother Goddam: The Story of the Career of Bette Davis*. New York: Hawthorn, 1974.

Dennis, Jeffrey P. *We Boys Together: Teenagers in Love Before Girl-Craziness*. Nashville, TN: Vanderbilt University Press, 2007.

Denton, Sally. *The Pink Lady: The Many Lives of Helen Gahagan Douglas*. London: Bloomsbury, 2012.

Dick, Bernard. *Hellman in Hollywood*. Rutherford, NJ: Fairleigh-Dickinson Press, 1983.

Dinnerstein, Leonard. *Anti-Semitism in America*. Oxford: Oxford University Press, 1994.

Douglas, Ann. *The Feminization of American Culture*. New York: Doubleday, 1988.

Edwards, Anne. *A Remarkable Woman: A Biography of Katharine Hepburn*. New York: Morrow, 1984.

Eleventh Report of the Senate Fact-Finding Sub-Committee on Un-American Activities. Sacramento: California State Legislature, 1961.

Ephron, Nora. *The Most of Nora Ephron*. New York: Random House, 2013.

Epstein, Cynthia Fuchs. *Woman's Place: Options and Limits in the Professional Careers*. Berkeley: University of California Press, 1970.

Fagan, Myron C. *Documentation of the Red Stars in Hollywood*. Hollywood: Cinema Education Guild, 1950.

—. *Documentation of the Red Stars in Hollywood, No. 3*. Hollywood: Cinema Education Guild, 1960.

Fairbanks, Douglas, Jr. *The Salad Days*. New York: Doubleday, 1988.

Faludi, Susan. *Backlash: The Undeclared War Against Women*. London: Chatto and Windus, 1991.

Feeley, Kathleen. *Mary Pickford: Hollywood and the New Woman*. New York: Routledge, 2018.

Filene, Catherine, ed. *Careers for Women, New Ideas, New Methods, and New Opportunities—to Fit a New World*. Boston: Houghton Mifflin, 1934.

Francke, Lizzie. *Script Girls*, London: BFI, 2000.

Friedrich, Otto. *City of Nets*. New York: Harper & Row, 1986.

Frost, Jennifer. *Hedda Hopper's Hollywood: Celebrity Gossip and American Conservatism*. New York: New York University Press, 2011.

Gaines, Jane. *Pink-Slipped: What Happened to Women in the Silent Film Industries?* Champaign: University of Illinois Press, 2018.

Galerstein, Carolyn L. *Working Women on the Hollywood Screen: A Filmography*. New York: Garland, 1989.

Gilbert, Julie. *Opposite Attraction: The Lives of Erich Maria Remarque and Paulette Goddard*. New York: Pantheon, 1995.

Goodman, Jonathan. *The Passing of Starr Faithfull*. London: Piatkus, 1990.

Grisham, Therese, and Julie Grossman. *Ida Lupino: Her Art and Resilience in Times of Transition*. New Brunswick, NJ: Rutgers University Press, 2017.

Gussow, Mel. *Don't Say "Yes" Until I Finish Talking: A Biography of Darryl F. Zanuck*. New York: Doubleday, 1971.

Hallett, Hilary. *Go West, Young Women!* Berkeley: University of California Press, 2012.

Hamilton, Ian. *Writers in Hollywood, 1915–1951*. New York: Harper & Row, 1990.

Hampton, Benjamin. *A History of the American Film from Its Beginnings to 1931*. New York: Dover, 1970.

Harvey, James. *Romantic Comedy in Hollywood from Lubitsch to Sturges*. New York: Da Capo Press, 1998.

Haskell, Molly. *From Reverence to Rape*. New York: Holt, Rinehart, and Winston, 1973.

Hecht, Ben. *A Child of the Century*. New York: Simon & Schuster, 1954.

Heinmann, Jim. *Out with the Stars: Hollywood Nightlife in the Golden Era*. New York: Abbeville, 1985.

Hellman, Lillian. *Scoundrel Time*. Boston: Little, Brown, 1976.

Hill, Erin. *Never Done: A History of Women's Work in Media Production*. New Brunswick, NJ: Rutgers University Press, 2016.

Hoopes, Roy. *When the Stars Went to War: Hollywood and World War II*. New York: Random House, 1994.

Hopper, Hedda. *From Under My Hat*. Garden City, NY: Doubleday, 1952.

——. *The Truth and Nothing But*. Garden City, NY: Doubleday, 1962.

Hutchins, Grace. *Women Who Work*. New York: International Publishers, 1934.

Hyams, Joe. *Bogie: The Authorized Biography*. London: W. H. Allen, 1971.

Irwin, Wallace. *North Shore*. New York: Houghton Mifflin, 1932.

Jurca, Catherine. *Hollywood 1938: Motion Pictures' Greatest Year*. Berkeley: University of California Press, 2012.

Kahn, Gordon. *Hollywood on Trial*. New York: Boni and Gaer, 1948.

Kaplan, E. Ann. *Women and Film: Both Sides of the Camera*. New York: Routledge, 1990.

Keefe, Maryellen. *Casual Affairs: The Life and Fiction of Sally Benson*. Albany: State University of New York Press, 2014.

Kelly, George. *Craig's Wife*. In *Three Plays by George Kelly*. New York: Limelight Editions, 1999.

Kennedy, David M. *Freedom from Fear: The American People in Depression and War, 1929–45*. New York: Oxford University Press, 2001.

Kessler-Harris, Alice. *Out to Work: A History of Wage-Earning Women in the United States*. New York: Oxford University Press, 1982.

Knopf, Christopher. *Will the Real Me Please Stand Up*. New York: BearManor Media, 2010.

Koppes, Clayton, and Gregory Black. *Hollywood Goes to War*. New York: Free Press, 1987.

Kurzman, Dan. *Left to Die: The Tragedy of the USS Juneau*. New York: Pocket, 1994.

Lane, Christina. *Phantom Lady: Hollywood Producer Joan Harrison, the Forgotten Woman Behind Hitchcock*. Chicago: Chicago Review Press, 2019.

Lang, Rocky, and Barbara Hall, eds. *Letters from Hollywood*. New York: Abrams, 2019.

Laville, Helen. *Cold War Women: The International Activities of American Women's Organizations*. Manchester: Manchester University Press, 2009.

Leff, Leonard J., and Jerold L. Simmons. *The Dame in the Kimono*. London: Weidenfeld & Nicholson, 1999.

Leuchtenburg, William E. *Franklin D. Roosevelt and the New Deal, 1932–1940*. New York: Harper & Row, 1963.

Lewis, Sinclair. *Babbitt*. New York: Harcourt, 1922.

Loos, Anita. *Kiss Hollywood Good-By*. New York: Viking, 1974.

Lupino, Ida, with Mary Ann Anderson. *Ida Lupino: Beyond the Camera*. New York: BearManor Media, 2011.

Maas, Frederica. *The Shocking Miss Pilgrim: A Writer in Early Hollywood.* Lexington: University Press of Kentucky, 2002.

Macgowan, Kenneth. *Behind the Screen.* New York: Dell, 1967.

Mahar, Karen Ward. *Women Filmmakers in Early Hollywood,* Baltimore: Johns Hopkins University Press, 2008.

Malone, Alicia. *Backwards and in Heels.* New York: Mango, 2017.

Marion, Frances. *How to Write and Sell Screenplays.* New York: Covici-Friede, 1937.

——. *Off with Their Heads: A Serio-Comic Tale of Hollywood.* New York: Macmillan, 1972.

Marx, Samuel. *The Gaudy Spree: The Literary Life of Hollywood in the 1930s When the West Was Fun.* New York: Franklin Watts, 1987.

Mason, Lucy. *To Win These Rights.* New York: Harper & Bros., 1952.

Mattson, Arthur S. *Water and Ice: The Tragic Wrecks of the Bristol and the Mexico on the South Shore of Long Island.* New York: Lynbrook Historical Books, 2009.

Mayne, Judith. *Directed by Dorothy Arzner.* Bloomington: Indiana University Press, 1995.

McCall, Mary C., Jr. *The Goldfish Bowl.* Boston: Little, Brown, 1932.

McConathy, Dale, with Diana Vreeland. *Hollywood Costume.* New York: Abrams, 1976.

McCreadie, Marsha. *The Women Who Write the Movies.* New York: Birch Lane Press, 1994.

McDowall, Roddy. *Double Exposure.* New York: Delacorte Press, 1966.

McGilligan, Patrick. *Backstory 2: Interviews with Screenwriters of the 1940s and 1950s.* Berkeley: University of California Press, 1991.

McGilligan, Patrick, and Paul Buhle. *Tender Comrades.* New York: St. Martin's, 1997.

McLean, Adrienne L. *Being Rita Hayworth: Labor, Identity and Hollywood Stardom.* New Brunswick, NJ: Rutgers University Press, 2004.

——, ed. *Glamour in a Golden Age: Movie Stars of the 1930s.* New Brunswick, NJ: Rutgers University Press, 2011.

Miller, Merle. *The Judges and the Judged.* Garden City, NY: Doubleday, 1952.

Mott, Frank L. *A History of American Magazines.* Cambridge, MA: Harvard University Press, 1957.

Mulvey, Laura. *Visual and Other Pleasures.* London: Palgrave, 2009.

Munby, Jonathan. *Public Enemies, Public Heroes.* Chicago: University of Chicago Press, 1999.

Naumburg, Nancy, ed. *We Make the Movies.* New York: W. W. Norton, 1937.

Navasky, Victor S. *Naming Names.* New York: Viking, 1980.

Nelmes, Jill, ed. *Women Screenwriters: An International Guide.* London: Palgrave, 2015.

Niven, David. *Bring on the Empty Horses.* London: Book Club Associates, 1976.

O'Brien, Pat. *The Wind at My Back.* New York: Doubleday, 1964.

Osborne, Robert. *Sixty Years of the Oscar.* New York: Abbeville, 1989.

Palmieri, Patricia Ann. *In Adamless Eden.* New Haven, CT: Yale University Press, 1977.

Peiss, Kathy. *Hope in a Jar: The Making of America's Beauty Culture.* New York: Metropolitan, 1998.

Pickett, Elizabeth Chevalier. *Drivin' Woman.* New York: Macmillan, 1942.

Porst, Jennifer. *Broadcasting Hollywood: The Struggle Over Feature Films on Early TV.* New Brunswick, N. J., Rutgers University Press, 2021.

Prime, Rebecca. *Hollywood Exiles in Europe.* New Brunswick, NJ: Rutgers University Press, 2014.

Prindle, David. *The Politics of Glamour: Ideology and Democracy in the Screen Actors Guild.* Madison: University of Wisconsin Press, 1988.

Rabinovitch-Fox, Einav. *Dressed for Freedom: The Fashionable Politics of American Feminism.* Urbana: University of Illinois Press, 2021.

Rainger, Ronald. *An Agenda for Antiquity: Henry Fairfield Osborn.* Tuscaloosa: University of Alabama Press, 1991.

Ramsaye, Terry. *A Million and One Nights.* New York: Simon & Schuster, 1926.

Robson, Cheryl, and G. Kelly, eds. *The Celluloid Ceiling: Women Film Directors Breaking Through.* London: Supernova, 2014.

Rogers, Ginger. *My Story.* New York: HarperCollins, 1991.

Rollyson, Carl. *Lillian Hellman: Her Life and Legend.* New York: St. Martin's, 1988.

Ross, Murray. *Stars and Strikes: Unionization of Hollywood.* New York: Columbia University Press, 1941.

Ross, Steven. *Hollywood Left and Right.* Oxford: Oxford University Press, 2011.

Rosten, Leo. *Hollywood.* New York: Harcourt Brace, 1941.

Russell, Catherine. *The Cinema of Barbara Stanwyck: Twenty-Six Short Essays on a Working Star.* Champagne: University of Illinois Press, 2023.

Russell, Rosalind. *Life Is a Banquet.* New York: Random House, 1977.

Sager, Catherine. *Across the Plains in 1844.* New York: Dodo Press, 2010.

—. *The Whitman Massacre of 1847.* Fairfield, WA: Ye Galleon Press, 1989.

Sampson, Robert. *Yesterday's Faces: Dangerous Horizons.* Bowling Green, OH: Popular Press, 1991.

Sanders, Marion K. *Dorothy Thompson: A Legend in Her Time.* Boston: Houghton-Mifflin, 1973.

Sarris, Andrew. *The American Cinema: Directors and Directions, 1929–1968.* New York: Da Capo, 1968.

Sbardellati, John. *J. Edgar Hoover Goes to the Movies: The FBI and the Origins of Hollywood's Cold War.* Ithaca, NY: Cornell University Press, 2012.

Schatz, Thomas. *Boom and Bust: American Cinema in the 1940s.* Berkeley: University of California Press, 1997.

—. *The Genius of the System.* New York: Pantheon, 1988.

Schickel, Richard. *The Men Who Made the Movies.* New York: Atheneum, 1975.

Schickel, Richard, and Douglas Fairbanks Jr. *The Fairbanks Album.* New York: New York Graphic Society, 1975.

Schulberg, Budd. *Moving Pictures: Memories of a Hollywood Prince.* New York: Stein and Day, 1981.

—. *What Makes Sammy Run?* New York: Random House, 1941.

Schwartz, Nancy Lynn. *The Hollywood Writers' Wars.* Lincoln, NE: iUniverse, 2001.

Short, Luke. *Ride the Man Down.* New York: Bantam, 1947.

Sigal, Clancy. *Black Sunset: Hollywood Sex, Lies, Glamour, Betrayal, and Raging Egos.* Berkeley: Soft Skull Press, 2016.

Sklar, Robert. *Movie-Made America.* New York: Random House, 1975.

Skolsky, Sidney. *Don't Get Me Wrong—I Love Hollywood.* New York: Putnam's, 1975.

Slotkin, Richard. *Gunfighter Nation.* Norman: University of Oklahoma Press, 1992.

Smuckler, Maya Montañez. *Liberating Hollywood.* New Brunswick, NJ: Rutgers University Press, 2018.

Smyth, J. E. *Nobody's Girl Friday: The Women Who Ran Hollywood.* New York: Oxford University Press, 2018.

——. *Reconstructing American Historical Cinema from Cimarron to Citizen Kane.* Lexington: University Press of Kentucky, 2006.

Snelson, Tim. *Phantom Ladies: Hollywood Horror on the Home Front.* New Brunswick, NJ: Rutgers University Press, 2014.

St. Johns, Adela Rogers. *The Honeycomb.* Garden City, NY: Doubleday, 1969.

Stabile, Carol. *The Broadcast 41: Women and the Anti-Communist Blacklist.* Cambridge, MA: MIT Press, 2018.

Stamp, Shelley. *Lois Weber in Early Hollywood.* Berkeley: University of California Press, 2015.

Stempel, Tom. *Framework: A History of Screenwriting in the American Film.* New York: Continuum, 1988.

Stewart, Donald Ogden. *By a Stroke of Luck.* New York: Paddington, 1975.

Studlar, Gaylyn, and Mathew Bernstein, eds., *John Ford Made Westerns.* Bloomington: Indiana University Press, 2001.

Tebbel, John William. *George Horace Lorimer and The Saturday Evening Post.* Garden City, NY: Doubleday, 1948.

Temple, Shirley. *Child Star.* New York: Headline, 1988.

Thomas, Bob. *King Cohn.* Beverly Hills, CA: New Millennium Press, 2000.

Thomson, David. *Showman: The Life of David O. Selznick.* New York: Knopf, 1992.

Tucker, Sherrie. *Dance Floor Democracy.* Durham, NC: Duke University Press, 2014.

U.S. Congress House Committee on Un-American Activities Hearings, 1951–52. Vol. 2. Washington, DC: U.S. Government Printing Office, 1951, 1952.

Viera, Mark. *Irving Thalberg: Boy Wonder to Producer Prince.* Berkeley: University of California Press, 2009.

Wallace, Eileen V. *Earning Power: Women and Work in Los Angeles, 1880–1930.* Reno: University of Nevada Press, 2010.

Wallis, Hal. *Starmaker.* New York: Macmillan, 1980.

Ware, Susan. *Holding Their Own: Women in the '30s.* Boston: Twayne, 1983.

Warner, Jack. *My First Hundred Years in Hollywood.* New York: Random House, 1965.

Warren, Douglas. *James Cagney.* New York: St. Martin's, 1983.

Whitfield, Eileen. *Pickford: The Woman Who Made Hollywood.* Toronto: Stoddart, 1998.

Wiley, Mason, and Damien Bona. *Inside Oscar: The Unofficial History of the Academy Awards.* New York: Ballantine, 1987.

Wilson, Victoria. *Barbara Stanwyck: Steel-True.* New York: Simon & Schuster, 2013.

Winfield, Betty Houchin. *FDR and the News Media.* Urbana: University of Illinois Press, 1990.

Winkler, Allan. *The Politics of Propaganda: The Office of War Information, 1942–1945.* New Haven, CT: Yale University Press, 1978.

Yoakum, Lola, ed. *TV and Screen Writing.* Berkeley: University of California Press, 1958.

Index

Academy Awards, 1, 3-4, 7-8, 10, 12, 95, 145, 181, 202
Academy Foundation, 156-57, 161
Academy of Motion Picture Arts and Sciences, 1, 7, 75, 83, 106, 139, 145, 155, 157, 222, 229; and Board of Governors, 1, 139, 161
Ackland, Rodney, 8
adaptations, 45, 47, 59-62, 65, 68-72, 85-89, 100-01, 109-110, 122, 124, 126, 160, 196
Addams, Jane, 213
Adventures of Davy Crockett, Boy Pioneer, 203-4
Affairs of Martha, The, 117
Ainsworth, Helen, 204
American Association of University Women, 153
Angel Street, 170. See also *Gaslight*
Anderson, Doris, 57
Ann Vickers, 59
anticommunism, 167, 170-71, 176, 188, 194, 201-2, 215
antifascism, 118, 129
anti-Semitism, 5, 118, 128, 142, 167, 182
Anybody's Woman, 86
Apartment, The, 212
Appointment with a Shadow, 207
"Aquarium Reverie," 22, 39, 41
Arbuckle, Roscoe ("Fatty"), 146
Arling, Joyce, 43
Arliss, George, 51
Armstrong Insurance Commission, 14

Arzner, Dorothy, 85-89, 100, 102, 130, 220
"As Cheaply as One," 52
Ashley, Chuck, 219
Auer, Mischa, 102-3
Authors League of America, 57, 83-84
Awful Truth, The, 92, 203
Ayres, Lew, 70, 123

Babbitt, 59-62, 66, 70-71, 109
Baby Face, 63
B pictures, 111, 115, 244n5
Bacall, Lauren, 157
Back Street, 77
Bacon, Lloyd, 150, 153
Bad and the Beautiful, The, 214
Bad Sister, 47
Baker, Herb, 203
Baker, Mary, 11, 73, 99, 102-5, 127, 156, 184, 194
Baker, Mel, 102
Baldwin, Earl, 208
Ball, Lucille, 199
Balmer, Edwin, 36
Bankhead, Tallulah, 28, 170
Banks, Miranda, 166
Banks, Polan, 47
Barretts of Wimpole Street, The, 95
Barrie, Wendy, 119
Barry, William E., 4
Barrymore, Ethel, 28
Barrymore, John, Jr., 198
Barthelmess, Richard, 48

Bartlett, Richard, 207

Barton, Durstine and Osborne, 23

Bates, Blanche, 28

Baum, Vicki, 78

Baxter, Warner, 85

Bean, Amelia, 212

Beau Geste, 110

Beaumont, Harry, 59

Beaux Arts Ball, 30, 33, 63

Beavers, Louise, 109

Beebe, Charles William, 29, 32

Beecher, Elizabeth, 137–38

Beery, Wallace, 53

Bell, Helen, 79

Bellamy, Ralph, 92, 216

Benchley, Robert, 35

Benjamin, Gladys Torrance, 15

Bennett, Constance, 152, 236n28

Bennett, Dorothy, 78

Benson, Sheila Franklin, 11, 45, 48–49, 69, 74, 97, 103, 126–28, 142–43, 169, 186–87, 217–21, 223, 228, 235n18

Benson, Walter "Spike," 219

Beranger, Clara, 78, 85

Bergen, Edgar, 98

Bergquist, Lillian, 143

Berlin, Irving, 8

Bessie, Alvah, 180

Beverly Wilshire Hotel, 161

Beymer, William G., 98

Bieberman, Herbert, 180

Big House, The, 38

biopics, 5, 8–9, 59, 61, 65, 81, 83, 105, 127, 151, 198–99, 213, 220, 224

Bischoff, Samuel, 60, 66, 89

Bitter Tea of General Yen, The, 63

Black, Donald, 172

Black Pirate, The, 26, 29–30

blacklist, 1930s, 58, 80, 90

blacklist, postwar, 94, 10, 110, 180, 186–96, 215, 223, 229

Blanke, Henry, 66–68

Blizzard of 1888, 26

Block, Ralph, 57, 138

Blondell, Joan, 34, 84

Blondie, 116

Blood and Sand, 85

Blood on the Moon, 196

Bogart, Humphrey, 30, 34–35, 38, 47, 73–74, 101–3, 129, 157–58, 194, 198, 204, 228, 243n34

Boland, Bridget, 206

Bombay Nights, see *Night in Bombay*

Bond, Ward, 151

Bow, Clara, 18, 59, 86, 146

Bowman, Lee, 120

Boxoffice, 118

Box-Office Maisie, 148

Boyd, William, 132, 207–8

Brackett, Charles, 2, 7, 80–81, 93–94, 96–98, 107, 135, 137–39, 157, 163, 172–73, 176, 182, 185, 188, 201–2, 205, 212, 219, 228, 253n54

Brackett, Elizabeth, 137, 172

Bradbury, Ray, 187, 208, 218

Bradshaw, George, 213

Bramson, David, 5–6, 11, 131–34, 142–44, 146, 157–58, 160, 164, 168–72, 180, 182–88, 197–98, 200–9, 212, 215, 217–19, 221–22

Bramson, Goldie, 132, 142

Bramson, Herb, 132

Bramson, Mary-David. *See* Sheiner, Mary-David

Bramson, Theodore, 132

Breaking the Ice, 99

Breen, Bobby, 99

Breen, Joseph, 70

Brent, George, 55

Brian, Mary, 46

Bricken, Jules, 199

Bride Wore Red, The, 102, 220

Bright, John, 166

Briskin, Fred, 205

Broadway, 34

Bromfield, Louis, 119

Bronco Buster, 196

Brontë, Charlotte, 37

Brooklyn Children's Museum, 28

Broun, Heywood, 30

Brown, Joe E., 160
Brown, Kay, 59
Bruce, George, 159
Bruce, Virginia, 92, 114–15, 131
Buccaneer, The, 98, 101
Buchman, Sidney, 90, 135, 138–39
Buck, Gertrude, 18
Buckingham, Tom, 62, 65
Buffington, Adele, 78, 188
Bullets and Saddles, 138
Burke, Arthur, 15, 17
Burke, Clarence (Tod), 5, 142
Burke, Francis, 15,
Burke, Katie Green, 20, 22, 151, 217
Burke, Lea, Lt., 147
Burnett, W. R., 70–71
Busch, Niven, 50, 59–60
Butler, A. E., 27
BUtterfield 8, 216
"Butterfly," 35

Cagney, Billie, 33–34
Cagney, James, 5, 6, 30, 33–34, 36, 38, 43, 50,
    54, 68, 70, 73–74, 83–84, 101, 103, 109, 127,
    129, 139, 152, 157, 168, 204, 222–23, 228
Cain, James M., 192
Caine Mutiny, The, 198
Cairns, Dorothy, 78
California legislature, 214
Canfield, Mark. *See* Zanuck, Darryl F.
Caples, John, 24
Capone, Al, 70
Capra, Frank, 8, 63, 85, 94, 176, 213
Captain Blood, 69, 82
Carlisle, Helen Grace, 99–100
Carrillo, Leo, 91–92
Carroll, Madeleine, 93
Carroll, Nancy, 48
Casablanca (1942), 72, 146, 215
Caspary, Vera, 78, 120
Castle, Irene, 18, 100
Caylor, Rose, 38, 89–90
Ceplair, Larry, 223, 240n12
Chambers, Marilyn, 220

Champlin, Charles, 221
Chandler, Harry, 200
Chapin, Anne Morrison, 78
Chaplin, Charles, 146, 172
Chatterton, Ruth, 50, 79, 86, 236n28
Cheaper By the Dozen, 25
Chertok, Jack, 203
Chevalier, Elizabeth Pickett, 119
Chicago Tribune, 146
Chicken Every Sunday, 168, 173, 185
China Seas, 88
Christopher Awards, 205–6
Christopher Strong, 85–86, 101, 220
Christy, Eileen, 198
Chodorov, Edward, 55, 84, 86, 91, 98, 241n42
Church, Claire, 78
Churchill, Bert, 60
Churchill, Winston, 129, 170
Cimarron, 59, 108
Cinema Art, 19
Cinema Education Guild, 214
Clement, Rufus E., 167
Cleveland, Grover, 13
Cleveland Museum, 27
Cobb, Irvin, 41
Cock and Bull, 107
Cocoanut Grove, 1, 4, 10, 102, 143, 181
Coe, Charles Francis, 147
Coffee, Lenore, 57, 77, 106
Cohan, George M., 5, 25, 42, 222
Cohen, Alfred, 57
Cohen, Emanuel, 98–99
Cohn, Harry, 6, 11, 84–85, 87, 89–90, 92, 94,
    115, 231n9
Colbert, Claudette, 85, 148, 158
Cole, Lester, 138, 164–65, 179, 180
Collier's, 22, 37, 52, 70
Collison, Wilson, 109, 111–12, 117, 120
Colman, Ronald, 59
Columbia Pictures, 11, 84–93, 115, 190, 208
Communist Party, 166, 189, 202–3
Conference of Studio Unions (CSU), 165–66
Confessions of a Nazi Spy, 129
Congo Maisie, 117

Congreso de Pueblos de Habla Española, El, 77

Connery, Sean, 218

Connolly, Mike, 214

Cooper, Gary, 1, 8, 81, 162, 198

Cooper, Jackie, 53

Cooper, James Fenimore, 28

Cooper, Olive, 78

Corey, Wendell, 216

Corn Is Green, The, 213

corpse rouging, 62, 82, 201

Costello, Dolores, 99

Cotton, Helen, 206

Court-Martial of Billy Mitchell, The, 198

Covered Wagon, The, 85

Coward, Noël, 8

Cowboys in the Clouds, 138

Craig's Wife, 84–90, 112, 147, 220, 241n41

Crawford, Joan, 44, 46, 49, 51, 119, 156, 158, 196, 220

"Crazy—Or Something," 37

Creelman, Eileen, 159

Creiger, Henry Edward, 13

Crisp, Donald, 157

Cromwell, John, 164

Crossman, Melville. *See* Zanuck, Daryl F.

Crouse, Russel, 37

Crowninshield, Frank, 33

Crowther, Bosley, 159

Crowthers, Rachel, 78

Cry Havoc, 158

Cummings, Mitzi, 78

Cummings, Ruth, 78

Cunningham, Ann Lee, 79

Daily Worker, The, 95

Dancing in the Dark, 173–74, 181, 185

Dangerous, 2

Dare, Irene, 99

Daring Years, The, 18

Dark Dame, 111

Dark Victory, 110

Daughter of the Dawn, 200

Daves, Delmer, 80, 173

Davies, Valentine, 185, 188, 215

Davis, Bette, 2, 4, 47, 50–51, 55, 63, 65, 74, 79, 82, 88, 102, 109, 131, 136, 163, 167, 169, 171, 194, 200, 213, 222, 224, 228, 247n3

Davis, Bobby, 4

Davis, Elmer, 145

Day, Laraine, 126, 158–60

de Acosta, Mercedes, 78

de Armand, Marjorie, 154–55

de Havilland, Olivia, 133, 171

DeMille, Cecil B., 69, 81, 97–98, 126–27, 162, 224

De Nevers, Lucille, 78

Dean, Bashford, 30

Dekker, Albert, 181

Delano, William Adams, 33

Delmar, Viña, 78, 92

Democratic Party, 14, 92, 96, 130, 136, 146, 166–67, 178, 181, 213–14

Derek, John, 198

Desirable, 11, 55–59, 62

Destry Rides Again, 110

Deutsch, Helen, 168

Dieterle, William, 67–68, 71, 73

Dillinger, John, 70

Dinehart, Alan, 48

Disney, Walt, 1, 115, 161–62, 166

Disraeli, 46, 59

Dix, Richard, 108

Dmytryk, Edward, 180

Dodge City, 110

Dodsworth, 59

Doherty, Edward, 154

Don the Beachcomber's, 213

Donlevy, Brian, 197

Doorway to Hell, 70

Douglas, Helen Gahagan, 92, 130, 136–37, 163

Douglas, Lloyd, 80–81

Douglas, Melvyn, 91–92, 129, 136, 214

Down to the Sea in Ships, 18

Doyle, Maxine, 61

Dozier, William, 172

Dr. Monica, 55

Dr. No, 207, 218
Dr. Socrates, 70–73, 80–83
Drake, Betsy, 185–86
Drake, Oliver, 137–38
Dramatic School, 104–7
Driscoll, Charles, 74
Drums Along the Mohawk, 110
Dunne, Irene, 59, 81, 91, 152, 205–6
Dunne, Philip, 7, 184
Durante, Jimmy, 172
Durling, E. V., 148
Dwight School for Girls, 16, 40, 54

Earnshaw, Fenton, 214
Eastman, Ruth, 32
Ebenstein, Morris, 43, 49
Eddy, Nelson, 63
Edwards, Cliff, 115–16
Eldredge, John, 65
Eleventh Hour, The, 216
Ellison, Harlan, 221
Elman, Irving, 216
Elston, Virginia, 79
Emergency Committee of Hollywood Guilds
    and Unions, 162, 164
Engle, Sam, 175
Ephron, Henry, 199
Ephron, Phoebe, 199, 211
Equal Rights Amendment, 17, 128, 140, 163,
    220, 260n27
Erickson, Carl C., 73
Estabrook, Howard, 165, 202, 224
Evelyn, Judith, 170
Everybody's Sweetheart, 81
Exodus, 214
Eye Street, 188

Fagan, Myron C., 194, 214
Fairbanks, Douglas Sr., 11, 19, 26, 28–39, 41,
    44, 53
Fairbanks, Douglas Jr., 43–51, 55, 76, 218
Faithfull, Starr, 216
Fashions for Women, 85
Fedderson, Don, 204–5

Federal Bureau of Investigation, 70, 167,
    194–95, 200–1, 252n31
Federal Theatre Project, 18
Felton, Norman, 216
Ferber, Edna, 22, 108
Film Daily, 28, 98, 147, 153–54
film history, sexism and exclusion of women,
    78, 220–24, 227–28, 251n19
Finkel, Abem, 73
Fitzgerald, F. Scott, 19
Five Star Final, 43–44, 46
Flaming Youth, 18
Flanagan, Hallie, 18
Fleming, Victor, 53
Flynn, Errol, 82, 146
Fontaine, Joan, 1
Ford, John, 87, 175, 195
Ford Television Theatre, 199–200, 217
franchises, 114, 116–17 123, 143, 207, 218. *See
    also* serials
Francis, Irene, 79
Francis, Kay, 45, 47, 49–50, 55, 68, 81
Franken, Rose, 78, 98, 160
Frankenheimer, John, 199
Franklin, Alan, 112, 127, 172, 186–87,
    218, 228
Franklin, Dwight, 4–6, 11, 25–43, 45, 48–49,
    51–54, 63–64, 67–69, 74, 81, 97–98, 101–4,
    127–28, 142–43, 157, 160, 169–70, 198, 211,
    218–19
Franklin, Gerald ("Jerry"), 112, 127, 172,
    186–87, 218, 228
Franklin, Jean Whittemore Dwight,
    26–27, 128
Franklin, Joseph, 26
Franklin, Sheila. *See* Benson, Sheila
Franklin, Sidney, 9
Frankly Over Forty, 171
"Fraternity," 125
Freed, Arthur, 125, 217
Freeman, Mona, 198
Freeman, Y. Frank, 2–4, 8, 11, 107, 118, 146,
    157, 203
"Friday Girl, The," 211–12

Frisco Jenny, 79
Froeschel, George, 8
From Here to Eternity, 89, 198
Front Page Woman, 80

Gable, Clark, 44, 85, 11, 132
Gardner, Ava, 213
Gardner, Marcella, 79
Garland, Judy, 110
Garrett, Oliver H. P., 567, 189
Garson, Greer, 4, 9–10, 163
Gaslight, 170, 222; see also Angel Street
Gelsey, Irwin S., 50
Gentleman's Agreement, 181–82
Gentlemen Prefer Blondes, 19
Geraghty, Tom, 57
German-Soviet Non-Aggression Pact, 117
Gibbons, Cedric, 53, 127
Gilbert, Doris, 189, 205, 216
Gillette, Don, 214
Gilligan's Island, 217
Ginger Rogers Finds a Bargain, 148
Gish, Lillian, 132, 171, 222
Gleason, James, 32, 52, 101
Gleason, Lucile Webster, 32, 54, 74, 101,
    109, 135
Gledhill, Donald, 140
Gluck, Carol Warner, 205
Goddard, Paulette, 104
Goldfish Bowl, The, 40–46, 49, 52, 207
Gold Rush Maisie, 114, 120–25
Goldwyn, Frances, 6, 231n9
Goldwyn, Samuel, 6, 59, 85–86, 108, 148,
    162, 224
Gombel, Mina, 61
Gone with the Wind, 100–1, 110, 119
Good Earth, The, 104–5
Goodrich, Frances, 57, 78–79, 106, 109,
    165, 196
Gordon, Ruth, 106
Grable, Betty, 163, 173–74
Graham, Sheilah, 6, 108–9, 143
Grand Street Follies of 1928, 34
Grant, Cary, 157, 185–86

Grapes of Wrath, The, 122
Great Depression, 9, 34, 36, 8, 52–55, 57, 59,
    92–93, 110, 114, 122, 125
Great Gatsby, The, 19
Great O'Malley, The, 81–82
Great Ziegfeld, The, 104–5, 114
Green, Al, 46, 205
Green, Howard J., 57
Green Light, 81–82
Gregory, Paul, 204
Grey, Lita, 172
Grey, Virginia, 115
Griffith, D. W., 19
Guilaroff, Sydney, 114
Gunga Din, 110
Gunman's Chance, 196

Hackett, Albert, 57, 196
Haight, Elizabeth Hazelton, 17
Haight, George, 131, 158, 170, 206, 249n38
Hale, Alan, 60
Halff, Robert, 144
Hamilton, Andrew, 14
Hamilton, Ian, 95
Hamilton, Patrick, 170
Hamlet, 200
Hamlet and the Three Eggs, 203
Hammett, Dashiell, 112
"Handed Down," 52
Hardie, Russell, 43
Hardy, Oliver, 73
Harrington, Julian, 22
Hartman, Don, 108
Hartmann, Edmund L., 208
Haskell, Molly, 221
Hawes, Elizabeth, 18
Hawks, Howard, 87, 157
Hays, Will, 28
Hayward, Lillie, 57, 65, 78–70, 196
Hayworth, Rita, 90
Heart of the Rio Grande, 196
Hecht, Ben, 38, 89
Helburn, Theresa, 28
Hell's Angels, 190

Hellman, Lillian, 78-79, 130, 140

Hemingway, Ernest, 19, 22

Henreid, Paul, 215

Henry V, 176

Hepburn, Katharine, 9, 59, 78, 86, 90,
    105, 220

Herbert, F. Hugh, 62, 126, 182-83

Herbert, Hugh, 68, 102

Herbert, Pamela, 126, 143

Herne, Chrystal, 84

Hersholt, Jean, 136, 157, 173, 176, 186

Higgins, Frank, 14

Hill, Ethel, 78

Hilton, James, 8, 162, 165

Hinton, Jane, 78

Hitchcock, Alfred, 199

Hodiak, John, 144

Hoffman, Joseph, 205

Hold Everything, 46

Holiday, 95, 123

Hollywood Anti-Nazi League, 117-18

Hollywood Canteen, 4-5, 131, 169

Hollywood Council of Guilds and
    Unions, 166

Hollywood Democratic Committee, 146, 181,
    202-3

Hollywood Reporter, The, 130, 171, 174,
    186, 214

Hollywood studio system, 9, 55, 76-77, 94,
    155-56, 163, 199

Hollywood Victory Committee, 145, 161

Hollywood Women's Club, 162

Hollywood Writers Mobilization, 140-41,
    145, 161, 168, 179, 181

Honky Tonk, 196

"Hoofer, The," 5

Hoover, J. Edgar, 185, 195

Hope, Bob, 8, 11

Hopper, Hedda, 2, 5-6, 135-36, 142-43, 148,
    16, 180, 184-86, 199, 202-3

"Horse with the Flaming Mane, The," 37, 54

Horwitz, Howie, 207

House Un-American Activities Committee
    (HUAC), 129, 178-80, 188, 195-96

Housewife, 79-80

Hovey, Tim, 208

How Green Was My Valley, 125

Howard, Leslie, 63-64, 73-74, 81-82, 104

Howe, James Wong, 8

Howell, Maude, 78

Hughes, Charles Evans, 14

Hughes, Dorothy, 79

Hughes, Eric, 224

Hughes, Howard, 189-95, 213, 215

Hughes, Rupert, 83, 257n9

Hummingbird, The, 29

Hunt, Julie, 250n21

Hunt, Marsha, 116-17

Hunter, Glenn, 28

Hunter, Ian, 115-16

Hurlbut, Gladys, 78

Hussey, Ruth, 115-16

Huston, John, 224

Huston, Walter, 59

Hymer, John B., 43

I Found Stella Parrish, 68, 81

I Love Lucy, 199

I Promise to Pay, 91-92

I'm No Angel, 56

Ide, Leonard, 62

In Caliente, 91

In Name Only, 110

In Our Time, 19

In Which We Serve, 8

Informer, The, 20, 83

Ingster, Boris, 58, 107

International Alliance of Theatrical Stage
    Employees (IATSE), 165-66

International Women's Day, 166-67

Interrupted Melody, 80

Intolerance, 77

Irish American community in Hollywood, 6,
    53, 101, 136, 165, 222

Irsky, Gregor, 162

It Happened One Night, 85

It's All Yours, 92-93

It's Tough to Be Famous, 42-47, 49-51

Jack Benny Program, The, 200
Jaffe, Sam, 11, 73, 150–54, 184
James Bond franchise, 206–7, 218
Janice Meredith, 79
Jarrico, Paul, 189–92
Jarrico, Sylvia, 190
Jazz Singer, The, 24
Jeffersons, The, 220
Jenk, Tom, 124
Jesse James, 110
Jessel, George, 173–74
Jezebel, 2, 102
Johnson, Erskine, 199
Johnson, Nunnally, 57, 122, 152
Johnson, Rita, 117, 170
Johnston, Eric, 176, 180, 253n71
Jolson, Al, 24, 24
Jones, Allan, 208
Jones, Jack, 208
Jones, Jennifer, 148
Jones, John Paul, 28, 127
Joyce, Ella, 79
Juke Box Rhythm, 209, 214
Jungle, The, 14

Kahlo, Frida, 128
Kandel, Judith, 79
Kanin, Michael, 8–9, 165
Kathleen, 125–27, 130–31, 217
Keeler, Ruby, 82
Keep Your Powder Dry, 158–60
Keighley, William, 60
Keller, James, Father, 205
Kellogg, Virginia, 78–79, 188–89
Kelly, Gene, 174
Kelly, George, 84–89, 112
Kendall, Chad, 204
Kennedy, George H., 214
Kenyon, Charles, 47, 67
Kenyon, Curtis, 214
Keon, Barbara, 99
Kerr, Laura, 94
Kerrigan, J. Warren, 69
Kibbee, Guy, 60, 62

King, Henry, 175
King, Louis, 175
King and I, The, 206
Kingsley, Darwin P., 14, 21, 32
Kingsley, Dorothy, 106
Kitty Foyle, 116
Knopf, Christopher, 208, 214, 221–22
Knopf, Edwin, 111
Korda, Alexander, 64
Koverman, Ida, 106, 132, 136, 155, 160, 163
Kramer, Cecile, 196
Krasna, Norman, 7
Krims, Milton, 81–82
Kruschen, Jack, 212–13
Ku Klux Klan, 118, 128

labor unions, 15, 57–58, 77, 94, 106, 155, 161–66, 176, 178, 189, 195
Ladies' Man, 47
Ladies of Leisure, 63
Lamarr, Hedy, 1
Lansing, Sherry, 223
Lardner, Ring Jr., 8–9, 168, 171, 179–80, 194
Las Vegas Story, The, 190
Lauber, Pauline, 168
Laughton, Charles, 204
Laura, 120, 173
Lauren, Sam, 7
Lavery, Emmet, 165, 168, 171, 176, 179–80, 188, 198
Lawrence, Viola, 87
Lawson, John Howard, 57, 77, 94, 138, 180–81
Lazarus, Erna, 79
Lean, David, 8, 77
Lear, Norman, 127
Leave It to Beaver, 208
Lederer, Charles, 170
Lederer, Francis, 93
Leeds, Andrea, 108
Lehman, Gladys, 77–79, 140, 155
Leigh, Vivien, 110
Lennart, Isobel, 106, 116, 190
Leroy, Mervyn, 8, 105
"Let's Not Pretend," 7

Levien, Sonya, 80, 101, 109

Lewis, Joseph, 138

Lewis, Sinclair, 9, 59, 61

Life Begins, 51

Life, Liberty, and Orin Dooley, 199

Lindbergh, Charles, 39, 40–41, 49–50, 118, 128, 246n20

Lindsay, Margaret, 220

literary adaptations, 58–59, 110. *See also* prestige pictures

Little, Barbara, 28–29

Little, Brown, 42–43

Little Caesar, 43, 46, 70

Little Foxes, The, 200

Little Lord Fauntleroy, 99

Little Women, 100

Loeff, Ted, 214–15

Logan, Helen, 78, 253

Lombard, Carole, 152

Lone Rider in Cheyenne, The, 138

Loos, Anita, 19, 57, 77, 79, 106, 158, 171, 184

Loos, Mary Anita, 184

Lord, Robert, 44–46, 70–73

Los Angeles Assistance League, 247 n3

Los Angeles Daily News, 99

Los Angeles Examiner, 6, 142, 188, 203

Los Angeles Times, 5, 97, 123, 130, 132, 135, 168, 197, 200, 202, 214, 221, 223, 228

Lotus Eater, The, 203

Love Affair, 110

Love Finds Andy Hardy, 96

Lovett, Josephine, 78

Loy, Myrna, 88, 214

Lubitsch, Ernst, 66

Lucey's, 7

Ludwig, William (Bill), 80, 96, 209

Lupino, Ida, 85, 190, 200

MacCracken, Henry Noble, 17, 20

MacDonald, Jeannette, 8, 63

MacLaine, Shirley, 212

MacLane, Barton, 70

MacMahon, Aline, 60, 81, 148

Macpherson, Jeanie, 98, 106

Madame du Barry, 84

Madison, Guy, 204

Maggie the Magnificent, 84

Magnificent Obsession, 80

Mahin, John Lee, 7, 83, 111

Mahoney, Jock, 208

Maibaum, Richard, 18, 206, 218

Maisie, 109–16

Maisie franchise, 5, 11–12, 79, 110–17, 119–26, 129–30, 143–48, 154, 159, 160, 168, 170, 196, 206–7, 212, 218, 221–22, 228, 252n36

Maisie Gets Her Man, 120, 123, 131

Maisie Goes to Reno, 114, 144

Maisie Was a Lady, 120, 123

Malloy, Doris, 78–79, 94

Maltz, Albert, 180

Man of Conquest, 108

Man Who Played God, The, 51

Manhattan Cocktail, 86

Mankiewicz, Herman, 38, 83

Mankiewicz, Joseph, 152

Manners, Dorothy, 199

Mannix, Eddie, 4, 6, 108, 136, 157, 163–64, 250n32

Marcus, Ellis, 216

"Margaret Browning Story, The," 205

Marie Antoinette, 105

Marie Antoinette, 95

Marin, Edwin, 116, 124–25

Marion, Frances, 8, 77, 79–80, 106, 109, 165, 171

Mark of Zorro, The, 28

Marked Woman, 102

Markson, Ben, 80

Marshall, Herbert, 126

Martin, Mildred, 88, 185, 197

Martin, Nell, 112

Marx, Harpo, 172

Marx, Samuel, 217

Mary Tyler Moore Show, The, 220

Mason, Sarah Y., 99

Match King, 61

Mathis, June, 10

Mayer, Louis B., 3, 7, 89, 105, 125, 155

McCall, John A., 12-15, 20-21, 58, 119

McCall, Leo, 13-15, 20, 23, 25, 38, 73, 142

McCall, Leo Jr., 16, 23, 32, 38, 45, 195

McCall, Mary Caldwell (Mazie), 13, 15, 20, 25-26, 32, 37, 73, 112, 131, 142, 217, 223

McCall, Mary C. Jr.: and the Academy Foundation, 157; accusations of communism, 167, 181, 194-95, 214; and advertising career, 23-24, 33; and Anglophilia, 118-19, 176; and awards, 215, 220, 222; and Bramson's domestic abuse, 169-70, 186; and broad coalition, 135-36, 163; and chair of Hollywood Council of Guild and Unions, 166; as chair of War Activities Committee, 3, 143, 145-48; and combating ageism, 171; and commitment to guild, 58, 96-97, 107-9, 137-38, 190; commitment to helping working women, 138, 140, 164; and contract wage increases, 107-8, 137-41; and death, 221-22; and declared anticommunism, 200-3; and defense of Hollywood, 156; and deterioration of relationship with Zanuck, 183-85; and divorce, 142; and Dorothy Arzner, 86-88; early writing career, 21-23, 35-36, 51-52; early years, 12-16; exposes KKK members in Hollywood, 118; and extramarital affairs, 44-46-47, 64, 74, 102-3, 127-30, 133-34; and films about women, 47-48, 84-87, 110-25, 130-31, 143-49, 158-60, 168, 174-75, 182-83, 196-97; and first screenplay, 47-50; and Harry Cohn, 89-90; and Howard Hughes, 189-93; and independence, 31; in Ireland, 20-22; joins Screen Writers Guild, 58; and media coverage of, 2, 5-6, 8, 12, 45, 89, 109, 124-29, 136, 142-43, 146, 148, 154-55, 163, 184-86, 202, 224; mentoring young writers, 80, 96, 209; and MGM, 101, 104-27; and MPA, 160-64; and novel, 39-43; and Paramount, 98-99; and pay inequalities, 60, 65, 67-68, 73, 137; as a political moderate, 12, 97, 163, 190, 195, 202, 215; and pregnancies, 36, 67-68, 164;

as president, 135-41, 188-93; and relationship with children, 126-27, 186-87, 228; and relationship with Franklin, 6, 31, 54, 63, 97, 101; and remarriage, 142-43; and RKO, 99; as role model for girls, 147-48; runs for president of guild, 118; and Screen Actors Guild, 54, 91, 98; and Screen Directors Guild, 94; and Screen Editors Guild, 189; and Selznick, 98-101; and sexism at Warner Bros., 67, 71-72, 90; struggles for work, 195, 200-4, 208; sues Hollywood Reporter; 214; and television career, 198-200, 204-9; as top-earner, 184; and Twentieth Century-Fox, 168-69, 173-75, 181-86; at Vassar, 16-20; as vice-president, 135, 138; and views of Hollywood's opportunities for women, 155-56; and Warner Bros., 42-45, 52-73; and women's role postwar, 167; and work for Democratic Party, 136-37; and writing philosophy, 21-22, 37

McCall, Mary Smyth Horan, 14

McCann-Erikson, 206

McCarey, Leo, 92

McCarthy, Mary, 79, 90-91, 164

McClave, Dorothy "Day," 102, 211

McCrea, Joel, 108

McCreadie, Marsha, 143

McDaniel, Hattie, 60

McDowell, Roddy, 125

McGuinness, James, 83

McGuire, Dorothy, 148

McHugh, Frank, 68, 101, 243n39

McLean, Barbara, 227

Mellett, Lowell, 3-4, 139, 145-47

Mencken, Helen, 34

Menjou, Aldolph, 186

Meredyth, Bess, 106

Merrill, Gary, 200

Merry, Merry Maidens, The, 99-101

Methot, Mayo, 102-3

Metropolitan Museum of Art, 27-28

Meyer, Elizabeth, 101

MGM, 3, 5-6, 8-9, 11, 53, 59, 63, 77-79, 85, 88, 92, 95-96, 101-27, 132, 136, 148, 150, 152, 154, 158, 160, 163, 165, 168, 184, 188, 190, 203, 206-7, 216-18
MGM Studio Club News, 136
Midnight, 110
Midsummer Night's Dream, A, 67-68
Miles, Norbert, 200, 204
Milland, Ray, 127
Miller, Alice. D. G., 78
Miller, Marilyn, 199
Miller, Seton I., 80
Millionaire, The, 204-5
Milne, Peter, 65
Miracle Woman, The, 200
Miss Madeira's School, 15-16
Miss Pinkerton, 79
Mitchell, Thomas, 152
Modern Mothers, 65
Money, Women, and Guns, 208
Monogram Pictures, 137, 236n29
Monroe, Marilyn, 201
Monsieur Beaucaire, 29
Montgomery, Robert, 54, 91, 101, 109, 206
Moore, Colleen, 18
Morehead, Agnes, 159
Morgan, Michele, 167
Morris, Chester, 91, 101
Morrow, Anne, 15, 40
Morrow, Elisabeth, 15, 40
Morrow, Elizabeth Cutter, 15
Motion Picture Alliance for the Preservation of American Ideals (MPA), 160-64, 168, 175
Motion Picture Association of America (MPAA), 176, 180, 188
Motion Picture Producers and Distributors of America (MPPDA), 147
Motion Picture Relief Committee, 130, 141, 186
Motion Picture Relief Fund, 11, 130-31, 136, 141, 146, 155, 157, 173, 176, 186, 204
Moultrie, Eliza, 169, 219
Mr. Belvedere Goes to College, 182-83, 185
"Mr. Nolan's World," 37

Mrs. Miniver, 4, 7-9, 146
Muir, Florabel, 79
Muir, Jean, 54-56, 58-59, 74, 79, 82, 129, 195
Muni, Paul, 70-73
Muray, Nickolas, 127-30, 133
Murfin, Jane, 57, 77-79, 94, 99, 119, 140, 155, 171
Murphy, George, 79, 109, 123
Museum of the City of New York, 28
Museum of Natural History, 27, 127

Nagle, Conrad, 119
Nana, 86
Nancy Drew, 116
Nathan, George Jean, 28
National Labor Relations Board, 57-58, 74, 80, 96, 103, 107-8, 166, 179
Naughty Marietta, 63
Navasky, Victor, 178
Negri, Pola, 28
Neilan, Marshall "Micky," 203-4
Nelson, Ham, 102, 130
Neufeld, Sigmund, 137
New Deal, 3, 18, 122, 129, 139, 146, 161-62, 166-67, 203
New York Post, 37, 89, 129
New York Times, 50, 58, 62, 89, 130, 167, 188, 223
New Yorker, 19, 22-23, 35, 39, 60, 185
Nichols, Dudley, 57, 83, 98, 168
Night in Bombay, 119
Night of the Hunter, The, 204
Ninotchka, 110
Niven, David, 72, 103, 243n34
North Shore, see *Woman in Red, The*
Notorious, 185
Now, Voyager, 2

Obringer, Roy, 49
Of Human Bondage, 63, 88
O'Flaherty, Liam, 20
Office of War Information (OWI), 3-4, 139, 143-48, 159
Oklahoma Kid, The, 110

Olcott, Sidney, 29
Old Maid, The, 110
Olivier, Laurence, 176, 200
On the Sunny Side. See "Fraternity"
On to Oregon, 174–75, 196
Ornitz, Sam, 180
Osborn, Henry Fairfield, 27
Outlaw, The, 190
Outside Looking In, 34
Owen, Seena, 78

Paige, Janis, 206
Panama Hattie, 129–30
Paramount Pictures, 2, 45, 47, 52, 69, 85, 99,
    103, 111, 139, 203, 214
Parker, Albert, 29
Parker, Dorothy, 1, 22, 77–79, 84, 98, 109, 130
Parsons, Harriet, 190, 200
Parsons, Louella, 2, 6, 45, 65, 68, 81, 86, 116,
    132, 143, 148, 159–60, 170, 206
Partos, Frank, 7
Passion Flower, 47
Patrick, Gail, 126
Paul, Alice, 17
Pearl Harbor, 129, 146, 148, 157
Peck, Gregory, 181, 214
"Peek A Boo," 23
Pelgram, Robert, 102
Perelman, Laura, 78–79
Perils of Pauline, The, 116
Perino's, 7
Perkins, Frances, 58
Perlberg, William, 173
Perry, Joan, 231n9
"Persian Rug Mystery," 35
Peters, Andrew James, 216
Peters, Susan, 158
Petrified Forest, The, 73–74, 239n34
phantom lady syndrome, 165
Philips, Mary, 34, 102
Photoplay, 102, 122
Pickford, Mary, 10–11, 28, 37, 44, 46, 67, 106,
    125–26, 155, 224
Pictorial Review, 36–37, 42–43
Pittman, Montgomery, 207–8

Plainsman, The, 69, 81
Pocket Full of Miracles, 213
Pomerance, William, 188
Possessed, 44
Potanina, Raissa, 167
Pre-Code, 48
Preminger, Jim, 220
Preminger, Ingo, 194, 220
Preminger, Otto, 115
Prescott, Thelma A., 164–65
Pressburger, Emeric, 8, 176
prestige pictures, 59, 62, 67, 85, 106, 108
Price, Vincent, 170, 222
Prickell, Justine, 37, 45
Pride of the Yankees, 8
Prisoner of Zenda, The, 95
Private Secretary, 199
Progressive Era, 14–15, 22, 213
propaganda pictures, 3, 140, 145, 148, 151,
    154, 159
Production Code, 55, 70, 111
Public Enemy, The, 43, 70
Purcell, Gertrude, 78–79
Putnam, George Palmer, 32
Puzo, Mario, 89
Pyle, Howard, 28

Quiet Man, The, 196
Quinn, Anthony, 132, 180

Radio Free Europe, 215
Radio Writers Guild, 189
Raft, George, 98
Raiders, The, 196
Raines, Ella, 158, 197
Rainer, Luise, 104–6, 171
Ramsaye, Terry, 156
Ramrod, 196
Random Harvest, 8
Range Busters, 137
Range Rider, The, 208
Rathbone, Basil, 109
Ratoff, Gregory, 173
Rauh, Stanley, 108
Ray, Nicholas, 196

Ready, Willing, and Able, 82

Reagan, Ronald, 222

Reap the Wild Wind, 127

Reckless, 88

Red Dust, 111, 113, 117

Redbook, 22, 36-37

Reed, Tom, 59

Registered Nurse, 65

Reinhardt, Elizabeth (Betty), 79, 115, 120,
    122-23, 126, 131, 155, 165, 173, 196, 200, 228

Reinhardt, Max, 67

Reisbord, Jeannette, 167

Republic Pictures, 108, 195-96

Republican Party, 3, 7, 14, 66, 129, 161,
    178, 204

Revolt, 48-50. *See also Scarlet Dawn*

Reward Unlimited, 148

Rich Are Always with Us, The, 50

Ride the Man Down, 196-97

Riffraff, 114

Rin Tin Tin, 76

Ringside Maisie, 144

Rio Grande, 196

Riskin, Robert, 85

Riskin, Victoria, 224

Ritter, Thelma, 212

Ritz Brothers, 203

Rivkin, Allen, 94, 99, 188

Robert Montgomery Presents, 206

Roberts, Marguerite, 57, 78, 140, 190, 196

Robeson, Paul, 165

Robin Hood, 28

Robinson, Casey, 68, 80-81

Robinson, Hubbell, 215

Rockefeller, John D., 14

Rockwell, Norman, 32

Rogers, Ginger, 105, 116, 148, 156, 190

Rogers, Gregory. *See* Zanuck, Darryl F.

Rogers, Howard Emmett, 83

Rogers, Jean, 144

Rogers, Lela, 155

Rogers, Will Jr., 198

Rooney, Mickey, 96, 116, 155, 245n20

Roosevelt, Eleanor, 4, 137, 165

Roosevelt, Elliott, 165

Roosevelt, Franklin D., 3-4, 7, 28, 53, 57, 74,
    137, 145-46, 163, 167, 179, 181, 213

Roosevelt, Faye, 165

Roosevelt, Theodore, 14, 28

Rosten, Leo (AKA Leonard Q. Ross), 58, 97,
    99, 168

Rouverol, Aurania, 96

Rouverol, Jean, 96

Royle, Selena, 152

Ruben, J. Walter, 5, 11, 92, 105, 108-9, 112,
    114-20, 131, 205

Ruggles, Charles, 99

Russell, Rosalind, 1, 87-88, 147

Ryskind, Morrie, 83

Sabatini, Raphael, 69

Sager, Catherine, 174-75

Sale, Richard, 184

Salmon, Lucy, 17

Sanders, Sydney A., 36-37, 42-43, 53

Sarah and Son, 86

Saturday Evening Post, 22, 211, 213

Scandal Sheet (1931), 47

Scarecrow, The, 28

Scarface, 70, 190

Scarlet Dawn, 50. *See also Revolt*

Scarlet Pimpernel, 64

Schallert, Edwin, 123, 130, 197

Schary, Dore, 168

Schenck, Joseph, 152-53

Schermer, Jules, 154

Scheuer, Philip K., 123

Schickel, Richard, 220

Schnee, Charles, 214

Schulberg, Budd, 7, 101

Schulman, Silvia, 99

Schwartz, Arthur, 173

Schwartz, Nancy Lynn, 260n35

Scott, Adrian, 180

Screen Actors Guild, 5, 74, 82, 84, 91, 94, 98,
    104, 109, 135-36, 138-39, 157, 248n17

Screen Directors Guild, 85, 94, 176, 220,
    248n17

Screen Gems, 206

Screen Guild Theater, 109

Screen Guilds Magazine, 82, 84, 95, 105, 124, 136

Screen Playwrights, 83, 97–98, 103, 107–8, 111, 180, 257 n9

Screen Publicists Guild, 132, 162

Screen Writer, The, 154–55, 175, 190, 209

Screen Writers Guild, 1–3, 5–9, 11, 57, 69, 73–85, 90–91, 93–98, 102–9, 112, 118, 120, 127, 129–30, 135–47, 149–50, 152, 154–55, 157, 161, 163, 165–66, 173–81, 185–95, 200–2, 225

Sea Hawk, The, 129

Sea of Grass, 196

Seaton, George, 188, 203

second wave feminism, 220, 260n27

Secret Bride, The, 62–63, 67, 71

Seldes, Gilbert, 37

Selznick, David O., 4, 99–101, 148, 164–65, 174, 224, 251n20

Selznick, Myron, 60

Sennwald, André, 58, 62–63, 239n10

Sergeant York, 151

serials, 116. *See also* franchises

Serling, Rod, 208, 216, 228

"Sesame Lollard," 35

Seven Brides for Seven Brothers, 196

"Seven Watchmen," 204

Shakespeare, William, 33, 67–68, 98

She, 136

"She Called Him 'Uncle Hugh,'" 216–17

She Done Him Wrong, 56

"She Said What She Meant," 52

Sheehan, Winfield, 182

"Sheila," 205–6

Sheiner, David, 218–20

Sheiner, Mary-David, 127, 165, 170, 172, 187, 201, 208, 210, 212, 215, 217–23, 228, 235n18, 252n41

Shining, The, 61

Shore, Jane, 78

Short, Luke, 196–97

Show Boat, 208

Show-Off, The, 84

Silver Bullet, The, 138

Sinatra, Frank, 213, 222

Since You Went Away, 148, 164, 204

Sinclair, Upton, 14, 74

Sitting Pretty, 181–83, 185

Skelton, Red, 123

Sklar, Robert, 220

Skolsky, Sidney, 6, 8, 124, 126, 129

Slesinger, Frank, 148

Slesinger, Tess, 78, 148, 231n12

Slim Carter, 207–08

Smith, Vernon, 57

Smith, Winifred, 19

Smoky, 175

Snowed Under, 84

So Big, 63

So Proudly We Hail!, 146, 158

Song of Russia, 190

"Sonnet For a Partnership," 31

Sothern, Ann, 5, 11, 115–16, 120–23, 129, 144, 158, 163, 199, 203, 206, 222

Spartacus, 214

Spewack, Bella, 109

Stage Door, 105

Stagecoach, 110

Stanwyck, Barbara, 62–63, 65–66, 200

Star Is Born, A, 100, 174, 186

Starr, Irving, 205, 257n29

Steel, Dawn, 223

Sterne, Meta, 79

Stewart, Donald Ogden, 95, 124

Stewart, Rosalie, 85, 241n35

Stewart, Wendy, Dr., 171

Story of Dr. Wassell, The, 127

Stratton, Dorothy, Lt. Com., 147

Street of Women, 47–50, 54, 76

Strickling, Howard, 156

strikes, 3, 57, 97, 138, 161, 165–67, 178, 188, 191, 193–94, 214, 224

Stromberg, Hunt, 119

Struther, Jan, 9

Stuart, Gloria, 48, 74

Stulberg, Gordon, 191–92, 256n61

Sturges, Preston, 152

"Subway Diamonds," 235

Sullivans, The, 150–56, 222
Susannah of the Mounties, 79, 125
Swanson, Gloria, 29
suffrage movement, 15, 17
Swing Shift Maisie, 114, 143–46, 148

Taft-Hartley Act, 178–79
Tall Texan, The, 196
Tarbell, Ida, 14
Tashman, Lilyan, 86
Taylor, James Monroe, 17
Taylor, Robert, 81, 132
Taylor, William Desmond, 146
Teesdale, Verree, 55
television, 188, 193, 198–209, 214–15, 217–20, 223–24
Temple, Shirley, 125–26, 130, 148, 155–56, 175, 185, 217
Tenney, Jack B., 129, 179, 184, 202
Tested Advertising Methods, 24
Theodora Goes Wild, 90, 109
There's No Business Like Show Business, 201
They Call It Sin, 79
Thin Man, The, 106
Third Man, The, 215
Thirer, Irene, 112
Thompson, Dorothy, 9
Thomsen, Robert, 188, 213
Thunderbirds, 197–98
Thunderhead, Son of Flicka, 175
Thurber, James, 35
Tobin, Genevieve, 65
Tom, Dick, and Harry, 190
Torch-Bearers, The, 84, 241n35
Torchy Blane, 116
Tourneur, Jacques, 148
Tracy, Spencer, 9, 83, 105, 161, 243n39
Traube, Rose, 5, 142
Treasure Island, 20, 53, 59, 63
Trinity College Dublin, 20–21
Trumbo, Dalton, 57, 80, 138, 140, 163, 179–80, 214, 224
Tuchock, Wanda, 78
Tugend, Harry, 98, 118

Tunberg, Karl, 188–92
Turner, Lana, 104, 158–59, 163
TV Guide, 205
Twentieth Century-Fox, 7, 78–80, 122–25, 131, 148, 152–53, 163, 168, 172–74, 179, 184–86, 195–96, 215, 227
Twilight Zone, The, 205, 207

Uncle Tom's Cabin, 115
Unger, Gladys, 78
Union Depot, 44
Union Pacific, 110
United Negro College Fund, 167
Universal Pictures, 47, 60, 80, 168, 206–07
University of California, Los Angeles (UCLA), 11, 104, 164, 182, 186, 215, 217
University of Southern California (USC), 209, 229
"Unknown Master," 52
Unterberger, Sally, 79

Vadja, Ernst, 104
Van Dyke, W. S., 53
Van Upp, Virginia, 78, 90, 152
Variety, 62, 102, 107–8, 127, 130, 144, 147, 173, 214
Vassar, Matthew, 16
Vassar College, 7, 16–20, 52, 104, 106, 183, 196, 215
Veltin School, 26
Viertel, Salka, 78
Virginian, The, 196

Wagner Act, 75, 96–97, 103, 178
Wald, Jerry, 7, 80
Wallis, Hal, 47, 54–60, 62, 65–74, 77, 80–81, 84
Walloping Wallace, 200
Wanamaker Galleries, 27
Wanger, Walter, 4, 157, 162, 172, 176, 182
War Activities Committee, 3–4, 6, 143–48, 158, 163–64, 180
War and Peace, 206
Ward, Luci, 80

Warner Bros., 2, 5, 8, 34, 38, 43-44, 46-50,
    53, 57-63, 65-88, 91-92, 98, 102, 116,
    118-19, 127, 130, 148, 150, 166, 179, 196,
    205, 214; and attacks on unionized
    writers, 84; and poor record of hiring
    women writers, 79-80
Warner, Jack, 2, 11, 45, 58, 64, 72, 74, 76, 81,
    90, 153
Warren, Earl, 3
Warren, Eda, 189
Watson, Minor, 61
Waxman, Percy, 35
Wayne, John, 127, 161
Weaver, William K., 157
Webb, Clifton, 173-74, 181-83, 185-86
Weidler, Virginia, 121, 125
Weisberg, Brenda, 79
Weisberg, Sheila J., 220
Welles, Orson, 181, 224
West, Claudine, 8
West, Mae, 56, 111
westerns, 46, 80, 110, 138, 175, 196, 200, 207;
    and written by women, 59, 80, 137-38,
    174-75, 196-97, 207; and writers paid less
    for, 80, 137-38, 196
Whales of August, The, 222
Wharton, Edith, 36
What Makes Sammy Run?, 7
What Price Hollywood?, 77
Wheeler, Burton K., 127
Whistler, James, 34
White, K. Alexandra, 171
White, Pearl, 42
Whitty, Dame May, 167
Whole Town's Talking, The, 87
Wilcox, Grace, 101
Wild Party, The, 86
Wilder, Billy, 7, 98, 139, 212
Wiles, Irving, 217, 223
Wilkerson, Billy, 170-71, 186, 214
Willkie, Wendell, 129
Wilson, Carey, 77
Wilson, Elizabeth, 196

Wilson, Michael, 188
Wimperis, Arthur, 8
Winn, Marcia, 146-47, 155-56
Wizard of Oz, The, 110
Woman in Red, The, 65-66, 100
Woman of the Year, 8-9
women: and employment in Hollywood,
    10-11, 77-80, 106-8; and employment in
    U.S., 9, 256n1; and films aimed at, 47, 81,
    85, 88-89, 99-100, 105-6, 110, 114, 116;
    and higher education, 15-17; and
    management of Screen Writers Guild, 77,
    79, 118, 165; and screenwriting, 77-80,
    99; and television, 199, 205
Women's Auxiliary Army Corps, 158-59
Women of Glamour, 92, 114
Wood, Sam, 161
"Wooden Shoes," 36-37
Woods, Frank, 57
Woollcott, Alexander, 28, 35
World War I, 3, 34, 40, 76, 166
World War II, 110, 128-33, 136, 138-60,
    163-68, 198
Wrap, The, 224
Wright, Muriel, 171
Wright, Teresa, 108
Writers Guild of America West (WGAW),
    135, 200, 208, 209, 214-15, 220, 222
Wuthering Heights, 110
Wylie, Philip, 155
Wyman, Jane, 116

Yankee Doodle Dandy, 5, 8
Yates, Herbert J., 195-97
Yeats, W. B., 54, 223
Yost, Dorothy, 78
Young, Robert, 115, 160
Young, Roland, 102
Youngman, Henny, 160

Zanuck, Darryl F., 38, 43-50, 54, 59, 63-64,
    76-80, 89, 120, 135, 136, 146, 152-53, 156,
    163-64, 168, 170, 173-75, 181-86, 194, 224